D1758715

THE BATTLE OF THE SEXES
IN FRENCH CINEMA,
1930–1956

The Battle of the Sexes
IN FRENCH CINEMA, 1930–1956

Noël Burch and Geneviève Sellier

Translated by Peter Graham

Duke University Press
DURHAM AND LONDON
2014

Translation © 2014 Duke University Press
All rights reserved
Printed in the United States of America on acid-free paper ♾
Designed by Kristina Kachele
Typeset in Garamond Premier Pro by Tseng Information Systems, Inc.

Library of Congress Cataloging-in-Publication Data
Burch, Noël, 1932–
[Drôle de guerre des sexes du cinéma français, 1930–1956. English]
The battle of the sexes in French cinema, 1930–1956 / Noël Burch and
Geneviève Sellier ; translated by Peter Graham.
pages cm
Includes bibliographical references and index.
ISBN 978-0-8223-5547-2 (cloth : alk. paper)
ISBN 978-0-8223-5561-8 (pbk. : alk. paper)
1. Man-woman relationships in motion pictures. 2. Motion pictures —
France — History — 20th century. I. Sellier, Geneviève. II. Burch,
Noël, 1932– Drôle de guerre des sexes du cinéma français, 1930–1956.
Translation of: III. Title.
PN1995.9.M27B8713 2013
791.43094409'04 — dc23   2013018959

ℛ

Contents

𝒜

Introduction

ALTHOUGH NEITHER of the authors of this book is a trained historian, historical research of the kind that has emerged in France over the past fifty years or so, and in particular the history of representations, no doubt sparked our desire to approach film analysis from a fresh angle. This required a considerable change of course on our part in view of the fact that the disciplines that nurture film studies in France, quite apart from the traditional areas of aesthetics and art history, have, since Christian Metz's key contribution to the debate, been linguistics and psychoanalysis.

Not that the history of the cinema has been unexplored territory in France: ever since Georges Sadoul's first comprehensive surveys of the subject, many researchers have focused their attention on an "art" which, although only just over a century old, has not always been very accessible. But among the multitude of angles from which such a protean object as the cinema can be approached — as both a technique, a language, an industry, a business, an art, a popular culture, an institution, and an instrument of propaganda — we feel that French researchers have so far failed to take full advantage of film's potential as an ideal area in which to study the history of representations.

This can perhaps be explained by the difficulty that film specialists and history specialists have in communicating with each other, the former often being enthusiastic cinephiles and too fixated on their subject of study (and love!) to be able or willing to use it as a way of achieving another end, the latter tending to instrumentalize the cinema as just one of several sources and to overlook its relative autonomy. Even the most pertinent historical work from our point of view (Ferro 1977/1988; Garçon 1984) articulates its argument around a non-cinematic factor (a political one in this case): films serve to gauge the impact of a political ideology on civil society or to confirm the existence of an ideology that opposes a given political regime. What we attempt to articulate here is an argument based on the films themselves.

The cinema, a collective cultural product in the way it is both produced and consumed, is probably an ideal medium for the expression of a social imaginary. But it does nevertheless also constitute a language in its own right, whose highly complex and very diverse codes (mimesis, narrative, fiction, characters, lighting, sets, spectacle, music, dialogue, and so on) require a specific approach of the kind that the art historian Pierre Francastel wanted to see applied to painting.

Our book is the result of our wish to combine certain aspects of contemporary historical research with our so-called inside knowledge of the cinema as an object and of the specific tools that have been developed to analyze it. Among the approaches that have changed the way we look at films, mention should also be made of the fairly recent discipline of cultural studies, developed chiefly in English-speaking countries, which seeks to understand the symbolic productions of a given society without reference to the evaluation grid imposed by the dominant culture. In France, Pierre Bourdieu's (1979/1984) revolutionary approach to the sociology of culture adopted similar criteria, but France's elitist view of culture is so pervasive that it acts as a hindrance to that kind of historical research, which is difficult to find anywhere except in the work of a historian like Pascal Ory (1989).

In the field of cinema, in particular, the relatively recent struggle — which has been crowned with success in France — to get the cultural legitimacy of the cinema recognized by both the intelligentsia and official cultural institutions has had the effect of encouraging the setting up of a pantheon of "great" directors at the expense of a more modern (and in some ways more relevant) approach to cinema as a collective cultural production. This is the approach we have adopted in our book.

Finally, the most recent but by no means least important ramification of the New History — the history of women, or rather the history of gender relations — has begun to emerge in France with the five volumes of Georges Duby and Michelle Perrot's *Histoire des femmes en occident* (1991), whose scientific value is enhanced by the authors' constant concern to weave together the material and symbolic dimensions of male domination of women that forms the basis of our societies. The historical precision of that collective work, which is based on the premise that sexual identities are not essences but relationships and differentiation processes inherent in a given society and period, lent a useful extra dimension to the work of English-speaking historians—particularly in the field of gender studies—which, while substantial, was all too often sub specie aeternitatis. Moreover most of those same historians' work on cinematic representations of gender was chiefly, if not exclusively, concerned with U.S. cinema. It fairly soon became clear to us that, ever since Laura Mulvey's (1975/1981) trailblazing essay, any analysis aimed at understanding the symbolic function of film and of its spectator as regards sexual relationships could not be applied directly to French cinema, for reasons that have precisely to do with history in general and cultural history in particular. We do, then, distance ourselves from the principal feminist theories in English-speaking countries insofar as we are unwilling and unable to lock ourselves into the notion that any analysis of representations of gender relations would be of interest only to women endowed with sexual awareness (an argument implicit in Modleski [1988]). Just as the French cinema continues to be aimed at spectators of both sexes without discriminating between them, we feel that gender relations concern men just as much as they do women. Equally, we have not followed the practice of most American feminists, who ignore the issue of class, for we feel that in the cinema of every period and in every culture that issue is profoundly interconnected with the issue of gender.

In the end, while we would like our work to be seen as part of the general framework of the struggle for sexual equality, we regard as of secondary importance the theoretical construction of a female spectator, which can be used as a basis for reassessing movies against the grain, so to speak, in other words, without paying any attention to a film's historical and social environment (Petro 1989; and, from a critical viewpoint, Williams 1988). We are more interested in identifying and understanding the generally conflicting and contradictory importance of gender relations at a given period, particularly since, in a country like France during the period under study, the spectator's position is resolutely male, in that the great majority of women, at least up until the 1970s, had internalized patriarchal values along with the secular and libertine connotations peculiar to France (Fraisse 1992; Rosanvallon 1993; Viennot 1995).

Our decision to focus on the period 1930–56 was motivated by various factors. First, as can be seen from publishers' catalogues, university degree courses, and art-house programs, most cinephiles and teachers of film studies are not overly familiar with French movies made before the New Wave arrived on the scene at the beginning of the 1960s and tend to look down on them, apart from a handful of established masterpieces. This can easily be explained by the history of film appreciation in France and in particular by the role played by *Les Cahiers du cinéma*, in whose pages were elaborated the theories of the future New Wave filmmakers who came to prominence at the end of the 1950s by elbowing aside the previous generation. But before pre–New Wave movies become totally incomprehensible once cultural benchmarks disappear, it is perhaps high time to rescue from oblivion those twenty-six years of French cinema, from the beginning of the talkies to the rise of the New Wave — a period notable in France for enjoying the highest cinema attendances and drawing on the widest social spectrum of filmgoers. From the end of the 1950s on, government support for high-quality cinema brought about a two-tiered system, auteur cinema and commercial cinema, a situation that persists today for better or for worse. Irrespective of the changing tastes that have, over the past forty years or so, led cinephiles to prefer Hollywood classics to French films over the same period, we felt it legitimate for us to look back over that production so as to understand its place, its function, and its significance in French society of the time. More crucially our intention was to focus on our recent past, certainly more useful than a study of Hollywood movies in helping us to understand where it is that *we* come from.

The choice of that period also seemed to us to be the right one for historical reasons: France was then going through the darkest and most traumatic years in its recent history; during the 1930s violent political clashes took place in an atmosphere of mounting ideological confusion; they were followed by the "phoney war," resulting in military defeat and the Débâcle, an unprecedented political and human disaster, which in turn led to four years of German occupation with its attendant miseries, suffering, and humiliation; finally came the Liberation, which marked both a deliverance and the end of an epoch, one in which France could still claim to be a great world power. That situation was confirmed by France's inability to escape the mechanism of the cold war, with the well-known impact it had on domestic politics. Ten years later, economic prosperity ushered in a new era, that of modernity and the consumer society. The "Brigitte Bardot bombshell" burst on the scene in 1956, the point at which we bring our study to a close.

Halfway through that period came the four years of the Occupation, which we have studied more particularly because, at a time when the French were going through the most painful ordeal in their history, the cinema occupied a very prominent place: along with sport, it was the only mass leisure activity that was authorized by the authorities and became, through the device of fiction, an outlet and an ideal means of expression for a society where the press and publishing were gagged by the dual censorship of Vichy and the German occupying forces. We were of the opinion that it was legitimate for us to delve more deeply into the film production of the time, which had hitherto been dismissed by film historians as merely a duller continuation of the cinema of the 1930s (Jeancolas 1983).

It was, on the contrary, on the basis of the abrupt change we noted between cinematic representation before the war and during the Occupation that we began to construct our argument, which seemed to be borne out by an equally marked shift that emerged in postwar cinema. Our definition of the corpus of movies we examined was geared to cultural history rather than a simple love of the cinema. So we watched, in the case of the 1940–44 period, a very large proportion of France's output (180 movies out of the 220 produced), while in the case of the 1930s and the postwar period we focused on a very broad sample of films that was representative of every genre and of every economic and cultural level, initially leaving aside all qualitative criteria, whether those of the time or later. Indeed as we progressed in our research, we felt the need to redefine those qualitative criteria, with the result that what we regarded as the "best" films were those that succeeded in dealing with the issues that were to be found in all films produced during that period in a sufficiently complex way to bring out its conflicts and contradictions, regardless of stereotypes. These movies were often the same as those in the film buffs' pantheon, but we approached them in a different way, which required us to eschew praise of their timeless beauty as created by some solitary genius and to demonstrate their extraordinarily acute approach to the problems of the time. As a result, certain other movies usually left out of the pantheon, often because they were not the work of established auteurs, came to be seen as more important.

As regards our choice of the central issue, it arose initially from our desire to take into account the specificity of the cinema, and of French cinema in particular, whose fictional material derives extensively from interpersonal relations between men and women and/or between people of the same sex. In other words, an analysis of cinematic representations of gender relations as a particular expression of a social imaginary enabled us both to respect the relative autonomy of our subject (fictional films do not touch much on politics in the strict sense of the term) and to avoid restricting ourselves to the myth of a timeless art devoted to the worship of beauty.

It was also the work of Ginette Vincendeau, a British-based French researcher, that supplied us with the starting point for our undertaking. In addition to her remarkable analyses of the Jean Gabin myth (1985; Gauteur and Vincendeau 1993), her main contribution to our understanding of French cinema in the 1930s arose from her observation of the way the image of an "incestuous couple" recurred in movies produced between the beginning of the talkies and the Débâcle of 1940 (1989). And we ourselves were able to verify that such movies typically portray a middle-aged man who enters into a more or less explicitly amorous relationship with a very young woman. As Vincendeau suggests, this pattern was probably overdetermined by factors that obtained at the time, such as the fact that the leading male stars were then elderly and met the requirements of the talkies because they had a background in the theater, where the presence of rather elderly young leads was considered quite normal. Such relationships were all the more unremarkable because bourgeois values encouraged marriage along those lines, particularly after the slaughter of the 1914–18 war (McMillan 1981). That pattern also signified, more powerfully than any other, the prerogatives of the father, whose power over women was indistinguishable from his power over children and, like French common law (the Napoleonic Code), maintained them in the same state of submission.

But to describe that narrative pattern as Oedipal, as Vincendeau does, runs the risk of producing a theoretical misinterpretation. We are happier with the other formulation she proposes: an incestuous pattern. Apart from a handful of movies labeled "realist," whether or not carrying the additional epithet "poetic," in which Jean Gabin usually has to face up to a domineering "unworthy father," the most characteristic feature of those prewar films is that the subject of the fantasy is never Oedipus or Electra (the female child, according to the young Sigmund Freud), but the father as representative of the Law who tries to oust the "son" in order to appropriate the "daughter." The term *incest* also makes it possible to tie that film theme in with a whole psychosocial paradigm in real life that extended well beyond arranged marriages between older men and young women, since sexual abuse of girls by men in a position of power over them is not just what a psychoanalyst might describe as a fantasy, as Nancy Huston (1979) and Marie-Victoire Louis (1994) have usefully pointed out.

Now if the origin of that pattern of the incestuous couple is to be seen as arising not from a universal, hence "innocent," psychical phase of human ontogenesis (if Freud is to be believed) but from a hidden yet very real violence in society, its widespread occurrence in the films of that decade (almost a third of all movies) begins to make sense. The sexual self-confidence of such portly Lotharios as Raimu, Harry Baur, Jules Berry, and Victor Francen, combined with the submissiveness of young women whose faces and names were so quickly forgotten, can be interpreted as a denial of the crumbling patriarchal edifice, a denial symptomatic of a fear of changes already under way (Sohn 1991/1994).

In the study of gender relations, it is commonplace to note that men as a whole, at all times and in all places, have displayed fear and mistrust of the female sex (Dinnerstein 1978). Given that context, under the particularly oppressive and outmoded patriarchy of 1930s France (McMillan 1981), such images of sexual submission by the child-woman were taken for granted and inevitably prompted some left-wing filmmakers to include examples of rebellion against the father. To be more specific, who was responsible for the fear of women that features in those films? Frenchmen (a facile generalization much loved by feminist writers)? French petit bourgeois? French intellectuals? The male community of filmmakers (in the broadest sense) and their boulevardier entourage? At the stage we have so far reached in our work, only this last hypothesis seems to us to be indisputable.

Or could it be that we are looking at a displacement of more directly political fears toward the register of gender relations, which in that case would be a smokescreen: fear of war, fear of the loss of national identity, fear of the Other? That is the hypothesis favored by French film historians when they observe a thematic regularity in the cinematic representation of relations between generations and between the sexes (Bertin-Maghit 1989; Garçon 1984; de La Bretèque 1977). However that may be, such representations also probably reflect a fear of real women — a fear exacerbated by modest social progress and the very reasonable demands of the feminist organizations of the time (Bard 1995).

These same issues take on a completely different complexion in the light of the startling revelations that emerged from our close examination of four-fifths of French films produced between 1940 and 1944 under the German Occupation and the rule of the Vichy government. What we see from start to finish during that period is a veritable supplanting of the Law of the Father by a fantasized "Law of the Mother." This reversal, which is to be found in almost all movies of the period, can be attributed, as we ourselves are tempted to do, to the trauma of defeat and the discredit that attached to a patriarchy closely associated with the Third Republic and its routed chiefs of staff. This hypothesis tends to substantiate, much more even than the incestuous pattern of the prewar period, the existence of a male social imaginary as well as its surprising changeability: fear and hatred of women vanished in no time at all (we noted that the change took place in a matter of months) and were replaced either by a rigid female figure on a pedestal, like some monument to discredited masculinity (an attitude typical of the traditionalist right and its mouthpiece, the right-thinking Catholic press), or by a dynamic figure that foreshadowed a future renaissance (a left-wing stance, as, for example, in Louis Aragon's novel *Aurélien* of 1944).

That male social imaginary in a state of crisis, which can be detected in the work of the great majority of male directors, has its left-wing and its right-wing versions (which comes as no surprise, given that we are talking about France, where this division is traditional). But how can one explain why so many movies are capable of being interpreted in various ways (*Le Ciel est à vous* [*The Woman Who Dared*], 1944, is the most celebrated example) and do not contrast as obviously with one another as the "unworthy fathers" of poetic realism did with the "complacent fathers" of the boulevard films or Marcel Pagnol's Provence?

Pierre Laborie (1990) notes that the prevailing atmosphere during the prewar period in France was one of political and ideological confusion. Yves Chalas (1985) argues that the Débâcle and the Occupation caused people in all sections of society — from Resistants to collaborators, from right-wing Vichyites (supporters of Charles Maurras, traditionalist Catholics) to left-wing Vichyites (followers of Paul Faure, then leader of the Socialist Party) and even apolitical believers in a wait-and-see policy — to yearn vaguely for "something else," which he describes as a "transcendence of liberal capitalism."

Let us look a little more closely at the argument — admittedly a controversial one — that some progressive aspirations emerged under Vichy. The theme of regeneration through women that can be found in the totality of film production at the time is comparable to the celebrated "return to the land" advocated by Philippe Pétain. Gérard Miller (1975) notes that this theme was initially "launched" by the exodus of June 1940, when French living in the north, east, and Paris region turned their back on the modern, urban, and industrial society that had been the cause of upheavals since 1936 and had failed to protect them against the invading Germans, and sought refuge in the agricultural south, which also represented a retreat into the past. Christian Faure (1989) points out that, independently of Pétain's propaganda, the Vichyite desire to promote the farming world resulted in the creation of a rural French ethnography (the opening of the Museum of Popular Arts and Traditions) and a major documentary school, the most famous example of which was Georges Rouquier's *Farrébique* (which was actually made after the war but grew directly out of one of Vichy's official programs). Today, now that the farming community, the landscape of France, and the quality of its farm products are under threat from the increasingly absurd principles of liberal capitalism, we can take a more dialectical view of that phenomenon: the aspirations embodied in France under Vichy both by the official theme of upgrading rural life and by the activities fostered by that promotion, can be seen to anticipate certain aspects of present-day ecology. In that light, it becomes easier to see that it is a mistake to describe the ideological ambiguity that informed civil society, at least during the first two years of the Vichy government, in solely pejorative terms.

Now the same is true of the aspirations reflected, for example, in the setting up of schools for women cadres, modeled after the celebrated Ecole d'Uriage for men, whose stated aim was to rectify the serious deficiencies of the Third Republic regarding the civic and social education of the national community's female members. Those hopes of a greater empowerment for both sexes in society, as well as for a new relationship for couples and a new conception of fatherhood (Delumeau and Roche 1990), greatly influenced the Occupation cinema.

Albert Camus, Emmanuel Bove, Jean-Paul Sartre, and Aragon were virtually the only writers at that time who exposed the male identity crisis triggered by the Defeat. However, in *L'Etranger*, *Le Piège*, and *Les Chemins de la liberté* (*Aurélien*, which was greatly influenced by Elsa Triolet, is a case apart), male self-doubt is accompanied by often violent misogyny, which is precisely what distinguishes these books by the literary elite from the great majority of films of the period. This difference between literature and cinema can perhaps be explained by the specific characteristics of the two artistic disciplines: the writer stands alone and is an heir to a French cultural tradition that gives pride of place to the male universe (Coquillat 1982). Although writers may be aware of the world around them, they do not write for it; they write for eternity.

The collective artist that makes a movie (that is to say, both the director's team and the milieu of film professionals) has an attitude that is more receptive to the world as a result of belonging to a group, and awareness of the ephemeral nature of film (which was much greater then than it is now) meant that people making movies were working in the present for the audiences of the time. And let us not forget the commercial dimension of the cinema, which encourages the collective filmmaker, whether consciously or not, to be receptive to the Zeitgeist—which in our view is not necessarily a bad thing.

However that may be, this complementarity between a male identity crisis and a regenerative view of the female is nowhere as patently obvious as in the cinema. True, in a handful of works for the theater — another collective art — we find female effigies surrounded by men in a state of crisis according to a pattern similar to that of the most typical movies of the period. And Pierre Laborie (1993) has pinpointed how the Catholic press of southwest France used Joan of Arc as a symbol of unity and solidarity during the same period.

The huge scale of the phenomenon in the cinema compared with its virtual absence from popular literature, for example, leaves several questions unanswered and probably touches on an area that has remained little explored up to now, at least in France: the specificity of various cultural practices, both individual and collective, in a given social formation at a given time. Taking the cinema alone, how did creators and technicians become mediators of the social imaginary — always supposing that such an identity crisis of the sexes falls under that heading?

The male identity crisis that regularly comes in the wake of a war, that supreme test of manly values (especially when it results in defeat), has begun to be investigated in the case of other periods and other nations (Theweleit 1987–89; Maugue 1987). As regards France in the 1940s, one could argue that as a result of the two national humiliations triggered by that war — the Débâcle followed by the Occupation, then the Liberation led by non-French forces — the male identity crisis should be divided into two phases: a collapse followed by a backlash. Following two complementary trajectories, the active and independent woman of the Occupation turns into a diabolical figure (*Panique* [*Panic*], 1946), whose actions are exclusively directed against men, whereas the complacent male turns into a victim (*Manèges* [*The Cheat*], 1949), as though echoing the image that the countless French prisoners of war had of themselves as they returned from their ordeal, terrified that women would no longer accept the submissive role they played before the war (Durand 1987).

Film representations of the postwar period are, however, highly contradictory; in the context of a dominant atmosphere of misogyny, and at a time when Beauvoir's *Le Deuxième Sexe* (1949) was poised to become a best-seller of the 1950s, a number of truly feminist movies, in the modern sense of the word, were produced. Often remarkable, like *Casque d'or* (*Golden Marie*, 1952), they attempted to reveal the workings of patriarchal oppression by demonstrating that it was also a burden for men.

Thus more than any other means of expression, in our view, the cinema reflects the destabilization of gender relations in French society of the 1940s that was triggered by political and military events. In this book we focus on their repercussions in the area of private life traditionally regarded as being governed by a different temporality (the *longue durée* of the history of mentalities).

The sensitivity of the cinema to upheavals in the area of gender relations brought about by war and the Occupation proves, if proof were needed, how political the private sphere is. Moreover our bringing to light a layer of meanings perceptible only (for the moment) in fictional films, which account for only part of cultural output, should also demonstrate how useful it can be to approach the history of the cinema as an autonomous area capable of telling us much more about the state of our societies, provided films are no longer regarded as a mere reflection, or counterreflection, of ideas elaborated elsewhere.

Our book takes the form of a triptych whose central panel consists of an overall analysis of the French cinema during the Occupation. Two "side panels" offer a more schematic overview of the prewar and postwar periods, each of which covers a decade. All three historical panels are accompanied by separate sections that analyze a number of movies — many of them well known, others little known — whose complexity we felt deserved special treatment. In each case, we try to demonstrate how the status of a masterpiece, whether or not recognized by cinephiles, derives not from some lofty isolation in the firmament of ideas and forms but from a particularly remarkable ability to bring out the contradictions of the period.

We warmly thank those who allowed us unrestricted access to their archives: Dominique Païni of the Cinémathèque Française, Michelle Aubert and the Film Archive Department of the Centre National de la Cinématographie, and Gabrielle Claes of the Cinémathèque Royale de Belgique.

In the case of prewar and postwar films, we have indicated their date of commercial release, whereas we have preferred to indicate the date when shooting began in the case of Occupation films, given the speed of events characteristic of that period and their effects on films as soon as production started.

Part I

THE PREWAR PERIOD, 1930–1939

ॐ

CHAPTER I

Panorama of a Cine-Family Romance

THE FIRST SECTION of this book, an overview of the 1930s, does not claim to be exhaustive. In focusing more particularly on an undoubtedly restricted number of films, we intend above all to illustrate the broad tendency that is characteristic of the French cinema during that decade: the "incestuous" father figure in his three variants—"complacent," "self-sacrificing," and "unworthy." Readers will have to accept our contention that all the films concerned are representative of production at the time, even if they do not always square with the image we may have today of a quality product. An unambitious movie like *Vous n'avez rien à déclarer?* (*Confessions of a Newlywed*, 1937, which, by the way, remains as funny as ever) can be as representative of the imaginary of a given period as a work that has been elevated by posterity to the rank of an auteur film—a postulate that is central to our whole approach. We also devote more extensive analysis to a number of films whose superior quality is generally recognized, while endeavoring to demonstrate how they go against the grain in their treatment of the major themes of the period—a characteristic that, in our view, explains their exceptional quality.

THE FOURTH VOLUME of *History of Private Life*, edited by Philippe Ariès and Georges Duby (1998), covers under a wide range of headings the period running from the French Revolution of 1789 to World War I; the fifth and final volume, *Riddles of Identity in Modern Times* (1998), deals almost exclusively with changes that have occurred only since 1950. Implicitly, then, the interwar period is perceived, as far as developments in that area are concerned, as a kind of no-man's-land between the old and the new society, in which the order of private lives remained intact within structures bequeathed by the nineteenth century, despite the fact that the area of public affairs was so remarkably eventful. The broad argument of that book is that France in the 1930s was still dominated by the omnipotent father figure, whose rule is analyzed as follows by Michelle Perrot in her chapter "Roles and Characters":

> Figurehead of the family as well as of civil society, the father dominates the history of private life in the 19th century. Law, philosophy, and politics all conspired to establish and legitimate his authority. . . . Deprived of the king, traditionalists sought to restore the father. Revolutionaries and republicans were no less eager to bolster his authority. . . . Republicans placed the keys to the city in the father's hands. . . . In the name of nature, the Civil Code granted the husband absolute superiority in the household and the father absolute superiority in the family; the wife and mother were legally incapacitated. (167–68)

The *pétroleuses* (female firebrands) of the Commune, the female workers in arms factories, and the *garçonne* look of the Roaring Twenties are misleading images; in fact Frenchwomen throughout the interwar period lagged behind their northern European sisters (almost all of whom had obtained the right to vote just after World War I, for example). James F. McMillan (1981), the author of the first sociological study of the condition of women during the Third Republic, sums up the situation in the 1920s as follows:

> Our argument is that contemporaries greatly exaggerated the extent of women's progress in the wider sphere [of work and civil rights] while failing to appreciate the significant ways in which the impact of the First World War reinforced rather than weakened the cult of domesticity. . . . Likewise, women continued to be discriminated against in most administrative jobs. . . . The new opportunities for girls in secondary and higher education were slow to produce any notable "feminisation" of the liberal professions. . . . The point remains nevertheless that in interwar France

there was no lack of signs to indicate the survival of an essentially patri-archal social order. (117–20)

But a cultural study by an American researcher, Mary Louise Roberts (1994), shows that "overestimates" of many phenomena affecting women and sexual identity in the years following World War I, although contradicted by statistics, do nevertheless reflect real and widespread concerns in society. According to Roberts, it was the fear of a blurring of the borderline between the sexes that underpinned the major debates in the 1920s about the "modern woman" and her androgynous look, about the relationship between mother-hood and sex, and about the tax status of the unmarried woman, against a background of both sexual freedom and natalism.

While one of the characteristics of the 1920s, in France as well as in Germany, for example, was a general and explicitly formulated concern about questions of sexual identity, the 1930s ushered in a normalizing repression whose emblem, in Roberts's view, was the introduction of more subdued fashions. From that perspective, it is probably significant that one of the most striking films of the period immediately after World War I in France, Abel Gance's *La Roue* (*The Wheel*, 1923), adopts an outspoken and anguished approach toward incestuous desire (which lies at the heart of sexual differentiation), whereas in the cinema of the 1930s, on the contrary, this same fantasy was both an object of denial and an increasingly commonplace theme. Ginette Vincendeau (1985) argues that Léo Joannon's *Vous n'avez rien à déclarer?*, based on a 1906 vaude-ville comedy by Hennequin and Veber, illustrates the "nostalgia" for live pre-war shows (vaudeville, *caf' conc'*) that was a feature of early talkies in France.

Let us summarize the convoluted plot and ideological argument of this film: a likable middle-aged entomologist called Papillot (Raimu) is about to emerge from the "cocoon" of sexual abstinence in which he is trapped at the beginning of the film. In order to do that, he follows a course that eventu-ally — in the very last shot — legitimizes his right to consort with young women on a regular basis, in this case with a charming demimondaine, Evelyne (Germaine Aussey). He feels entitled to do so in view of the fact that his rather un-attractive wife (Marguerite Templey) has been having a long-term affair with a preposterous bourgeois (Alerme); that the great love of his student years, Angèle (Pauline Carton), has become a toilet attendant in a cabaret; that his shy young assistant, Edmond (Pierre Brasseur), now his son-in-law, has, with expert coaching from the wife he has recently married, Paulette (Sylvia Ba-taille), managed to emerge from his own "cocoon" (the traumatic result of a coitus interruptus on his wedding night); and that the two insects that have obstinately refused to copulate since the beginning of the film finally get down to it too, thus providing ample proof that coitus is a natural thing.

The successive displacements of this scenario are typical of the denial of incest that was characteristic of the cinema of the period. After deciding to help his son-in-law to overcome the unfortunate repercussions of his wedding night on a train (a customs officer burst into the compartment of his sleeper at a critical moment — hence the title of the film), Papillot first goes to see a scatty psychoanalyst (Saturnin Fabre) and, in a scene added by the film's adapters, describes his young friend's misadventure. The psychoanalyst clearly believes that Papillot is describing an imaginary friend who simply serves to disguise a similar mishap he has himself experienced. Although this suspicion is belied by the actual text, the episode reveals the true argument of the film, whereby the beneficiary is not "the son" but the father. Later on, in a curious scene, Papillot finds himself sitting alone with Paulette one evening in the drawing room; they both seem to want to tell the other something but are unable to express it and end up simply saying goodnight. This scene, which serves absolutely no purpose in an otherwise perfectly linear context, reveals the film's subtext: the incest taboo, whose transgression the beautiful and obliging dancer, Evelyne, enables Papillot to enact at the end of the movie.

We would argue that the term *nostalgia* that Vincendeau applies to such a film is not entirely apt; the use of themes from turn-of-the-century vaudeville results here in such far-reaching changes that it would be more accurate to talk of an incestuous construction specific to 1930s cinema than of a nostalgic escape into the past. When the film's scenario is compared with the original text, it in fact emerges that this incestuous dimension, on which the whole adaptation hinges, was totally invented by the adapters. In the original, the relationship between the father-in-law of the traumatized young man and the prostitute who is supposed to help the latter to "recover his pride" is a mere starting point that is taken for granted, and the typically turn-of-the-century theme of the play is social advancement through marriage, the son-in-law in this case being a wealthy aristocrat, not one of the father's employees (Kaussen 1992). Far from being a passive reflection of the enduring patriarchal system, the film is a plea, specific to its period, in favor of threatened privileges, whereas the original play, written at a time when those privileges were taken for granted, simply attempted to use a certain sexual hedonism as a smokescreen for some not very commendable social ambitions.

In order to look at Vincendeau's observations in greater detail, we drew up a list of some three hundred films (out of the thousand specifically French productions that came out between 1929 and 1939) where this "incestuous" father-daughter relationship can be observed. The regular recurrence of that theme is confirmed by the analyses found in *Générique des années 30* (Lagny et al. 1986: 177–200), based on a systematic classification of leading roles in the cinema during that decade. It is a surprisingly high figure, which lends that cinema a homogeneity comparable to that of popular cinema in Japan, Hong Kong, or India, with their endlessly repeated narrative devices, and is in sharp contrast with the American cinema, where conformity is more often organized according to genre.

But we also observed that the sampling of the father by Vincendeau (1989) makes no distinction between the three aspects of the incestuous fantasy actually found in that cinema, namely "the complacent father," "the self-sacrificing father," and "the unworthy father." About half the instances feature a "complacent father." These are films in which the father's power is reinforced, sometimes in an explicitly sexual manner (*Vous n'avez rien à déclarer?*), but more often implicitly (*Justin de Marseille*, *Abus de confiance* [*Abused Confidence*]), where denial does not lead to any enactment, not even through a displacement, as in Joannon's film. That kind of father, whether or not in quotes, was often played at the time by Raimu, but also on occasion by Charles Vanel (*Carrefour* [*Crossroads*]), Jules Berry (*Arlette et ses papas*), and Pierre Blanchar (*La Nuit de décembre* [*Night in December*]), among others.

The rest of these incestuous fathers fall into two categories: "the self-sacrificing" figures, chiefly played by Harry Baur but also by Erich von Stroheim, and "unworthy" fathers, not so much "inadequate" as downright evil. Those in the latter category, unlike the two others, no longer play a central role but serve as an antagonist to a younger male central character. Often featuring in movies made by left-leaning French directors, the most memorable incarnations of that role are those of Jules Berry (*Le Crime de Monsieur Lange* [*The Crime of Monsieur Lange*], *Le Jour se lève* [*Daybreak*]) and Michel Simon (*Le Quai des brumes* [*Port of Shadows*]).

While the "complacent" father was easily the dominant figure during the first half of the decade (a period that saw the triumph of filmed vaudeville) but became statistically less common after 1936, the theme of the "self-sacrificing" father, which gained ground after that date, was nevertheless well represented from the beginning of the sound era. As for the "unworthy" father, he was essentially a phenomenon that appeared after the Popular Front and went hand in hand with the (modest) development of poetic realism.

Now the way these different fathers fall into distinct periods is only one of several indications which suggest that the resonance of this theme of incest is not simply one more proof of patriarchy's enduring sway; it is much more a reactive and exorcizing ritual organized by a well-defined community of male filmmakers. For, although all had a complex relationship with their milieu, class, and sex, most strove to dispel the threatening clouds that hung over patriarchal power, capitalist order, and national identity.

For despite its apparently solid foundations, patriarchal legitimacy suffered various setbacks in 1930s France that could not have escaped the notice of any Frenchman: in 1935 legislation abolished a father's right to administer corporal punishment; in 1938 the same fate befell marital rights. On three occasions, the National Assembly voted in favor of granting women the vote (the last time in 1936), no doubt because the MPs were aware that the more conservative Senate would block the decision. The tyranny of the Napoleonic Code continued to be a burden on women, and natalist concerns resulted in the introduction toward the end of the decade of the Family Code, which tended to intensify the confinement of women to their maternal function.

Meanwhile, however, the strikes on an unprecedented scale that hailed the victory of the Popular Front in 1936 traumatized the social counterpart of private patriarchy, that is, the hierarchy of the workplace. And those strikes followed in the wake of the clashes of 1934, which could then be seen as marking the definitive failure of the far-right leagues that felt open nostalgia for the father. It is equally well known that some sections of the middle and lower-middle classes were very worried about the "foreign invasion"—that of Italian and Polish immigrant workers, of refugees from Spain, and of Jews hounded out of central Europe (Schor 1985: 168–70)—which was "eroding" a national identity whose connection with the Law of the Father is better expressed in German than in French (*Vaterland*).

ℜ The Godfather of the Nation and His Goddaughter

A young American woman researcher, Lynn Kirby (n.d.), has done pioneering work on the converging representations of xenophobia and the "national identity crisis" familiar to historians in a number of major films of the period, in particular Maurice Tourneur's *Justin de Marseille* (1934), Jacques Feyder's *La Kermesse héroique* (*Carnival in Flanders*, 1935), and Marc Allégret's *Gribouille* (*Heart of Paris*, 1937). Her analysis of Tourneur's movie, in particular, throws original light on the connection between xenophobia and a reaffirmation of the power of the father—a complacent one, to say the least.

Justin (Berval), a prominent Marseille gangster who hates violence (an idealistic picture cooked up by the scriptwriter Carlo Rim with the permission of the city's underworld), is the benevolent patriarch par excellence; a humorous and affable man who never loses his cool, he rules over a likable gang of crooks, as well as a kind of "private" pseudo-family made up of two children and a grandmother, and a "street" family representing the People and consisting of winsome young women selling shellfish in Marseille's old port. The struggle Justin wages against the Other throughout the film begins paradoxically when he does a favor to a "good" foreigner, a Chinese drug trafficker who is on the level. But in so doing he simply dishes up the familiar cliché image of unobtrusive Chinese who keep out of the news (Schor 1985). Shown solely in their den at the end of a telephone line, these Chinese are not part of Marseille. Justin does them a good turn by foiling the plans of a much less well-behaved rival gang that has robbed them—a gang made up of Italians and banked by "a man who dresses like an Englishman." Justin ends up executing their leader (discreetly offscreen), thus ridding the city of a heterogeneous element who does not stick to the rules and has, in addition, killed his one real buddy in the gang, a gentle, simple-minded man known as Le Bègue (the Stutterer), played by Pierre Larquey. It is then almost by chance, at the end of the film, that Justin unintentionally "inherits," with the most honorable intentions, the innocent young creature who, at the beginning of the story, is cynically seduced by Tonio, an apprentice pimp scheming to send her "around the world in a pink nightie."

She is one lucky girl! In a key scene at the beginning of the film, the young pimp, impatient to get his way with her and bent on luring his victim into a shady hotel, ignores her romantic outpourings at the sight of the night sky. In the final scene, after preventing the young woman from committing suicide and taking her under his wing, Justin turns his back on the same hotel and walks away arm in arm with her while himself waxing lyrical about the stars— and the beauties of the city of Marseille. Lynn Kirby demonstrates convincingly that in this film Marseille stands for France and that the gentle patriarch who respects very young women (but keeps them on hand) embodies the defender of the Nation against an alliance between a figure who conjures up an image of "perfidious Albion" and a vulgar and brutal Italian behind whom the specter of fascism can be detected: Carlo Rim's anarchist-leaning populism was typical of many left-wing intellectuals.

Another aspect of the complacent father, associated with a very different political option, can be found in the character of Jacques Ferney (Charles Vanel) in Henri Decoin's *Abus de confiance*. Actually he is not as complacent as all that, since he harbors a guilty secret. The film itself harbors another, that of a certain nostalgia that still thrived in 1936. It is one of the few films of the period that has a woman as its central character, Lydia (Danielle Darrieux, the first young female "star" of the French cinema). At the outset, the movie charts with genuine seriousness the gradual changes in the condition of women, as well as some of the obstacles that hindered them, which was fairly rare at the time.

Throughout the first part of the film, where the visual style is similar to that of the emerging school of poetic realism, Decoin shows in an almost didactic manner how Lydia, an orphan and a law student, is exposed to examples of male aggression of various kinds. These range from the pimp lurking in the cemetery where she has just buried her last relative to the hotel owner who wants the rent she owes him to be paid "in kind"; from the prospective employer seeking a secretary willing to "work for him at home in the evening," who turns down a polyglot but overweight supertypist in favor of the pretty Lydia, to the nice student who tries to take advantage of his impecunious friend by getting her drunk and taking her to a hotel. With the exception of the student, a socially indeterminate preadult, all these exploiters of poor women (including the restaurant owner who stops giving her credit) belong to what could roughly be described as the petite bourgeoisie. The few people during this first part of the film who want to help her in a disinterested way are, on the other hand, mostly from a working-class background: a restaurant waiter, a woman oyster vendor, and, above all, her best female friend, who suggests to Lydia the idea of the swindle that gives the movie its title.

The idea is that Lydia should turn up at the home of a wealthy and eminent historian with documents that her friend had found by chance and that seem to prove that she is the man's illegitimate daughter, the fruit of an affair with a woman in his youth whom he abandoned and who subsequently died. Ferney, the historian (Charles Vanel), leads a quiet and contented life, surrounded by his books and enjoying the unobtrusive solicitude of his wife, Hélène (Valentine Tessier), at their Versailles villa (the lighting and camera style of these scenes belong to the "theatrical" cinema of the period); appropriately enough, Ferney's special area of research is the Ancien Régime.

Needless to say, the generous patriarch takes into his home the fruit of his guilty love with just a quiver of excitement whose ambiguity is reinforced by his wife's jealousy; she initially suspects him of having an affair, wrongly as far as the apparent context is concerned, but whose possibility is reinforced in the audience's mind because they know he is not her father. The couple end up

Charles Vanel and Danielle Darrieux in *Abus de confiance*, 1937. Courtesy of Raymond Voinquel and Loulou Marx, Cinémathèque française.

adopting the orphan, even after the truth is revealed. They help her to embark on the first steps of her chosen career as a barrister and entrust her to a husband worthy of her, who is none other than Ferney's double—his young assistant, Pierre, who is following in his footsteps. Here the choice of an actor whose charm is a little insipid (Pierre Mingand) throws a singular light on the film's subtext, which was already clear from the posters and the credit titles: the true couple is the "incestuous" couple, and the marriage (in fact an arranged one) is no more than a convention designed to safeguard the incest taboo.

In 1936 the social message of this fable was clear: a certain emancipation of young middle-class women is inevitable, but in order for the patriarchy to retain control, it is necessary not only to reaffirm the authority of fathers but to return to the legendary age of a benevolent monarchy, to a society run by an elite of enlightened intellectuals who have objective affinities with the "true workers" and who are not only above base pecuniary considerations (associated with the petite bourgeoisie) but respectful of women. Though we need not necessarily suspect Decoin or his scriptwriter Pierre Wolf of having supported Action française, there is here a strong whiff of that monarchist, antirepublican movement.

It is worth looking a little more closely at this virginal and enterprising young woman, as it is her like who are most often subjected to the amorous attentions of our potbellied fathers. Evelyne (Germaine Aussey), the demimondaine in *Vous n'avez rien à déclarer?*, a kind of courtesan who is almost extradiegetic, is more an amused spectator of Papillot's clowning than a true character; while Papillot's daughter (Sylvia Bataille) looks deceptively as though butter wouldn't melt in her mouth, but when the time comes she knows just how to initiate her timid husband. But that role is more usually played by the kind of modern and dynamic young woman embodied by a whole series of actresses with short careers (from Madeleine Ozeray and Josette Day to Jacqueline Delubac and Jacqueline Laurent), and above all, after Léo Joannon's *Quelle drôle de gosse* (1935), by Danielle Darrieux. Along with Viviane Romance, Edwige Feuillère, and Michèle Morgan, Darrieux was one of a quartet of women who made their mark on prewar French cinema at a time when there were very few leading female roles (barely more than 5 percent of all movies produced in France).

What is at stake in the patriarchal imaginary, embodied in the figure of the "modern young woman," is a more and more urgently needed control of the "new woman," who goes out to work and thus risks breaking free from men. This phenomenon is bluntly portrayed in Jacques Deval's *Club de femmes* (*Girls' Club*, 1936), a movie that may seem to go against the general trend of the period in that it features no patriarch but nevertheless takes place from start to finish under the "father's gaze."

A group of resolutely modern-minded young women are cooped up in a kind of secular convent well out of sight of any men and therefore more likely to expose themselves spontaneously to the male gaze of the camera; Claire (Danielle Darrieux) and her chums romp around mostly in shorts, sun suits, or negligees. True, they are employed outside the establishment (and offscreen) but, we are led to believe, only while waiting to find a husband. In the course of five interwoven but broadly independent plots, the road to modern normality is carefully signposted: Claire is flanked by three rather sordid counterexamples—a tragic lesbian doomed to be unhappy in love (Else Argal), a cynical Swede who sells her body in order to rise in society (Betty Stockfeld), and a working-class telephone operator (Junie Astor) who, out of a sense of class solidarity with her pimp friend, finds him prey he can easily exploit. All these transgressions are of course punished (the Swede is abandoned, while the lesbian poisons the telephone operator out of female solidarity).

The transgression committed by Claire, who is an amiable sort of rebel, is more harmless. All she does is break the rule that no man is permitted to

Eve Francis, Danielle Darrieux, and Raymond Galle in *Club de femmes*, 1936. Courtesy of
Vincent Rossell and Pierre Le Fauconnier, Cinémathèque française.

enter the Club. It is a funny, lighthearted transgression that bears the stamp
of positivity: the young woman contrives to get her boyfriend (a nice but insignificant student and certainly not a potential husband) into her room in the
course of a kind of reversal of a barracks-room comedy routine that naturally
involves his dressing up as a woman. In other words, in the fantasies current in
Deval's boulevardier milieu, the ideal preparation for marriage includes a combination of sexy work (Claire is a music hall chorus girl) and laddish pranks
that can even involve an illegitimate birth. (A fifth narrative thread centered
on a secret pregnancy is treated in the same jolly conspiratorial manner.) These
audacities are of no consequence, since they are comical, titillating, and liable
to provide sexual training for a future woman partner. Once the fracas caused
by the discovery of Claire's boyfriend has died down, the matron who runs
the Club (Eve Francis) intervenes for the last time. She is an authoritarian
mother figure, slightly ludicrous, as is only to be expected, but who, when the
time comes, acts as a spokeswoman for the paternal comprehension we suspect
is waiting in the wings, reminding everyone that the whole episode is just an
interlude leading up to wedding bells. This is lighter and bawdier (there is no
longer any question of virginity) than the approach adopted by the moralizing

Jean-Louis Barrault and Madeleine Renaud in *Hélène*, 1936. Courtesy of Cinémathèque française.

Abus de confiance. But both films embody the same phantasmatic determination to control a femininity that is beginning to cause alarm.

To illustrate the quasi-hegemony of the theme of incest throughout this decade, we should now turn to *Hélène* (1936), by Jean Benoît-Lévy and Marie Epstein (along with Marguerite Viel, the only French woman director making feature-length movies at the time). The central character of *Hélène* is one of the most "modern" of the period. Adapted from a novel by Vicky Baum, the film is anchored in the tradition of central European proselytizing feminism, which scarcely had any equivalent in French literature or cinema of the time. Hélène Wilfur, a poor young woman student played by Madeleine Renaud, takes on the job of assistant to her chemistry teacher, Professor Amboise (Constant Rémy), so she can afford to continue her studies. Pierre Régnier (Jean-Louis Barrault), a young musician who has been forced by his father to study medicine so he can follow in his footsteps, is in love with her. In desperation he commits suicide after making her pregnant. Hélène gives birth to her baby and goes back to work, only to discover that her professor, who is devastated after being left by his wife, has given up his research. She manages to persuade him to go back to work with her.

Although a denunciation of institutional machismo (Hélène has difficulty convincing the authorities of her skills as a researcher) and of the power of the father (resulting in the suicide of Régnier, who is torn between his musical talents and his father's pressure on him to pursue studies for which he is unsuited), the film's dénouement enables it nevertheless to fit into a French template. After having had to put up with the run-of-the-mill misogyny of Professor Amboise in order to succeed in her studies, Hélène eventually becomes his work colleague — and a great prop to his morale after his wife leaves him to pursue a career as an opera singer. In those days, it was only because of this last-minute rallying around the father figure that a film was able to argue in favor of women taking male jobs. This augured ill for the future of feminism in France.

℘ Martyrs of the Sex War

In 1931 Julien Duvivier directed an adaptation of Irène Némirovsky's bestselling novel, *David Golder*. The movie, which is the first striking example of a talkie that features a sacrificial father figure, has in our view the heuristic merit of doubly combining a defense of speculative neoliberalism with a certain "cultural" anti-Semitism and a (barely denied) fantasy of father-daughter incest with thoroughgoing misogyny. The main work of this film resides in a chain of displacements that both naturalizes and obscures these various discourses through a process of accumulation.

David Golder (Harry Baur) is a prominent Jewish financier of the kind frequently caricatured in satirical journals that had been peddling a petit bourgeois and anticapitalist form of anti-Semitism for more than half a century. But in the movie as well as in the novel, Golder is a good Jew, an assimilated Jew. Harry Baur, incidentally, was not Jewish at all (Le Boterf 1995: 12–13). He is simply a leading financier like any other (the first displacement), a self-made man who managed to pull himself up by his own bootstraps and escape the Odessa ghetto. But above all he is just an ordinary husband (the second displacement), ruining his health to make more and more money so as to maintain his scandalously spendthrift and idle wife and daughter, who live surrounded by a bevy of effeminate hangers-on in a villa on the Côte d'Azur.

In order to make it clear from the start that the Jewish element in Golder has nothing to do with his being a ruthless financier (in the opening sequence, he drives a rival to ruin and suicide), he needs to be flanked by another profiteer whose blatantly Jewish characteristics visibly square with the codes of ordinary racism at the time. By dividing the traditional target of French anti-Semitism into a good subject (the assimilated Jew who makes his capital work for him) and a bad one (a "wog" and unproductive hoarder), the film achieves in two sequences the major ideological shift that within the space of a century gradually severed anti-Semitism from its anticapitalist roots (Leon 1971).

Harry Baur and Jackie Monnier in *David Golder*, 1931. Courtesy of Cinémathèque française.

In the Némirovsky novel, the character called Soifer (the "bad Jew") appears only very briefly toward the end of the book. In the Duvivier movie, on the other hand, he plays a prominent role during two long sequences. The only friend and confidant of Golder, the big-time speculator, he is a caricature of the Jew from the ghetto and gets contemptuous looks from his friend's Aryan manservant; he owns a fortune (in the form of diamonds because he mistrusts banks) but walks on tiptoe so as not to wear out his heels. This is undoubtedly one of the most anti-Semitic portraits to be found in the cinema of the period, where such depictions were commonplace (Garçon 1984).

But the second operation of the film involves shrouding this anti-Semitism with straightforward male solidarity aimed at combating consistently predatory women. In this confrontation, the world of audacious and modern finance can lend a helping hand to the most archaic form of Jewry: when telling Soifer about the funeral of his unfortunate rival, Golder makes no secret of his disgust at the cupidity and ugliness of the man's widow. This way of turning Golder above all into a victim of women makes both the defense of speculation (made out to be an exciting and productive game) and the anti-Semitic distinction between the good and the bad Jew seem to be the most commonplace and normal thing in the world.

In the last account, Golder is simply an ordinary man who is exploited, "like all the others," by a shrewish wife (who, on the other hand, is interested solely in a bad, extravagant use of money). How can he avoid transferring his desire (albeit sublimated) to a daughter who is just as much a spendthrift as her mother but is also superbly beautiful and responds to just the right degree to his incestuous caresses? Indeed while the daughter's affection is portrayed as superficial and self-interested, her father's desire is seen to be natural and touching.

The high point of the film is the harrowing clash between Golder, who has been struck down by his first heart attack, and his castrating wife, Gloria (Paule Andral), who stands over his bed and screams that he is not the father of his beloved Joyce (Jacky Monnier)—which has the effect of adding spice to the subtext, since the incest taboo loses its power. And yet to save his "daughter" from the life of poverty she would have had to endure if he decided to retire in the hope of giving his weakened heart another lease of life, Golder gets back to work again. He returns to his roots in the land of the Soviets (!) and manages, after a hard-fought struggle, to win a ninety-nine-year concession in a rich oilfield. But he dies of exhaustion on the boat that is bringing him back to France, while new emigrants, crowded together on the deck, chant a gloomy folk song; he has become an exile like the rest of them, sacrificed on the altar of all-devouring female idleness.

The selective anti-Semitism of this film arises from the internal contradictions of the Jewish community at the time, where long-assimilated Jews rubbed shoulders with others who had just arrived from central and eastern Europe; its defense of speculation originates in Némirovsky's background as the daughter of upper-middle-class parents driven out of their country by the October Revolution. But the film's anti-Semitism is also typical of a wide section of the press at the time, while its defense of speculation was designed to quell the doubts that had been surfacing since the 1929 Crash. The extreme misogyny of the film, while shared by Duvivier and Némirovsky as individuals (the latter apparently had problems with her mother), is also part and parcel of the period: it arises from the anxieties prompted in many men (and indeed many women) by such figures as the garçonne and other New Women.

But we need to look more closely at the two-pronged nature of this misogyny, for it is a model that persisted for a long time in the French cinema and is to be found in many postwar movies, such as *Manèges*, *Voici le temps des assassins* (*Deadlier Than the Male*), and *A double tour* (*Leda*); it involves a mother who, because of her age, is no longer sexually attractive (her lover is interested only in her money) and whose greed and pettiness are such that they are perceived to be purely sadistic (or as the revenge of the woman who is no longer desired). This is the figure of the bad "mother" — in quotes because the same figure can equally well be a wife, mother-in-law, aunt, or someone else, the key element being that she is excluded from the circuit of desire and persecutes the main male character.

In Duvivier's movie, Joyce's cruelty is unconscious, for Golder's "daughter" is as ingenuous as her mother is cunning. The innocence of this spoiled child is no doubt the signified of the pastoral holiday sequence in the Basque Country, where the young woman accompanies her conceited young lover while back home her parents are tearing each other apart. The English-sounding names of the two women (perfidious Albion again!) and their parallel predations demonstrate that Gloria is simply what Joyce will eventually become, and that it is the proximity of the young body of this unwilling enemy that will in the last account prove fatal to the father, incapable of resisting her charms because he is a man — an argument similar to that justifying prostitution on the grounds that it prevents men raping women, given men's "irrepressible" sexual urges (Corbin 1978).

One of the most clear-cut formulations of this two-pronged misogyny — "ugly or beautiful, young or old, they're all bitches" — is a greatly admired movie by Jean Renoir, *La Chienne* (*Isn't Life a Bitch?*, 1931). Renoir's prestige as a director is such that no analyst of the film seems to have attached the slightest importance to the barrage of hatred it directs at women, first in the person of Adèle (Magdeleine Bérubet), who sadistically prevents her shy husband, Maurice (Michel Simon), from pursuing his harmless hobby, then in the person of the stupid and cruel prostitute, Lulu (Janie Marèze), with whom the humble accountant is unlucky enough to fall in love. At most, some commentators mention this feature as a passing stylistic trait that can be put down to Renoir's problems with the actress Catherine Hessling, from whom he had just separated. And yet one needs to look no further than *David Golder*, *La Belle équipe* (*They Were Five*), *Mollenard* (*Hatred*), *L'Homme de nulle part* (*Feu Mathias Pascal*), and many other movies in order to understand that we are dealing with figures that were commonplace in the French cinema of the time.

What is original about the character played by Michel Simon is that he is a persecuted rather than a self-sacrificing man, and one who, through a regressive process of male bonding (he becomes a Boudu-like clochard in the company of his wife's first husband), achieves a kind of tragicomic tranquility, far from the females of the species. This rather pathetic ending, combined with Renoir's powerful use of images and sounds, is probably what rescues the film from being aggressively misogynistic, notably in its presupposition that women's involvement with artistic creation of any kind is bound to be ill-fated (the wife who prevents her husband from painting, the prostitute who dies as a result of trying to pass herself off as an artist).

Also at the beginning of the decade, the same mother-daughter couple is condemned by more left-wing authors than Némirovsky and Duvivier, or indeed Renoir at that time. True, at the beginning of Jean Grémillon's *La Petite Lise* (*Little Lise*, 1930), the father, Berthier (Pierre Alcover, too young for the part but with the appropriately symbolic burliness), has already killed his wife, who cuckolded him, and spent time in the Cayenne penal colony. After serving his sentence, he contacts his beloved daughter, "little Lise" (Nadia Sibirskaïa), in Paris. Unfortunately she is in love with the ne'er-do-well André (Julien Bertheau) and is forced to sell her charms to elderly men. (The incestuous disavowal is emphasized in the scene where the young woman returns to her room dreading a visit from her "client" and instead finds her father, who has just returned from Cayenne.) She is eventually implicated in a murder along with her lover — but it is Berthier who deliberately takes the blame and is sent back to the penal colony. *La Petite Lise*, directed by Grémillon from a script by Charles Spaak in 1930, demonstrates that just before making the extraordinary *Daïnah la métisse* — an antiracist and antimacho film — the two men were capable of depicting a Jewish usurer (the man murdered in *La Petite Lise*) almost as caricatural as Soifer in *David Golder*. Is there a contradiction here? Or does it simply show that, at the time, ordinary anti-Semitism (and misogyny) was commonplace in both left-wing and right-wing circles, whereas anticolonialist awareness was gaining ground. Renoir probably would not have directed, in the 1930s, his *Le Bled* (1928), a glorification of the white "civilizers" of Algeria.

If we have pointed up these flaws in the works of two great progressive auteurs, it is because the theme of incest, which chiefly concerns us here, and which is in the last account just one form of defense against Difference, not only is not restricted to certain genres but can be found just as frequently in unpretentious movies as in films that posterity regards as masterpieces — and that were in some cases very popular in their time (*Les Bas-fonds* [*The Lower Depths*], *Le Quai des brumes*). We clearly need to avoid reading into these films the sociocultural dichotomy that emerged in the cinema and its public from the New Wave on. In the 1930s and 1940s all French films, even Renoir's and Grémillon's, were aimed at the general public. Irrespective of explicitly political shades of meaning, they all drew on the same ideological basis as regards the relationship between men and women and the idea of the Nation. Indeed the greatness of certain movies by Renoir, Grémillon, Jacques Feyder, Pierre Chenal, and Marcel Carné resides in their way of treating these same motifs in dialectical fashion and sometimes calling them into question. We shall later examine some of these successful films that go against the grain of tradition.

ℛ The Incestuous Love That Dare Not Speak Its Name

We have already seen, in *Vous n'avez rien à déclarer?*, an example of a disavowal of incestuous desire (the scene at the psychoanalyst's). Yet similar tropes indicate the presence of such a motif in several other such films. Disavowal can take the form of a misunderstanding (*Vous n'avez rien à déclarer?*, *Arlette et ses papas*), a lie (*Abus de confiance*, *Gribouille*), or a deception (*Tempête*).

One classic example of the "complacent father" is Camille Morestan (Raimu) in Marc Allégret's *Gribouille* (1937). This melodramatic vaudeville is informed from beginning to end by disavowal (in the form of an "innocent" lie). Morestan, the *gribouille* (short-sighted fool) of the title, wears a proletarian cloth cap and a thick sweater and runs a sporting-goods shop. He is called for jury duty at the trial of a Russian orphan, Nathalie (Michèle Morgan), who is one of life's casualties. He gets her acquitted, then takes her under his wing and brings her home to his family, where he passes her off as a friend's daughter who has been entrusted to him. He then spends the rest of the movie denying to himself and to his wife not only the fact that his protégée is foreign but that he is in love with her. Embroiled in an Oedipal rivalry with his son Claude (Gilbert Gil), he ends up seizing a statuette of Joan of Arc that sits imposingly on the shop's cash register and knocking out the beautiful troublemaker. The symbol is ambiguous, in that it brings an emblem of the French nation into conflict with a foreigner who is herself a woman and the victim of a male world. The dénouement of the film is also ambiguous: after knocking Nathalie unconscious, Morestan goes out without saying a word in order to give himself up to the police. His wife reassures her son, "Don't you worry, we'll save her for you." But at the time of the quarrel, Nathalie firmly intended to leave the household, and there had been nothing to suggest that she was in love with Claude. And when Morestan's wife overtakes her husband to tell him that the young woman is unharmed and to persuade him to come back home, the film ends with her gently scolding him with a conciliatory "You silly old *gribouille*!"

A happy ending seems unlikely, to say the least. Indeed what could the happy ending be, since the spectator inevitably identifies with Gribouille? Should the foreigner be expelled in order to preserve the identity of the family-nation, or should her otherness be brought under control by marrying her off to the son (resulting in Morestan's actually becoming her "father" in order to fuel the incestuous fantasy, a situation that has been implicitly called for since the beginning of the movie)? Both solutions are problematic. By contrasting the unexcitingly handsome Claude with Morestan's energy and generosity, the film refuses to settle one way or the other the father-son rivalry and leaves Nathalie with the task of making her choice — after the end of the movie. Already the patriarchal fantasy is less confident here than in *Abus de confiance*, a film that left the Darrieux character without any chance of escaping the boring young academic; she could only submit to the Law of the Father (who was too certain of his power ever to give himself away by bashing somebody over the head).

Finally, an example of a disavowal that involves a piece of narrative trumpery is to be found in *Tempête* (1939), an unusual film by a little-known director, Bernard Deschamps. Erich von Stroheim portrays one of the most exemplary sacrificial fathers of the second half of the decade. A big-time international swindler named Korlick, wanted by the police of many countries, decides to go into retirement in Paris. There he is determined to find "the love of his life" (Annie Ducaux), who is now married to the prefect of the Paris police. In the course of a furtive meeting during a ball, the young woman and the aging adventurer embrace passionately in a way that would seem to leave little doubt as to the nature of their relationship, and the film now appears to be the story of a secret love affair. It is only at the very last moment that both the audience and the by now suspicious prefect (André Luguet) come upon the couple in their love nest — only to discover that they are in fact father and daughter, separated by Korlick's career in crime. Korlick proceeds to sacrifice his life in order to save his daughter from a blackmailer (thus paying the price of his "incest" at the level of the subtext). This itinerary of incestuous anxiety (the search for the lost daughter) is paralleled by an equally hopeless quest for a national identity: in the opening New York sequence, we see Korlick in blackface for the purpose of his last major swindle before retiring to Paris, but a redemptive return to a problematic motherland was in any case out of the question for the eternally stateless Stroheim, "the man who spoke every language with a foreign accent."

Light is thrown on the various ploys that so many French movies of the period used to indicate the presence of the theme of incest, barely disguised beneath the surface of the manifest narrative, by the work of an American scholar, Janet Walker (1999). In her analysis of the Hollywood movie *Kings Row* (Sam Wood, 1942), adapted from a best-selling novel whose central theme was incest, she demonstrates that the "removal" of that motif from the

Annie Ducaux and Erich von Stroheim in *Tempête*, 1939. Courtesy of Roger Corbeau, Cinémathèque française.

screen version (as required by the Hays Code) is indicated in both the text and the intertext (trailer, launch campaign, reviews) by many "scars" — displacements, substitutions, denials, and so on. Walker posits that "in the psychological Hollywood cinema, the sexual trauma [of incest] operates as a *textual trauma*, which asks filmic mechanisms to come up with an answer they cannot provide, thus producing a fragmented text." This is all the more true because it is not only young women's Oedipal desire (a scandalous fantasy) that needs to be censored but also the incestuous violence of fathers (actual sexual abuse). Indeed these are the extracinematographic themes to which this incest motif points, even in such frothy films as *Vous n'avez rien à déclarer?* and *Arlette et ses papas* — a recurring motif throughout a whole decade of French cinema. A fundamental key to the difference between Hollywood and French cinema at the time could be as follows: U.S. cinema represses any representation of incest, even when displaced (couples made up of an older man and a young woman are virtually nonexistent), whereas French cinema plays with fire, repeatedly portraying incestuous pairings (always from the father's point of view, since the woman's Oedipal fantasy can only be a construction on the part of the female spectator, except perhaps in *Hélène*), but contriving through a host of subterfuges never to name them.

ℛ *Two Extreme Instances: Sarati and the Baker*

In contrast with all these roundabout representations of incest, we know of only one movie from the period that actually shows incest being committed while at the same time indicating, more effectively no doubt than any other film, the hidden sociopolitical and economic undertones of the sacrifice the father is required to make. André Hugon's *Sarati le terrible* (1937) shows the defeat of patriarchal prerogative, linking it with the structural transformation of the economy that modernizing sections of the bourgeoisie saw as unavoidable. The film combines in ambiguous fashion the figures of the unworthy and the self-sacrificing father in the person of Sarati (Harry Baur), who is the true hero of the story despite the presence of a rich young man who makes off with the woman. The film provides the key to a whole period — that is to say, it depicts the efforts of the male imaginary to implement a "painless break with the nineteenth century" — at the same time remarkably foreshadowing the typical scenario of Occupation films (*Premier rendez-vous, Le Val d'enfer* [*Valley of Hell*]). The film is set in the present-day port of Algiers. Sarati, whose earring suggests his "non-Aryan" origins (compare Golder's "Aryan manservant"), is the uncouth and brutal manager of a boardinghouse for dockworkers. He lords it over his little world, whip in hand (even thrashing his mistress, whose charms have faded with age but who, unlike the usual stereotype of the period, stands up to the bully and on occasion protects his victims). There is just one ray of sunshine in Sarati's life, his niece Rose (Jacqueline Laurent), whom he has brought up in the place of a brother who died and upon whom he lavishes an affection that is quite unambiguous.

The Sarati character involves a contradiction that is only superficially solved by the extraordinary charisma of Harry Baur: how to get the spectator to identify with such a repulsive main character, who beats up workers who owe him money, who nearly rapes his ingénue niece, and whose sole interest in life is amassing money (to guarantee his niece's future, of course) — all attributes that are firmly condemned throughout the movie. And yet these antisocial traits are undeniable manifestations of Sarati's masculine vitality, which, however excessive, is immensely entertaining. What is more, Sarati vents his violence by turns on shadowy figures of "niggers" and "North Africans" devoid of narrative consistency, on an elderly Arab servant and a drunken homosexual (Jean Tissier), both caricatures of abject cowardice. And who can blame Sarati for lusting after his niece Rose, considering the way she hangs around the house in scanty attire?

The sequence where Sarati yields to temptation says a lot about the way the film, however accusatory it may be, persists in placing us on the side of the desiring father: having gone for a walk with his niece, he suddenly sees her stretched out on the grass at his feet, with her blouse half open, behavior that is hardly in character or justified by anything at that point in the narrative. When Sarati ventures to touch her, it is implicitly because "women just ask for it." And his niece's revulsion, which leads to her falling into the arms of the young Count Gilbert de Kéradec (Georges Rigaud), is not totally convincing; Sarati does not come across as entirely guilty.

And yet the aim of the movie is indeed to portray the defeat of the tyrant, the fall of a certain archaic form of patriarchy. The idea is not of course to emancipate either the female character or the exploited workers but to find them a more reasonable and legitimate master. In this film the solution to the crisis of the patriarchy is no longer to be found in a fantasized return to the paternalistic paradise of the Ancien Régime.

True, the young man comes from a Breton family of country squires, but if he turns up penniless one day in Algiers it is precisely because he has broken off his ties with them and their "degenerate" decadence. And if he ends up defeating Sarati by taking his niece away from him it is because he has joined forces with a good patriarch (Charles Granval), who runs a company in the port. Together they launch a sweeping plan to modernize the port, which will eventually, it seems, abolish unskilled labor and, along with it, the "archaic" exploitation identified with Sarati's outrageous behavior. Symbolic of this handing over of power is the phallic shotgun that bears engraved on its stock the coronet of Gilbert de Kéradec's noble family and that he tries to sell to Sarati as soon as he arrives in Algiers — but that the latter finds too beautiful, too expensive, and "too heavy to bear."

However, while the rather colorless young man is the positive hero of the film and a living embodiment of a future governed by an "enlightened" colonial and patriarchal brand of capitalism, Sarati, whose charisma in the eyes of the average spectator implies that he would somehow have deserved to possess the young woman, ends up being the tragic hero of the story. Leaning over the bed in which the beautiful Rose is sleeping after her wedding night, Sarati abandons his prerogatives (his power and his virility) in spectacular fashion: he castrates himself with a huge knife that he earlier confiscated from a lodger he handed over to the police. Just so there is no doubt in our minds as to the meaning of his act, it is preceded by another scene, which was even more unusual for the period, in which Sarati's friend Granval, the dockworkers' "good boss," gently confronts him with his incestuous fantasies. The poignant castration scene—a personal tragedy that brings to a close a film that advocates a harmonious mutation of capitalism—sounds the death knell of the old order, whose violent demise is predicted, but in a much less compassionate way, by the masterpiece that would soon bring the period to a close, Jean Renoir's *La Règle du jeu* (*The Rules of the Game*; Browne 1982).

During the first half of the 1930s, Hugon's specialty was Provençal movies (e.g., the Maurin series with Berval). But the true master of that cinematic genre, Marcel Pagnol, offered, in the same year that *Sarati le terrible* came out (1937), a far more imperious solution to the incestuous-patriarchal dilemma. Pagnol's trilogy had already featured one of the earliest representations of the complacent father with Raimu's portrayal of César. His *La Femme du boulanger* (*The Baker's Wife*, 1937) is an out-and-out defense of the incestuous-patriarchal order, which "everyone realized was unnatural" but whose survival was believed to be a requirement for civil peace and national unity.

Ginette Leclerc, one of the period's emblematic "sluts" who is cast in the film's title role, comes across curiously as a character whose voice is scarcely ever heard—in a film filled with talkative men—and who is largely absent from the screen. Unable to resist the charms of a handsome young shepherd (as the village schoolteacher points out, humans are basically animals), she rides away into the dawn with him. Her escapade coincides with that of her "double," the household she-cat, which later comes crawling home at the same time as her mistress. Such was the unabashed misogyny of the period.

The movie constantly stresses the "naturalness" of the attraction that brings together a handsome shepherd (always seen alone with his animals) and a beautiful young woman married to a paunchy old man. But it is also worth noting that the shepherd is Italian—and haunted by the fear of God—whereas the likable baker, whose naïve and blind passion drives him to drink and a form of suicide, is a staunch republican and something of an agnostic. In this sense, he stands halfway between the schoolteacher and the priest, whose philosophical squabbles are meant to satirize the Church-state conflict still very much alive across the nation, symbolized by Pagnol's apolitical village. The search for the wayward wife, followed by the reuniting of the ill-assorted couple—a mismatch that the film both denounces and justifies in more or less the same breath—eventually heals all the dissensions in the village: farmers who have been enemies for generations make it up in the interests of a good cause—that of bringing back to the village the wife of the excellent baker so that he relights the ovens that out of despair he allowed to go out; the schoolteacher will wade out to the lovers' inaccessible island refuge with his enemy the priest riding on his back, frightening away the shepherd and prompting the flighty wife's return to the fold.

The makeshift love nest of the shepherd and the runaway wife, reminiscent of Robinson Crusoe's shack, is contrasted significantly with the baker's comfortable home; the film carries the message that while middle-aged men are not exactly a bargain they do offer young women from a poor background a security that is not provided by men of their own age. The decisive role played somewhat reluctantly by the priest, who is made to look ridiculous throughout the film but the mere sight of whom is enough to make the superstitious shepherd flee in terror, shows that in Pagnol's republican and secular village the Church still has a role to play, which is to keep women and young men on the straight and narrow. To the extent that it recognizes fathers' desires as "unnatural" (ill-suited to woman's animal nature), this movie might be considered more clear-sighted than most. But in fact it is yet another exorcism, which proves that it is better to be portly, good-natured, witty, and French than young, good-looking, cowardly, and Italian. (In a lengthy monologue the drunken baker lashes out at those who serenade "our women" in a language "we" cannot understand.)

A certain lucidity gets in the way of the film's message, which does not quite manage to conceal the arbitrary nature of the final surrender, where the tearful speechlessness of the frustrated and chastened wife signals both submission to the Law of the Father and relinquishment of freedom, youth, and pleasure. If the prodigal daughter can be seen smiling through the flames of the oven as she reverts to being the baker's wife (by agreeing to be his "younger sister," as one witness of her disappearance had already believed her to be), it is obviously a forced smile. She has agreed to a self-mutilation which the movie shows to be indispensable to social order, while shedding a discreet tear for a muted — or rather very muted — regret for the death of desire.

It is a movie that contains curious Vichyite overtones long before the term existed, but, as we shall see, the Vichyite cinema almost never relied on the restoration of patriarchal order as its driving force. It is edifying to compare *La Femme du boulanger* with *Le Val d'enfer*, which Maurice Tourneur directed during the Occupation and which features Ginette Leclerc in a very similar role. True, it is one of the very few films of the period that continues to believe in the survival of patriarchal power, but the character played by Leclerc is anything but silent and clearly will not put up for long with a man incapable of satisfying her. That is why she has to be brutally murdered so that the discredited patriarch may redeem himself by becoming reconciled with the son he once rejected. In Pagnol's film, on the other hand, the theme of sexual inadequacy, although made explicit in the bedroom scene where the baker is clearly uninterested in his wife's physical desires, is ultimately swept aside by her last-minute return to hearth and home, and her conjugal duties; indeed the shot showing her relighting the oven is full of sexual connotations (fire = desire).

Departing for once from our historical perspective, it is disturbing to note that *La Femme du boulanger* continues to be enormously popular, as can be seen from the frequency with which it is shown on television, and that everyone's favorite scene, which never fails to elicit a sympathetic smile, comes when the cat, on its return home, is scolded by the baker in an ultrareactionary lecture about the animality of woman and her need for a domestic interior that will protect her from her instincts and from the dangers of "the savage world out there."

ℛ Berry, the Father Burned in Effigy

It would no doubt be excessively auteurist to argue that Jean Renoir and Jacques Prévert "invented" the figure of the "unworthy father" in their great optimistic movie of 1936, *Le Crime de Monsieur Lange*, which heralds the end of capitalist exploitation and the dawn of a new era. Batala (Jules Berry) is the villainous boss of a small business who exploits the women under his command even more than his workers. This was a well-established figure in the imaginary of the French workers' movement, to which the makers of the film and the October Group of left-wing writers, of which Prévert was a member, all subscribed.

In her analysis of the discourse on women in the late nineteenth-century working-class press, and more particularly on the oppression of working women by the potbellied bourgeois men, Christine Dufrancatel (1979: 167) notes, "Women's destiny is not thought of as a separate problem. Women are above all seen as the symbol of moral and social issues. . . . The deterioration in the status of working-class women when they are obliged to work, the resulting violence suffered by their bodies, the inhuman conditions of their motherhood, and their reduction to the state of sexual object represent a deterioration of the class as a whole and affect men through women. . . . The man's body depends on the woman's body. And the body is a class issue."

The repugnant Batala, who has sex with very young women on his office settee without a thought for the consequences and exploits their charms against his enemies, is an unworthy father by virtue of his class position. The first decisive defeat he suffers, after he has fled his creditors and the law and before his return disguised as a priest and his death at the hands of Monsieur Lange, is the miscarriage of one of his female victims, which is greeted with gales of laughter by all the inhabitants of the building.

Le Crime de Monsieur Lange, the Utopian film par excellence, highlights women's work, chooses as its hero the gentle Monsieur Lange (played by René Lefèvre, who is a kind of anti-Gabin), and sees American comic books as the source of male violence. (This is the other meaning of Arizona Jim, the righter of wrongs thought up by Lange.)

It is well known that the three Utopian movies that Renoir "offered" the Popular Front were virtually unique for their time. But as regards what it is generally agreed to call the pessimistic current of left-wing cinema — poetic realism in the strict sense — the unworthy father becomes an obligatory presence. One such figure is Michel Simon, the lecherous shopkeeper in *Le Quai des brumes*, who threatens the virtue of Nelly (Michèle Morgan), the unhappy young woman placed in his care, and whom the deserter from the Foreign Legion (Jean Gabin) has to kill in order to free her. It is often overlooked that this ending, which is extremely pessimistic from a male point of view (the Gabin character dies), is much less so from a woman's point of view, since Nelly, although losing the man she loves, also loses her oppressor and escapes with her life. But it may be that this meaning escaped the notice of the makers of that Manichaean and manipulative movie, which likens the freedom Nelly finally enjoys to that of the stray dog that goes back on the road after the death of his ephemeral master (a curious parallel to the cat in *La Femme du boulanger*, released the same year). But this emancipation is objectively inscribed in the film-text — and in the libertarian hatred of patriarchy that envelops it — and it is open to the kind of reading against the grain that is always useful to highlight the contradictions of a film, a milieu, or a period. And it is a fact that with the appearance of the unworthy father the borderlines between categories of femaleness become blurred.

The most famous unworthy father of the period is Monsieur Valentin (Jules Berry) in that masterpiece of poetic realism, *Le Jour se lève*, a film that constantly flirts with the incestuous fantasy and Oedipal rivalry, the two driving forces of the genre. But poetic realism had no monopoly on the unworthy father figure.

Thomas Elsaesser (1984: 278–83), in a stimulating survey of films made in

Pierre Brasseur, Michèle Morgan (back), and Jean Gabin in *Le Quai des brumes*, 1938. Courtesy of Cinémathèque française.

France by German émigrés before World War II, notes that their chief characteristic is their hybrid nature, a mixture of genres, styles, and motifs borrowed indiscriminately from Berlin, Hollywood, and Paris. Shot in 1936 by the most prolific of those émigrés, Robert Siodmak, *Le Chemin de Rio* (*Woman Racket* or *The Traffic in Souls*) combines French paternal melodrama with the German-American lighthearted police drama. Siodmak films two stories that only rarely intersect: the first is an investigation by a Franco-German couple of journalists (Kate de Nagy and Jean-Pierre Aumont) who are stereotypically dynamic and determined to break up a white slave trade network (their squabbling rivalry maintains the "necessary" separation of sex and work by bringing them together as a couple only at the end of the film); the second story is an extraordinary fight to the death between two father figures, one of them the apparently harmless ("complacent") Blanco (Charles Granval) and the other the more blatantly "unworthy" Moreno (Jules Berry). Here it is precisely the failure to prevent private life from spilling over into professional life that proves the undoing of the two men.

The movie opens with the suicide of an innocent young woman (Sylvia Bataille) in a luxurious brothel in Latin America. Back in Paris, Moreno, a big shot in the white slave trade, discovers that the woman concerned, on whom he has set his heart, was sent out there against her will by his partner, Blanco. Wild with anger and grief, he wants to take his revenge on Blanco, but just as his henchman Pérez (Marcel Dalio) is about to kill him, Moreno restrains him because he has just realized that Blanco is the father of a very beautiful young woman he adores and who knows nothing of her father's shameful activities. Now the camera moves closer to the Blanco family dinner taken on the terrace of a luxurious villa in an upper-crust district, with Moreno and Pérez lurking behind the garden bushes like spectators separated from the stage by foot-lights—a situation that seems to emphasize the bourgeois family's theatrical hypocrisy. Henceforth the revenge plotted by Moreno will be a fate worse than death: he manages to seduce the young woman (a rather implausible scene that attests precisely to the power of the father in the cinema) and gets her sent off to Rio with a contingent of female chorus girls—easy dupes, like her, because of their desire for financial independence, and fleeing, like her, the authority of their parents. When the boat is already at sea, Moreno goes to break the "good news" to Blanco, who catches him off guard and stabs him to death. This is a film that provides an overview, in the form of a darkly humorous and multi-form caricature, of the major motif of the French cinema of the time and heralds in its own way the twilight of the father.

Finally, *L'Entraîneuse* (*Nightclub Hostess*, 1938) was the first feature made by Albert Valentin, an unjustly forgotten director whose full talent blossomed during the Occupation. The film portrays with exceptional realism the hypocrisy characteristic of actual patriarchal power—what McMillan (1981) calls its double standards—in the person of a rich company boss who is a good-natured autocrat at home and an exploiter of young women when in town.

The beginning of the movie offers this critique in capsule form: chief executive Monsieur Noblet (Félicien Tramel) presides over a board meeting where his moral and professional qualities are praised by all. A few minutes later we see him in a nightclub, after the camera has crossed an alleyway typical of poetic realism. There Suzy (Michèle Morgan), the eponymous *entraîneuse*, or nightclub hostess, for once turns down a proposition from a client (Noblet) in order to keep an appointment with her true love, who abruptly declares he is leaving her. She takes the news in her stride (her lover is clearly no great loss) but feels the need for a change of scenery. So she sets off for the Côte d'Azur and takes board and lodging with a fatherless family of good bourgeois standing. Gradually the widow, her daughter, and her three sons "adopt" the young woman. While two of the three sons are hilarious examples of male

Fréhel, Michèle Morgan, and Claire Gérard in *L'Entraîneuse*, 1938. Courtesy of Cinémathèque française.

smugness (one a budding capitalist, the other a young yachtsman), the third (Gilbert Gil) is a gentle intellectual whom Suzy could easily marry—if it did not turn out that the uncle of the three sons, a part-time patriarch, is none other than Noblet, the company director she had spurned. Without revealing the identity or the past of the "creature" he finds ensconced with his relations, he makes it clear to her in a private conversation that there can be no question of her planned marriage taking place—and cold-bloodedly offers to support her financially.

Without further ado, Suzy returns to Paris and her nightclub job. But the movie does not leave things at that; the patriarch, who seems to the audience (and to her) to have changed his mind for the better, comes looking for her in her nightclub, only to repeat his offer in the same cynical terms. She throws champagne in his face and reluctantly seeks the protection of a disillusioned playboy, who offers to take her on a world tour, while the camera lingers in close-up on the ravaged features of the singer Fréhel as she bewails the tragic fate of women.

It is true that the pessimism of this film, and indeed of most films of the poetic realism school, reflects the political disappointment caused by the in-

Félicien Tramel and Michèle Morgan in *L'Entraîneuse*, 1938. Courtesy of Cinémathèque française.

creasingly timorous policies of the Popular Front. But it also reflects, in a less time-specific way, a form of lucidity characteristic of left-wing circles as to the inextricable nature of patriarchal oppression. And yet the only alternative open to Suzy is prostitution or marriage; in other words, this left-wing denunciation of sexual exploitation as class oppression (and solely as such) reveals the specifically French limitations of male thinking, even when it is progressive.

ℛ *Gabin: Nobody's Son*

L'Entraîneuse is undoubtedly a most unusual film for its period in that it leaves its heroine to face the bad father on her own. But in the seminal movies of the poetic realism school, *Le Quai des brumes* and *Le Jour se lève*, an intercessor called Jean Gabin steps between the bad father and his putative "daughter." Ginette Vincendeau (in Gauteur and Vincendeau 1993) brilliantly describes how the Gabin myth was built up, from Julien Duvivier's *La Bandera* (*Escape from Yesterday*) onward—the myth of a masculinity that is both ideal and doomed to die, an object of identification for men who doubt (and who project those doubts on "the people"), and an object of desire for women. In her subtle analysis of *Pépé le Moko* (*moko* is slang for a man from Toulon) and

La Belle équipe, she demonstrates, among other things, how Gabin's masculinity is placed on display (his music hall numbers) and defined as a kind of acceptable middle ground within a group composed of "excessive" masculinities (the womanizer, the brawler, the moneygrubber, and so on). The process is similar to the one that constructs an ideal femininity in *Club des femmes*. But Gabin's masculinity is also constructed in a confrontation with more or less negative female figures, whether the two versions of the slut (*garce*) — the "poor" version (Line Noro in *Pépé le Moko*, Viviane Romance in *La Belle équipe*) and the "rich" one (Mireille Balin in *Pépé le Moko* and *Gueule d'amour* [*Lady Killer*]) — or more complex figures such as the tragic woman with a mysterious past (Michèle Morgan in *Le Quai des brumes* and *Remorques* [*Stormy Waters*]), or the deceptively innocent young woman (Jacqueline Laurent in *Le Jour se lève*).

The distinction between the rich and poor bitch, which constitutes one of the essential points of conjunction between the problems of class and of sex in the French cinema of the period, may not have been adequately examined to date. Augusto Genina's *Paris-Béguin* (*The Darling of Paris*, 1931), the first film in which Gabin starred, as well as the same director's *Prix de beauté* (*Beauty Prize*, 1930) and Marcel L'Herbier's *Le Bonheur* (1935), pose the problem as it existed at a time when the notion of the proletarian hero was still in gestation: that of the power of the showgirl (Conway 1992) and, by extension, the kept woman (often one and the same person), a power perceived both as dangerous for the man of the people (that repository of ideal masculinity) and as a source of tragic isolation for the woman herself (which in return restricts her power).

The plot of *Paris-Béguin*, a minor melodrama in the tradition of the Italian "diva films" of which Genina was one of the leading exponents, and the plot of *Le Bonheur*, based on a successful play by Henry Bernstein, are surprisingly similar despite their very different sources: an adulated star — a music hall artist (Jeanne Marnac) in Genina's movie and a film actress (Gaby Morlay) in L'Herbier's — is frustrated by the impotence of the men around her (in both films she works with a homosexual who serves to point up her deprivation and has a gigolo lover who is far from virile) and discovers physical love in the arms of a man of the people. From *Paris-Béguin*'s populist perspective, the story is about a small-time crook (Gabin early in his career) who dies an unpleasant death as a result of a doubly feminine fatality, embodied by both the star and his rejected girlfriend, who in a fit of pique betrays him to a dangerous accomplice. He dies in front of a huge poster of the star as he was just about to join her, while she, having experienced physical love for the first time in the arms of her one-night burglar-cum-rapist, sums up the pathos of the situation on stage in a *chanson réaliste*. Although rather crudely made, the film is extraordinarily premonitory, particularly in the way it shows Gabin caught between those two key figures, the rich bitch and the poor bitch.

In the boulevard version offered by *Le Bonheur* just as the Popular Front came into being (the play and the film are virtually contemporary), the virile working-class man is in fact a déclassé militant anarchist (Charles Boyer) who abandons the woman he loves when he discovers she has agreed to appear in a film that exploits their love affair; he disappears from her life, contenting himself thereafter with her image on the screen — and his memories. In Genina's right-wing version, the love that has been rendered impossible both by the treachery of the "poor bitch" and by the class barrier of the "rich bitch" results in the tragic death of an outlaw who could have stepped straight out of the pages of a book by Francis Carco. In the more left-leaning version of L'Herbier and Bernstein, a Malraux-style rebel ends up furiously refusing to accept a society of pretence. This to-ing and fro-ing of the same gender matrices between right and left is an essential feature of this kind of cinema, which is totally devoted to papering over the cracks in the edifice of masculinity. As we shall see, this same narrative pattern would be repeated during the Occupation in a radically different spirit (*L'Amant de Bornéo*), after the type of masculinity embodied by Gabin and Boyer had been swept away by the trauma of the 1940 debacle.

This theme of the rich woman who has everything but whose physical needs can be satisfied only by a man of the people continued to sustain the Gabin myth in two important movies by Duvivier and Grémillon, directors even more clearly at ideological odds than Genina and L'Herbier. Duvivier's *Pépé le Moko* treats the populist theme of the tragic hero — Gabin — whose predicament as a Parisian gangster holed up in the Casbah of Algiers could easily be read as the loneliness of the new settler-worker, fleeing not the Paris police but the economic crisis and beleaguered by an Arab society marked by strict sexual segregation and where male homosexuality goes more or less undisguised. This theme is present in the person of the strange Inspector Slimane (Lucas Gridoux), clearly fascinated by his prey. Pépé's nostalgia for his working-class Paris is awakened by his encounter with Gaby (Mireille Balin), a kept woman from the rich part of the capital, and is a variant of the already mentioned anxiety about national identity; the film exploits all the themes of difference as experienced at the time.

For a right-wing anarchist, even one as misogynistic as Duvivier, the tyranny that money exerts over Gaby, the object of Pépé's impossible love that will

Mireille Balin and Jean Gabin in *Gueule d'amour*, 1937. Courtesy of Cinémathèque française.

prove his undoing, is seen more as a social fatality than as evidence of women's duplicity; it requires all the authority of the colonial police to persuade the unhappy woman to return to the fold of her wealthy, corpulent protector (Charles Granval). In the case of the left-wing Grémillon, despite his many feminist films, the Balin character in *Gueule d'amour* (Madeleine) comes off worse in the end. The movie begins both as a comment on the Gabin legend and an exercise in sex-role reversal: Lucien Bourrache, known as "Gueule d'amour" ("pretty boy"), a ladies' man in the Spahis regiment in Orange, can have any woman he wants. But when he is demobbed and returns to Paris he discovers that without his fine uniform, nobody is interested in him anymore. He also finds out that Madeleine is kept by a rich bourgeois and is not prepared to give up her comfortable existence for a love affair with a plebeian typesetter. For a time the female character is treated like her opposite number in *Pépé le Moko*, as a prisoner of a social logic (even if the cynicism of a mother who pimps for her daughter in typical boulevardier fashion is somewhat over the top). But when Gueule d'amour admits defeat and leaves Paris to open a modest bistro in Orange, Madeleine (perhaps a trifle artificially) turns into one of the most out-and-out bitches of the period: she pesters him again, taunting him with quite extraordinary sadism, notably by wounding the pride of his best friend, René (René Lefèvre), who has fallen in love with her, and finally driving Lucien to murder her.

In André Beucler's novel, which was written ten years earlier, the class difference was not perceptible — Madeleine is a totally mysterious creature who "devours" men out of an "animal" need — and the social criticism that Grémillon and the scriptwriter Charles Spaak weave into that framework is specific to their milieu and their decade. *Gueule d'amour* is a perfect example of the contradiction, in the left-wing discourse of the period, between its class argument and its "gender argument." In Geneviève Sellier's (1989: 26 ff.) view, the conscious argument used by Grémillon and Spaak is here a class criticism: Bourrache's fatal mistake is that he is not mistrustful enough of the cynical and hypocritical behavior of the wealthy classes — and of the women who belong to them. But in this film, as often at the time, these mores are indistinguishable from the all-consuming power of female sexuality. Just as the Jews, in the years leading up to the Holocaust, were a commonplace emblem of the evil power of money — Grémillon and Spaak had no qualms about murdering a grotesque Jewish usurer in *La Petite Lise* — wealthy women, with their frustrations, their nymphomania, and their frigidity, symbolized the harmful decadence of their class. And that kind of iconography was not the exclusive preserve of the left. For instance, in another Duvivier movie, the indolent mistress serves as a sign of depravity, lolling about the home of the evil schemer in *La Tête d'un homme* (*A Man's Neck*, 1932), who uses a foreign student to murder the aunt from whom he will inherit a fortune. These are not innocent metaphors for political conflict as understood by the male tradition of historiography. In *Gueule d'amour*, Grémillon and Spaak, as left-wing intellectuals, are aware of the division of society into classes and the resulting injustices, but as private individuals they sense the indescribable threat of the woman as a "natural" vector of social contradiction.

ℛ *The Downward Drift of the Bitch Stereotype*

The "poor slut," a figure as old as populist literature, is more of an animal than anything else. Her fate is consubstantial with an unbridled sexuality, of which she is, at a pinch, a prisoner just as the "rich bitch" is a prisoner of her financial dependence. In the French cinema of the 1930s, that figure was virtually invented by and for Viviane Romance, even though she did no more than elevate to the rank of myth a prototype no doubt created by Catherine Hessling under the curiously sadistic direction of her husband Jean Renoir (*Nana*, 1925) and in Hollywood by Marlene Dietrich under Josef von Sternberg's rather more masochistic direction (Studlar 1993; Duvivier had originally thought of casting Dietrich in the role of the bitch in *La Belle équipe*).

The movie that propelled Romance to stardom in 1937 was Genina's *Naples au baiser de feu* (*The Kiss of Fire*), where she is the cause of Tino Rossi's suffering while at the same time stealing the show. But the film that established the actress as the ignorant and wicked bitch she was to play in many movies to come was *La Belle équipe* (1936), the negative version of *Le Crime de Monsieur Lange*. It is she who, in the "pessimistic" ending turned down by the producer, causes the ultimate failure of the workers' cooperative: Duvivier's visceral misogyny blends admirably with his philosophical pessimism.

Romance, aware of the misogynous manipulation to which she was being subjected, attempted to resist being typecast as a stupid, grasping bitch (Romance 1986). By 1938 she had become the highest paid female star in France, and thanks to her own efforts, a few dissenting movies did manage to see the light of day. We analyze *La Maison du Maltais* (*Sirocco*, 1938) elsewhere. But it is worth dwelling on an even less well known film, Marc Sorkin's *L'Esclave blanche* (*Pasha's Wives*, 1939), since it is one of the few movies of the period that criticizes patriarchal order. The film proceeds in the manner of Montesquieu's *Lettres persanes*; the customs it criticizes are ostensibly those of Islam. But it is hard to imagine that the more aware female spectators of the film in 1939 would have failed to spot the very French target of the satire, given in particular the familiar faces of its main actors. Romance plays Mireille, a Parisian woman who has married a high-ranking Turkish official, Vedad Bey (John Lodge; the casting of this insipid American actor was perhaps designed to save the character from the rain of brickbats and provide a happy ending). No sooner has she arrived in Turkey to settle down with him than she realizes that the fate of women in a Muslim country is "barbaric" to a degree that is intolerable for a European woman: she is not allowed either to appear in public with her husband or to go out alone, and her sixteen-year-old sister-in-law (Louise Carletti) is about to be married to a potbellied dignitary she has never met (Saturnin Fabre). Mireille's indignant rebellion (Romance is extraordinarily convincing in this role as a righter of wrongs) fails, of course, to change local customs, and the volte-face of the bey, who ends up following her when she decides to return to France, is not very plausible. But the film remains a scathing indictment of the patriarchy of others.

ℛ *Feuillère, the Marked Woman*

To complete this picture of the family romance in the French cinema of the 1930s (but which does not claim to be exhaustive), we come now to the strong woman, or rather the shrew to be tamed, a role Edwige Feuillère specialized in. Hers is an extreme instance but is highly revealing, as it demonstrates how intolerable it is for the patriarchy that women should rise to a position of power. From 1936 (*Lucrèce Borgia* [*Lucrezia Borgia*]) to 1948 (*L'Aigle à deux têtes* [*The Eagle with Two Heads*]), unaltered by the upheavals of defeat and liberation, Feuillère's image remained that of a beautiful, haughty, inaccessible, and above all formidably efficient woman, whether as high-society thief (*J'étais une aventurière* [*I Was an Adventuress*], *L'Honorable Catherine* [*The Honorable Catherine*]), legendary spy (*Marthe Richard au service de la France* [*Marthe Richard*]), or seductress who avenges women (*La Duchesse de Langeais* [*Wicked Duchess*]), which was why the taming of this shrew always had to be exemplary.

An emblematic example of this constantly renewed humiliation comes with the climax of *Marthe Richard au service de la France* (Raymond Bernard, 1937), where Richard comes to tell the man she loves, Baron Erich von Ludow (Erich von Stroheim), a German espionage officer, that she has succeeded in her assignment, which was to sink the fleet of submarines he was responsible for protecting. Without batting an eyelid, Ludow stops caressing the keys of his beloved piano, picks up a syringe, and injects himself with a lethal poison, and Richard, who has been victorious in the male sphere of war, is defeated in the female sphere, that of feelings, naturally assumed to be more important to her. Thus the story ends with its supposed heroine shattered by Ludow's act of supreme virility and reduced to the role of dumbfounded, powerless spectator of her lover-cum-enemy's tragic death.

But the most violent punishment occurs in *L'Emigrante* (*The Emigrant*), by the Catholic director, Léo Joannon (1939). Christiane (Edwige Feuillère), the owner of a nightclub in Antwerp, is the mistress of Tino, a dangerous gangster (Georges Lannes), who showers her with diamonds but apparently gets little in return: Christiane loves *only* diamonds. Indeed when Tino, who has to go into hiding after a failed robbery, takes back the jewels from Christiane, she has no hesitation in denouncing him to the police in order to recover her gems. But the gangster breaks out of jail, and now it is Christiane who must run for her life. She manipulates a pathetic character named Monrozat (Pierre Larquey), who is already the victim of a flighty wife and wants to emigrate to South Africa; she ships out with him using the unfaithful wife's passport, then gives her pitiful friend the slip when, after suffering a heart attack, he has to be taken ashore during the voyage, finally dying alone in a hospital crying out Christiane's name. Meanwhile she has stayed in hiding on the liner, where she seduces a naïve and noble-hearted officer, François Champart (Jean Chevrier),

Edwige Feuillère in *L'Emigrante*, 1939. Courtesy of Cinémathèque française.

with a fable about a cruel husband. But a crippled, spiteful Asian woman lets the cat out of the bag. Champart is dismissed from his post, and after refusing to accept money from Christiane, joins the émigrés in the hold. Everyone now heaps scorn on her because of the way she has treated Monrozat and Champart. Embroiled in her predicament as a woman who is at last in love (yet another wealthy, frigid woman discovering desire in the arms of a man of working-class origin), she saves her soul by sacrificing her beloved diamonds to put up the guarantee the South African government demands of émigrés — before being shot in the back by Tino, who has finally tracked her down (a dénouement reminiscent of *Le Quai des brumes* — and in a sense Feuillère is here the female Gabin of the late 1930s). The town founded by Champart and the émigrés is, naturally, called Christiana.

Thus, at the risk of making their story implausible, the authors are forced to multiply the negative traits of the female character, in order both to neutralize the star's exceptional charisma and to pave the way for the sinning woman's Christian redemption (for which we are prepared by her confrontation with a character even more wicked than she is, the ugly Asian woman who holds a grudge against the beautiful European woman and spies on her out of jealousy). The movie bluntly reveals the Catholic subtext of the discourse about

Edwige Feuillère and Jean Chevrier in *L'Emigrante*, 1939. Courtesy of Cinémathèque française.

women in France at that time: only a canonical ordeal—involving both love and suffering—can exorcise the threat posed by a woman who is literally diabolical because she lays claim to her independence. During the Occupation, at a time when the Catholic right was in power in France for the first time in a hundred years, this figure of the powerful woman shifted curiously in the direction of a more secular and sometimes feminist image; even when she is "defeated" (as she continues to be at the end of all the films she appears in), she is the one who notches up the most points, so to speak, and we no longer get the impression that the match was rigged in advance.

Libertarian populism of both right and left incorporated its *ressentiment* and its fantasies — only remotely related to the realities of class struggle — into the family romance of the time. While right-wing auteurs (Duvivier, Genina) made absolutely no secret of their fear and hatred of women by portraying wicked bitches and pimping mothers, their left-wing counterparts often allowed their worries about male identity and gender to peep through at a time of great ideological confusion.

With hindsight, we can see that it is undoubtedly the struggle between Gabin, himself doomed to die, and a string of women who are more or less wicked but always *fatales*, a string of fathers who are more or less unworthy but always condemnable, which seems to dominate the second half of the decade. And yet once he became a star Gabin deliberately restricted the number of roles he took and became increasingly involved in the quantitatively insignificant school of poetic realism. Indeed Gabin's prestige in the eyes of the general public probably hinges more on its identification with the image of a "new" virility as against the prestige of aging stars than on a commitment to left-wing libertarian populism (Carné, Prévert, Renoir, Grémillon).

In fact "the good old Saturday Night yarns," to quote François de La Bretèque's (1977) phrase, continued to feature fathers who were almost as "complacent" as before (Pierre Blanchar as a famous pianist in Kurt Bernhardt's *La Nuit de décembre*, 1939, meets, twenty years after the event, the spitting image of a woman he fell in love with at the age of thirty — who turns out to be his own daughter); self-sacrificing fathers, as pathetic as ever (Harry Baur in the title role of Robert Siodmak's *Mollenard*, 1938, escapes from his martinet of a wife to embark on virile adventures in the Far East but is forced by old age and illness to submit to the tender mercies of the horrible termagant, until a last-minute rescue by his devoted crew allows him to die at sea); and unworthy fathers, as repugnant as they are colorful (Michel Simon in Pierre Chenal's *Le Dernier Tournant*, 1939, a drunken oily skinned husband who is killed mainly out of disgust). These rituals of power and conspiracy would be abruptly put on ice for four long years by the invading tide of Panzers, the debacle of the army in 1940, and the frantic flight of the old men in charge of the Third Republic. They could never again be resumed in quite the same way.

ℛ

Film Analyses

ℛ *LE GRAND JEU*
  (Jacques Feyder, 1934)

In her important essay on Jean Gabin, Ginette Vincendeau (Gauteur and Vincendeau 1993) contrasts Jacques Feyder's *Le Grand jeu* (1934) with the actor's classical movies, arguing that it is a "woman's film." If by that she means a film that is aimed at women, her viewpoint is surely mistaken, if understandable. Since most British and U.S. feminist studies have focused mainly on Hollywood cinema, women researchers from that background are naturally tempted to detect Hollywood marketing templates in European cinema. That form of segregation does not, however, exist in European culture, whether cinematic or literary, as Molly Haskell (1977) noted with reference to the cinema in a book that, although now outdated, contains many shrewd observations.

If Vincendeau's assertion implies that the makers of *Le Grand jeu* intended to appeal to women, that is not particularly justified either. True, the film does not conform to the misogynistic patterns current at the time, and it uses as its mouthpiece a woman who sees straight through men; it puts its finger on the fantastical essence of male desire. But those who see *Le Grand jeu*, whose narrative viewpoint is male almost from beginning to end, as a kind of "woman's film" or "woman's melodrama" overlook the specificity of the French cinema.

They forget that Jacques Feyder and Charles Spaak, both individually and together, were used to making family films that approached issues of sexual roles from a critical standpoint, an approach all too often believed, in the United Kingdom and the United States, to be culturally inaccessible to men. *Les Nouveaux Messieurs* (1928), based on another scenario that Spaak wrote for Feyder, is a political satire, a genre not regarded as particularly appealing to women. And yet its female central character (played by Gaby Morlay), who is torn between two politicians, one of them right wing, the other (Albert Pré-jean) a social democrat, is forced by the opportunistic hypocrisy of the latter to yield with a heavy heart to the inescapable power of the former. Feyder's *La Loi du Nord* (1939, 1942), also scripted by Spaak, is an adventure film and therefore aimed more specifically at a male audience, but it proposes a sancti-fication of women that foreshadows that to be found in the whole of French Occupation cinema. Finally, *Le Ciel est à vous* (1943), which Spaak wrote for Jean Grémillon, is a family film par excellence that stands apart from the forty-odd women's melodramas made during the Occupation precisely because the dominant viewpoint in many of its key scenes is male. And yet it is no doubt the most feminist film of the whole French cinema up until 1970.

On the other hand, if Vincendeau's assertion is taken to mean that *Le Grand jeu* is "objectively" aimed at women in that it can be understood only by female audiences (to whom some U.K. and U.S. feminists attribute a socially constructed, if not innate, awareness of gender), she is probably right as far as the present day is concerned, in particular with regard to U.K. and U.S. audi-ences. But that does not tell us much about the status of *Le Grand jeu* in the cinema of the time, when in France above all — and this is still broadly the case today — a great majority of women internalized the male viewpoint on mascu-linity. It could be that the movie was, in a sense, incomprehensible at the time.

Textually, anyway — assuming that textuality is indeed to be found at the interstice of a text and a society — *Le Grand jeu* is aimed both subjectively and objectively at women, but even more so at men (if only because it can be super-ficially seen as an action film). It is an object lesson in the pitfalls of the male ideal, in what Elisabeth Badinter (1997) has described as the difficult and frag-ile construction of the masculine identity.

Le Grand jeu, which was released in 1934, exploits the mounting popularity of the theme of colonial wars and the Foreign Legion, triggered by Abd-el-Krim's rebellion in Morocco and the sporadic military operations that fol-lowed the end of the Rif War (1921–26) up until the 1930s. The framework of the narrative seems to be drawn from a novel by Pierre Loti dating from the "great period" of colonial conquests, *Le Roman d'un spahi* (1881), which was adapted for the screen in 1914, then again in 1936: a weak man flees the woman who has brought about his downfall and recovers his manhood while fighting in Africa, but at the cost of his life. The most celebrated and probably the most typical of the dozen or so French movies devoted to that theme in the 1930s is Julien Duvivier's *La Bandera* (1935), in which a hood from Paris who has stabbed his mistress to death takes refuge in the Spanish Foreign Legion and redeems himself by dying heroically in an apotheosis that is dragged out in frenzied fashion; it consists of a grandiloquent roll call of the dead in the course of which the character played by Robert Le Vigan, the sole survivor of a patrol wiped out by the "dirty Arabs," lists the names of the martyred dead.

At first sight, *Le Grand jeu* seems to follow a similar pattern. Pierre (Pierre Richard-Willm) is a Parisian playboy whose childish behavior includes risking his life at the wheel of his sports car "for no reason in particular," unless it be to impress Florence (Marie Bell), an elegant Parisian courtesan on whom he is squandering his fortune. The ruin that is staring him in the face and the fact that his upper-class family insists that he leave France, combined with his mistress's icy refusal to accompany him, set him on the classical path that will turn him into a Man: he joins the Legion, loses touch with women and his family, and dies heroically. But in *Le Grand jeu* there is no escaping from women, for they are in men's minds.

It is well known that the rule which governs the fighting community of the Foreign Legion requires its members to forget the past and the murders or crimes they may have committed, to forget their feelings and everything that used to make up their private sphere, and therefore to forget the world of women (women in general, of course, as opposed to prostitutes). Now what exasperates Pierre's army buddy, a White Russian (Sacha Pitoëff) who has radically repressed his past, is the obsession that is gnawing at his roommate's mind: the memory of the woman who ditched him so heartlessly after ruining him financially and whom he continues to love even so.

So Pierre goes to weep on the maternal shoulder of Blanche (Françoise Rosay). The hard-boiled manager of a bar for legionaries, she is the film's key character in that she has excluded herself from the circuit of desire; the very first time she appears, she calmly explains to a fellow tradesman, a good-looking man who makes her an honest proposition, that she is really "sick and tired" of men. And typical of the men concerned is Clément (Charles Vanel), her despised husband, a spineless creature and "unworthy father" par excellence who harasses sexually the women he employs.

When Pierre moans to Blanche about his painful memories of "that woman," she remarks, "That's all in your head." Blanche's voice is that of the movie. Proof of this can be seen in her gift for fortune-telling. Twice in Pierre's case, and once in that of Irma, a prostitute, she reads their cards (spreading out *le grand jeu* of the title for them, a sign that she is to play a central role in the movie),[1] and all her predictions turn out to be true. She foresees that Pierre will murder her husband, and she tells him he will see "that woman" again, a prediction which proves to be doubly true and which structures the whole film in such a way that at the end, when she predicts Pierre's death, we know that that, too, will take place.

On the surface of the text, then, she is a true fortune-teller. But we are in a movie, and neither this film nor any of the previous or subsequent works of its makers shows any particular belief in the irrational. So if the character played by Rosay (Feyder's wife in real life) knows the rest of the story, it is because she is in a sense outside the story; she is like the chorus of a Greek tragedy who draw conclusions as the story unfolds. And when she says to Pierre, "That's all in your head," she reveals the truth of the movie.

This is what conditions the status of the character called Irma when she appears before a dumbfounded Pierre one evening in a soldiers' dive. Irma is a small-time prostitute thinly disguised as a singer. Her touchingly awkward performance ("Gaiement, gaiement"), where she is lost in a very long shot of the bar where she performs and her voice is half-drowned by the hubbub, is already an admirable satire of the playacting that women have to put on in order to appeal to men — perfect playacting in the case of her plump girlfriend, whose dynamic and artificial gaiety satisfies Pierre's Russian friend but is something that Irma is quite incapable of putting on.

Irma, who is Florence's lookalike (the two roles are played by Marie Bell, though Irma's voice is dubbed by Claude Marcy), is also her counterpart; she sells her charms in soldiers' cabarets just as Florence did in luxury villas. The economics of prostitution, from catering to casual clients to being a kept woman, lies at the heart of *Le Grand jeu*, which is only superficially about the Foreign Legion; warfare as such takes place exclusively out of frame, and the only "battle scene" — a general shot teeming with people — is the extraordinary invasion of the red-light district by legionaries back from the front line, who pounce on women and carry them off in their arms like prey.

What causes problems for Pierre when he believes he has found his beloved

---

1. *Le grand jeu* is the most advanced and complex layout in Tarot fortune-telling.

again, dressed in the rags of a common prostitute, is Irma's voice. On the surface of the text, this is the only aspect of her character that distinguishes her from Pierre's memory of the woman he idealized (and with good reason!). Yet this difference is charged with meaning: Irma's grating working-class voice is at the opposite pole from the high-pitched, snobbish, and eminently "feminine" voice of her lookalike, the high-class prostitute. As soon as they meet, Pierre says to Irma, "Just sit there and look pretty!" In other words, "Be content to conform to the idea of the woman I have in my head." In any case, Irma is under no illusions, for when she prepares to do what a prostitute does for a client, she says to him, "And I won't say a word, since that's what you like," underlining the need most men have to fantasize during sex.

Up until that first night of love, the camera adheres exclusively to Pierre's viewpoint (apart from a brief introductory scene in Blanche's bar). But at breakfast time we realize that the rather "cow-like" Irma has fallen in love with Pierre. She suggests they shack up together and shows him her meager savings. But Pierre ups and leaves, slamming the door behind him, after tossing a few banknotes on her bedside table. We sense that he is both sickened by the sordid nature of the situation and by the initiative taken by the woman. But this scene also looks like a displaced representation of the psychophysiological differences between men and women that cause so many misunderstandings: the fits and starts of male desire compared with the longer, gentler curve of that of women.

Now it is at that precise moment that the movie takes a new turn, briefly but in such a way as to affect the whole of the rest of the narrative: the camera remains alone on the tearful and hurt Irma in an unusually lengthy shot that constitutes the first of three moments where the movie adopts the woman's viewpoint. The accumulation of similar signs, followed by a disabused conversation between Irma and Blanche centered on women's having to cater to the male need for illusion, encourages us little by little to look at Pierre critically rather than pityingly. That being the case, the theory he thinks up whereby some kind of metempsychosis has taken place (he believes Irma to have been Florence "in another life") can only be interpreted for what it is: a desperate attempt at bringing fantasy to life. And all the more so because Florence, who in the course of her fleeting appearances in Paris has already been presented to us as a frivolous and selfish love object and a poor choice hardly deserving of the passion Pierre strives to maintain, is shown in an even less favorable light when Pierre bumps into her in a Casablanca street, just as he is preparing to return to France with Irma. When he tries to persuade her to take up with him again, Florence's cynicism is now plain for all to see, but so is her lucidity. "If you love me, it's because of my beautiful clothes and my jewelry," was the gist of what she told him when they first parted. She knows full well she is just an image up for sale, and now it is a wealthy sheikh who foots the bills (compare the Madeleine character in *Gueule d'amour*).

Pierre's eyes are opened at last. He turns his back on the beautiful image that no longer exists for him. He resorts to a white lie to part from the passive Irma, who loves him but does not square with his fantasy, and rejoins the Legion.

Looked at in isolation, or in the context of the legionary cycle, this final rejection of women and of love in favor of war and death may seem highly ambiguous, confirming the old misogynistic maxim "The more beautiful they are, the more sluttish they are, so the best thing is to do without them." And yet by that final stage in the movie, the audience's identification with Pierre has been so undermined, and his credibility as a clear-sighted man so eroded, that many spectators are prepared to identify no longer with the firebrand whose fate has been sealed by his typically male illusions, but for a few minutes with Blanche. As she observes how Pierre's sick masculinity has fouled things up, while at the same time trying to bond with him by getting drunk in his company, she lays out for the last time the cards of the *grand jeu*, which tell her he is soon to die. When the bugle rings out, calling on the legionaries to leave for the front line, Pierre walks out of frame and the camera lingers for the third time in the movie on a female figure silently lamenting the folly of men. Just as the masculinity of the working-class Jean Gabin, according to Vincendeau (Gauteur and Vincendeau 1993), is enhanced *a contrario* by his entourage, here the vain masculinity that Pierre, the elegant aristocrat, can achieve only by dying is parodied with varying degrees of subtlety by the male characters surrounding him in the diegesis. When Irma hangs flycatchers (what an admirable metaphor!) from the ceiling of the bistro, unintentionally flaunting her legs, in a series of flattering low-angle shots, to the lecherous gaze of the idle proprietor (Charles Vanel), the scene makes perfectly explicit the theme of the man who "fantasizes over an image"; this spectacular reification of a woman's body leads directly to his murder by Pierre.

The refusal by the former Russian officer to talk about his feelings makes him the perfect icon of men's blindness about themselves. Emotionally crippled because he has repressed "the feminine" in him and accepting death out of weariness with life, he is the subject of a funereal tribute on the part of Pierre and Blanche (they burn his belongings), which suggests that this rejection of his innermost self and of his past is already a form of death.

Finally, the comical warrant officer played by Pierre Larquey, who is too old for active service but is keen to prove to everyone that he is a Man by demanding that he should be allowed to go to the front, sheds light on the derisory character of bellicose masculinity. This derision is given a political extension by one of the few scenes that actually take place in the combat zone: some men are building a road, and a legionary remarks, "These guys are pretty ungrateful. We build roads for them, but they still shoot at us!" The fatal "progressive" illusions of colonial oppression have rarely been denounced in such lapidary fashion.

Although the auteurists (and Georges Sadoul of all people!) have dismissed *Le Grand jeu* precisely because of the way it calls sexual roles into question, the film is indeed the masterpiece it has been described as by some mainstream film historians, not because it can be classified as existing on some remote planet of absolute art, floating high above the "banalities" of the French cinema of the period, but because it gets fully to grips with the themes that lay at the heart of popular cinema at the time: warlike and tragic virility, the wealthy "slut," the prostitute with the heart of gold. In so doing it transcends those themes but without ever losing sight of either their primacy or their popular following.

ℛ *LA MAISON DU MALTAIS*
(Pierre Chenal, 1938)

Usually classified by sloppy film historians as falling into the category of poetic realism, *La Maison du Maltais* differs radically from that genre, at least if "poetic realism" is understood to take as its model the sociometaphysical and Manichaean fatalism of Marcel Carné's *Le Quai des brumes*. True, it is a film about fatality. But that fatality is explicitly social and in no way Manichaean; in it, all the characters have their light and dark sides, including Rossignol, the corrupt private detective played by Louis Jouvet, a kind of cynical voyeur who, in the course of a crucial scene, seems to effect a *mise en abyme* of the spectator's role when he eavesdrops, through the wall of a hotel used by prostitutes (from his "seat in the stalls"), on the melodrama that is life itself.

While Rossignol, a character who appears quite late in the movie, reminds spectators of their place, the central figure of Matteo (Marcel Dalio), who is present from the very first scenes, is redolent of the filmmaker's vocation as a serious entertainer and perhaps also the Utopia the film proposes (but with no illusions), that of a society in which salaried work is no longer the main driving force, a "Gorzian" society, as we might say nowadays (Gorz 1988). Matteo is a storyteller who strolls through the streets of a North African port, providing everyone with little favors involving gratification of one kind or another, but accepting payment only from the wealthy. In the course of a single sequence, he brightens up the dull daily life of a craftsman with one of his stories, strokes the head of a child as he walks past, and persuades a merchant to give him some food by reminding him that he once found a woman to pleasure him. Matteo lavishes on anyone prepared to listen a philosophy of life that harks back to Paul Lafargue and his *Eloge de la paresse*: "Working is fine for those who have nothing else to do. . . . I listen to the breeze and the sea, and I wait."

But this "oriental paradise" is abruptly replaced by another world, one that reminds us we are somewhere in the French Empire: a nightclub-cum-brothel for Europeans where among the women selling their charms are a German, Greta (Jany Holt), and Safia (Viviane Romance). Behind this trashy luxury, a harsher reality soon makes itself felt: Greta has a worrying cough, and her potential client, a portly army officer, suddenly remembers he has an urgent rendezvous. Poor Greta has no choice but to return to the sleazy hotel where the women who work at the nightclub are housed. Greta is Safia's "dark side," embodying the tragic future of women who share this lot. The cut from the nightclub to the hotel emphasizes that link; initially a high-angle long shot leads us to think that it is Greta who is returning, whereas it is in fact Safia, who will find Greta in her bed in a sorry state: Rosina, the hotel keeper (Fréhel), has withheld Greta's key because she has not paid her rent (Greta is no longer a prosperous hooker). And yet, as Greta remarks, "Rosina's not a bad sort."

In *La Maison du Maltais* everyone has to play his or her social role, even against character. Rosina is as far removed from the sympathetic café owner in *Le Quai des brumes* who gives Gabin the clothes of a painter who has committed suicide (Robert Le Vigan) as she is from the lecherous hotelier in *Abus de confiance*, who insists on Lydia's (Danielle Darrieux) paying her rent in kind.

A parallel is drawn between Greta's predicament here and that of Matteo, whose father cannot accept his refusal to become enslaved by a salaried job and will not let him into the family home, "the house of the Maltese," an old windswept shack by the seaside. The deeper structure of the movie consists of a comparison between two forms of exploitation: the exploitation of men by men (specifically that of peoples colonized by the white man) and the exploitation of women by men. The innocent Matteo wanders through the streets of the town, constantly hoping to meet his "princess," as he explains to his dockworker friend (Gaston Modot), who has perfectly integrated into both the legal and the illegal regimes of colonial labor, as we shall see.

It is Safia's anger at Rosina's obstinate, if regretful, attitude toward Greta that brings about her first contact with Matteo; in a rage she throws the piece of underwear she is washing over the balcony into the street. The storyteller picks it up, then is flabbergasted by the beauty of the woman who comes down to retrieve it. True to her image as a "slut" (see *La Belle équipe* et al.), Romance/ Safia casts a provocative look at the innocent Matteo, who cannot takes his eyes off her breasts, before going back upstairs.

The fetishistic characteristics of this case of love at first sight are, however, a red herring. The gentle Matteo woos Safia assiduously, and she realizes that he is not like any man she has ever met. Following an altercation in the nightclub, Safia agrees, contrary to all the spectators' expectations, to take up Matteo's suggestion that she find refuge with him in the house of the Maltese. This is the first of a series of veritable narrative provocations that the filmmaker seems to revel in, contrasting with the conventions of the cinema of the time. The provocation that sets the tone of the movie is undoubtedly the decision to give the role of the male lead, Matteo, to Marcel Dalio, an actor more commonly cast as a treacherous "wop" or, at best, "a poor Jew." Allowing him to enjoy the favors of Viviane Romance, the sexiest star of the period, is an outrageously daring move. (In *Naples au baiser de feu*, in which they both appeared the previous year, Dalio served as a foil to the crooner Tino Rossi.)

The film also runs against the expectations of contemporary audiences by casting Dalio as a worker. For with a woman to support, Matteo in turn has to integrate into the economy of exploitation, in this case by becoming a dockworker, a particularly grueling job for a poet who has never used his hands. This marks the beginning of Matteo's descent into reality. The social articulation between Safia's withdrawal from the colonial economy of prostitution and Matteo's entering that of workers' exploitation, its counterpart, is expressed by an ellipse: Safia needs only to take Matteo's hand, thus recognizing the link that now unites them, for him to be shown at work in the following shot.

Matteo has abandoned his Utopia of a free man in order to free an exploited woman and construct with her the Utopia of a couple. But there are certain barriers you cannot break down with impunity: when an overjoyed Safia tells him she is pregnant, he immediately gets involved, along with his dockworker friend (Modot), in arms trafficking so as to top up his meager income. He falls into a police trap and is unable to get back to Safia. She is once again confronted with the tragic fate of prostitutes, in the person of her friend Greta, whose colleagues have had to club together to repay what she owes the owner of the brothel and allow her to go and die in a hospital. After being thrown out of the house of the Maltese by Matteo's father, who blames her for his son's misfortunes, Safia wanders off into the desert and ultimately faints from hunger. She is rescued at the last minute by a wealthy and kindly French archaeologist, Chervin (Pierre Renoir), whose only passion up to then would seem to have been a fetishistic attachment to ancient statuettes. (He is reminiscent of the central character in Wilhelm Jensen's novel *Gradiva*, analyzed by Freud [1907/2003], who falls in love with a young woman whose features remind him of a bas-relief in Pompeii.) Once Safia has recovered, Chervin prepares to return to France. When he realizes she has nowhere to go, he asks her to marry him.

Here the film lays bare the "incestuous" pattern of the cinema of the period, since the constraining financial dimension of their union is made plain for all to see, but without either Safia or her protector being condemned for all that; in this film, to quote Jean Renoir's celebrated but widely misunderstood remark about his own *La Règle du jeu*, "everyone has their reasons." The makers of *La Maison du Maltais* refuse to confine this male character to the typology of our three fathers (complacent, sacrificial, or unworthy) and lend him a contradictory personality, both generous and restricted by gender and class determination. Finally, the movie stresses the similarity and difference between the male and female conditions of the oppressed: just as Matteo is drawn inevitably into the path of delinquency, Safia can only sell her body.

When we next see Safia in Paris, now the wife of the grand bourgeois Chervin and mother of the little girl she conceived with Matteo, she is quite unrecognizable. This transformation causes the archaeologist's more malicious friends to voice the age-old obsession with the "prostitute-cum-chameleon" (Corbin 1978):

— He's said to have fished her out of a souk!
— Worse than that!
— In any case, she's a very good hostess!
— She's familiar with salons![2] (*laughter*)

But in the course of the same scene we realize that Safia is not just putting on an act but has at last managed to shake off the prostitute's straitjacket: ashamed of her ignorance but clearly intelligent, she has been attending lectures at the Collège de France. In this she has gone beyond her kindly husband's expectations: "Do you imagine I want a scholar for a wife? I love you as

---

2. *Salon* = drawing room or brothel parlor.

you are!" — in other words as a sex object, the living replica of the statuettes of Venus he used to caress so affectionately. If everyone has their reasons, everyone also has their limitations.

At this point, allow us to stress the movie's other major singularity: its rejection of the unity of genre. We have already moved on from an exotic tale to a realistic melodrama and the world of boulevard theater; the movie is now about to turn into a gangster film. This discontinuous framework, which offers a succession of genres without their being woven into each other, reflects the radically different social milieux of the protagonists on either side of the Mediterranean, and it admirably serves Chenal's purpose, which is to confront the various forms of human exploitation in such a way as to reveal their deep-seated similarity.

When he is released from prison, Matteo can think only of tracking down the woman he loves. His quest takes him from the Orient of the *Arabian Nights* to the symbolic heart of the colonizing world: the Paris underworld. There he is taken under the wing of a petty thief, Gégène (Raymond Aimos), and becomes the immigrant worker who is always on hand to run minor errands. In this little secret world, a parody of both capitalist free enterprise and patriarchal oppression, Matteo suffers the fate in metropolitan France of any street peddler or road sweeper.

Logically enough, it is through her little girl that Safia happens to get wind of Matteo (the child tells her mother about a story she heard from the lips of a "gentleman" she met in a park). The innocence of Matteo, who is constantly surprised by how nasty his employers are, partakes as much of the innocence of childhood (a pre-exploitive state, so to speak) as of the fantasy Orient of "idleness" and its indifference to worldly goods. Also in line with the logic of the film, whose tone can be described as one of "optimistic pessimism," and whose characters are all generous at heart (even Rosina, the hotel manageress, helps to pay off Greta's debt), is Safia's decision to sacrifice the great love she still feels for the gentle father of her child. In a sordid hotel room, she forces herself to behave like a "slut" so as to disgust Matteo and protect her little girl's happiness. This scene also reveals to us the true narrative function of Rossignol, the corrupt detective whom Safia has hired to track Matteo down and who, from the room next door, describes to his beautiful, glacial, and cynical secretary the ins and outs of Safia's sacrifice. The caricatural Rossignol, a kind of Shakespearean mercenary, is above all the character responsible for the film's dénouement: after having given a running commentary on the play-acting going on in the hotel room, it is he who puts Safia's marriage to the test by blackmailing her. Interestingly, so as to get into Chervin's apartment, he assumes a perfectly appropriate disguise for a blackmailer by passing himself off as a representative of a religious charity, who has come to take advantage of a bourgeois citizen's uneasy conscience.

Safia's subterfuge is such a success that Matteo, after learning his lesson, suddenly bursts into the adult world. On his return to the gangsters' hideout, he loses his temper, knocks out his drunken boss, and replaces him as gang leader. This further coup de théâtre, although rather implausible in its suddenness, is nevertheless perfectly logical at a subtextual level precisely because of that suddenness, since it seems to resolve energetically the fundamental dilemma facing any colonized people: between submission and violent revolt, there can be no middle course.

Matteo's transformation into a caricatural underworld boss sporting a dinner jacket and with women draped all over him once again echoes the parallel destiny of Safia, who has been transformed into a society lady. The two sides of the coin, so to speak: the free and loving bodies in the Maltese's house, in their loose-fitting and flowing materials, now wear the stuffy attire of "civilization."

Matteo eventually finds out that Safia was putting on an act, that their child has survived (the fact that it is a girl, as Safia had always wanted, poses no problem to the feminine man he remains at heart), and that she has been thrown out of her husband's apartment as an indirect result of being blackmailed by the corrupt detective. In one last moment of symmetry, it is now Matteo's turn to sacrifice himself: he forces his way into Chervin's home, not to attack him but to prove Safia's innocence. Then, putting on his storyteller's clothes again, he shoots himself in the head and, in the movie's very brief closing shot, "returns" to the house of the Maltese, the mythical home of happiness "before the Western invasion."

True, Safia, who disappears abruptly from the movie, fares better than the man she loves in that she emerges with wounds that will heal from this parallel itinerary of two oppressed persons, the prostitute and the Arab. Thanks to the sacrifice of the gentle male figure, she earns a place in high society for herself and her little girl. Before the child was born Safia was chiefly concerned to spare her daughter the ordeal of selling her body. By locating this dénouement off-screen, the film seems not to begrudge her the luck she has had. As for Matteo, his death is the price to be paid for a twofold transgression (condensed at the level of the signifier by the casting of Dalio against type): first there is the transgression of a colonized subhuman who overcomes the class and "race" barrier (although the character he plays is Maltese, which was more acceptable at the time than Arab, it is significant that Dalio, like Chenal, was Jewish); then there is the transgression of the gentle male figure, who is forced, by an all-conquering Western world, to play the macho contrary to his own values.

There is probably to be found in the background to all this an idealization of the Orient that was part of a long-standing tradition of the French intelligentsia (to wit, Gérard de Nerval, Eugène Delacroix, and Gustave Flaubert), whose racist and phallocentric undertones have been denounced by Edward Said (1978/2003). But Chenal had been friends with the Surrealists in his youth, and their idealization of the Orient was of a very different kind, a penetrating critique of white male domination and workaholism in the West. In the 1930s, the film's critique of work was perhaps too idealistic to have been seen as radical. And yet the respective experiences of Safia and Matteo say a lot about the two subjugations that have left their mark down the centuries, that of "exotic" peoples and that of women. And the movie's pessimism is a very different kettle of fish from the Manichaean romanticism favored by Marcel Carné, Jacques Prévert, and others. It is much more in line with the great tradition of critical realism dear to Jean Renoir and Jean Grémillon, which can also be found in movies by Albert Valentin, Louis Daquin, Claude Autant-Lara, and Jacques Becker.

◈ LE JOUR SE LÈVE
(Marcel Carné, 1939)

Le Jour se lève was the first screenplay written by Jacques Viot, a young art dealer who lived in the apartment adjoining Marcel Carné's. According to Carné (1989), one day in 1938 Viot brought him a story just three pages long that immediately captivated him because of its use of flashbacks, which had never been used before in French films. Carné managed to persuade Gabin to play the central character (François) and Jacques Prévert to put aside his own projects and collaborate with Viot. Viot was responsible for the adaptation, while Prévert wrote the dialogue. Neither of them showed any particular enthusiasm for this collaboration, Carné observed, but he was satisfied with the result.

Audiences were somewhat disconcerted by the novelty of the narrative device, to such an extent that without Carné's knowledge the producer inserted an explanatory message before the credits: "A man has committed a murder. . . . Locked up and besieged in his room, he recalls the circumstances that led him to become a murderer." Thom Andersen (Andersen and Burch 1994) has pointed out that the flashback technique was originally used in films made in the Weimar Republic and then became very common in American noir movies, whereas nowadays it is little more than a hackneyed narrative device used by scriptwriters who have run out of inspiration.

Under the influence of André Bazin's (1983) celebrated analysis of *Le Jour se lève*, it became traditional for cinephiles to highlight the combination of realism and poetry in what they saw as a twentieth-century tragedy set in a working-class suburb. More recently Maureen Turim (1990/2000) demonstrated that the dual temporality around which the movie is constructed (with three flashbacks) is intended not so much to make concrete the mechanisms of memory as to illustrate François's compulsive desire, extinguished only by his death. The only psychical device used by this narrative construction is associative memory (a snapshot of François, the mirror, the wardrobe, the brooch, the teddy bear, and the door of François's tiny room). Throughout the movie, objects serve both as metaphor and as metonymy, but also as objects of a fetishistic fixation.

Turim also analyzes the way the film employs the codes of melodrama by lending an unparalleled complexity to the figure of the hero and to the two female characters, who can no longer be reduced to the traditional contrast between the pure young woman and the fallen woman. Turim suggests that the film's social realism may also be interpreted as a displaced self-portrait of the filmmakers themselves. We shall explore that line of inquiry by reexamining an idea once formulated with reference to François's jealousy of Valentin: "When one remembers that taboos about faithfulness and a woman's virginity above all form part of petit bourgeois ideology, one may question the innocence of that romantic projection" (Sellier 1981). The figure of the worker and the choice of Gabin to play such parts embody, in the work of Carné and Prévert and in the context of the populist cinema of the period, a positive male image with which the public as a whole (men and women) could easily identify. The film does not become any less complex — on the contrary — when we analyze the hero's relationship with women in terms of the critique of gender relations as shaped by the patriarchal ideology interiorized by all men, even the best of them. The attribution of this virginity taboo to the working-class masculinity of the period (if indeed it was historically specific) strikes us as debatable. On the other hand, what we know about the double sexual standards predominant in French society at the time (McMillan 1981) suggests that this taboo, which is attributed to the Gabin character, François (in contrast with the broadminded Jules Berry character, Valentin), weighs heavily on the whole of society, including presumably the progressive filmmakers who tried to denounce it.

As confirmation of this critical dimension, the dual female character proposed by *Le Jour se lève* breaks away from the stereotypes found in the poetic realism movies of the time, from *La Belle équipe* to *Gueule d'amour*. It suggests that the spectator should question the traditional Judeo-Christian contrast between the Madonna and the whore, not in order to conclude with another stereotype along the lines of "they're all sluts" but to demonstrate on the contrary that "real" women are kept against their will in fantasized straitjackets made by men.

Edward Baron Turk (1989: 152 ff.) analyzes the first encounter between François and Françoise (Jacqueline Laurent) as a mise-en-scène of the male erotic fixation on the image of the flower-woman, as it emerged from the Romantic tradition and was revalorized by the Surrealists (to whom Prévert was close). Françoise's immobility, as she stands in a flimsy dress at the entrance to the workshop holding a pot of azaleas, and François's protective garb, which shows only his eyes — in short the whole arrangement of the scene underlines the way the male gaze constructs the image on which it is going to fix itself, irrespective of the woman who exists behind that image. The fixation is facilitated by the contrast between the nightmarish science-fiction atmosphere of the workshop and the delightfully archaic aura of this "young woman in bloom," who seems to have sprung from the paradise of the preindustrial era. But Carné goes further than that: the azaleas that suddenly wilt as they come into contact with the noxious miasmas of the workshop convey, of course, the deadly horrors of François's manual labor. They may also symbolize a posteriori Françoise's lost virginity, something that François later discovers to his horror.

The film's discourse nevertheless keeps its distance from François's idealized view of the young woman: the dichotomy he constructs between the dream woman he loves and Clara (Arletty), the real woman he sleeps with, is clearly shown to be fantasized and brings about the final disaster. From that critical standpoint, the greenhouse flowers that wilt can be interpreted as an ironic warning about the fragility of fantasies. The later scene in the greenhouse returns to the same theme: idealized love is shown to be a mental construction by François as Françoise lies down on the bales of straw, clearly signaling that she would like some kind of more sensual contact, after she has agreed to stop seeing the man whose name François does not even mention for fear he may cast a shadow over the ideal image of his loved one.

The movie's entire complexity is no doubt to be found in this oscillation between François's viewpoint, which structures the narrative through the use of flashbacks, and the signifying elements that put that viewpoint in perspective and may prompt spectators to ask themselves about the deeper causes of the tragedy suffered by the young man. From the start of the film, the way François shuts himself up in his room after killing Valentin represents rather clearly the illusory and desperate creation of a refuge against the outside world — the construction of a cocoon that is both symbolized and barricaded by the wardrobe which, as Bazin remarks, serves to wall up the room like a tomb. This is an eminently regressive process in which death looks very much like a return to the mother's breast; at the end François huddles in a corner of his bed in the blind spot of his room, which cannot be reached by police fire, as though yearning to curl up in the wall.

The movie, then, draws a parallel between François's obsessive, regressive, and fetishistic character and his Manichaean view of women, while at the same time offering an objectively more complex view of the female characters than his. This is particularly noticeable in the case of the aptly named Clara, whose undemonstratively independent behavior from the moment she first appears is rather unusual in a film of that period. Turk notes the contrast between the sophisticated and feminine clothes she wears for her role in Valentin's animal act (a tutu, spangles, a décolleté, black stockings, and stiletto heels) and the perfect naturalness with which she approaches François at the bar of the cabaret. She tells him about her problems as though they had long been friends and manages to get him to unbend despite the jealousy he feels as he notices Françoise's wonderment at the way Valentin gets his dogs to perform. In a very different role from the highly literary character she plays in *Hôtel du Nord*, Arletty is here a "real" woman who works and has feelings. In the transformation that Carné subsequently caused her to undergo when immortalizing her as Garance in *Les Enfants du paradis* (*Children of Paradise*; Turk 1989; Sellier 1992), there is an idealizing dimension that is not yet present in *Le Jour se lève*. On the contrary, Clara here gains in authenticity what she has lost as a wisecracking working-class broad, and the movie sees male neurosis as the reason for the fact that, despite her charm and common sense, she fails to appeal to François, who is interested only in her body as he dreams of eternal love with Françoise, whom he dares not touch.

Françoise herself seems different from the idealized image François has of her. We are led to believe that when she first meets him she already has a settled relationship with Valentin. As she tells François unselfconsciously later on in

Jules Berry and Jean Gabin in *Le Jour se lève*, 1939. Courtesy of Raymond Voinquel, Cinémathèque française.

the movie, "He has always been very nice to me. . . . He's been the only man like that . . . until you came along." As both lover and substitute father figure for Françoise, a state orphan, Valentin acts as an initial love fixation that is easy to understand. There are a few hints that it would not take much for her to lose interest in him, once she knows that François loves her. When Valentin leaves Françoise at the cabaret door to go and have it out with Clara, she remarks bitterly, "Well, that's my evening ruined." We may suppose that she is thinking of François, whom she has just left to join Valentin.

Later on in the greenhouse, when François tells her how disgusted he is with the scheming Valentin, she simply suggests he should stop seeing him; then, as she lies down on the straw bales in an inviting manner that François does not seem to understand, she hands him the brooch Valentin gave her. "It's yours now. . . . It's the thing I was most attached to; I've always worn it," she says before adding, in the familiar *tu* form, "I love you." This whole scene clearly indicates to anyone with eyes and ears (but not to François, who is blinded by his fantasies) that she has put Valentin behind her and is ready to enter into a relationship with François. This is confirmed by what follows, when Valentin complains to François that Françoise does not want to see him any more. In the scenes that follow the murder, when Françoise lies on Clara's bed talking deliriously, she can think only of François, despite the fact that Valentin has only just died.

But the thoughts going through the minds of the two young people never converge. François, who is no shrinking violet when he first visits Françoise (he more than once suggests they make love), behaves quite differently once he discovers the existence of Valentin. The comparison between his eagerness in that first scene and his overcautiousness in the second is edifying. Instead of making love to her, he mumbles, "I love you. . . . You've a pretty body. . . . You're fragile. . . . You know what? You're like a little animal. . . . When I first set eyes on you with your flowers, I immediately wanted to be happy." Here we have all the stereotypes of the eternal feminine, fulfilling their function as a denial of the woman as an independent and responsible individual. François has fashioned an image that belongs to the vegetable and animal world, but overlooks the human being. After his declaration, he leans over her and kisses her on the corner of her mouth, as though paralyzed by respect for her. Before our eyes, he sets up the pedestal on which he places her, as though foreshadowing the statue of the goddess played by Garance in Baptiste's pantomime (*Les Enfants du paradis*).

A little later, when François comes to break it off with Clara, another incoherence is highlighted. When she sees how gloomy he seems, she remarks, "To judge from the way you look, you'd think it was *me* who was ditching you! You're too much of a softie . . . Too sensitive. . . . I tell you, you make me laugh, the whole lot of you!" ("The whole lot of you" refers of course to the male confraternity, of which François is, in Clara's eyes, just another specimen, and one almost as unsavory as Valentin.) The spectator's desire to see François and Françoise happy together is undermined by the churlish way he treats Clara—an indication of his unconscious submission to patriarchal values.

This alienation is confirmed by François's love-hate relationship with Valentin, who comes across as a subjective rather than an objective barrier standing in the way of François's relations with women. Before he even appears, Valentin the dog trainer is implicitly singled out as an obstacle to François's desire; it is at the point where François sits down on Françoise's bed in a blatant play for her that she gets up to go and meet Valentin. Later, when François sprawls on Clara's bed waiting for her to join him, Valentin turns up and interrupts their tête-à-tête. Instead of making love to Clara, François goes downstairs with Valentin. By telling the two men to leave because she does not want to hear what they have to say to each other (about Françoise), Clara clearly indicates that a form of complicity has been established between

François and Valentin. Indeed François has taken Valentin's place between Clara and Françoise, reproducing the same typically patriarchal dichotomy in the use he makes of women (those you sleep with and those who are worthy of your love). This alienation displayed by François becomes clear for all to see in his final scene with Valentin, who shows he is aware of what is going on when he tells François, "I absolutely had to see you privately in a man-to-man talk," in other words, within the framework of male chauvinist rivalry.

Although François tries to push Valentin out of a window, he is incapable of kicking him out of his room; he seems to be literally paralyzed by what Valentin is saying, a condition reinforced by cross-cutting between mobile shots of Berry and static shots of Gabin's tense face as he keeps his eyes trained on him. On three occasions, François tries to cut short his older rival when he talks about his knowledge of young women. The attempted defenestration is prompted by Valentin's remark, "Women are complicated, aren't they? Young women are mysterious, aren't they?" Their second clash is triggered by an allusion to the brooch, which symbolizes Valentin's sexual link with women: "A pretty gift to make to a child . . . What do you want to know?" And the shooting is François's response to Valentin's ultimate provocation: "Since she took to me, didn't she? . . . The girl and I, we . . . [laughs] I'd have been wrong to have had any scruples. . . . I love young people. . . . [laughs] You're interested, aren't you? Do you want chapter and verse?"

In fact François cannot silence the voice of the father within him — the voice that considers women to be objects and tells us we need to make sure we have sole ownership of them. When Valentin chucks his pistol onto the table, he symbolizes the transfer of patriarchal power from which François cannot escape (Carné 1989: 109). François ends up killing him, even though Valentin, on his own admission, has lost Françoise. "You'd better shut that mouth of yours!" ("Tu vas la taire, ta gueule"), egregiously ungrammatical in French, shows that in François's mind Valentin is above all a voice, that of the Law of the Father.

We find in *Le Jour se lève*, in a particularly complex form, the "incestuous" problem of 1930s cinema. As in many films with Gabin, it is treated from the point of view of the "son" who tries to tear the "daughter" away from the "bad father." The hero believes he has found the perfect match in the shape of a young woman who, like him, has no family, but then discovers she has already been confiscated by a totally cynical "father" who is at once unworthy, authoritarian, and incestuous. Valentin's cynicism is emphasized in the scene where he gets François to believe that he is Françoise's father and tries to prevent him from seeing her again, on the pretext that the young worker suffers from ill health and has no future. When Valentin's fatherhood is revealed to be a lie, the incest taboo is ridiculed at the same time as the patriarchal claim to exclusive possession of young women is exposed.

But the movie also shows that it is impossible for François to kill the father symbolically; he kills Valentin because he cannot free himself from the patriarchal Law, from which he will escape only through his own death. It is a desperate acknowledgment of the powerlessness of sons in the face of their fathers' cynicism, which foreshadows the Débâcle and Pétain's confiscation of power. François's unhappiness arises from his enslavement by patriarchal images: the omnipotence of the father and the fetishization of female virginity. He is incapable of being happy with Clara, a figure who offers a combination of beauty, generosity, affection, and maturity. And his fetishistic fixation on Françoise prevents him from realizing who she really is: a young woman with whom he could be happy if he accepted the idea that she could love him despite having loved another man before him.

The murder scene depicts the two men holed up in a little room under the eaves as though trapped by the suffocating logic of male values, where each tries to sap the other's virility through challenges related to the possession of women. A kind of macabre complicity brings the two men together in this scene, as when Valentin finds just the right sort of language to wound François, while François goes along with Valentin's suicidal urge. If Valentin is the quintessence of the bad father, François cannot escape a certain form of objective connivance with the patriarchal values that alienate him.

The great strength of *Le Jour se lève* is that it does not restrict itself to a Manichaean description of class alienation. True, François is financially exploited by invisible bosses and believes it is his work that is killing him. But unwittingly he also bears the brunt of the patriarchal system in the private sphere. While Valentin symbolizes the power of attraction which the discourse of the Father exerts over women (according to Clara, Valentin has a degree in philosophy!), the film above all highlights the pregnancy of that discourse over all men, even when they belong to the oppressed classes and, in the movie's subtext, even when they are progressive intellectuals.

LA RÈGLE DU JEU
(Jean Renoir, 1939)

This film, which was made in total freedom by a filmmaker at the height of his powers and the peak of his success, had a most unusual career: an unprecedented flop on its release in 1939, it was banned immediately after the declaration of war, unsuccessfully rereleased in a shortened version in 1945 and in 1959, and finally resuscitated in its original form in 1965, when it was hailed by the critics (Vanoye 1989). Nick Browne (1982) brilliantly analyzes the way Renoir resorts to theatricality in order to suggest that "the society within the film is pictured for the audience as preoccupied with its self-image" and "acts out its own destruction" until the death of the young aviator "discloses the aggression latent in civilised society," not so long after the publication of Freud's *Civilization and Its Discontents*. Browne also highlights the function of cultural icons in the movie (theater, painting, sculpture, architecture) as a way of examining how members of the dominant class represent themselves to themselves, whereas class relationships are expressed by mirror devices in both the literal and the figurative sense, where servants identify with the image their employers have of them. This political analysis of the film and of its critical dimension in relation to the troubled period when it was made (1939) nevertheless leaves aside the representation of gender relations. And yet Renoir stresses the importance of that theme in the credit titles, where the male and female casts are listed on two separate title cards.

The opening sequence, which cuts between shots of the arrival of André Jurieu (Roland Toutain) at Le Bourget airport and scenes where Christine (Nora Gregor) is in her boudoir preparing to go out for the evening, contrasts the aviator's male world — exterior night — with the brightly lit female world of the aristocracy; on the one hand we have a manifestation of popular enthusiasm where a woman radio reporter is swallowed up by the crowd, and on the other the refinement of a boudoir where mirrors and net curtains perfectly set off a society woman's delicate beauty. Moreover, this narrative and iconographical contrast is heightened dramatically by the aggressive and bitter remarks the aviator makes on the radio about a woman, and the spectator realizes, as Christine turns off the radio, that the remarks, without any regard for conventions, are being directed at her.

In other words, the movie opens with a brutal confrontation between a male and a female world, the first characterized by modernity, youthfulness, and spontaneity, and the second by luxury, refinement, and fragility. Sexual differences overlap with class differences as well as blurring them, given that the young aviator from a working-class background who is promoted to the status of national hero is in love with a female aristocrat. The social prestige that here attaches to a flying exploit and, in Jean Grémillon's *Gueule d'amour* (1937), to a military career lends the young commoner an attractiveness he interprets as love. In both films, that illusion ends in tragedy.

But in the film's opening sequence the two worlds are also, separately, built on a complicity with another individual of the same sex, with André opening his heart to his friend Octave (Jean Renoir) and Christine, the marquise, quizzing her chambermaid, Lisette (Paulette Dubost), about her relationship with men. Relations between women as portrayed by the film are marked by sexual rivalry or class domination, whereas male friendships are numerous and of many kinds. In addition to the couple formed by André and Octave, which can be interpreted as a doubling (see Browne 1982), relations between Octave and Robert, Marquis de La Cheyniest (Marcel Dalio), between Robert and Marceau (Carette), and finally between Marceau and Schumacher (Gaston Modot) are all founded on a complicity that excludes a third party: complicity between men against women, complicity between lawbreakers against an upholder of the law or vice versa. Like all his colleagues, Renoir draws on the pattern of male friendship typical of 1930s films (e.g., *L'Equipage* [*Flight into Darkness*], *La Belle équipe*, *Gueule d'amour*), which is seen as an ideal community not contaminated by desire or sexual disruption, in other words by women. But following on from his earlier movie, *La Grande illusion* (*Grand Illusion*), he stresses the crucial nature of social differences, irrespective of any fleeting moments of imagined complicity felt by the male characters. For instance, Schumacher and Marceau first clash because they have to defend incompatible interests (the gamekeeper versus the poacher), then they are rivals for a woman's affections, before finally joining forces after they have both been sacked by the marquis.

Robert's complicity with Octave, and then with Marceau, cannot survive their class difference, and the friendship between Octave and André often looks like emotional blackmail. All the male relationships in *La Règle du jeu* function as more or less short-lived alliances in the class war and the battle of the sexes. The small number of alliances between women can perhaps be interpreted as a sign of their dominated status and isolation, something that is further heightened by Christine's foreign background. When, after discovering that her husband is having an affair with Geneviève (Mila Parély), Christine goes to see Geneviève and suggests they team up together (a proposal that never comes to anything), she demonstrates her ignorance of the rules of the sex war in France, which is based on division between women.

The subject of the movie is indicated by a series of disruptions of the rules governing sexual relationships in Parisian high society, the main rule being the keeping up of appearances, which André infringed by talking about his love life on the radio. But the second disruption is caused by the little personal secrets that Christine, who comes from another culture (her father was an orchestra conductor in Salzburg), reveals to her urbane husband, Robert, who is so moved by this token of marital trust that he decides on the spot to break with his mistress.

Because of the same need for truth and sincerity, André and Christine are both in their different ways hindrances to the proper workings of the dominant classes' libertine codes. They both come from elsewhere, from another class or another country, and the sexual and class differences between them are partly cancelled out by their shared relationship of exteriority to the rules of the game. One of them gets killed, and the other has to fall into line with the deadly rigidity of those rules that lurks behind their congenial and permissive trappings. Initially Robert displays a remarkable broadmindedness when he decides to forget all about the mini-scandal centered on his wife. And Christine may at first strike the spectator as a charming, if rather irresponsible young woman.

But this light vein proves to be an illusion as soon as the film's long preamble comes to an end, when Geneviève, who is told by Robert of his intention to leave her "in order to deserve [his] wife," threatens to tell Christine about his unfaithfulness. The marital trust whose virtues Robert discovers somewhat tardily proves impracticable for a libertine aristocrat like him. Behind all the politeness one can sense the cruel law of upper-class mendacity, from which one cannot escape any more than from a pact with the devil. The clash between the marquis and his mistress is filmed in a series of close-ups that isolate each of them in turn next to a bust of Buddha, whose inhuman immobility they seem to ape even as they try to express sincere feelings.

The clutter of art objects in Geneviève's flat shows her to be just another fetish in Robert's collection; from the very beginning of the movie he is shown surrounded by the musical automata that fascinate him. These objects, only marginally connected with legitimate art, are intended to show Robert's relationship with the world: a never-satisfied fetishistic possessiveness directed at objects that imitate the appearance of life and that their owner believes he commands although he does not know how they work. The spectator cannot fail to see the connection between this obsessive love of automata and the form that love takes in the patriarchal system.

Robert's relationship with women is indeed like that of a collector: Christine is a beautiful object he shows off but whose inner feelings he does not seem interested in delving into. In their Paris mansion, he stands outside his wife's bedroom door waiting to say good morning to her by kissing her hand, while

Octave lolls on her bed. At their château, La Colinière, he bids her goodnight in similar fashion, and the camera lingers on Christine as she shuts her bedroom door with a melancholy air and asks her chambermaid, "Tell me, Lisette, wouldn't you like to have children?" So saying, she highlights the sexual and emotional frustration she feels.

The pride with which Robert exhibits his new hurdy-gurdy, "the crowning achievement of [his] career as a collector," is very similar to his pride in Christine when she introduces André to the guests at La Colinière; she has perfectly performed the role assigned to her. The jealousy that later causes the marquis to behave like an "Italian navvy" is consistent with the same proprietary attitude. It is only later that he becomes "civilized" again, when offering to step aside in favor of André if that is what will make Christine happy. But given how the movie ends, one may legitimately have doubts as to the sincerity of his offer. Renoir's choice of Dalio to play the marquis (he had initially thought of Fernand Ledoux) confirms the satirical dimension of the character, with his small stature, affected politeness, and very visible makeup. Usually cast as a traitor or in supporting roles, Dalio is here cast against type, as in *La Maison du Maltais*, so as to shatter the flattering image that French aristocrats like to give themselves and that was perfectly embodied by Pierre Fresnay in *La Grande illusion*. Another of Renoir's provocations is the way he alludes to Dalio's Jewish origins by attributing them to the marquis himself during the celebrated scene in which the servants are eating in the kitchen and the cook ridicules his colleagues' racism by praising his employer's gastronomic refinement.

On the other hand, in the course of the complicated to-ing and fro-ing that takes place within the confines of La Colinière, the role of Octave, played by Renoir himself, remains mysterious. Browne (1982) shows how Renoir, through this exuberant character who does not dominate the situation any more than anyone else or represent "a centre of moral consciousness," attempts to represent his own refusal "to exempt himself from the objectivity of the critique which in his capacity of director he undertakes." But from the point of view of gender relations, it is worth noting that Octave, who is the equivalent of the confidant in eighteenth-century drama, plays this role successively vis-à-vis André, Christine, and finally Robert. This relative lack of sexual differentiation is underlined by his chubby physique and his easygoing and childlike manners; he goes into Christine's bedroom with the same casualness as her chambermaid, and more easily than her husband, and the way he fondles Lisette has more to do with playing games than with an expression of desire.

During the fancy-dress fête that the marquis organizes at La Colinière in honor of André, Octave is disguised as a bear, with a galumphing manner that suggests his lack of virility. This is further emphasized by the fact that he is unable to extract himself from his costume, which acts like a straitjacket — and makes him impotent — while the other men run after Christine (both literally and figuratively). An explanation for Octave's ill-defined sexuality can be found in the pathetic scene where he opens his heart to Christine on the château terrace. By way of compensation for his lack of social definition (a failed musician, he is no more than a parasite in this milieu), his self-inflicted castration makes him acceptable because he presents no danger. But the system hangs together only because of the confidant's smiling affability. It all falls apart the moment Octave confesses he is in love with Christine.

André is the positive version of Octave: his professional success, similar to that of an artist, gives him the feeling he can transgress social barriers. He still has the youthfulness that makes him desirable, and which Octave has lost. These illusions will cost him his life. Octave is objectively responsible for the death of this other version of himself: it was he who introduced André to Christine, and it is his confession to Christine that he is in love with her, in violation of the implicit rules that govern his acceptance by this milieu, that brings matters to a head. His departure from La Colinière at the same time as Marceau, who is in love with Lisette, confirms the demise of the illusions about a world that is incapable of integrating the Other and therefore already potentially dead.

In this representation of several types of unhealthy masculinity, we need also to take into account, at the level of the servants, the contrast between Schumacher and Marceau. The gamekeeper uses his gun to defend his proprietary rights over his wife, just as he defends the estate of his employer, the marquis; the poacher's approach to sex is purely playful. "Whether you want to seduce a woman, leave her or keep her," he says to the marquis, "you have to make her laugh." So on one side we are shown a deadly and murderous seriousness, and on the other a lightheartedness that is potentially just as dangerous, and their complementarity is underlined by the two men's collaboration in the final murder. The Germanness of the Alsatian gamekeeper, stressed by the marquise, herself an Austrian, also gums up the works; like her, he refuses to accept the lies that govern this world and "disrupts the service" with his marital problems. Like André, he does not respect the barrier between the private and public spheres.

Schumacher and Marceau also reflect two aspects of the marquis's identity, the former his patriarchal authority, and the latter his womanizing. The film's depiction of male power in the dominant class boils down to banning poaching on one's own land while poaching oneself on other people's land. This implies that women form part of one's heritage.

And when women neglect or misunderstand that status, they must pay the price. In the film's very first sequence, Christine, in conversation with Lisette, is shown to be ignorant of the rules that will later be brought home to her harshly through public humiliation. Her chambermaid, on the other hand, knows the rules and tries, in vain, to get round them. Even Geneviève, who seems to be not only familiar with those rules but capable of turning them to her own advantage, ends up stripped of everything, ridiculed and infantilized. The way the society of the time regards women as minors is constantly stressed; although Christine is able to receive André in her bedroom, it is out of the question that he should be able to show himself at her side in public, as he would like. Her luxurious residence seems from the start to be a kind of gilded cage, which contrasts with the skies that are André's domain. Finally, for André to be able to come to La Colinière, Octave first has to obtain Christine's agreement, but he also has to negotiate the permission of her husband, on whom everything depends in the end.

La Règle du jeu analyzes the way gender and class relationships intertwine. Although André goes as far as attempting suicide (by crashing his car) in order to persuade his friend Octave that he has to see Christine again, he is completely paralyzed when she finally responds to his desire. The marquise's social status makes her both desirable and untouchable to the young aviator (as indeed it does to Octave, who does not dare any more than André to manifest his physical desire for Christine, except in a playful manner). And even when she decides out of pique to take a lover, none of the three men she makes a play for in the course of the wild fête in the château is capable of responding to her desire. Saint-Aubin is a wimp whom André eliminates by punching him in the face, but even André himself turns out to be paralyzed by what he sees as the proprieties, and Octave dares to kiss Christine on the mouth only after she has specifically asked him to. With his rifle shot, Schumacher, the patriarchy's enforcer, puts an end to Christine's efforts to escape her alienated status as a bourgeois wife. It is with a hangdog look that she returns to the fold, leaving her husband with the task of explaining André's death to the guests.

The character of Lisette, Christine's double on another social plane, enables Renoir to bring out the way class membership affects gender identities. From the first, Lisette shows she knows more than her employer about the question of relations with men. With a typically Parisian volubility, she ridicules Christine's wish to remain on merely friendly terms with a member of the opposite sex: "Friendship with a man? Don't make me laugh!" What's more, she consciously uses her job to keep her distance (both literally and figuratively) from her husband, Schumacher, who works as a gamekeeper at La Colinière while she is a chambermaid in Paris. Even when she is at the château she strives to exercise her freedom as a woman in the interior space to which she is confined, taking advantage of her husband's obligation to remain outside. Precisely because Schumacher persecutes Marceau, she pretends to make overtures to the former poacher with a joyful cynicism that is reminiscent of the sly soubrette characters of theatrical tradition. It is she who triggers the chase through the rooms of the château and takes advantage of the party atmosphere to flirt with Marceau under her husband's very nose. While Christine exhausts herself trying to run after men who are incapable of complying with her desire, Lisette enjoys getting men to run after her. But her carefree attitude disappears the moment her mistress's interests are at stake.

When she realizes that Octave has decided to leave the château with Christine, Lisette reacts violently, turning herself into an objective ally of the patriarchal order, under the pretext of protecting the marquise. After André's murder, she barely finds time to bid Marceau farewell before flying to Christine's assistance and summoning the butler: "Quick, Corneille, we're needed!" — a phrase that admirably expresses the specific alienation of servants vis-à-vis their masters. Thus in using her job to break free from her status as a wife, Lisette gains in the end not a greater freedom but another servitude. She escapes from a master by placing herself in the service of a mistress.

While Renoir entitles all his characters to be sincere and categorically refuses to play one against the other, he does not allow the spectator to be taken in by this ubiquitous sincerity, which does not prevent illusions any more than it does the exercise of power. This is brought home to us by the movie's tragic end, which involves an objective and subjective alliance between men who are apparently rivals or from different social backgrounds, an alliance aimed at forcing all women to fall into line with the patriarchal order. In the end, gender domination transcends class differences.

"In these times when everyone lies," to use Octave's phrase, Renoir shows that gender relations are overdetermined by the social decomposition taking place in the dominant class. The confusion of feelings that imbues the whole film, without calling into question the characters' sincerity, mirrors the ideological confusion that, according to Pierre Laborie (1990), is the chief characteristic of prewar French society. The alliance between Love and Death (Browne 1982) in the central episode of the fête at the château symbolizes the return of the repressed in a society solely concerned with its image and incapable of controlling its impulses. The sudden appearance of Schumacher (whose German-sounding name is probably no coincidence) gives concrete expression to this return of the repressed and structures the social, national, and gender dimensions of the crisis affecting that fast-degenerating society.

Thus analysis of gender relations in *La Règle du jeu* confirms the political acuity of a movie that, unlike other great films of the same period (*Le Jour se lève*, *Pépé le Moko*), does not base its social critique on an idealized view of love but shows that gender relations are shot through with the contradictions of society.

☆ REMORQUES
(Jean Grémillon, 1939–41)

It has often been said that Jean Renoir's *La Règle du jeu* was in 1939 the first "modern" movie in the French cinema. What is probably meant by that is that it does not conform to the traditional patterns of the "family romance" we have already examined (the incestuous pathos of the sacrificial father, for example), any more than it does to the conventions of the boulevard or the rather naïve noir realism of poetic realism.

Before war broke out, Jean Grémillon started work on *Remorques*, a film based on a novel by Roger Vercel, adapted for the screen by André Cayatte with dialogue by Jacques Prévert. Although the movie does not have the stature of Renoir's masterpiece, it can claim to be equally groundbreaking in the history of the ambiguous and complex cinematic modernity that was to blossom during the Occupation (in Renoir's absence) with *Falbalas* (*Paris Frills*), directed by Renoir's former assistant Jacques Becker, as well as *Douce* (*Love Story*), *Marie-Martine*, *Sortilèges* (*The Bellman*), *La Fiancée des ténèbres* (*Bride of Darkness*), *Secrets*, and indeed Grémillon's own *Lumière d'été* and *Le Ciel est à vous*.

Remorques is a movie of exemplary simplicity, whose plot can be described in a few lines. André Laurent (Jean Gabin) is captain of a tug and employed by a sea rescue company. For many years he has enjoyed an uneventful (and childless) marriage with Yvonne (Madeleine Renaud), an exquisitely sensitive but totally conventional woman. In the course of a difficult rescue operation he meets Catherine (Michèle Morgan) and has a brief affair with her. Catherine persuades him to drop his job and break up with his wife, who is suffering from a serious disease she has been keeping secret from her husband. Her final moments and her death put an end to André and Catherine's romance. She leaves town and he goes back to his job.

In fact this backdrop, which is both melodramatic and pseudo-documentary in style, elaborates a discourse about alienating masculinity and the social construction of gender roles, themes that were virtually unknown in the French cinema, apart from one or two movies by Pierre Chenal, Jacques Feyder, and Jean Renoir.

The encounter between Catherine and André, which sets the plot as such in motion, has many elements that are reminiscent — no doubt deliberately — of the opening of Marcel Carné and Jacques Prévert's *Le Quai des brumes*: nighttime, the sea, the beautiful female passenger of a cargo boat in distress, and her loathsome husband, Marc (Jean Marchat), a crooked captain who is prepared to allow his ship to sink so he can claim the insurance money and who seems to be keeping his wife prisoner. But this character, who has something in common with the Michel Simon character in *Le Quai des brumes*, disappears from the movie once André has disposed of him with a punch in the face. From that moment on, these elements, which smack of poetic realism, are swept aside by the psychological realism that was to become the hallmark of the movies made by Grémillon at the height of his powers.

The first sequence of the film displays a low-key populism often associated with Renoir but present in Grémillon's work before Renoir's, notably in the dance-hall sequence of *Maldone* (*Misdeal*, 1928) and that of the Bal Nègre in *La Petite Lise* (1931). And yet the striking feature of the wedding banquet in honor of a young member of the tug's crew and his bride is André's embarrassment when the doctor of this small Breton port, who is presiding over the banquet, asks him to say a few words. He declines, arguing that he is not used to public speaking. "That's enough talk," he adds, "we've come here to have fun!" Then he opens proceedings by inviting the bride to dance with him. Throughout the movie he responds in similar fashion when his wife asks him for tokens of his love or begs him to take an interest in her worries about the meaning of life: André is incapable of expressing his feelings or of saying what effect this wedding has had on him, for example. He does not like to talk about "all that." His wife's fear that he might be lost at sea — which is in fact fear of her own death — is something he does not want and cannot bring himself to hear.

On the other hand, he is a man who obeys a very strict moral code: when his drunken cook directs a torrent of abuse at "the Dutch boat," a rival tug, André

Michèle Morgan and Jean Gabin in *Remorques*, 1939–41. Courtesy of Cinémathèque française.

orders him to sober up immediately under the water pump. During the dance-hall scene he ticks off a member of his crew who is showing an interest in "the wife of Tanguy," the first mate, a woman notoriously unfaithful to her husband, "a happy cuckold" who is incapable of sticking up for himself and refuses to face the truth. On several occasions during the first part of the film, André intervenes on this issue, taking to task a joker who pretends he is afraid of being gored by Tanguy,[3] and then, when Tanguy's unfaithful wife has yet again absconded, urging him to leave her. In the end, André, by now "disgusted by men's gullibility," looks on helplessly as the wife returns to the fold and defuses her husband's pathetic anger with a few blatant lies and a broad smile.

In a few scenes, then, Grémillon sketches the portrait of the "he-man," engrossed by his job, his men, his competence, his duty, all lumped together under the heading of "the sea" by his wife, who accuses him of loving the sea more than her and who imagines that "the sea is wreaking its revenge" when the wind whistles past the house and causes a framed diploma to fall off the wall. He is a man who represses his feelings and requires little more of his wife than that she should make him coffee and help him write his reports and who

---

3. In French and other Latin languages, a cuckold is said to "have horns" growing out of his head.

imposes on those around him a petit bourgeois moral code that he regards as a natural law.

The same representation of masculinity had been constructed for more than five years previously by such movies as *Pépé le Moko* and *La Belle équipe* (Gauteur and Vincendeau 1993), with, in particular, the same presence, surrounding "Gabin the hero," of a band of men designed to define *his* masculinity by contrast as falling into the category of the happy medium: the newly wed young man he mothers, the drunk he castigates, the cuckold he reasons with, or Bosco (Fernand Ledoux), the philosopher he "allows to talk." The average spectator (male, but possibly also female) may have been able to find here, at any rate during the first half of the film, a construction similar to that of prewar movies, despite the many clues that suggest a fundamental questioning of this image of masculinity. The questioning is engineered by two female characters who have absolutely no equivalent in Gabin's previous movies (including *Maria Chapdelaine*, despite the presence of Madeleine Renaud) and who in *Remorques* undermine masculine values as embodied by Gabin the hero.

Renaud is a case apart in the cinema of the late 1930s, a period that coincides with her encounter with Jean-Louis Barrault. In the few films she still agreed to appear in, this great actress often embodies the "true woman": neither slut nor ingénue, she typically plays an active housewife or an office worker, and if she is loved by anyone — by her unhappy university professor (Constant Rémy) in *Hélène* or by the cobbler (Pierre Blanchar) in *L'Etrange Monsieur Victor* — it is never as a sex object for the male spectator to ogle at but in relation to a particular narrative situation that justifies the choice of the male protagonist irrespective of that spectator's programmed desire. In *Remorques* Yvonne was once loved by André, but it is clear that their marital relations have got bogged down in routine.

Although at a certain level of narrative coding (and probably the coding of male spectatorial, or "masculinized," perception), Captain Laurent's wife has become a classic pain in the neck, the insistent and embarrassing questions she asks her husband are reiterated and enlarged upon by Catherine, the sex object he seeks as a refuge from the boredom of married life. This runs against the classical pattern found in such movies as *La Chienne*, among others.

At first sight, the character played by Michèle Morgan is perfectly identical to those she played in *Le Quai des brumes*, *Gribouille*, and *L'Entraîneuse*: the woman with a tragic past. In this respect, *Remorques* even looks very much like a sequel to *Le Quai des brumes*, since it was in Le Havre, where she was dying of boredom, that she was spotted and seduced by the odious Marc, so he could take her off "to his part of the world." It is only later that she realized the true nature of the man, for whom being married boiled down to owning a woman. When, as a result of the shipwreck, André and his crew pull her out of the lifeboat she has decided to board against her husband's wishes, she escapes for good from his overbearing guardianship — and thus ceases to resemble Morgan's previous roles.

Unlike the beautiful and mysterious woman of *Le Quai des brumes*, a kind of blank page on which every male spectator can project his fantasy, Catherine in *Remorques* has always had her private feelings, her own personality, and her desire, none of which was ever recognized by other people or ever communicated to other people, until her encounter with Captain Laurent. Those private feelings are symbolized by her "secret name," which she reveals to him: Aimée. She is very different from the passive effigy that the Gabin character shields from the designs of villains (in *Le Quai des brumes*) or that the Raimu character protects from vicissitudes and prejudices (*Gribouille*). Her fundamentally active role here involves challenging male certitudes before she goes off into the night to live her own life.

The rightly celebrated scene by the sea where André shows Catherine around the empty house he intends to rent for himself and his wife after he retires is conducted, however poetic it may be, like a kind of therapy. On the beach André immediately confesses to having a mental block:

André: I hope you don't mind going for a walk with a man who doesn't say anything.
Catherine: When people are silent, it means they have lots of things to say to each other.

Later, in the house, Catherine asks him about his marriage. "I hate that sort of question," he snaps. When, after she goes upstairs without asking, André, irritated, asks her, "Where are you going?" She replies, "I'm curious!" She becomes more aggressive once he has joined her, obviously trying to break through his defenses:

André: *I'm* just a straightforward man!
Catherine: No, you're not. Straightforward people don't make such a fuss about concealing what they think. They're not ashamed of their desires or their pleasures. You're not straightforward, you're like other people, like men, you're too scrupulous, too tactful, and there are always things going through your mind.... Why, at this very moment, you're thinking things that nobody will ever find out about. And even

if you wanted to talk, if you wanted to be sincere, you wouldn't be able
to, you'd talk nonsense, involuntarily, so as to hide everything.

It is in this house, where André intends to move with his wife, that he fleetingly finds freedom in intercourse.

The retirement fantasy of the workaholic André — a retirement his wife
longs for so she can get closer to her husband again before her own death,
of which she has a foreboding — is not at all experienced by André from that
standpoint: it is more in a spirit of pique, a reaction against his subjection to
the big capitalist company that employs him and that encroaches increasingly
on his independence as a tugboat captain who is proud of his skills and of the
camaraderie he enjoys with his men. When André complains to his employers
about how he was swindled by Catherine's husband, who severed the towline
just as his cargo ship in distress reached the harbor mouth in order not to have
to pay the rescue fee, they refuse to support him. This makes André fly into
a rage, all the more so since some members of his crew were injured in the
course of what was a tricky rescue operation, in particular the young newlywed, who lost a finger and was not able to spend his wedding night with his
wife. For in this film, Gabin retains the positive characteristics of the conscientious worker, which had long formed an integral part of his image (compare
the methodical burglar in *Paris-Béguin*, 1931). But Grémillon is the only director who shows (already to some extent in *Gueule d'amour*, 1937) that these
qualities are also the shield that conceals his masculine frailty. André's destabilization is indicated by his change of attitude toward Tanguy; following his
brief tryst with Catherine in the empty house, he apologizes to his first mate
for having tried to dictate to him what he should do. He has understood that
life is more complicated than he thought.

But in fact it is too late for Captain Laurent: his wife is already dying when
he is sent for at the hotel where he has joined Catherine, and she dies a few moments after his return to the couple's home. His grief is such that the news of a
ship in distress initially provokes no reaction in him. But when he is told that
the ship concerned is none other than his Dutch rival, which is constantly referred to during the movie but never seen, he decides, out of solidarity toward
foreigners who also have to face the dangers of the sea, to join his crew and set
out to sea. Remarkably for 1939, in the context of a cinema where rejection of
the Other as a reaffirmation of national identity was the instinctive reaction
of almost all filmmakers, Grémillon and his scriptwriters deliberately and unambiguously emphasized their rejection of xenophobia.

A word should be said about the documentary nature of the film, which in the view of most commentators (and indeed of Grémillon himself) was seriously compromised by the need, in the context of the war, to film maritime exteriors in the studio, with special effects and scale models. From a realistic point of view, it is probably true that this is a shortcoming, but the artificial dimension thus lent to the portrayal of male labor helps to highlight, at the expense of the picturesque, what can today be seen as the true subject of the movie: the overvaluation of labor in human life and the barrier that this overvaluation erects between the sexes in a patriarchal society.

Alexis Roland-Manuel's extraordinary score, half-spoken and half-sung, with liturgical overtones reminiscent of the great lyrical works of the 1930s (such as Arthur Honegger's *La Danse des morts* and Darius Milhaud's *Christophe Colomb*), which is used precisely during the scenes on the tug, carries the same message in that it "contaminates" labor through the sacred, in the sense that Georges Bataille (1967) meant by that opposition. He argued that the great founding principle of Western civilization is a rigorous separation between the sacred, gratuitous domain of Eros and the profane, utilitarian domain of labor. For Bataille, that principle is a kind of ontological necessity, but feminist thinking has long posited that this compartmentalization and the repressions that arise from it are mutilations imposed by patriarchal society. All Grémillon's subsequent work centers on that contradiction, which is today more clearly perceived, and it is this that makes him the most "modern" filmmaker of his generation.

Part II

THE GERMAN OCCUPATION, 1940–1944

Fathers Take a Backseat

CHAPTER 2
Castrated Fathers

———————————
———————————

MEETING IN NATIONAL assembly in Vichy on July 10, 1940, the two houses
of the French Parliament gave full constituent powers to an eighty-four-year-
old retired marshal, Philippe Pétain, who, after being asked to form the last
government of the Third Republic on June 16, had just requested and agreed
to an armistice on terms imposed by Hitler. The Vichy ballot was passed by
569 votes to 80, with 20 abstentions (and in the absence of the Communists,
who were ineligible).

Nine months later, on April 22, 1941, the German-owned production company Continental, benefiting from the initiative that the occupying power had
seized by prohibiting any French film from being made in the northern zone
for eight months, produced the movie that was to become, in August 1941, the
first notable success of the Occupation period: Henri Decoin's *Premier rendez-
vous* (*Her First Affair*). This film marked the return to the screen of Danielle
Darrieux, who had remained in France after the Débâcle and was historically
the first young female star of French cinema. Her rise to that status toward the
middle of the 1930s may have been more or less consciously perceived as a sign
that the ascendancy of the father was possibly about to be eroded.

But *Premier rendez-vous* also marked the point at which Fernand Ledoux,
after more than fifteen years of good and faithful service playing lugubrious

individuals who served as a foil to the leading characters, gained top billing in his own right. In nine other films shot before the Liberation in which he played a father or father figure, Ledoux descended from such patriarchal icons of the 1930s as Raimu, Sacha Guitry, Jules Berry, Harry Baur, and Victor Francen — but put across a completely different image. The huge success of Decoin's movie was undoubtedly due partly to the lavishness of its production, to its finely honed direction, and to the fact that more than a year before the release of *Les Visiteurs du soir* (*The Devil's Envoys*) it was perceived by the public, if not the critics, as signaling the renaissance of French cinema. But this was mainly due to the prestige of its female star and not to Ledoux's performance, despite its remarkable qualities.

Micheline Chevassu (Darrieux) is a fresh-faced and innocent-looking teenager who has run away from her orphanage. She goes into a deserted and rather unprepossessing café, where she has a rendezvous with someone she contacted through the lovelorn ads, and whom she naturally imagines to be young and good-looking. The only customer in the café is Nicolas Rougemont (Ledoux), who has plastered his greased hair over his balding head and has the demeanor of a man "long-defeated by life." He finally decides to approach the young woman and admit, with a sad little smile, that he is the person she is expecting to meet. Then, to dispel the enormous disappointment he can see on her face, he immediately reassures her by claiming he has come with a message from his nephew, who was unable to come to his rendezvous with her and who is indeed young and good-looking.

Premier rendez-vous, then, is a film that begins with a denial of the "benevolent" incestuous impulse. But Rougemont immediately embarks on a rather alarming course of action, which, because of his sinister behavior and the dramatic music on the sound track, looks suspiciously like an attempt at abduction. Actually, although the film casts him fleetingly in this ominous role, it soon transpires that he is in fact a pathetic teacher at an expensive private secondary school who cannot control his pupils. He ends up taking the orphan into his quarters at the boarding school; everything is aboveboard, and the atmosphere becomes almost that of a happy family.

In other words, the movie begins by detailing in reverse, and via a succession of denials ("I'm not the person who desires you," "I'm not abducting you," "I'm keeping you here only until my nephew arrives"), the incest scenario as it features both in the minds of actual fathers and in the narratives of so many prewar films. True, despite his denials, the old man is cured of his reprehensible desire only after an outburst of Oedipal jealousy directed at his nephew,

Pierre (Louis Jourdan), who has fallen in love with Micheline; the scenario had to avoid simplifying the lesson it was putting across and leave a little hope for those spectators who could identify with Nicolas, along the lines of "I know perfectly well, but even so . . . ," which is precisely the repressed hope of the character, if not of the subtext. But in *Premier rendez-vous*, unlike similar films from the prewar era, the early scenes between Micheline and Nicolas created a barrier between the two that was insurmountable both for Nicolas and for the male spectator: the incestuous desire is rejected by the father himself, when he anticipates the young woman's refusal by symbolically castrating himself. The movie begins where *Sarati le Terrible* (*Sarati the Terrible*) ended, thus indicating that the days when audiences were not bothered by the potbellies of actors like Raimu and Baur were over. In this case, the unsightliness attached to aging is emphasized from the start; it is shown to be a subject of repulsion, then of pity.

The first indication of the surprising frequency of this figure that was to mark French films as soon as production got under way again on June 9 of that same year, 1941, came with *Premier Bal* (*First Ball*), which Christian-Jaque made for André Paulvé, one of the best producers of the period. In it, playing opposite two young actresses (Marie Déa and Gaby Sylvia), Ledoux plays a role that is in a way the next stage in the ordeal of fathers during the Occupation: the castrated and mothering father, endearing but doomed to die.

So it was that, during the months following the most humiliating defeat in France's history, two distinct groups of leading professionals in French cinema, one operating in Paris in the occupied zone, the other in the so-called free zone, adopted critical variants of an incestuous fantasy that had been hugely preponderant during the previous decade. And in both *Premier rendez-vous* and *Premier Bal*, the actor chosen to embody that rejection was Fernand Ledoux, playing an amiable failure.

True, the ostensible motive, including in the minds of the makers themselves, may have been in both cases to make a romantic comedy that would help people to forget the hard times they were going through. But the male tendency to see no serious significance in romantic matters suggests that what may in this case have been unintentional is all the more revealing about the deeply rooted attitudes of such milieux (the cinema, the small world of the Parisian intelligentsia, and so on) at that particular moment in French history.

The last decisive twist in *Premier rendez-vous* before the de rigueur happy ending is the spectacular scene where Micheline steps in between the pathetic teacher and his unruly pupils, whom she tells in no uncertain terms that they should be ashamed of themselves. This spectacular female incursion into the circle of masculinity has its logical follow-up: when Micheline is once again cooped up in her prison-cum-orphanage, the boys storm the building to free her and her fellow inmates from the clutches of their phallic and cantankerous headmistress, who represents the old order. Here, then, a sympathetic but discredited father figure is contrasted with a young woman capable of acting decisively, but who functions above all as a regenerative effigy for men — two poles that structured a very large number of movies of widely differing ideologies produced in France during the Occupation.

As we have seen, in the cinema of the 1930s, the Law of the Father chiefly manifested itself in the symbolic or actual possession of a young woman who was (symbolically or actually) his daughter. That pattern was radically disrupted in the films produced during the four years of the Occupation. True, there were still plenty of patriarchs; they were a key feature of some thirty-five melodramas acting as vehicles for Pétainist propaganda. But even in those movies, when a young woman must submit to the Law of the Father (this is true of some twenty films), it almost always causes havoc, which it is then the work of the film to repair.

Premier rendez-vous is not the only important movie of the period that admonishes middle-aged men tempted to exert their power over young women. Another striking example is Maurice Tourneur's *Le Val d'enfer* (*Valley of Hell*, 1943), one of the few films produced by Continental that was strictly speaking a melodrama. (The genre was much more a specialty of French producers, and more particularly Vichyite producers.) In it Gabriel Gabrio plays Noël Bienvenu, a rugged-faced, prickly, and inarticulate widower. A kind of man of the woods who has difficulty controlling his violent tendencies, he slaps his son in the face in front of an examining magistrate who has just charged the boy with theft. "My apologies, but my hand did that all on its own," he mumbles as he turns his back on his unworthy son.

Then an old friend who is on his deathbed after suffering an industrial accident asks Bienvenu to look after his daughter, Marthe, who has become a prostitute. Marthe is played by Ginette Leclerc, by that time the "slut" par excellence of the cinema of the Occupation following Viviane Romance's decision to switch to playing more virtuous characters than before. When Marthe sees the intimidating figure of Bienvenu walk into her sordid hotel room, she is at first convinced, and understandably so, that a policeman — that supreme manifestation of the Law of the Father — has "yet again" come to question her following the arrest of her pimp. Bienvenu, who operates a quarry in Haute-

Provence, takes this dark-haired and voluptuous city girl into his home. She soon agrees to marry him, despite feeling no sexual desire for him, attracted as she is solely by the prospect of protection and social advancement. She makes praiseworthy attempts to remain faithful to her husband and fulfill her wifely role, but human nature being what it is, she ends up cheating on him with a younger man, Barthélémy (Lucien Gallas).

The slut is now less of a total slut than she used to be in prewar films; she is almost always capable of redeeming herself (Ginette Leclerc in *Le Corbeau* [*The Raven*]), even though death catches up with her (Mireille Balin in *L'Assassin a peur la nuit*, Leclerc in *Le Dernier sou* [*The Last Penny*]). Here she ends up being killed by Bienvenu's double, a kind of village idiot who suddenly emerges from the maquis, a recurring figure of Destiny throughout the film. Bienvenu can then look forward to the future, as embodied by his son, whose follies he has forgiven.

This optimistic ending is in line with official propaganda, but it goes further than that because of the character of Grandfather Bienvenu (Edouard Delmont), a frail, garrulous antipatriarch, constantly putting his son on guard against marriage to a woman whom this undisputed but wrong-headed patriarch will be incapable of satisfying. It was very rare at the time for a film to highlight a sexual problem in this way — and in so doing it relativizes other aspects of the film that could be regarded as Pétainist.

For in the last account, Bienvenu is an impotent patriarch who has delusions about himself. This mirrors the image that an increasing number of French were going to have of their head of state, a world-weary old man who desperately tried to get people to believe that he personified law and order, which was patently in the control of the invader. In his diary, Jean Guéhenno (1947) described the uneasiness he felt on hearing Pétain on the wireless: "June 17, 1940: . . . An old man who no longer has the voice of a man but talks like an old woman told us at 12.30 pm that he had sued for peace last night."

Pierre Laborie (1990) has demonstrated that as public opinion moved away from Vichy — but as "Pétain worship" persisted — the weakness and vulnerability of that "poor old man" were key elements in the expression of support for the head of state as a person. Although it remained unformulated by the great majority of people at the beginning of the Occupation, the figure of Marshal Pétain was the embodiment of a defeated, humiliated, wounded, and moribund patriarchy that was perfectly suited to that moment in history. That was the (open) secret that cinematic representations of the father were apparently alone in admitting out loud. Irrespective of the more explicitly traditionalist propaganda put out by Vichy, this blunt refusal to condone the father's "incestuous" desire means that a movie like *Le Val d'enfer* falls into a gray area where certain objectively progressive aspects of the rejection of the Third Republic by a "loose conglomeration of Vichyite movements" converge with the deeper aspirations of a people who in their majority did not identify politically with Pétain's government (Chalas 1985). In view of its recurrence, this neutralization of the "lecherous" father on twenty occasions during the four dark years of Occupation can be seen as tantamount to a ritual slaying of the father as portrayed in 1930s cinema, who is defined by his relationship with a young woman — whether he conquers her, sacrifices himself for her, or exploits her. And it could be argued that in the imaginary of the group of men then making films such "fallen" fathers personified the social, political, financial, and above all military patriarchy that was henceforth seen as having failed to achieve its universalist ambitions.

An ailing patriarchy as a sociopolitical metaphor, even if there is far more to the film than this, works remarkably well in Marcel Carné and Jacques Prévert's celebrated *Les Visiteurs du soir* (1942), in the persons of the couple formed by Baron Hugues (Fernand Ledoux), the powerless sovereign of a drowsy kingdom, and Baron Renaud (Marcel Herrand), a megalomaniac knight of warlike and sexual virility to whom Hugues is about to give away his daughter. In the end both men, caught up in the coils of their masculinity, are thwarted by the rebelliousness of the betrothed maiden, by their own ludicrous pursuit of an unattainable woman (Arletty), and by the arrival on the scene of a devil much nimbler than themselves (Jules Berry). This has been interpreted as an allusion to the traumatic defeat of French troops by invading Panzers and Stukas in 1940 (Turk 1989). In the bittersweet banquet scene, Hugues's unsullied daughter, Anne (Marie Déa), sitting between two oppressive incarnations of the patriarchal order — her father and her future husband — wittily lays claim to her right to look at another man (in this case, the gentle Alain Cuny); this is the point of departure for an exemplary disruption of the organization of sexual roles.

This indictment of the patriarchal power's erstwhile key action — the taking control of young women — is illustrated in particularly spectacular fashion (even though it has remained curiously invisible to critics and historians) by a film regarded, along with *Les Enfants du paradis* (*Children of Paradise*), as the official masterpiece of the Occupation years: Louis Chavance and Henri-Georges Clouzot's *Le Corbeau* (1943). It has become customary to describe this movie either as anti-Vichyite or as fascistic (right-wing anarchistic), thus confining it to the two alternative extremes of French society at the time. So far, apparently no one has stressed the extent to which this film squares with the Zeitgeist and even the propaganda of the period. This can be seen in its hostility to abortion, but also in its disavowal of the incestuous father: at a literal level of the scenario, which it would be a mistake to ignore, for the root of evil in this film is an unnatural marriage between Pierre Larquey, here cast against type as a pompous old man but a character who serves as a vehicle for the film's "metaphysics," and the blonde Micheline Francey, an ocean of passion beneath a cool surface of propriety.

True, the noir atmosphere of *Le Corbeau* (which is in marked contrast with all other films of the period, apart from three or four), its overt expression of female desire, and its attack on the authority of the great and the good preclude its being categorized as a merely Vichyite movie. This ambiguity suggests rather that we should not try to trace the origin of the spontaneous themes of the cinema of the period either solely in the imagination of the author or subject or in official propaganda, even when they also feature in that propaganda. The great quality of many Occupation films is perhaps generated precisely by that tension between the Vichyite content and the progressive content of certain major themes.

Another (ingenious) way of bringing the curtain down on the incestuous fantasy of the 1930s was the curious to-ing and fro-ing through time between Françoise Monier (Madeleine Sologne) and her husband, Robert (Jean Marchat), in André Zwoboda's *Croisières sidérales* (*Sidereal Cruises*, 1941), one of the very few French science-fiction movies. The two protagonists play a couple of scientists who are preparing to take off into the stratosphere in a kind of blimp. But a car accident puts Robert out of action, and his wife is forced to go on the trip with just Lucien (Carette), her ham-fisted assistant. A mishap encountered by their space vehicle takes them into a kind of fourth dimension, from which they return after what seems to them to be only a few weeks, but is in fact twenty years for the inhabitants of the Earth. So we end up with Françoise finding herself married to a man old enough to be her father. But such mismatches were no longer allowed in the post-Débâcle cinema. So on the next voyage, a luxury cruise to a planet where Pétain's National Revolution seems to have been put in place, with a definitive Return to Nature, it is the husband who travels alone so his wife can catch up with his age and erase any trace of the incest fantasy, now shelved along with other unusable accessories for the duration of the Occupation.

Along with the twenty or so films (out of a corpus of 220) in which the temptation to commit "incest" is punished, one could list more than sixty others during that period that highlight a father who has always already been castrated, an endearing or ridiculous character who can in no way embody the Law. A typical example of that kind of role is Maloin, the character played by Fernand Ledoux in Henri Decoin's *L'Homme de Londres* (*The London Man*, 1943), based on a novel by Georges Simenon. Maloin is a lumbering figure who has been given a stoop by fate and by his very Pétainist guilt feelings, but who is also trampled on by his sarcastic wife and his young, fresh-faced daughter, who gently disapproves of the presents her father gives her with suspect money. Decoin and his scriptwriter Charles Exbrayat made this daughter very different from the original character in Simenon's prewar novel, who works as a servant in another family and is a colorless, mindless woman totally submissive to her father's wishes. As far as adaptations of novels or plays are concerned, such changes, which were frequent and similar in type, provide striking proof of the specificity of this period in French cinema.

Another significant symptom is the fate suffered during the Occupation by the great patriarchal figures of the prewar period, such as Raimu, Harry Baur, and Jules Berry. Although they continued to play the same sorts of roles, their power seemed somehow undermined by the sea change that had just occurred. In the four movies in which Raimu appeared between 1940 and 1944, the figures of authority he embodied crumble, thus marking a change from characters like César or Gribouille, "complacent fathers" whose virility remains intact. In Decoin's *Les Inconnus dans la maison* (*Strangers in the House*, 1942), he ends up giving a Vichyite lecture to the worthies of a small town, accusing them of neglecting the future by leaving their children to their own devices—thus playing the role of the towering authoritarian father of his earlier films. But before this thoroughly Pétainist redemption he plays an alcoholic barrister incapable of taking the stand in court. In Georges Lacombe's *Monsieur la Souris* (*Midnight in Paris*, 1942), Raimu is a former music teacher turned tramp who briefly plays amateur detective and righter of wrongs but returns to his former condition once he has solved the crime because his hatred of the police prevents him from readapting to the social order. Decoin's *Le Bienfaiteur* (*The Benefactor*, 1942) is in a sense a remake of *L'Etrange Monsieur Victor*, in which a respectable citizen of a small town turns out to be a formidable gang leader in Paris. But this theme is given a new twist: the transgressive father has only one ambition, which is to go straight and abandon his phallic power. (He dies as a result of the goodness of his heart.) Finally, the scriptwriters who adapted Balzac's novel *Le Colonel Chabert* for René Le Hénaff's movie of the same name (*Le Colonel Chabert*, 1943) saw fit to go one better than the original by making their antihero a crippled survivor of the Napoleonic wars (it was apparently Raimu's idea that he should have lost an arm), who on his return to civilian life realizes that women no longer obey him. The scene at dinner where Rosine (Marie Bell), who used to be Chabert's wife but has remarried and inevitably become his enemy, has to cut up his meat turns this miserable veteran into an emblem of the period.

Harry Baur acted in only two films during the Occupation before being arrested and tortured by the Gestapo in 1942; he died in 1943. In Christian-Jaque's *L'Assassinat de Père Noël* (*Who Killed Santa Claus?*, 1941), he plays an old globe-maker and innocuous mythomaniac who drinks too much and whose daughter escapes him into a world of dreams. In Maurice Tourneur's *Péchés de jeunesse* (*Sins of Youth*, 1941), a kind of remake of Duvivier's *Carnet de bal* (*A Dance Program* or *Life Dances On*) with a reversal of sexual roles that is typical of the period, Monsieur Lacalade (Baur), a wealthy, lumbering, and frighteningly authoritarian bachelor delves into his prewar past in search of the numerous offspring he spawned, then abandoned in various places. But whereas the femme fatale Christine (Marie Bell), in Duvivier's movie, tracks down the men who were left devastated by their relationship, Lacalade discovers that his sons and their mothers, though none of them very well off, have managed perfectly well without him. An emblematic scene comes when Emma Vacheron (Marguerite Ducouret) explains that a picture she bought at a flea market portraying an officer thought to have died during the war acted as a perfect ersatz father while she was bringing up her son.

Finally, Jules Berry, who had played both complacent fathers in vaudevilles (*Arlette et ses papas*) and sacrificial fathers in melodramas (*Le Chemin de Rio*) and who was the archetypal unworthy father of poetic realism (*Le Crime de Monsieur Lange*, *Le Jour se lève*), enjoyed a prolific career during the Occupation. Particularly notable were his roles as a pathetic father, as, for example, in Albert Valentin's *Marie-Martine* (1943), where he plays a pulp novelist who is given a proper dressing-down by his young wife (Hélèna Manson) in a startling scene where she mocks the "master's" childish behavior, or as a sad clown on the run in *L'Homme de Londres*. In *Les Visiteurs du soir*, Berry plays what was his most celebrated role at the time, a kind of "boulevard devil" whose dominant presence overshadows that of the two other fathers, played in a declamatory manner reminiscent of the Comédie-Française. One racy exchange of dialogue seems to encapsulate the way Berry had changed since the days when he could play Gabin's torturer in *Le Jour se lève*. Here Gilles (Alain

Cuny), who has been robbed of his memory by the devil and can remember neither his master nor his sweetheart, Anne (Marie Déa), walks past the couple she seems to form with Berry and says to the devil, "What a pretty little thing! Is she your daughter?" "No, she's certainly not my daughter!" the devil replies in a fit of pique.

Of all the actors who left their stamp on the Occupation period, the castrated father par excellence was indisputably Pierre Larquey. Unlike Ledoux, he did not switch to playing a different kind of character after 1940, and indeed he was only rarely given leading roles. But he was constantly present on cinema screens, more or less typecast as the castrated father, in such movies as Louis Daquin's *Nous les gosses* (*Portrait of Innocence*, 1941), where he plays a kind of detective who sees himself as Sherlock Holmes and would like to be the father of abandoned children, or as a pathetic and bullied figure in Robert Vernay's *Le Père Goriot* (*Father Goriot*, 1944), a remarkable and now forgotten film scripted by Charles Spaak and released after the Occupation.

Larquey also appeared in many Pétainist melodramas aimed at female audiences, in which he may be regarded as a kind of unintentional intruder who does not fit into the movie's conscious ideological viewpoint. Of all the great popular successes of the Occupation, Jean Stelli's *Le Voile bleu* (*The Blue Veil*, 1942) was one of the most explicitly Vichyite, more notably in its treatment of the Louise Jarraud character (Gaby Morlay), with her strong traditionalist Catholic overtones, than in its censure of Third Republic mores and institutions, which were the subject of a national consensus (Chalas 1985). But the Larquey character, a pathetic toy merchant who is hopelessly in love with Louise and whose every appearance on screen concludes with the breakage of an object (including the tragic scene of his fatal heart attack), is anything but Pétainist — unless of course that epithet is subversively understood to mean that the marshal is the derisory father par excellence, the *Connétable du Déclin* celebrated by the *zazous*.[1]

This castrated father figure is to be found in all the major genres we have identified for this period. We will go on to discuss the actor Saturnin Fabre, who played a *zazou* father in many movies. But worth mentioning here are Jean Debucourt as the shy, mothering father who limps his way through that great noir tragedy, Claude Autant-Lara's *Douce* (*Love Story*, 1943), and the inimitable Alerme, who, in an unusually emotive scene that contrasts with the boulevard lightness that bathes the rest of Jean-Pierre Feydeau's *L'Amant de*

---

1. *Connétable du Déclin* is a pun on the historical Connétable Du Guesclin.

Bornéo (1942), takes leave of Arletty while promising, on behalf of a whole generation of roués, to give up his philandering.

Even though they are meant to embody the "true" tradition, the patriarchs of certain seminal films in the hard-line Pétainist mold are greatly diminished characters, to wit, the quivering, querulous, and bent figure of Monsieur des Lourdines (Constant Rémy) in Pierre de Hérain's 1942 movie of the same name, or Peyrac (Thomy Bourdelle) in Léon Poirier's *Jeannou* (1943), doomed to failure though remaining stubborn and dignified in his plus-fours. Their task is to pass on the torch to two young couples, who in the first instance will keep conservative rural values alive and in the second will embody the compromise between technocracy and the land. Indeed it may even be argued that it is precisely the way the father figure is discredited in these two movies that undermines their Pétainist ideology and makes them still watchable today.

A handful of patriarchs resist. This is true of François Ascarra (Charles Vanel) in one of the best-known productions of that type, Jacques de Baroncelli's *Haut-le-vent* (*Above the Wind*, 1942). François, a larger-than-life colonial who was able to escape France's "emasculation" (this is one of the rare movies of the period that allude to the Defeat) because his Basque father emigrated to Latin America, returns to France in 1940. We see him resolutely striding around the family estate, which he eventually prefers not to sell; he decides to remain in France in its hour of need, setting an example to everyone, and to get his son to marry a young woman of the people and of the land. Vanel, who sported the *francisque*, the decoration he had been awarded by Vichy, when he went on demonstrations in Paris during the Occupation (Ragache and Jean-Robert 1988), played two other similar roles during that period, in Jean-Paul Paulin's *La Nuit merveilleuse* (1940) and Jean Dréville's *Les Roquevillard* (1943). But his thickset, determined figure was also to be seen in the whole range of paternal roles typical of that contradictory period, from the weak and unpleasant fathers in Pierre Billon's *Le Soleil a toujours raison* (1941) and André Berthomieu's *Promesse à l'inconnue* (*Promise to the Unknown One*, 1942) to the "extreme" patriarch who is doomed to die a lonely death in Dréville's *Les Affaires sont les affaires* (1942) and a mothering, "feminine" anti-patriarch in Jean Grémillon's *Le Ciel est à vous* (*The Woman Who Dared*, 1943).

To conclude this initial survey of the various manifestations of the father, mention has to be made of a remarkable movie made immediately after the Liberation, in which Vanel plays François, perhaps the most caricatural patriarchal peasant of his career—the very personification of pigheadedness. The aim of Dréville's *La Ferme du pendu* (*Hanged Man's Farm*, 1945) is to put paid to the Pétainist idealization of the peasantry, in particular with a dénouement that looks like an ironic echo of the typically edifying endings of Vichyite films: the child of François's sister, whom he once drove out of the family home, is running to where the old man has collapsed over his plow in the middle of a field, shouting that his mother has finally given him permission to stay with his uncle, who adores him. The film ends before the child realizes that François has died of a heart attack, the same fate as that suffered by another caricatural patriarch in an earlier Dréville movie, *Les Affaires sont les affaires*. But this recurrent feature should be interpreted not so much as an auteurist touch as the expression of an antipatriarchal theme that was particularly evident during the Occupation and that went back to the tragic confrontations between Jean Gabin and the evil father in prewar films. Such clashes were to die out only in the 1950s, with Gabin's second career as a spectacularly triumphant patriarch.

Women in the Service of the Patriarchy

PROBABLY THE MOST distinctive feature of the French movie scene between 1940 and 1944 is the reversal of the relationship between male and female characters and actors. The prewar cinema gave pride of place to male leads, whereas Occupation films, irrespective of their ideology or artistic ambition, tended much more often to place women in positions of power. This is paradoxical in the light of the scorching attack launched by Vichyite ideologues on all manifestations of female independence (Bordeaux 1987; Muel-Dreyfus 1996/2001), and all the more so because during that period French filmmaking remained an almost exclusively male preserve.

Recourse to female effigies was not new; according to a tradition that goes back to Antiquity, from Pallas Athene to Joan of Arc and Marianne, iconography offers a wealth of female images that embody society's fundamental values (Warner 1976, 1985). The French cinema during the Occupation tended to idealize female figures in a way that directly reflected that logic of the effigy. A succession of women, from Gaby Morlay to Madeleine Sologne, made possible an imaginary reconstruction of the national and moral identity that had been badly battered by the humiliation of the defeat, the German Occupation, and France's two million POWs and people deported under the Compulsory Labor Service scheme to work in Germany. It was an ambiguous tribute that presupposed an obfuscation of women's actual experience and point of view. But the very nature of the cinema — with its "ontological realism," as André Bazin was to describe it in 1958 (2009) — and the talent of certain auteurs often caused those effigies to evolve into more complex characters that also reflected other aspirations.

With this new preeminence of female characters, the genres themselves began to evolve. The theatrical model of boulevard comedy, which had such resonance in the 1930s, gave ground to melodrama, which had evolved from eighteenth-century bourgeois dramas via Balzac, Victorien Sardou, and Henry Bernstein — a serious genre centered "on conflicts of morality and feelings, which often gave pride of place to a female character" (Corvin 1992: 850). It is no surprise that the Vichy regime, in its obsession with moralizing, should see melodrama as its ideal form: almost all overtly Pétainist films fall into that category and advocate a form of happiness compatible with the Law of the Father.

But as can be seen in U.S. melodramas (Lang 1989), the genre made it possible to take note of the oppression of women, which had mostly been obfuscated by the discourse of Hollywood action films and French boulevard movies. The large number of melodramas made during the Occupation (about ninety out of a total of 220 movies) also formed part of that trend, which flourished once the Defeat had eroded a number of patriarchal convictions.

Gaby Morlay, a leading light of the prewar boulevard genre on both screen and stage, became the icon of Pétainism during the Occupation in such films as Jean Stelli's *Le Voile bleu* (1942), which went down in history as the quintessence of Vichyite cinema, Robert Péguy's *Les Ailes blanches* (1942), and Jean Faurez's *Service de nuit* (*Night Shift*, 1943). Whether a nun or a "lay nun" (a nanny or a switchboard operator), the Morlay character would typically give up all aspirations to personal happiness in order to set right a society that traditionalist Catholics saw as blighted by all the vices of the Third Republic: pleasure-seeking, lacking parental responsibility, full of adultery, venality, selfishness, personal ambition, and so on. More dispenser of justice than figure of charity, she would take charge of the values of a temporarily diminished patriarchy (as a result of the Defeat) and with her unwavering gentleness manage to persuade everyone to repent their sins. The very embodiment of Judeo-Christian guilt feelings, she would achieve her ends by disguising a figure of authority beneath an apparent submissiveness. The blue veil of the nanny and the white wings of the nun, like the switchboard operator's cape, make her invulnerable; a universal mother, she renounces commonplace terrestrial motherhood (Louise Jarraud in *Le Voile bleu* lost both her husband and child during the 1914–18 war), just as the childless Marshal Pétain derived his paternal dignity from the Battle of Verdun and extended it to all the French.

But whereas political propaganda relied on patriarchal admonishment to put its message across, the cinema, concerned as it was to edify audiences in an appealing way, chose melodrama as its register because, through the intervention of the female, it could give priority to feelings. Morlay functioned as a kind of female marshal of the French cinema, symbolically carrying out a program of moral regeneration in line with Pétainist plans for young people. For while the parents' generation could not always be relied upon to mend its ways, its influence over the younger generation needed to be neutralized: hence the strategic role played by female educators who replaced inadequate or unworthy parents. The last shot of *Le Voile bleu*, where the new leaders of a regenerated society gather around a Christmas tree to pay tribute to their aged nanny, mirrors the Vichyite posters that showed young people surrounding the marshal and more generally the religious iconography of Christ and the Virgin Mary ruling over a community of the blessed.

Such films take the form of a series of episodes or sketches that list the social ills that need to be combated. The construction of Yvan Noë's *La Cavalcade des heures* (*Love around the Clock*, 1943), for instance, hinges on the intervention of a kind of *dea ex machina* called Hora (Pierrette Caillol), the incarnation of the final hour when everyone has to account for their acts before the Creator. In the course of several sketches, this effigy of the dispenser of justice sets about reforming or punishing a series of people: a worker who rebels against his condition (Jean Daurand); a selfish bureaucrat, Léon (Tramel); a fame-seeking sportsman, Massardier (Jules Ladoumègue); an unworthy mother (Gaby Morlay); an unscrupulous unemployed worker, Antonin (Fernandel); a bourgeois epicurean, Maurice (Charpin); a singer who cannot come to terms with his success, Charles (Charles Trenet); and a man on death row who refuses to accept his punishment (Jean Chevrier). No one can escape the verdict of this female figure of authority, who has more in common with the vengeful God of the Old Testament than with the God of love found in the Gospels. In this respect, the movie is particularly revealing in its portrayal of the moral attitudes that imbue Pétainism: it was an ideology that emerged from the most conservative tendencies of Catholicism and was characterized by a fundamental mistrust of human nature, at the opposite pole not only from Rousseauist optimism but also from the more progressive brand of Catholicism advocated by the Ecole d'Uriage and the review *Esprit*.

In *La Cavalcade des heures*, Morlay, as a flighty woman of the kind she often played in her prewar movies, is a mother who neglects her child so she can devote herself to her (disreputable) lover; when she visits her son at his boarding school, the clock is stopped by Hora, thus forcing her to abandon her lover to his fate (he is wanted by the police) instead of running away with him. This episode illustrates a prime truth of Vichyite morality: a mother's duty is incompatible with a woman's desire; she is no more capable of acting spontaneously like a good mother than she is of feeling affection for an estimable man. This is what necessitates the intervention of a superior moralistic, policing authority (Hora-Pétain), who forces human beings to do what is right, even against their will. This extreme form of Pétainist melodrama leaves little room for complexity or suspense. But what these female figures lose by being excluded from the circuit of desire is compensated for by their active nature: they are "militant" women, and the spectator identifies with such characters who survive a series of ordeals like the male hero of an action film (mutatis mutandis).

In movies made during the Occupation, a woman's renunciation of her desire becomes the key issue of another kind of Pétainist melodrama, in which, curiously, Viviane Romance specialized. Typecast before the war as a bitch or femme fatale, she made a U-turn by embodying a long-suffering heroine in a whole series of films, from Abel Gance's *Vénus aveugle* (*Blind Venus*, 1940) and Edmond T. Gréville's *Une femme dans la nuit* (*A Woman in the Night*, 1941) to Maurice Cloche's *Feu sacré* (*Sacred Fire*, 1941) and Léon Mathot's *Cartacalha* (1941). Even more than in the case of Gaby Morlay, the significance of her new direction can be assessed both from the actress's change of register and from the emblematic nature of her new persona. *Vénus aveugle*, for example, describes the slow and painful transformation of a pagan image (her portrait is on posters all over town advertising a brand of cigarette) into a Christian icon (a blind woman sitting on a pedestal, around whom the whole community ends up rallying). The film describes the veritable ordeal she has to go through between those two states, which is marked from the beginning by a reference to blindness, a recurrent theme in Occupation cinema, which is contrasted with the motif of "the Marshal's blue eyes" to be found in Vichyite iconography (Miller 1975).

But the scene where Clarisse (Romance) belts out a popular song containing the bitter and vengeful refrain "I hate you men!" to an audience of rollicking sailors in a quayside café displays a complexity that goes much further than that of a mere propaganda film for the National Revolution. For while at the outset Clarisse tries to exploit her good looks in order to earn a living, she also falls victim to the possessive desire of her lover, Madère (Georges Flamant), who wants to prevent her from singing in public. When he returns to her side, it is in order to bring her his little girl, whose mother has abandoned them, and to start a new family, thus demonstrating that his selfish possessiveness has been superseded by a generous openness toward the community. But in order to achieve her new status Clarisse has to give up any idea of autonomy, as is signaled by the metaphor of blindness. She no longer exists outside the maternal role she has been allotted by the community that worships her.

This convergence of idealization and misogyny can also be found in Jean Delannoy's *Fièvres* (1941), a blander Pétainist melodrama in which Jean Dupray (Tino Rossi) recalls his unfortunate experiences as an unworthy father who abandoned his virtuous wife, Maria (Madeleine Sologne), for a wealthy "slut," Edith Watkins (Jacqueline Delubac), whom he left, only to fall into the clutches of a working-class "slut," Rose (Ginette Leclerc); his only salvation is the convent, where he can celebrate his love for the ideal woman by singing Franz Schubert's "Ave Maria." The contradiction that runs through prewar cinema here becomes perfectly explicit: a woman who desires is dangerous, and the only way of keeping her in check is to turn her into an icon.

Guillaume Radot's *Le Bal des passants* (1943) concentrates these two complementary aspects of male fantasies on a single character. At the beginning of the movie, Fabienne Ozanne (Annie Ducaux) is a selfish, shallow woman who prefers to live out her passionate love without burdening herself with a child (she has an abortion), but after going through a long series of ordeals, she becomes a perfect mother who is prepared to wait as long as is necessary for the man who abandoned her.

But these sorrowful effigies sometimes escape the reductive pattern of Pétainism, as in the final and most sordid episode of *Le Voile bleu*, where Morlay ends up as a maid of all work in a family that consists entirely of women stricken by poverty and loneliness and faced with children who have become unmanageable because of their mother's illness and their father's absence. They symbolize the financial and moral destitution of mothers who had to fend for themselves during the Occupation—the 800,000 wives of POWs struggling to feed their children with the government's ludicrously small allowances, to make up for the lack of a "paternal authority" in a totally disrupted sociopolitical context, and to defy public opinion, always quick to level the charge of adultery against women left without any male supervision (Bordeaux 1987; Fishman 1991).

In a more complex mode, Madame Manu (Héléna Manson) in Henri De-coin's *Les Inconnus dans la maison* (1942) and Gérardine Eloi (Gabrielle Dor-ziat) in Louis Daquin's *Le Voyageur de la Toussaint* (1942) transcend the limits of the *film à thèse* because of their depth of character and their ability to re-sist the general atmosphere of hypocrisy and corruption on their own and in silence; they fight for those they love, not for power or money. Their struggle allows them to escape from the straitjacket of pure effigies and turns them into real characters. In Decoin's movie, Madame Manu, the destitute widow who works as a cleaner so as to be able to bring up her son, Emile (André Reybaz), does not qualify as one of the irresponsible parents attacked by the barrister Hector Loursat (Raimu). In Daquin's film, Gérardine, who is driven to mur-der out of love for her son, is transfigured by her moving defense of him when faced with Gilles Mauvoisin (Jean Desailly).

In a less austere but similarly emotional mood, André Berthomieu's *L'Ange de la nuit* (1942) portrays the selflessness of Geneviève (Michèle Alfa), who enables Jacques Martin (Jean-Louis Barrault), a young sculptor blinded dur-ing the 1940 war, to overcome his despair on returning home and to fit into society again. The movie's main theme is the acute anxiety of returning pris-oners about readjusting socially and their obsessive fear that their wives may have been unfaithful (Durand 1987). The movie exploits both themes: Gene-viève, a penniless student who, just before the outbreak of war, is taken charge of by a kind of student cooperative, repays this generosity by herself taking charge of Jacques at a time when she has no news of her fiancé, Bob (Henri Vidal). In devoting herself to the blind sculptor's "rehabilitation," even to the point of marrying him, she is unfaithful to her fiancé, who later reappears un-hurt, but faithful to the great patriotic cause. Jacques's blindness, through the dependence that results from it and the symbolic castration it implies, reflects more generally the traumatic effect of the Defeat on soldiers and, more gener-ally, on males. Men expect women to help them recover their lost manhood, their social creativity, and their power. The film explicitly spells out the price that women have to pay, which is a renunciation of their own desire, embodied here in the relationship between Bob and Geneviève at the beginning of the movie. This positive portrayal of a reciprocal love relationship prevents the movie from being classified as orthodox Pétainist and makes it more in line with "progressive" Catholicism or the ideology of the Communist Resistance. True, Geneviève is an angel, but she accepts her sacrifice in the full knowledge of what it entails and in no way pays for any sin. Her pain is that of a woman, not of a repentant slut. As for Barrault's remarkable performance as a blind man laboriously trying to resurface into a world in which he has lost his bearings, it is powerful enough to evoke genuine distress much more than some ideology of redemption through suffering.

The women who die so that the patriarchal order can be restored are usually mothers, since daughters have to ensure population renewal. In Pierre de Hérain's *Monsieur des Lourdines* (1942), this division of roles between Madame des Lourdines (Germaine Dermoz) and Sylvie (Claude Génia) works perfectly when they set about bringing Anthime des Lourdines (Raymond Rouleau) back to the ancestral home.

Paul Mesnier's *Patricia* (1942), one of the most popular Occupation films despite being shot on a technical and artistic shoestring, relies successively on the mothers' generation, in the person of Mademoiselle Pressac (Gabrielle Dorziat), and on the daughters' generation, as represented by Patricia (Louise Carletti), to implement Vichy's educational and regenerative program, culminating in the grand finale of the return to the land. Both women are active and efficient "militants," whereas the male characters either do nothing but talk, such as the hilarious priest (Alerme), or are beyond redemption, such as the father who has been corrupted by Paris (Aimé Clariond) and Fabien (Jean Servais), a suicidal artist.

This notion of the handover from one generation to another, one of Pétain's pet themes, coincided with the emergence of new actress figures, most of them young and blonde, in melodramas where the modesty of their (new) position is reflected in the casting. Thus the angelic faces of actresses like Janine Darcey, Michèle Alfa, Blanchette Brunoy, Josette Day, Madeleine Sologne, Yvette Lebon, Juliette Faber, Annie France, Claude Génia, Irène Corday, and Assia Noris bring a touch of light to stories often governed by a male figure, usually a patriarch firmly entrenched in his ancestral values. Charles Vanel (who was a convinced Pétainist in real life) specialized in such Vichyite figures attached to the land, "which at least doesn't tell lies" (Miller 1975: 136). The interchangeable patriarchs who feature in Jean-Paul Paulin's *La Nuit merveilleuse* (1940), Jacques de Baroncelli's *Haut-le-vent* (1942), and Jean Dréville's *Les Roquevillard* (1943) are invariably flanked by a pure young woman who, with all her Marian virtues (chastity, humility, gentleness), embodies the same attachment to the land, the family, and tradition.

In such movies, in order to thwart the corrupting city, which succeeds for a time in causing the son of the family to stray from the straight and narrow, the young daughter remains in her village, devoting herself to some task that is useful to the community, such as teaching in a primary school (Janine

Darcey) in Jean-Paul Paulin's *Cap au large* (1942). If it so happens that the young woman herself yields to temptation, she will subsequently throw all her energies into restoring the values she has transgressed, such as Patricia (Josette Day) in Marcel Pagnol's *La Fille du puisatier* (*The Well-Digger's Daughter*, 1940) and Mireille (Janine Darcey) in Jean Boyer's *La Bonne étoile* (1942).

Jeannou (Michèle Alfa) in Léon Poirier's *Jeannou* (1943) introduces an interesting variant by trying to reconcile the ancestral values embodied by her father, Peyrac (Thomy Bourdelle), with the modernist values upheld by her mining engineer fiancé, Pierre (Roger Duchesne). Thanks to the young woman's intervention, Pierre first shakes off the evil influence of Frochard, a financier (Saturnin Fabre) solely interested in stock market quotations, then finally agrees to wait until the patriarch dies before exploiting the coal the estate contains. Thus the movie, which is little more than a propaganda film despite the beauty of the Périgord landscape, resolves in fantasy and thanks to the mediation of a female figure the debate that Vichy never settled between technocrats and traditionalists. The only possible happy ending to this type of film is the formation of a new couple with the patriarch's blessing, since the female character's only function is to facilitate the handover. It is probably true that this sudden flurry of female figures embodying fidelity to ancestral values stems from the age-old identification of the female sex with Nature, the Earth, the Sea, and the permanence of the human race, whereas the male sex is more involved in Culture, History, Progress, Creation, and so on (Guillaumin 1995).

Despite its nonconformist reputation, *Les Inconnus dans la maison*, a Continental film which Henri-Georges Clouzot adapted for Henri Decoin from a Georges Simenon novel, conforms to a similar pattern: it is thanks to his daughter, Nicole (Juliette Faber), that Hector Loursat (Raimu) recovers his self-respect, and the end of the movie confirms the installation of a young couple with the blessing of a reconstituted patriarchal authority. When Loursat the barrister makes a blistering attack on unworthy parents (a category for which he himself qualifies as well), he uses as his yardstick the ideal patriarchal family, which he subsequently does his best to embody. In following this course, the film faithfully carries out the Pétainist program, something that is confirmed by the way it singles out a scapegoat in the person of the "foreigner," played by Mouloudji.

But Nicole is not just a Pétainist effigy; her influence over a gang of youngsters at odds with society who are implicated in a murder stems from a maturity that can also be seen in her relationship with her drunken father. Childishness is here an essentially male preserve — and has no age limit. The price to be

Raimu, André Reybaz, and Juliette Faber in *Les Inconnus dans la maison*, 1942. Courtesy of Cinémathèque française.

paid for this disparity between men and women is the virtual disappearance of such elements as desire; it is very hard to believe in the existence of a great love story involving Nicole and Emile (André Reybaz), a man whose docile self-effacement is more to be expected from a younger brother than from a fiancé.

One movie encapsulates and transcends all these female effigies of the Occupation: Robert Bresson's *Les Anges du péché* (1943). The playwright Jean Giraudoux, who wrote the script in collaboration with Bresson, had a crucial influence on the movie. Hailed on its release as a "genuine masterpiece" by all the critics, the film is set in a world from which men are in theory excluded: a convent. In it Sylvie, Renée Faure, Jany Holt, Marie-Hélène Dasté, and Paula Dehelly play, respectively, an iconic righter of wrongs, a snooty woman, a slut who has renounced her selfish desire, an effigy of suffering, and an utter altruist, all of them swept along by a collective ambition to regenerate the world — an ambition symbolized by their religious order, devoted to the rehabilitation of female delinquents. From the start of the movie, the dynamism of this female institution is highlighted; we witness meticulous preparations for a secret nighttime operation (not without extracinematic significance in 1943) carried out in masterly fashion by the mother superior. We discover, after the event, that the purpose of the operation is to rescue Agnès, a former prosti-

Mila Parély and Renée Faure in *Les Anges du péché*, 1943. Courtesy of Cinémathèque française.

tute (Sylvia Monfort), from the clutches of her pimp, who is waiting for her as she is released from prison; the nuns successfully foil the ambush set up by a gang of thugs. A far cry from its colorful representation in prewar films, prostitution is here denounced as a stranglehold exerted over women by a violent male power. The convent is portrayed as a refuge from that violence in a manner characteristic of a time when Pétain claimed to be protecting France from external violence by keeping it on the sidelines of a world conflict. While the convent's tutelary figure, the prioress (Sylvie), guarantees an effective protection for its inmates against the outside world — a domain of male power that manifests itself solely in the form of repressive forces (crooks or policemen) — she does not claim to evade the law; the murderess who is hiding in the convent will not be denounced, but she finally gives herself up under the moral pressure of her "sisters."

On the other hand, the film settles its score with the Catholic bourgeoisie through its portrayal of the mother of Anne-Marie Lamaury (Renée Faure), a conformist upper-class woman who refuses to allow her daughter to rub shoulders with former delinquents. It counters that attitude by offering a "progressive" conception of religion, which could also be found at the time at the Uriage School, which was set up with Vichy's blessing before being disbanded by Pierre Laval in 1943, and which turned out to have been a breeding ground of Resistants. The convent in *Les Anges du péché* advocates an ideal of sisterliness that ignores class differences, but the upper-class Anne-Marie has to take a long, hard road (which proves fatal to her) in order to achieve that ideal. Generous but turned in on itself, the convent as imagined by Giraudoux and Bresson reflects in its own way Catholic milieux during the Occupation. But the fiction of this female world that finds salvation by surrounding itself with the most impervious cordon sanitaire possible can more generally be interpreted as a radical broadside against the repressive and unjust nature of patriarchal law.

What all these idealized women of the Occupation cinema have in common, irrespective of their complexity and their degree of autonomy in relation to Pétainist ideology, is an effacement of desire, that is, the female reality that is the most terrifying for male power, precisely because it is the least controllable by it. During that period of submission to a foreign power, which was temporary but very real for most French people and which jeopardized all the traditional images of manhood, the idealization of female figures and the effacement of such elements as desire were a compensatory way of reassuring the male identity, even though the other side of the coin was a consciously or unconsciously depreciative portrayal of that identity.

CHAPTER 4

Misogyny Lingers On

FOR CENTURIES, comedies written by France's leading playwrights, from Molière to Jacques Feydeau, have displayed a certain casual misogyny that has never been problematic. Even today it is rare for schoolchildren to be told by their teacher that Molière's *Les Femmes savantes* expresses a fear of women. In the program notes accompanying the TV revival of a 1930s movie featuring Edwige Feuillère, a powerful woman who always ends up defeated, it is very seldom that we find the epithet *misogynistic*.

But under the Vichy government, with its cult of women—which could take more progressive forms than is widely believed—any public expression of misogyny seemed to be taboo. Only Paris-based *collabos* (collaborators) still dared to flaunt such views. (They tended to be the same people who also made no secret of their anti-Semitism.) And in view of the fact that those two ways of hating difference are to be found in the madness of Nazism, starting with *Mein Kampf,* may we be permitted to digress for a moment?

It is not entirely true, as François Garçon (1984: 179 ff.) contends, that Vichyite cinema contains no anti-Semitic images. His argument is based mainly on the fact that in *Les Inconnus dans la maison* there is no reference to the Jewishness of the character played by Mouloudji, a Jewishness that is spelled out in Georges Simenon's novel, on which the movie is based. This argument is hardly convincing, since the character continues to be referred to as a *métèque* (wop), a term current during the prewar period. (It should be remembered that the French brand of anti-Semitism, which is cultural and religious rather than "racial," regarded Jews primarily as foreigners.) But, more important, Garçon fails to mention the two caricatural Jewish financiers played by the archcollaborator Robert Le Vigan in Jean Dréville's *Les Affaires sont les affaires* (1942) and Jean-Paul Paulin's *L'Homme qui vendit son âme* (*The Man Who Sold His Soul to the Devil*, 1943). He also overlooks the figure, still very recognizable today, of the treacherous hawker Jéricho (Pierre Renoir) in *Les Enfants du paradis* (Sellier 1992), a role originally due to have been played by Le Vigan, who was only too delighted to portray such characters.

But broadly speaking, Garçon is right: it is true that on the whole French filmmakers showed great restraint in this respect, including people notorious for their anti-Semitism, such as Claude Autant-Lara. Similar restraint can also be observed in Occupation movies as regards misogynistic images, in contrast to prewar productions, where misogyny was much more the rule than xenophobia or anti-Semitism. This is almost entirely true of the two genres — melodrama and romantic comedy — which together accounted for a majority of films at the time. But misogyny was also somewhat less apparent in the genre where it was traditionally de rigueur: the boulevard movie.

The fact remains that the most consistent, if not the most aggressive, misogyny of the period is indeed to be found in the thirty-seven movies based more or less closely on boulevard plays. And yet it would be a mistake to interpret this (as most film historians do) as knee-jerk behavior on the part of authors clinging to their prewar preconceptions. On the contrary, those who went in for misogyny at the time, while mostly not left-wing or classifiable as anti-Vichyite collaborationists, did however make a political point, something that might be called, as a reaction against the "idolization of women" that was rampant at the time, an act of "male chauvinist resistance."

Take, for example, Pierre Billon's *L'Inévitable Monsieur Dubois* (1942), one of the most successful Occupation movies, which is immediately recognizable as a modern variation on *The Taming of the Shrew*. Hélène Mareuil (Annie Ducaux), a glacially beautiful, self-possessed woman wearing a haute couture trouser suit and hair drawn up tightly into a bun, gets into a convertible sports car and sets off at top speed along a road on the Côte d'Azur. Suddenly she loses control of her car, plows into a motorcycle with a sidecar coming the other way, and ends up in a ditch. The man on the motorbike, Claude Orly (André Luguet), an athletic, distinguished-looking Bohemian wearing goggles, is unhurt.

He immediately sets his heart on Hélène, who runs a perfume-manufacturing company. (The film is set near the town of Grasse, perfume capital of France.) Claude, who is a painter, wants to sketch the woman there and then, but the beautiful Hélène is in a hurry—and apparently impervious to male charm. She gives him the slip, leaving him a blank check as his only reminder of her.

Claude's aim throughout the movie will be to pin down the elusive Hélène, not only on the posters he designs for the firm she runs (where he gradually makes himself indispensable) but in the role of mistress-cum-wife, which she pretends to disdain until alcohol gets the better of her autonomy. She fends him off persistently and wittily. She does not lose her cool when Claude forces a kiss on her in her office; while he wipes his lips in front of a mirror, she phones the head of the research department and tells him that his so-called indelible lipstick is worthless. Although the heroine's resistance is highlighted more than it would have been in a prewar movie, Claude ends up winning a woman's heart—and probably a perfume company as well.

The most salient feature of the history of the Parisian theater during the Occupation was the fierce struggle that pitted those who had opted for collaboration (led by the critic Alain Laubreaux) against the "Judaized" boulevard tradition, personified in their view by the playwright Henry Bernstein, who had fled to the United States. This situation enabled "serious" drama—plays put on by the Cartel, an association of four stage producers founded in 1927, and those written by Paul Claudel and Jean Giraudoux, for example—to enjoy hitherto nonexistent official and financial support (Added 1992).

Film critics, whatever their political complexion, adopted a more or less similar stance, demolishing with a single stroke of the pen each boulevard movie as it came out, castigating the vulgarity of the genre and promoting the celebrated notion of "cinematic specificity." This notion was espoused by critics of all tendencies, from Jacques Audiberti in *Comoedia*, Roger Régent in *L'Oeuvre*, and Arlette Sarrazin in *Révolution nationale* to "François Vinneuil" (Lucien Rebatet's pseudonym) in *Paris soir* and *Je suis partout*, Georges Blond in *L'Oeuvre*, and Léon Daudet in *L'Action française*. Unlike theater and literary critics, those who wrote on the cinema, even the most radically fascist and racist of them, refrained, by a kind of tacit agreement, from mixing up art and politics. It was this that helped to give currency to the notion of an "escapist" cinema, despite the fact that films made during those dark years portrayed the real world just as much those of any other period, but simply in a more coded manner than before or after the war.

Whatever the truth of such assessments, boulevard films continued to appeal to audiences, as did plays that easily held their own against productions by the Cartel: Léo Joannon's *Caprices* (1941), pure boulevard written for the cinema, was one of the great hits of the period, as were other movies in more or less the same tradition, such as André Cayatte's *La Fausse maîtresse* (*Twisted Mistress*, 1942), Richard Pottier's *Picpus* (1942), Henri-Georges Clouzot's *L'Assassin habite au 21* (*The Murderer Lives at Number 21*, 1942), and Marcel L'Herbier's *L'Honorable Catherine* (1942). Numerically the genre accounted for almost 17 percent of movies produced during those four years. But if the statistics of the Film Industry Organization Committee regarding the number of tickets sold had survived, it is fair to assume that they would have shown that boulevard films in fact cornered a much greater share of takings over that period.

Now apart from a few notable exceptions, particularly Bernstein's plays, misogyny and male chauvinism were the two driving forces of the boulevard plot. Boulevard cinema during the Occupation conformed to that rule, but never did it purely and simply perpetuate the codes of prewar cinema. In some cases such films went so far as to turn their misogyny on its head, in movies portraying "madwomen" who are in fact not mad at all. In other cases, it was the official "idolization" of women that was turned on its head. In some films he directed, the boulevard playwright Yves Mirande, for example, under the guise of the conventions of an accepted genre, took malicious pleasure in thumbing his nose at the rather sanctimonious female effigies already associated with Pétainist cinema. In the film he wrote for Henri Decoin, *Le Bienfaiteur* (1942), set in a remote French village, the exaggeratedly upper-class diction and all too perfect manners of Suzy Prim, playing a Lady Bountiful character idealized by Moulinet (Raimu), a gangster disguised as a "benefactor," should clearly be interpreted as a take-off of Gaby Morlay's roles as a sanctimonious do-gooder.

This boulevard misogyny is directed at a very precise target. Postadolescent femmes fatales like Lana Turner who were a feature of the film noir genre that was beginning to take off in the United States did not appear at all in French films of the time. The halo that surrounded young people, the "hope of tomorrow," was not found solely in official propaganda. Also virtually nonexistent (and in any case unrecognizable) is the prewar bitch. Apart from when it attacks the occasional shrewish concierge or overpossessive widow, the boulevard cinema's typical target is an attractive, active woman well into her thirties. The task facing the male central character of the movie is either how to deprive her of the power she has acquired, whether it be sexual or financial, as in the case of Hélène Mareuil in *L'Inévitable Monsieur Dubois*, or how at all costs to escape the (demonized) power exerted, for example, by Blanche (Lise Dela-mare) in André Zwoboda's *Farandole* (1944).

Blanche is a discreetly elegant, slim woman whom we meet in an ultrachic nightclub. Her table companion is a trim, fit-looking banker played by André Luguet (yet again), who became a veritable icon of boulevard dandyism. (He played eleven roles during the Occupation, when he enjoyed the height of his film career.) But although the couple look like glitterati, they have dark secrets: the banker realizes he is ruined, and Blanche, after being told the truth about him by a malicious third party, coolly refuses to let him sleep with her any more. He gets his revenge (or so he thinks) by committing suicide while she is on the phone to him.

This sordid story is reminiscent of Marc Allégret's *Félicie Nanteuil* (*Twilight*, 1942), a movie affected both by the misogyny inherent in Anatole France's naturalism and by the Vichyite encouragement of guilt feelings. But there is a difference: in Allégret's film the revenge of the person who commits suicide, Cavalier (Claude Dauphin), is totally successful (in patriarchal terms); his ghost in the mind of poor Félicie (Micheline Presle) destroys her relationship with Robert de Ligny (Louis Jourdan) and forces her to seek solace solely in her profession as an actress—and therefore endure a state of loneliness which, as we all know, is bound to be tragic for a woman.

In *Farandole*, on the other hand, Blanche is not in the least put off her stride, and in the final episode of a not always very well put-together *film à sketches* we find the same cynical Blanche in the same nightclub, sitting at the table of the man who told her that her lover was penniless and who has now taken his place—momentarily. For another, even more rotund schemer soon whispers in her ear the news that her new lover is about to be ruined in turn, with, one supposes, similar consequences.

But let us examine the movie chronologically, since it provides a signifi-cant portrait gallery of various types of women portrayed in the cinema of the period and gives us some idea of how old and new images can cohabit in the same minds. The second episode introduces us to a prostitute (Paulette Du-bost) who is never at a loss for words and holds her own against her pimp; she is the whore with a heart of gold, now a well-known character but very rare at that time. The apparent contradiction between these two women who both make a living by selling their charms arises simply from the fact that they em-body two aspects of everyday sexism: on the one hand, a fear of the diaboli-cal talent that prostitutes have always been thought to possess, that of being able to ape society women perfectly (Corbin 1978), and on the other, the cult of the working-class prostitute, the only autonomous woman — apart from the nun — accepted by the classical patriarchal vision. Indeed in this respect, boulevard misogyny and the Pétainist idolization of women (Gaby Morlay as a nun) go hand in hand. And if the scriptwriter Henri Jeanson was provoking the Vichyite censors when he included a scene showing prostitutes and their clients, he did so in the same spirit as in the following episode, where Morlay is cast in the role of a scatterbrained actress reminiscent of the characters she played before the war. All of which was standard stuff on the boulevard stage.

But the boulevard spirit of this film seems also to have been impregnated by the dominant tendency of the period. For it also offers an extraordinary effigy of the female victim of men, played by Jany Holt, here as luminous as a Bresson angel, and who is on trial for having (accidentally) killed her lover's wife. This kind of tragic female figure is not entirely absent from boulevard films (she can be found in Bernstein), but she also derives directly from the most authentic inspiration of film melodramas of the period, such as *L'Ange de la nuit*.

In fact almost all these boulevard movies are receptive to the Zeitgeist. Take, for example, the screen adaptation of Denys Amiel's 1932 play, *Trois et une*. The play portrays a "vamp" who makes three brothers suffer when they fall in love with her. She gets her just deserts when the brother who eventually wins her heart dumps her and goes back under his mother's wing alongside his less "fortunate" brothers. In Roger Richebé's *Romance à trois* (1941), the adaptation by Richebé and Jean Aurenche of *Trois et une*, a number of alterations to the plot show that times have changed. In the play, the vamp character, Huguette, is presented as "a classic *femme fatale*, the eternal feminine," and when the curtain rises at the beginning of the play she has already seduced all three brothers and wormed her way into the family home. In the movie, on the other hand, Huguette (Simone Renant) is a kind of empty shell, a passive icon at whom the men throw themselves in an almost reflex action of virility, in the course of three rather satirical scenes when they first meet (added for the purposes of the film). And there is another crucial difference: whereas in the play the womanizing brother shows the cynical tart the door, in the film it is Huguette who forestalls this move by slipping out of her hotel just as Charles (Fernand Gravey) turns up with the intention of having it out with her.

A characteristic of all these boulevard movies, even those that most clearly show the impact of the Occupation, is a dose, in varying degrees, of what might be termed libertine misogyny. René Jayet's *Vingt-cinq ans de bonheur* (1943), based on a novel written during the Occupation by a woman, Germaine Lefrancq, tries basically to justify the husband's extramarital escapades by pointing to the wife's parallel philandering. At the same time, the movie is shot through with the cult of youth and of the future, guilt about the past, and the *zazou* (zoot-suiter) spirit of the period.

Actually boulevard misogyny creeps into every possible type of scenario, from dramas marked by poetic realism (*A la Belle frégate*) to detective films (*Les Caves du Majestic*) and even edifying melodramas. The whole substance and interest of Georges Lacombe's *L'Escalier sans fin* (1943) derives from the way it contrasts two sisters, Emilienne (Madeleine Renaud), who embodies a rather unsexy form of Pétainist virtue, and Anne (Suzy Carrier), a typical example of boulevard "fresh meat." Boulevard and hatred of independent-minded women carry the day, even if Pierre (Pierre Fresnay) is forced to exchange his sleazy nightclub for a stud farm in Normandy in order to get his hands on Anne's desirable body.

Anyone interested in exploring the cinematic complexities of misogyny at that time would be well advised to examine the interaction of genres. André Cayatte's *La Fausse maîtresse* (1942) seems at first to mark the defeat of boulevard and its misogyny, as well as the demise of melodrama and its effigies, as a result of the appearance of the New Woman, who escapes their thrall. This is both because the New Woman emerged from the optimistic comedies of the period and because in this film she was embodied by Danielle Darrieux. As soon as the star makes her appearance, boulevard (tinted with melodrama) joins a losing battle with Darrieux as Lilian Rander, an audacious circus acrobat (one of a series of sporty and independent young women who were a novelty for the period). She bursts into a men's gymnasium and manages to bully a gutter-press journalist into promising to retract a libelous article. She does this through physical intimidation, overtaking her fleeing prey on a rope like Tarzan.

True, in case we should forget we are dealing with a desirable woman, she also does a striptease on a trapeze, but it is a sequence that does not fit in with the rest of the movie. And it is clearly as an emblem of France and the New Woman that Lilian is wooed by René Rivals (Bernard Lancret), associated at first with a typically boulevard décor and situation, in which he seems to be increasingly ill at ease: just as he is about to become the lover of a frustrated wife, Hélène (Lise Delamare), a neglected, narcissistic, and rather melodramatic figure, and thus cuckold his best friend, Guy (Jacques Dumesnil), he is forced to pretend he is the outrageous acrobat's lover in order to avert the husband's suspicions.

Typically boulevard male self-importance is also undermined in another respect: René, Guy, and all the other young men in the movie play for a rugby team (the film is set in the Roussillon area), but the image they project of themselves is much more infantile than it is virile. They enact a complicated and grotesque ritual whenever they meet and spend most of their time trying to escape their marital duties by having stag parties. This mild mockery can probably be put down to the uncertainties about sexual roles that were typical of the cinema of the period, as can the way an endearingly weak father, Rander (Alerme), is lusted after for cynically self-interested reasons by a cigar-smoking virago, the lion tamer Laetitia (Monique Joyce). This latter character is perfectly at home in the boulevard battle of the sexes and is intended, in an utterly conventional way, to spare Darrieux the stigma of masculinity and to enable her in the end to give up her independence gracefully and marry René. As we can see, it is no easy task to unravel the various strands of such a movie, but it is these tensions between genres and ideologies — on top of the vitality of the Darrieux character — that make Cayatte's film interesting, for all its disconcerting humor.

It is hardly surprising that the most virulent and sordid misogyny of the period is to be found in a fascistic film (only two or three were made during this period): Louis Cuny's *Mermoz* (1942). Here we have Hélèna Manson playing Mermoz's asexual mother; the only scene in which she appears shows her rushing out of the hospital where she works as a nurse into the arms of her son and future hero in a kind of idealizing giant shadow show. Throughout the film, Mermoz carries out his aerial feats "while thinking of his mother," as an edifying voice-over informs us. When he is reported missing over the Atlantic, and when a subjective tracking shot moves forward to bring his mother the fateful news in the antechamber where she is waiting, no sooner is her image glimpsed than it dissolves into a shot of the sea — a very meaningful visual pun: *mère* (mother) is pronounced the same way as *mer* (sea).

Women are few and far between in this men's movie, but their representation is highly significant. We see society women in cocktail bars who lose interest in their dull husbands and go weak at the knees in the presence of the inaccessible hero; tempting dancing girls in Rio de Janeiro whom he succeeds in resisting by abruptly closing the shutters of his hotel room; a Berber prostitute who continues to smile stupidly (she does not understand French) while men treat her like a cur, in the shack in North Africa where Mermoz turns up with a female monkey as his only flying companion. We can detect here the two poles — the "white" woman (the Madonna, the mother, the nurse, and so on) and the "red" woman (in the double sense of prostitute and revolutionary, in German and in English) — that structure the fascist imaginary (Theweleit 1987–89; E. Ann Kaplan 1986).

More disturbing is the almost equally virulent misogyny to be found in Jean Delannoy's *Pontcarral, colonel d'Empire* (1942), one of the very few films that was widely recognized by audiences at the time as having a subversive, "Resistant" intention. According to what Delannoy said after the war — during which he, like his male lead, Pierre Blanchar, had played an active role in an underground network — his aim was indeed to galvanize the patriotism and spirit of resistance of the French people by telling the story of a soldier of the Empire who persists in refusing to submit to the restored monarchy and organizes raids against what he believes to be an illegitimate authority. When faced with the final image of the movie, where present-day cavalrymen parade past a memorial erected in Algeria in Pontcarral's memory, audiences would have had no difficulty being reminded of the Free French Forces who were then fighting in North Africa — though such vaguely patriotic images also appealed to supporters of Vichy, but not to the occupying power, which insisted on several bits of dialogue being cut.

In any case, Blanchar's sinewy, athletic physique and clipped repartee in no way corresponded to the characteristics of a "castrated father" or those of a "gentle male figure." And the character goes on to confirm his physical and moral strength in his love affairs, which, despite the reputation of *Pontcarral, colonel d'Empire* as an action movie, take up a good half of its running time of 125 minutes (which was exceptionally long for the period).

For when Pontcarral's "subversive" virility is forced to ease up by force of circumstance and he retreats to his estate, he proves to us that his manhood has remained intact by taming a beautiful horsewoman from the old aristocracy, Garlone (Annie Ducaux once again), whom he marries out of sheer bravado and whom he rapes before killing her lover in a duel. The movie highlights the violence of this marital clash much more than did the novel on which it was based, where Garlone is seen more as the victim of a marriage below her station than as a shrew needing to be tamed. The film stands almost completely alone, along with its fascistic counterpart, *Mermoz*, in suggesting that in order to retrieve a warlike spirit that was annihilated by the humiliation of the Defeat, the minority of men capable of taking up arms and resisting first needed to reaffirm their imperious virility.

This interpretation would seem to be confirmed by a movie that emerged from another tendency within the Resistance. When he adapted Roger Frison-Roche's novel *Premier de cordée* in 1943, the Communist director Louis Daquin intended to pay tribute to the heroism of the *maquisards* who held out against the Germans in the mountains of the Vercors and the Margeride. And yet this men's film, which centers entirely on the virile setting of new challenges to oneself (in this case the challenge of scaling a surprisingly phallic-looking peak), contains curious undertones. Daquin (1980: 48) himself admitted that he had been deluded by the spirit of the novel as well as that of the period.

The representations here are not crudely misogynistic, as can be judged from the key scene in which the female lead, Aline (played by the sweet blonde Irène Corday), undertakes to help the main male character, Pierre (André Le Gall), who has suffered from vertigo since a bad fall, to retrieve his manly courage. She drags the reluctant young man into a harmless enough climb, challenges him to start up the rock face, and, when he hesitates, bravely does so herself. But she loses her footing after a few meters, slips, and calls for help. The man then rushes to save her, overcoming his vertigo thanks to his chivalrous act. The woman has carried out, unintentionally and as a result of her weakness, her duty as a nurse. From that point on, the editing elides the rest of the episode and sidelines Aline in favor of some parallel action depicting the death of the father. The film closes with Pierre, now cured of his fears, setting off with a group of climbers roped together, all of them male, of course, while his fiancée looks on admiringly. The only position that women could occupy in the maquis, unlike their role in urban networks, was that of a nurse.

In a prewar film, such a formula would have been unremarkable. But during the Occupation, this defense of virility was incongruous, and the parallel with *Mermoz* is as obvious as it is uncomfortable. Also uncomfortable is the parallel with one of the other fascistic movies of the period, Léo Joannon's *Le Carrefour des enfants perdus* (*Children of Chaos*, 1943), which portrays an "experimental" hostel for delinquent teenagers founded by former prisoners, where only a "real" man — played by René Dary, as it happens — can quell the youngsters' irrational and indiscriminate rebellion.

The film features another "female auxiliary" rather similar to Aline temperamentally and physically. (She is played by the blonde and diaphanous Janine Darcey.) Her role is even a little more positive than that played by Irène Corday, because in her capacity as a specialized social worker in children's prisons she is genuinely competent: she knows how to detect a knife that has been hidden in a sock and herself exerts a certain authority over all the unsociable youngsters. But the purpose of the movie is to demonstrate that only a firm-handed leader can succeed in rehabilitating these teenagers by means of a ritual reminiscent of the *Chantiers de Jeunesse*, Vichy's youth camps—and not so very different from Frison-Roche's vision of mountain climbing.

At the end of the Occupation the appearance on the French film scene of Maria Casarès, newly graduated from the Conservatoire and on her way to the Théâtre National Populaire and the Comédie-Française, seemed to herald the advent of a serious, cultivated misogyny, a misogyny that would differentiate itself both from the insipid version of it found in poetic realism and from boulevard's libertine caricature, and would on occasion elevate itself to the level of "metaphysical" drama. It is curious how that great actress was able to embody so naturally the two faces of misogynistic imagery. In Jean Cocteau's screenplay for Robert Bresson's *Les Dames du bois de Boulogne* (*The Ladies of Bois de Boulogne*, 1944), she already plays the sexy but deadly Death character that Cocteau was later to cast her as in his movie *Orphée* (*Orpheus*). In *Les Enfants du paradis*, the last major production before the end of the Occupation, which was released to international acclaim only after the Liberation, Casarès personifies the domestic aspect of the eternal feminine, the moralizing, boring woman, the faithful wife, the millstone, the anti-Arletty, in short the anti-mystery. Using her son as a pretext to hound Baptiste (Jean-Louis Barrault) even when he is in the arms of the woman of his dreams, she seems to embody a negative image of all the women's melodramas of the Occupation, with their moralizing and their preaching of duty and self-sacrifice. It is an attack at least as caustic as that which targets Emilienne (Madeleine Renaud), the social worker excluded from the circuit of desire in *L'Escalier sans fin*.

But misogyny appears in another, subtler guise in Marcel Carné and Jacques Prévert's movie: the ultimate cruelty of the ambiguous Garance (Arletty) when she slips away from her one-night lover and disappears into the crowds on the Boulevard du Crime. Arletty/Garance, objectively speaking as a woman seeking independence and a victim of her condition, but from a male point of view an angel and slut rolled into one (Sellier 1992), seems to encapsulate on her own all the contradictions of a period that, at least in the minds of male filmmakers, severely tested the power relationship between the sexes.

CHAPTER 5

Absent Men, Fleeing Men

―――――――――――
―――――――――――

CONTRARY TO WHAT historians often suggest, not all films made during the Occupation were set in a "vaguely contemporary" period (Jeancolas 1983). As our research stands at present, we can identify fifteen movies that are explicitly set at the time of the Defeat and Occupation, either through a verbal or visual allusion (*Donne-moi tes yeux* [*My Last Mistress*], *Falbalas*, *Signé: Illisible*) or through a direct historical reference (*L'Ange de la nuit*, *L'An 40*, *L'Appel du bled*, *Après l'orage*, *Le Carrefour des enfants perdus*, *Départ à zéro*, *La Femme perdue*, *La Fille du puisatier*, *La Grande meute* [*The Big Pack*], *Haut-le-vent*, *Le Mistral*, and *La Nuit merveilleuse*). Four other movies contain more or less explicit allusions to the situation at the time: *L'Escalier sans fin*, in which Pierre (Pierre Fresnay), who has a gunshot wound and is trying to escape from the police, finds refuge with Emilienne (Madeleine Renaud); *Ne le criez pas sur les toits* (the energy shortage); *Farandole* (the episode of the roundup of Jews); *Le Voile bleu* (the sadness of a home without a man); and *Le Père Goriot*, where Vautrin is on the run from the police after being denounced by a couple of petit bourgeois inmates of the Vauquer boardinghouse.

Now one of the major topics of these movies—and of many others, as we shall see—is the lack of menfolk: 100,000 died in 1940 and 1.5 million others were taken prisoner; soon 700,000 men would be sent to work in Germany under the Compulsory Labor Service scheme; there were 60,000 *maquisards* and 120,000 fighters in the Free French Forces, not counting all those who had been imprisoned or deported. Men were indeed in short supply during the Occupation.

Thus *L'Ange de la nuit* centers entirely on the conscription of its two male protagonists, Jacques (Jean-Louis Barrault) and Bob (Henri Vidal), one of whom returns blind, and the other . . . too late. *La Fille du puisatier*, which was shot in two phases, before and after the Débâcle, weaves into its plot both the absence and the return of those who have been mobilized, with the similar ingredient of a soldier who is believed to be dead because there is no news of him — a direct allusion to the traumatic conditions of the Defeat in 1940. Other films transpose the tragedy of loss to World War I: in Robert Péguy's *Les Ailes blanches* (1942), Claire (Gaby Morlay) has become a nun because the man she once loved, who was separated from her by her father for financial reasons, died in the war — in the arms of a nurse whom he was unable, because of his blindness, to recognize as the woman he loved. As for the celebrated *Le Voile bleu*, whose central character, again played by Morlay, was widowed during World War I, it depicts transparently in its final episode the pitiful fate of prisoners' wives, who alone had to bear the moral and financial burden of the family.

The idealization of women in films of this period stems from a male fantasy and in no way reflects any changes in the actual balance of power in gender relations. But it is nevertheless legitimate to speculate that the ordeals and anonymous heroism of prisoners' wives, and their self-managed methods of organization (Fishman 1991), may have constituted — through the press, which regularly reported on them, and through the actual experiences of filmmakers' friends (there were prisoners from every level of society) — a major source of inspiration for this impressive portrayal of absent, missing, or "castrated" men, or men on the run, and of their counterparts: women whose desire was frustrated, saintly women, and women of action.

The arduous daily life of such women was not often directly depicted on screen. It is probably *Félicie Nanteuil* that best reflects the most sordid aspects of the lives of such war widows, in the literal as well as the figurative sense, who were constantly spied on in their home, district, or village by all those good people who ensured they were not unfaithful to their absent husband (or to the memory of a dead husband) and remained unfailingly in mourning for him, whether they liked it or not. Vichy introduced special legislation that punished prisoners' wives found guilty of adultery (Bordeaux 1987). In fact the great majority of such women took little advantage of their husbands' absence to become independent, preferring instead to patiently await their return, knitting sweaters, making up parcels, and fervently maintaining the veneration of the paterfamilias (Fishman 1991).

On the other hand, the grand narrative of male absence was fantasized in a good forty or so movies, which, without directly evoking the situation at the time, had symbolic echoes that were more complex than a mere lamentation or illustration of the present. Essentially centered as they were on the flight of men, those movies highlighted male responsibility.

Here again, it is tempting to see in the omnipresence of this latter theme a mere reflection of a real world where French troops fled from the Germans, where whole villages fled the war and the occupying forces, where POWs tried to escape from their stalags, where young workers went AWOL from the Compulsory Labor Service and joined the maquis, and where Jews and Resistants tried to escape from the Gestapo, went into hiding, or were hidden by others, and so on. This "rhyme" with reality, including the "reality" of propaganda posters urging people to return to the land, for example, cannot be dismissed. This is true with regard to cinematic escapes to the countryside (ranging from *Fièvres* and *L'Assassin a peur la nuit* to *Le Corbeau* and *Adieu Léonard*) but also to situations where a man goes into hiding, as in such dramatic movies as *Le Baron fantôme* (*The Phantom Baron*), with the corpse of Baron Julius Carol (Jean Cocteau) enclosed in an underground chamber, and *L'Auberge de l'abîme*, where the wounded Jacques Eymard (Roger Duchesne) hides in a cave, as well as comedies like *Pension Jonas*, with Barnabé Tignol (Pierre Larquey) trying to flee the world in the belly of a whale in the Natural History Museum, and *Madame et le mort*, where Armand (Henri Guisol) hides in a hotel room, letting the world think he is dead. And contemporary spectators must surely have interpreted as an episode of some (unthinkable) movie about the Resistance the scene in *L'Escalier sans fin* where Pierre (Pierre Fresnay), after being shot and wounded by his mistress, flees into the night, only to find refuge in the flat of Emilienne (Madeleine Renaud), who gives him first aid.

But let us explore this theme more closely. Two strangers meet when hiding in a train compartment at night. They are both on the run. One of them is Pierre Gohelle (Paul Bernard wearing a trilby), a dangerous gangster who has escaped from prison, and the other is Alain Ginestier (a very young Jean Marais), a bank clerk who has made off with the takings. That is the opening of Christian-Jaque's *Voyage sans espoir* (*Voyage without Hope*, 1943), undoubtedly the most noir of the movies belonging to a genre that was banned in principle, especially during the first years of the Occupation: poetic realism.

Before the war, the man on the run was one of the typical features of poetic realism in the broadest sense (quite apart from established masterpieces by Jean Renoir, Jean Grémillon, Julien Duvivier, Marcel Carné, and a few others). One could even categorize a whole swath of those films as being about men on the run. We have men who are fleeing from France or from Europe (*Le Paquebot Tenacity* [*s.s. Tenacity*], *Mollenard*), fleeing from the consequences of a murder, whether it be justified (*Le Crime de Monsieur Lange*) or committed in the heat of the moment (*La Bandera*), fleeing more generally from the long arm of the law (*Pépé le Moko, Pension Mimosas*), fleeing from one's class and one's family (the young country squire in *Sarati le Terrible*, the ruined playboy in *Le Grand jeu*), fleeing poverty, working-class conditions, and women (*La Belle équipe*), fleeing from a wife or from marriage (*La Chienne*), fleeing from a colonial war and the army (*Le Quai des brumes*), or simply fleeing from everything (*Marius, Boudu sauvé des eaux* [*Boudu Saved from Drowning*], *L'Homme de nulle part, Les Bas-fonds*). Each of these flights is a regression, usually into a world of male bonding, a form of regression celebrated in *La Chienne* and *Boudu sauvé des eaux* (though as a result of Renoir's personal and political development this is no longer the case in *Les Bas-fonds*). It is a regression that turns out to be a mirage in *Le Paquebot Tenacity*, but that becomes, from *Le Grand jeu* and above all *La Bandera* on, a kind of boastful yet desperate journey toward death, where femmes fatales are generally waiting to deal the death blow.

At first sight it is not surprising that all the Occupation films that echo that forbidden genre contain the theme of flight in one form or another. In *Le Corbeau*, for instance, we have Dr. Rémy Germain (Pierre Fresnay) fleeing his town, his eminent medical past, and the after-effects of an emotional trauma. In *Lumière d'été*, Roland (Pierre Brasseur) flees on a motorbike to escape his failed career as a theater designer in Paris. In *A la Belle Frégate*, René (René Dary) evades his romantic duties toward Yvonne (Michèle Alfa). And even in *Les Enfants du paradis*, there is the flight of Baptiste (Jean-Louis Barrault), first from Garance (Arletty), then from his family responsibilities.

But most striking is the fact that this theme of male flight is to be found in all the major genres (except perhaps in upbeat comedy) during the Occupation. The forty movies concerned fall more or less equally into two genres, melodrama (whether Pétainist or not) and tragedy, and the theme is also found in almost all the handful of comedies we describe as *zazous*. It is as much a distinctive feature of that genre as it was of poetic realism.

But this archetypal poetic realist narrative is affected by the climate of the period. It is true that for characters like those played by Jean Marais in *Voyage sans espoir* and Roger Pigaut in *Douce*, the dream of escape is still a tragic impossibility, but it now leads to the death of the loved woman, a sacrificial feature typical of the Occupation. Before the war, in *Pépé le Moko* and *Le Quai des brumes*, for example, it was the man who was sacrificed in the presence of a helpless woman. While in the great majority of other Occupation films escape is also a regression, it also turns out to be a narrative sleight of hand — from which one can return alive. Having become a symbolic and moral issue, escape is something that in various ways concerns all groups making up the nation. It no longer has the nihilistic meaning that the pessimistic intellectuals at the end of the 1930s saw in it, nor in every case the edifying meaning lent it by Vichy's traditionalist ideologues.

Running away is explicitly singled out in Pétainist melodramas as a Bad Solution, as a mistake to be paid for. In Jacques de Baroncelli's *Haut-le-vent* (1942), the erstwhile escape to Latin America of a Basque peasant seen as responsible for the suicide of an enemy's son is "redeemed" by the return to France, in 1940, of his wealthy descendant (Charles Vanel), who is prompted by the misfortunes of his native land to stay put. André Hugon's *Le Chant de l'exilé* (1942) tells a fairly similar story, in which the Tino Rossi character's flight from France is triggered by what at first seems to be a murder; when it turns out that the victim was only wounded his stint in the colonial labor camp is cut short.

We find the same theme in Jean Delannoy's *L'Assassin a peur la nuit* (1942), certainly an unambitious work but one that performs several ideological functions at the same time: the flight of a Parisian master thief, Olivier Rol (Jean Chevrier), following a murder of which he has been accused, results in a return to the land (approved of by the movie) and enables him to avoid (again with the film's approval) the wrong sort of domestic arrangement with the slut he knew before the war, the gold-digging Lola Gracieuse (Mireille Balin). Rol's encounter with an archetypal example of the Young France in the person of Monique (Louise Carletti) results, after many a twist and turn, in his finally giving himself up to the police; since Lola, with her dying breath, has redeemed herself by admitting that it was she who committed the murder, Rol will be able to join his beloved in the near future.

As for the exile of the aristocratic Baron Roland de la Faille (Raymond Rouleau), whose return to France marks the beginning of Christian-Jaque's *L'Assassinat du Père Noël* (1941), it has certainly turned him into a "gentle male" figure but proves to have been as vain as the imaginary journeys that provide an escape for globe-maker Gaspard Cornusse (Harry Baur), a castrated "Father

Christmas," mothering and drunken. Another morally disastrous flight, and one regularly found whenever a movie wheels out the hackneyed theme of the "return to the land," is to be found in *Monsieur des Lourdines*, where Monsieur des Lourdines's son, Anthime (Raymond Rouleau, who gives a remarkable performance in a difficult role), is doubly punished for his escape to high society in Paris. His mistress ditches him when he can no longer afford to maintain her, and he has to accept that he has been guilty, through his irresponsible handling of his finances, of having ruined his elderly parents. (His ultimate offense, that of causing his mother's death, is kept from him, but it is one for which the spectator takes responsibility on his behalf.) Naturally punishment has its positive side: Anthime ends up going back to the land to marry his sagacious and clear-sighted childhood friend and to comfort his elderly father and ensure his succession.

But Vichyite propaganda also contained motifs that objectively went far beyond Catholic traditionalism and sometimes coincided with broader aspirations. One of the most prominent of such motifs is the condemnation of men's evasion of their responsibilities, no longer explicitly national responsibilities but those involving the emotions and the family—a motif already present in prewar movies but rarely highlighted, and never depicted as a typically male chauvinist form of behavior involving both fear of and contempt for women.

We find that type of evasion castigated in a whole range of moralizing films. In *Le Voile bleu*, an unworthy, thuggish father (Jean Clarieux) forces his wife to hand their son over to a nanny so they can go into exile in Indochina; he is reprimanded for this by a police superintendent. In *Service de nuit*, a pathetic traveling salesman (Carette) tries to escape his marital commitments throughout the movie and dreams of an escapade with a young thing; he is reprimanded by Suzanne (Gaby Morlay). In *Le Bal des passants*, a pianist, Claude Amadieu (Jacques Dumesnil), tries to escape from his wife, whom he regards as unworthy, so he can go on a tour of Latin America; his own little girl upbraids him implicitly when he finally decides to return home. In *L'Homme de Londres*, a melancholy clown (Jules Berry) flees from the wife and children he has left in England in an ill-fated search for a stash of holdup money and dies in sordid circumstances; his wife reprimands him posthumously.

It may seem odd that we see a progressive dimension in the way Vichyite moralizing condemns such abandonments of home and family. The problem is more or less the same as that facing anyone who attempts to decipher the American "spinster" figures who destroy saloon bars and take part in the temperance campaigns of the turn of the nineteenth century, as caricatured in the films of D. W. Griffith and others. For us modern (and particularly male) spectators, it is difficult to see a fear of real-life militant women in such images; it is even harder to detect behind those images, in other words in the real world, not only (and in any case not always) sanctimonious moralists but also brave and clear-sighted feminists who fought against the violence that drunken husbands regularly inflicted on their wives.

Similarly it is difficult for us today to realize that such melodramas, even the most Pétainist of them, formulated complaints and demands with which, at a deeper level, millions of women could identify. But another element also comes into play: as cinephiles, there exists within us — men as well as women steeped in the same history of the cinema and cinephilia — a reflex that devalues the moralist and naïvely sentimental dimension of melodramas or upbeat comedies as compared with the cynicism and pessimism of a director like Julien Duvivier, for example. Our brand of cinephilia will always prefer a "masculine" and "noir" movie like *Le Corbeau* to a "feminine" and "rose-tinted" movie like *L'Ange de la nuit*. And one wonders how male spectators reacted during the Occupation when they were so often faced with a type of movie that the British and U.S. film industries directed specifically at women (the weepie). That said, the best French movies at the time managed to dialecticize the "female" and the "male" — gender relations and the class struggle, feeling and intelligence, "soppy" and "noir," as in *Le Jour se lève*, *La Règle du jeu*, *Remorques*, *Lumière d'été*, *La Duchesse de Langeais*, *Marie-Martine*, *Douce*, and *Falbalas*.

It could be argued that during the Occupation noir realism and, to a certain extent, boulevard cynicism acquired an objectively subversive dimension which they did not have before the war and which their postwar versions no longer possessed. It turns out, for both similar and contrasting reasons, that representations of male flight that were distinctly over the top, that showed no respect for anything or anyone, could be even more subversive during the dark years.

Take, for instance, Denis (Fernand Gravey) in Marcel L'Herbier's *La Nuit fantastique* (*Fantastic Night*, 1941), a penniless and overworked medical student who falls asleep among some crates of flowers he is supposed to be unloading at a street market and who takes refuge in a dream where he meets the Woman of the Future, who has rebelled against her overpossessive father and gives him as good as she gets. Take Barnabé Tignol (Pierre Larquey) in Pierre Caron's *Pension Jonas* (1941), a *clochard*-like figure who has taken refuge in the belly of a whale in the Natural Science Museum and who is determined to share his life solely with animals until the day human beings improve. In the same movie, Marmotte (Roger Legris) spends the whole time falling asleep in order to escape being questioned by his villainous associates. Or take Félicien (Carette) and Ludovic (Charles Trenet) in Pierre Prévert's *Adieu Léonard* (1943), who flee from, respectively, the terrorism of phoney Parisian intellectuals and the imperatives of capitalist economism to enjoy a simple way of life based on popular traditions. Similarly in René Lefèvre and Claude Renoir's *Opéra-musette* (1941) the composer Leroy (Maurice Teynac), who at the beginning of the movie is thought to have committed suicide, teams up with the strolling accordionist Lampluche (René Lefèvre).

At a time when the regime was essentially totalitarian and when intentionality, whether Utopian or utilitarian, was omnipresent, it has to be recognized — without in any way disowning what we have already said about the stigmatization of a certain form of male cowardice — that the movement we describe as *zazou* because of the chord it struck in certain sections of the "dissident" youth at the time had a salutary and liberating effect. Such movies differ from the largely conformist cinema of the period in that they do not induce guilt feelings and they validate flight.

It is perfectly possible to interpret *Adieu Léonard* and *Opéra-musette* as ambiguous films. The escape to the countryside and the positive nostalgic image of the small trades of yesteryear have an obvious parallel in Vichyite propaganda. But libertarian left-wing attitudes also rejected the inhuman society spawned by capitalism: the anarchist-leaning Prévert brothers shared that rejection not only with René Lefèvre, who was active in the Resistance, but also, whether they liked it or not, with those progressive Catholics who espoused Pétainist ideology for a time.

In a fair number of film comedies, whether zazou or not, the fleeing man has an enterprising woman in tow, who shields and organizes his flight while at the same time assuming in a sense the role of the male. Totte (Suzy Delair), the live-wire manicurist who takes charge of the ethereal Maxime (Paul Meurisse) in *Défense d'aimer*, and Clarisse (Renée Saint-Cyr), the young woman from the provinces and avid reader of detective novels who becomes a crime reporter and detective in Paris by standing in for Armand Le Noir (Henri Guisol) in *Madame et le mort* are just a couple of examples of young "superwomen," who act as a kind of positive reverse image of fleeing men, which was one of the most original and significant creations of the Occupation cinema.

Women Take Control of Their Destiny

IN MAY 1941 Maurice Cloche, who had made his first movie, *Ces Dames aux chapeaux verts* (*The Ladies in the Green Hats*), four years earlier, started shooting *Départ à zero*, a film shot entirely on location in the southern town of Castellane. It features a group of more or less amateur filmmakers who are making a 16mm documentary. Cloche's film itself seems to have been shot on a shoestring, with a budget barely greater than that of its young protagonists, a bit like a holiday movie in which a minimum number of scenes are filmed indoors, probably because of inadequate lighting. The movie is explicitly set at the time it was produced (the young men have all just been demobilized), and its very flimsy criminal plot, which is woven into a story involving a château bequeathed to two penniless young cousins, consists in a struggle against black marketeers which the film takes only half seriously.

On the other hand, it takes its title very seriously. The aim of the very young ex-servicemen (their enemies, the traffickers' bosses, played by Yves Deniaud and Félix Oudart, are middle-aged men) is to get off to a fresh start—that is, a fresh start with France—and with a woman, of all people, as their leader: Madeleine Sologne as a brunette in her first starring role. This is a very far cry from Gaby Morlay as a governess and righter of wrongs, Renée Faure as an "angel of sin," and even Michèle Alfa as an "angel of the night."

For any spectator unfamiliar with Sologne's career apart from the celebrated *L'Eternel retour* (*The Eternal Return*), the movie has a surprise in store. Instead of the slim, tightly clad, solemn, and statue-like body of Isolde as conceived by Jean Cocteau and Jean Delannoy in that movie, *Départ à zéro* portrays an agile, athletic young woman bursting with extraordinary energy. And she speaks her mind. She makes it quite clear to the group of young men whose leader she has rapidly become that they cannot expect her to do the cooking. She is at the origin of their project to make "a serious documentary on the region" and the driving force behind it. So that when she disappears, kidnapped by the gangsters, her companions feel that without her leadership they cannot go on with the film (even though she did not originally belong to the group that turned up at the château with a movie camera).

The following year another, more professional movie, also shot in the unoccupied zone, displayed certain similarities to *Départ à zero*: Christian Chamborant's *Signé: Illisible* (1942). It was a more lavish production and its plot is more elaborate. In a provincial village, a number of young men from a good background disappear one after the other, and a series of anonymous letters ending with the words *signé: illisible* (signature: illegible) are sent to wealthy inhabitants — including a "castrated father," played by Marcel Vallée, who collects rare stamps and plays with toy soldiers. The letters demand that the recipients carry out acts of social solidarity, such as donating hoarded black market food supplies to those in need. Soon the anonymous "rascals" make more sweeping demands: "The young men will be released when something has changed!"

The mystery is finally solved by Carlier (André Luguet), a film director looking for locations who winds up playing detective because he has been mistaken for a police inspector from Paris. But the audience has been on the side of the kidnappers ever since the camera followed one of the young village girls — the cast is largely female and the movie has no romantic male lead — as she enters a ruined castle where a whole "mafia" of women are holding the missing rich kids hostage. The latter are accused variously of having raped a young woman, abandoned a pregnant girlfriend, and so on. On occasion the young women even keep the braggarts at a healthy distance by threatening them with a truncheon. The intentions of the female conspirators are clearly stated from the outset: they want to change society. And because it is a movie, they win out in the end. The film closes with a shot of them all cycling away, singing, "Something has changed!"

Collaborationist Paris-based critics, who had no scruples about castigating Vichyite- commissioned movies such as *Patricia* or *Le Bal des passants*, apparently liked this lighthearted and briskly directed film with a message. This was not true of Jacques Siclier, who in his memoirs, written more than thirty years after the event, dismissed the movie as an example of "feminism with a Pétain-ist window-dressing" (Siclier 1981: 89). This is an expression worth examining in greater detail. It would seem to refer to the notion that there existed a truly feminist side to Pétainist propaganda (as in this case, "Let's hand over power to women, who will know how to impose a fairer society"). It is true that, with Vichy's blessing, women set up *écoles de cadres féminins* (schools for female executives), based on the model of the Uriage School, which were placed under the same supervising body as Uriage in 1941 and which set out to remedy the failings of the previous regime as regards women's civic and social education. But Vichy's official propaganda and its mouthpieces placed exclusive emphasis on women's traditional roles: *Kinder, Küche, Kirche* (children, cooking, and church). The need for paid female labor, brought about by the shortage of manpower and the occupying forces' war effort, was experienced as a painful contradiction by the traditionalist Catholics who enjoyed power in the Vichy government (Duquesne 1966; Azéma and Bédarida 1992; Muel-Dreyfus 1996/2001).

What *Signé: Illisible* contains is rather a spontaneous expression of "unofficial feminism" on the part of men who, in the context of that period of collapse, disappointment, and a discredited patriarchy, felt the need to create active and demanding female effigies that were unprecedented in the French cinema. This tendency had much in common with Faurism, and even with left-wing Catholicism (see Emmanuel Mounier and *Esprit*), but certainly not with some putative Pétainist version of feminism, in the ultraconservative sense that *Pétainist* is generally understood to mean.

The exceptional feminist message of the film can also probably be traced to the personality of its scriptwriter, Jean Boyer. The previous year, Boyer had scripted and directed *Romance de Paris* (1941), in which Jeannette (Yvette Lebon), after falling into the clutches of a bad guy, gets to know a woman (Claude Marcy) whom we guess to be a prostitute. This woman makes startlingly forthright and clear-headed remarks about the male chauvinism of their two pimps, who are drinking and playing cards at a nearby table.

Another indication that the climate of the period did indeed encourage implicitly or explicitly feminist discourses on the part of many men working in the cinema is provided by the adaptation that Marcel Aymé and Pierre Bost made for Louis Daquin of a now forgotten novel by Pierre Véry, *Madame et le mort* (1943). It tells the story of a young woman from the provinces, Clarisse Coquet (Renée Saint-Cyr), who learns how to rise above her (historically and

Henri Guisol and Renée Saint-Cyr in *Madame et le mort*, 1943. Courtesy of Cinémathèque française.

typically female) status as a passive reader of books (in this case, detective novels). She fantasizes about her favorite author, the famous Armand Le Noir (Henri Guisol), before becoming the active subject of the movie in the place of the male author. As she follows the man she believes to be her idol in Paris, the young woman witnesses his murder — actually that of a man who has been passing himself off as Le Noir. Stunned by the news of his own death, Le Noir decides to go into hiding in a little hotel in the Passy district of Paris. Clarisse tracks him down there and persuades him to let her conduct investigations as she pleases. Le Noir remains holed up in the hotel so he can finish the novel he is working on and write articles on the affair that will provide for them both — and which she of course will sign, since he is "dead."

This unusual confusion of sexual roles seems to have proved such an embarrassment to Pierre Ducrocq, a critic on the collaborationist review *La Gerbe* (May 22, 1943), that he devoted two paragraphs to the movie without once mentioning the name of the female lead or the part she plays — quite an achievement. In his view, the main detective in the film is Armand Le Noir. In fact Le Noir never does more than formulate vague and useless hypotheses, whereas the boundlessly energetic Clarisse, with the help of Daquin's lively directing, does all the investigating and spells out the solution.

But the most interesting exercise here is to compare the adaptation with the original. Although written in the third person, Pierre Véry's novel (published in 1932) is seen through the eyes of Charles de Bruine (Pierre Renoir). His gaze lingers more than once on Clarisse's body, very quickly turning her into a sexual object — something that Daquin's camera never does. The novel is above all the story of how Le Noir seduces Clarisse, and is given added spice more than once by his show of jealousy and by two attempted rapes by the bad guys (which do not feature in the film).

In the film version, Clarisse manages to extricate herself neatly and unaided from every predicament she finds herself in, whereas in the book Véry has the novelist leave his hiding place on several occasions, and more particularly to rescue the young woman from the clutches of an overinsistent young hood. The book lingers much longer on the "trials and tribulations of the creative process" experienced by Le Noir in his hotel room, while Clarisse's adventures are almost peripheral. In the last account, the novel is all about a male fantasy (though not devoid of irony): well-known author tries — successfully — to seduce beautiful female admirer.

It comes as no surprise that this kind of reversal or blurring of sexual roles and the emergence of young women who give impetus to the action (there are no fewer than thirty-five such movies in our corpus) should be found above all in comedies. Other such characters that come to mind are Totte (Suzy Delair), the saucy manicurist in *Défense d'aimer*; Irène (Irène de Trébert), the dynamic self-made singing and dancing star in *Mademoiselle Swing*; and Irène (Micheline Presle), the enterprising "ghost" in *La Nuit fantastique*, among many others. The comic register enabled audiences and critics alike to make light of representations that even today remain opaque for most French males. And yet such female figures were in large numbers on the screens of the Occupation, even if most spectators and critics did not yet possess the conceptual framework that would have enabled them to talk about them, or perhaps even simply to understand them along the lines that seem so obvious to us today in the light of the cinema of the period as a whole.

But women who take control of their destiny also feature in more serious movies. A few months after the shooting of the Daquin film, Renée Saint-Cyr, an unfairly underestimated actress, portrayed a darker yet just as determined version of female autonomy in *Marie-Martine*, a fine movie by Albert Valentin (who worked as a scriptwriter for Jean Grémillon and directed *L'Entraîneuse* from a script by Charles Spaak). In it she plays Marie-Martine, who puts up a passive but indomitable resistance to the depraved Loïc Limousin (Jules Berry) and avenges once and for all the victims of the "evil incestuous

Jean Marais and Simone Renant in *Voyage sans espoir*, 1943. Courtesy of Cinémathèque française.

father" Berry played in so many of his movies in the 1930s. Also worth mentioning are the many female leading roles in movies we analyze elsewhere: Odette Joyeux as a young aristocrat who rebels against her family and her class in *Douce*; Danielle Darrieux as Lilian Rander, a dauntless acrobat in *La Fausse maîtresse*; and above all Madeleine Renaud as Thérèse Gauthier, a fearless aviator in *Le Ciel est à vous*.

But there is one film, Christian-Jaque's *Voyage sans espoir* (1943), that deserves special analysis because, of all the movies of the period under discussion, it is the one that most explicitly claims to have its roots in prewar poetic realism — an aesthetics notoriously excoriated by Lucien Rebatet (1941) in an anti-Semitic pamphlet — and because it marks a spectacular break away from the misogyny usually found in such movies. It constitutes in our view one of the most convincing demonstrations of the difference between prewar and Occupation cinema. Adapted by Pierre MacOrlan, Christian-Jaque, and Marc-Gilbert Sauvajon from a story by Georg Klaren and Maurice Krol, *Voyage sans espoir* got a cool reception from the critics, who saw it purely as a poor pastiche. One cannot help suspecting that there is a connection between this general dismissal of the movie and its reversal of sexual roles as compared with the classic films of Marcel Carné and Jacques Prévert, Julien Duvivier, and others.

From the start, we are given all the ingredients of poetic realism: a confined, nocturnal world glistening with rain, where chance meetings are the rule and where Fate lies in wait in the person of the unpredictable police inspector Sorbier (Louis Salou), who humorously fills in the gaps in the narrative and foreshadows, in a more lighthearted mode, the character played by Jean Vilar in Carné's *Les Portes de la nuit* (*Gates of the Night*). But we do not get Mireille Balin playing a demimondaine who has nothing much to do (as in *Pépé le Moko* or *Gueule d'amour*), Viviane Romance as a slut beyond redemption (as in *La Belle équipe*), or Michèle Morgan quaking with fear in the hands of an evil guardian (as in *Le Quai des brumes*). Instead we have Simone Renant playing Marie-Ange, a level-headed, competent woman who initiates most of the action, mediating between three men rendered helpless by circumstances, and enjoying a one-night stand with the gentlest of them. At the opposite pole from Jean Gabin and the rough-hewn nobility of his disenchanted proletarian persona, Jean Marais here plays Alain Ginestier, a naïve bank clerk who has made off with the takings and whom Marie-Ange has to protect against the machinations of the evil and cowardly Pierre Gohelle (Paul Bernard). It is this character, a direct descendant of Pierre Brasseur's role in *Le Quai des brumes*, who forms the link between the two movies and the two cinematographic periods. But the element that has disconcerted critics past and present is the lack of differentiation between the three male antagonists, who all bear the stamp of "the feminine" (including the great Lucien Coëdel as a bashful lover who has lost all hope). The standoff between Jean Gabin and Jules Berry was more clear-cut!

In the course of the dangerous game she chooses to play out of love, Marie-Ange loses her life. But the movie's final scene resolves the apparently hybrid nature of the work by combining the female sacrifice that was de rigueur in Vichyite films in the strictest sense with the nihilist irony of poetic realism. As Ginestier is about to get on an early train to Paris at Marie-Ange's instigation in order to return the money he has stolen, he enjoys a final kiss from his sweetheart, who conceals from him the fact that she has just been fatally wounded by Gohelle. The death of this female Gabin crystallizes the moving heroism that the male imaginary of the French cinema attributed to women during the four wartime years.

𝒜

CHAPTER 7

The Zazou *Film*

A DISSIDENT STYLE DURING THE OCCUPATION

FROM AUGUST 1940 on, the Germans banned all English-speaking movies in the occupied zone. The French found themselves cut off for five years from a film culture that accounted for 50 percent of all movies released before the war. One of the side effects of this shortage was doubtless the extraordinary vogue for *le swing*, that is, jazz stripped of its prewar arrangements. Django Reinhardt became its leading figure when the Hot Club de France organized the first Festival of French Jazz at the Salle Gaveau in December 1940.

It was Johnny Hess, Charles Trenet's first partner, who coined the word *zazou* (zoot-suiter) in a 1939 song entitled "Je suis swing," which he adapted from a song by the American jazz singer Cab Calloway. But it was the Occupation that turned zazou into a social phenomenon, or at least a rallying cry for some urban youth, which prompted an angry response from Vichy and above all from the collaborationist press (Loiseau 1977; Rioux 1987). For while the zazous were to be found in a limited age bracket (between eighteen and twenty-five), their refusal to be ideologically indoctrinated was broadcast loud and clear:

> The men wear a baggy jacket that flaps against their thighs, tight trousers tucked into big unpolished shoes and a tie made of canvas or coarse wool. But as that is not enough to distinguish them from many other Parisians, they use salad oil, in the absence of grease, to give a shine to their rather

overlong hair, which hangs down over a soft collar held in place in front by a horizontal pin. Their attire is almost always completed by a fur-lined jacket which they are most reluctant to take off, and which they willingly continue to wear when wet, since they only really come into their own in the rain: one of the rites dear to them consists in delightedly dragging their feet in water and muddying their trousers, and exposing their thick, greasy hair to rain-showers. As for the women, they use animal skins to conceal their polo-neck jumpers and very short pleated skirts; their ex-aggeratedly square shoulders are in contrast to the men, who let theirs slope; long curls of hair spill down over their necks; their stockings are laddered and their shoes flat-soled and heavy; they are armed with large umbrellas, which remain obstinately unopened whatever the weather. (*L'Illustration*, March 23, 1943)

The zazous could also be distinguished by their marked penchant for entertainment of all kinds, particularly dancing (preferably imported from the United States). The "dancing schools" that mushroomed everywhere got around the ban on dance halls and balls.

Jazz musicians and club owners feared that the unruly zazous could get them into trouble, while at the same time feeling nothing but contempt for their musical ignorance. Accordingly, they very soon rejected these rebellious youngsters, who used music as an excuse to express their rejection of the moral order and their love of the United States. From the summer of 1942 on, hounded by the Vichyite and German police who conscripted them to work in Germany in the Compulsory Labor Service scheme, the zazous began to adopt a lower profile. But the zazou spirit lived on until the end of the Occupation. Its legacy was perpetuated after the war by Boris Vian and Juliette Gréco in the cellars of Saint-Germain-des-Prés.

According to the collaborationist press, the zazou or "swing" spirit (the two terms were used synonymously) boiled down to this: "Not taking anything seriously, not doing anything the way other people do, not doing anything in general, spending a lot of time in bars, being ignorant, making dull and meaningless remarks, being immoral, being incapable of fixing a demarcation line [*sic*] between what one can do and what one must not do, having no respect for the family, denying love, loving nothing but money, above all looking disillusioned, and on top of all that trying to pass oneself off as an intelligent 'type'" (Yves Ranc, *L'Oeuvre*, March 4, 1942).

This portrait, which would be hilarious in another context, suggests that offhandedness and derision were becoming weapons of resistance against the Zeitgeist, against both Vichyite moralism and fascist dragooning. And to counter the aggressive and murderous virility of the collaborationist militia, the zazous used their way of dressing and talking (men adopting a falsetto voice, women using a deep voice) as a provocative way of blurring sexual codes. That this was disturbing to many was clear from the way militia tracked down young zazou men and shaved their heads. The same hounding of deviancy can be seen in the banning of a production of Jean Racine's *Andromaque* staged by Jean Marais. Marais was accused in the collaborationist press "of offering too blatant a representation of depraved and shamefully emasculated young *zazous*. This is the most egregious example of decadent emasculation that one can find, and that such an individual should have tackled one of our most immortal masterpieces and twisted its meaning thus is an act of vandalism" (*La Francisque*, February 1944). Since the relationship between Marais and Jean Cocteau was already notorious at the time, this lumping together of homosexuality and the zazou spirit went without saying in circles and during a period where any deviation from sexual normality was seen as a threat.

Apart from these small groups of marginal youngsters, the two main vehicles of the zazou spirit were songs and movies. Trenet too was violently attacked by the collaborationist and "right-thinking" press because he adopted not only swing rhythms but the zazou spirit, as expressed in such songs as "Swing Troubadour" and "La Poule zazoue" ("The Zazou Chick"). Each of the four films he shot during the Occupation helped to popularize his lively music and the surrealistic and prettily absurd lyrics that went with it; but the zazou spirit of those films was also provided by other characters, as in *Romance de Paris*, in which Robert Le Vigan, cast as a preposterous patriarch, engages in an extravagant domestic quarrel with his daughter and his wife, sung in the style of a fin-de-siècle operetta.

In *Adieu Léonard*, the Prévert brothers, Jacques and Pierre, parody a *soirée poétique* in the home of Bernardine Léonard (Denise Grey), a patron of the arts, where her "great friend" recites a poem with the delicately lyrical refrain "Sonnez, sonnez, cloches de Corneville" (Ring, ring, the bells of Cuckoldsville) in the presence of her cuckolded husband Félicien (Carette), who unintentionally interrupts the session when his cigarette explodes. (He runs a joke and novelty shop.)

But while the cinema of the Occupation is more "serious" overall than prewar cinema, a trend of lighthearted derision can be detected in a certain number of films, all held in contempt by critics past and present. And this is by no means a case of reconstruction after the event: *Pension Jonas, Adieu Léonard,* and *Mademoiselle Swing* undoubtedly became cult movies for the zazous (Loiseau 1977: 105).

What strikes one most today about Pierre Caron's *Pension Jonas* (1941), apart from its undeniably shoestring budget (it was initially banned by the censors for "idiocy," then discreetly released), are its abrupt changes of tone. It tells the improbable story of a tramp called Barnabé (Pierre Larquey) who has set up home in the belly of a stuffed whale in the Natural History Museum, while Professor Tipule (Alfred Pasquali) combs the streets of Paris in search of a hippopotamus that has escaped from the zoo. Yet the fact that Pierre Véry and Roger Ferdinand worked on the adaptation and dialogue of the movie (though they removed their names from the credits) would suggest that *Pension Jonas* is something more than a mere shoestring farce. All the patriarchal figures are equally grotesque, from the museum's director, dismissed because he lost the hippopotamus, to Professor Tipule, obsessed with his thousand-year-old Tibetan egg, which explodes in front of a gathering of notables and society ladies, while two lovers strike up a lighthearted song and a gang of remarkably incompetent thieves desperately tries to track down the egg. We are somewhere between the Prévert brothers and the Marx brothers. And although there is no denying that the movie's furious pace owes something to vaudeville, there is an extra ingredient—the spirit of the Surrealists' *Cadavre exquis*, a parlor game similar to Consequences—which sets it very clearly apart from the spirit of, say, Eugène Labiche's theater, as it does from the various knockabout farces that Fernandel continued imperturbably to act in.

Adieu Léonard, which displays the same zany and cheeky spirit, pits a merry bunch of unconventional characters against the established order in a story that unfolds without the slightest regard for the codes of narrative or genre. Charles Trenet, who plays the central character, Ludovic Malvoisin, appears only in the second part of the movie. His casting as an appealing "happy fool" confirms the fact that the milieux of swing and the heirs of Surrealism joined forces to resist indoctrination by Vichy and Berlin.

Whether in movies adapted from operettas, such as Richard Pottier's *Défense d'aimer* (1942), or in musicals that combine highbrow, folk, and light music in burlesque fashion, such as Pottier's *Mademoiselle Swing* (1941) and René Lefèvre's *Opéra-musette* (1941), the zazou style uses music to ridicule seriousness. In *Opéra-musette*, Saturnin Fabre plays Monsieur Honoré, the composer of *Une Fille d'Amaltète*, a delightful parody of turn-of-the-century modernist French opera. During rehearsals, in which all the villagers take part, the cellist Marga (Gilles Margaritis) smashes with every stroke of his bow anything that comes within reach—which he immediately offers to repair, naturally causing even more irreparable damage. Swing also serves to ridicule the folk music that was so dear to Vichy; in Pierre Caron's *Ne bougez plus* (1941), Paul Meurisse and Annie France sing the following lyrics to a swing tune:

> I, who am not zazou,
> No, no, no, I'm not swing,
> I greatly prefer the old tunes from home.

And in *Mademoiselle Swing* there is a very swinging concert in which the musicians run the gamut of all the French provinces, parodying their folk music, then transforming it with jazzy rhythms. Then the members of the Club Swing d'Angoulême (all of them young women) go on stage and sing a swing version of the traditional *Mon père m'a donné un mari*. This episode is practically a documentary of Johnny Hess's tours.

Mademoiselle Swing, which seems to us today to be a perfectly harmless French-style musical, was due to come out in April 1942, at the height of the virulent anti-zazou press campaign, but its release was cancelled by the German censors, who regarded the words "One must defy destiny!," sung by Irène de Trébert, as a provocation. She took steps to have the decision reversed, and two months later the movie was released. It got a very favorable reception, not just in young zazou circles but also from such critics as Jacques Audiberti, who wrote in *Comoedia* (no. 53, 1942), "Only the cinema can afford to bring out a brilliant and sensational movie like *Mademoiselle Swing* at a time when swing is in bad odor!"

Another characteristic of zazou films is the way they flout realist conventions, using actors who rely systematically on either understatement or hyperbole: Paul Meurisse made a brilliant debut in *Défense d'aimer* playing the totally spineless son of an overexcited businessman, Gavard (Gabriello), "the fastest talker in the world." The zazou style also displays a total indifference to the conventions of genre, whatever they may be. Deliberately heterogeneous, it merrily combines musical comedy (preferably swing), chase sequences, ham acting, and every conceivable form of satire, parody, and pastiche.

The same spirit seems to have rubbed off on a wide range of filmmakers. It can be detected, for instance, in Robert Desnos and Roland Tual's *Bonsoir Mesdames, bonsoir Messieurs* (1943), with dialogue written under a pseudonym by Henri Jeanson. It is a zany satire of the radio world, in which Jean Parédès sings ditties under the name of the "tenor with no voice," whom the scenario contrasts with the great Jacques Jansen as a tenor with a voice.

Suzy Delair (drinking) and Paul Meurisse (standing) in *Défense d'aimer*, 1942. Courtesy of Cinémathèque française.

But quite apart from this penchant for screwball comedy, zazou movies opt resolutely for an attitude that ridicules patriarchy. All the young male leads can be defined as "gentle male" figures who do everything they can to escape the patriarchal straitjacket and confrontation with the law, just as the zazous refused to confront the totalitarian regime that was oppressing France, preferring instead to take refuge in "futile" areas (music, dance, café life, clothes) raised to the status of "true values," and to ridicule imposed values.

The male leads in zazou movies do not derive their attractiveness from the traditional attributes of virility. On the contrary, they delight in letting their female partner lead them by the nose. Pierre Dornier (Pierre Mingand), a swing singer in *Mademoiselle Swing*, very soon allows himself to be swept along in the wake of his brilliant admirer, Irène Dumontier (Irène de Trébert), singer, tap dancer, and composer rolled into one. Maxime Gavard (Paul Meurisse), in *Défense d'aimer*, is roused from his lethargy by the energetic Totte (Suzy Delair), who has decided to "teach him how to live." (There is a delightfully funny scene of working-class conviviality in a railway carriage, where Gavard, a rich daddy's boy, almost faints at the sight of Totte refusing to stand on ceremony and joining her genial fellow passengers in partaking of Camembert cheese, dry sausage, a hard-boiled egg, and some cheap red wine drunk straight from the bottle.) In *Ne bougez plus*, the same Meurisse, playing an absent-minded photographer working for Le Studio d'Art, run by one Farfadou (Guillaume de Sax), is seduced by Geneviève (Annie France), the dynamic manager of the studio, who ends up persuading him to join her in a fast and furious jive session. René Lefèvre, a scriptwriter, dialogue writer, and director of *Opéramusette*, also appeared in the film in the role of Lampluche, an accordionist who unwittingly usurps the identity of a highbrow composer. Lampluche spends most of the time worrying about whether Jeanne (Paulette Dubost) is really in love with him. She has great difficulty in convincing him in the end that "it is he she wants" and not the real composer Leroy (Maurice Teynac), a caricature of a stylish but straitlaced ladies' man. In *Bonsoir Mesdames, bonsoir Messieurs*, François Périer gives a delightful performance as Dominique Verdelet, a man as shy with women as he is audacious in his job as a radio journalist. His friend Sullivan (Carette) has to contrive a very complicated scenario, complete with country picnics and a scene of put-on jealousy that enables Dominique to end up romping in the hay with the beautiful Gaby Sylvia.

In all these movies, the "good father" figures (played by Pierre Larquey, Carette, and Saturnin Fabre, for example) rival each other in their permissiveness and their understanding of the younger generation; in *Ne bougez plus*, playing a caricature of a king on the run, Fabre systematically decorates everyone he meets, kissing them on the mouth in a ritual that makes a mockery of Marshal Pétain's ceremonious awards of medals. As for the small number of "strict fathers," they are irreparably ridiculed and/or neutralized (Farfadou in *Ne bougez plus*, Gabriello in *Défense d'aimer*).

Finally, alongside this gentle but systematic mockery of gender relations and power figures, the zazou movies were virtually alone during the Occupation in continuing to espouse populism. In view of the fact that the prewar period, and in particular the Popular Front, which was accused of having contaminated the French people with its "spirit of pleasure," was in bad odor under Vichy, it was not a good idea to resuscitate that image of the people as a "good object" that was largely responsible for the charm of poetic realism. Much preferred was the Pétainist viewpoint, which abandoned the very idea of social class in favor of the great family formed by the employer and his workers (*Le Val d'Enfer, Au Bonheur des Dames*) and the landed gentry and their peasants (*Haut-le-vent*). Alternatively all social classes were treated with the same condescending contempt (*Le Voile bleu, Le Corbeau, L'Escalier sans fin*), which boiled down to the same thing.

On the other hand, the populist spirit can be found in zazou movies, as, for example, in the convivial scene in *Défense d'aimer* where passengers in a train compartment share their picnic, or in the character played by Suzy Delair in the same film, a humble manicurist at Le Grand Hôtel so resourceful that she manages not only to teach the son of the house the facts of life, but to impose herself as the brains behind Daddy's company. Populism is also shown in a favorable light in *Opéra-musette*, the film by René Lefèvre that celebrates the delights of open-air restaurants where everyone dances to the sound of the accordion (an explicit nod in the direction of *La Belle équipe*).

The main argument of *Ne bougez plus* (the plot of which is impossible to recount) centers on some tramps who are believed to be kings, and vice versa, without the spectator's ever being able to work out who is who. The main thing is that the whole team working for Le Studio d'Art (a hilarious parody of Studio Harcourt in Paris), after being sucked into the wake of the tramp-cum-king, has a great time thanks to a reversal of all normal hierarchies (an iconoclastic motif if ever there was one, at a time when hierarchies of all kinds were religiously respected). In *Bonsoir Mesdames, bonsoir Messieurs*, Sullivan (Carette), an honest local photographer who loves outings in the country and pretty girls, is himself a tribute to Jean Renoir. As for Pierre Prévert's *Adieu Léonard* (1943), the Prévert brothers' contribution almost naturally implies the presence of populism. This last characteristic confirms, then, the discreetly but resolutely subversive nature of these apparently lightweight burlesque movies, which Roger Régent (1948), among others, unkindly dismissed at the time as "mindless."

The zazou spirit can also be detected in certain movies that obey the codes of previous eras, in particular in boulevard comedies. René Jayet's film adaptation of the play *Vingt-cinq ans de bonheur* (1943) features a couple of old-fashioned spinsters, Aunt Béatrice and Aunt Lucie (Jeanne Fusier-Gir and Marcelle Monthil), who indulge in delightful fantasies about the poetic talents of their nephew André (André Reybaz), to the point of ardently declaiming a poem by Victor Hugo which the young man, under pressure from his aunts to write, has passed off as his own. In another addition to the original play, the birthday celebrations of the mistress of the house are disrupted by the sudden appearance of five enormous Doberman pinschers in succession, one of them made of plaster (all the guests having plumped for the same birthday present), while one of the guests, Blondel (Gabriello), desperately tries to read out his congratulatory poem. The same Blondel, a bank manager, spends the rest of the movie bemoaning the demise of his female cat, whose empty basket he takes to the office. This example is of particular interest because Germaine

Lefrancq's original play, which was premiered in 1941 and had a successful run until 1943, contained none of these zazou features. One may perhaps legitimately speculate that it was Jean-Paul Le Chanois, coauthor with Lefrancq of the adaptation, who injected this ingredient into the movie at a time when he was a member of the Communist Resistance. Gabriello, who may legitimately be described during this period as a zazou actor, infects Continental's very serious adaptations of Georges Simenon—*Picpus*, *Cécile est morte*, and *Les Caves du Majestic* (*Majestic Hotel Cellars*)—by turning Lucas, the sidekick of Inspector Maigret (Albert Préjean), into a good-natured bumbling idiot that foreshadows "Béru" (Bérurier), who assists Superintendent San-Antonio in Frédéric Dard's detective novels.

Even Pétainist films were sometimes infected by the insidious zazou bug. In André Zwoboda's *Une étoile au soleil* (*A Star to the Sun*, 1942), a rather feeble comedy advocating a return to the land, we are suddenly treated to a scene that ridicules that edifying theme: its central character is Pierre Merlerault (Jean Davy), an aristocrat who devotes his energies to the land while his father, Adalbert (Léon Walter), leads a life of debauchery in Paris. Pierre brings his noble progenitor back to his ancestral estate in the hope of getting him to espouse Pétainist values. But just as we begin to think that the father has been won over, we see him turn up disguised as a farcical peasant, talking in a jargon that could have come straight out of a Molière comedy and pretending to behave like a Neanderthal. Explaining that they are indeed returning to the land, the father and his accomplice then have a good laugh in the presence of Pierre, who is furious at being ridiculed.

There are plenty of other such examples, but even more surprisingly we find traces of that lighthearted mockery in auteurs like Marcel L'Herbier, who was well known for his seriousness and his elevated conception of culture despite having often yielded to commercial pressures since the arrival of talking pictures. His *La Nuit fantastique* (1941) is no potboiler, and the wonderment that gripped audiences and critics alike during the summer of 1942 was a response to a "veritable cinematographic work," as Roger Régent (1948) pointed out. But those who attribute the style and qualities of the film to the personal stamp of its scriptwriters (Louis Chavance, who was responsible for the scenario, and Henri Jeanson, who wrote the dialogue while in hiding) are probably missing the element that connects this charming reverie with its period, namely the zazou spirit. It can be detected from the start in the presence of an outlandish character who literally sleeps on his feet while his mistress cheats on him with a kind of Russian con man. A little later on, Denis (Fernand Gravey) follows Irène (Micheline Presle), the beautiful woman he has dreamed of (is she a real or imaginary character?), into a cheap restaurant, where her father, Thalès (Saturnin Fabre yet again), and her fiancé, Cadet (Jean Parédès, the future "tenor without a voice" of *Bonsoir Mesdames, bonsoir Messieurs*), are waiting for her. There ensues a totally zany exchange of dialogue in which each character makes the most preposterous remarks in a totally natural way. In the movie as a whole, everything that seems to be part of Denis's supposed dream is informed by the picaresque zazou spirit which flouts plausibility and prefers players whose acting is the least "natural," like the celebrated Fabre, who appears in almost all such movies.

Fabre, a brilliant supporting actor in prewar movies whose charisma and voice left their stamp on Julien Duvivier's *Pépé le Moko* (1936) and Henri Decoin's *Battement de coeur* (1939), became a master of deadpan humor during the Occupation. He could lend papal solemnity to the most incongruous of remarks, as in his celebrated "Hold your candle . . . upright!" in Albert Valentin's *Marie-Martine*, words that, in the role of Uncle Parpain, he barks three times at his wretched nephew, Maurice (Bernard Blier), who has come to ask him for advice on how to conduct his love life.

The fact that the zazou spirit can be found even in serious genres at the opposite pole only confirms the importance of the trend, which remains little known because it belongs to a marginal culture, a culture of pastiche and tongue-in-cheek humor. Another reason the phenomenon has been underestimated is probably because of the oblique way it took part in resistance against Nazi-Vichyite oppression. While the collaborationists understood perfectly well the implications of the zazou spirit, it prompted reservations among "true" Resistants, who saw it not as a nonconformist student response but "as a false front for social maladjustment, idleness and various types of black-market trafficking on the part of privileged youths hanging out on the Champs-Elysées with no financial problems" (Ellenstein 1980: 142). In the view of the film critic and novelist Jean-Louis Bory, who had been a zazou himself, "*Zazouisme* was a form of dandyism; the 20th-century dandy reacts against preaching; he opposes the established order through provocation" (quoted in Loiseau 1977: 115).

The manifestations of the zazou spirit took the form of a cultural trend rather than that of a political movement during a period long perceived in purely political terms, and its neglect by historians is a further indication of the inadequacy of this traditional approach to the Occupation. Besides, the zazou movement carried the seeds of one of the decisive postwar conflicts, one that would put generations on a collision course.

A Woman Faced with Her Desire

THE FRENCH CINEMA from 1940 to 1944 was often imbued with Pétainism, even in its apparently paradoxical form involving an idealization of female figures. But it also evinced an element that, compared with the 1930s, was as novel as it was unexpected in the climate of the Occupation: the evocation of female desire, treated as such and in a serious manner, without any anxiety or hostility. Such a phenomenon would alone suffice to indicate the profoundly contradictory nature of the period. True, the misogynistic view of female desire had not disappeared, but it is to be found above all in boulevard movies or in the most mediocre examples of Pétainist propaganda, such as Jean Boyer's *La Bonne étoile* (1942), an ersatz version of a typical Marcel Pagnol movie, in which Mireille (Janine Darcey) becomes infatuated with a hood, Maurice (Andrex), before seeking consolation in the arms of Auguste (Fernandel).

Even boulevard cinema seems to have adjusted willy-nilly to the new trend. Pierre-Jean Ducis's *L'Etrange Suzy* (*Strange Suzy*, 1941) and Georges Lacombe's *Florence est folle* (1944) mark a similar attempt to take into account this new image of a woman who tries to express her desire. In both films, a bourgeois wife frustrated for too long by the straitjacket of marriage fakes madness in the hope of getting her husband to behave more lovingly. The madness of Suzy (Suzy Prim) in *L'Etrange Suzy* and Lucile (Annie Ducaux) in *Florence est folle* takes the form of their replacing their bourgeois reserve with the sexual aggressiveness of a courtesan in order to make their husbands realize that they (still) feel like making love. Each couple ends up by coming together again and integrating that particular dimension, which the husband in a boulevard play or film would traditionally seek away from home. The new element is that it is the woman alone who takes the initiative. Henri (Albert Préjean) in *L'Etrange Suzy* and Jérôme (André Luguet) in *Florence est folle* are initially horrified by the change they see in their wives but end up getting the message and going along with it.

In boulevard such issues as desire can be treated only in this lighthearted way and without undermining male power. In the populist and naturalist tradition, on the other hand, female desire, which is dangerous when embodied in the character of the slut, of which poetic realism offered so many variants, undergoes a more thoroughgoing change. Georgia (Germaine Montero) in Pierre Billon's *Le Soleil a toujours raison* (1941) and Marthe in Maurice Tourneur's *Le Val d'enfer* (1943) react against an oppressive matrimonial situation. Their desire is frustrated by authoritarian patriarchs (the characters played by Charles Vanel and Gabriel Gabrio, respectively), forcing them to seek an outlet elsewhere, not always successfully. In Jacques Prévert's scenario for *Le Soleil a toujours raison*, Georgia, after failing to seduce Tonio (Tino Rossi), manages to leave her jealous old husband thanks to Gabriel, a peddler (Pierre Brasseur); the pregnant Marthe, on the other hand, is abandoned by her lover and ends up being killed by her husband's avenging "double." As a result, the alluring slut is turned into a victim of patriarchal oppression. Tourneur's film, which was produced by Continental, is more ambiguous than the Prévert script directed by Billon; Marthe's "accidental" death is also made out to be the punishment of an unfaithful wife and facilitates a happy ending that brings together three generations of the family in a paradoxically Pétainist style for a movie produced by the Germans.

The issue of guilt and redemption that is characteristic of this period also informs another Continental-produced movie, André Cayatte's *Le Dernier sou* (1943): it describes the catharsis of Marcelle Levasseur (Ginette Leclerc), a run-of-the-mill slut who turns into a tragic figure so deeply in love that she sacrifices her life for a young sportsman, Pierre Durban (Gilbert Gil), who does not even love her. But the tragedy is clearly tied in with the oppression of women by the patriarchy: Marcelle is doubly exploited by her boss, Stéfani (Noël Roquevert), who sleeps with her and uses her sexuality to ensnare the suckers he swindles; she is forced to continue that kind of work to protect Perrin (René Génin), an irresponsible grandfather who has compromised himself. In the eyes of the young sportsman she falls for, she will never be anything other than an easy lay.

This questioning of the stereotypes of female desire takes an unusual form in Albert Valentin's curious film, *A la belle frégate* (1942), a kind of parodic remake of *La Belle équipe*, in which René Dary and René Lefèvre, respectively, take on the roles played by Jean Gabin and Charles Vanel in the earlier work. The movie engineers a change of perspective in favor of the female lead, played by Michèle Alfa (the total antithesis of Viviane Romance). The narrative hinges not on the search for work by a group of unemployed pals but on the female conquests of some sailors on a spree. Pierre (Carette), a mute (Aimos), and Félix (Azaïs) try to outdo René (Dary) in male chauvinist piggery. Whereas in *La Belle équipe* spectators could unhesitatingly identify with the handsome Gabin and reserve their pity for the cuckolded husband (Vanel), Valentin's movie deliberately places a dividing line between the spectators' identification with the nice guy, Jean (Lefèvre), and with René the womanizer, a small-time Casanova, a wimp puffed up with virile vanity. In the film's central episode, having attempted in their different ways to seduce Yvonne (Alfa), the two pals demand that she choose between them: Jean has given her a stuffed animal, while René has strutted his stuff in a boxing ring. From the moment the amiable Yvonne opts for the ladies' man, spectators have an unavoidable feeling of uneasiness—all the more because the film delights in recounting what follows solely from the point of view of Jean, the genial loser, who tries to see the woman again at the following port of call, whereas his rival prefers to go on a pub crawl with his chums. We have here the favorite settings and situations to be found in poetic realism (a port, sailors' bars, and a melancholy pretty woman whom an unscrupulous guardian tries to lure into his clutches), here reduced to their sordid reality, without the film's ever lapsing into the self-indulgent doom and gloom of postwar movies (compare *Dédée d'Anvers* [*Dedee* or *Woman of Antwerp*]).

The persistent misogyny of prewar poetic realism and Gabin's ambivalence as a male figure (Gauteur and Vincendeau 1993) are hinted at in this movie, which seems to display in a darkly uncomfortable mode the unspoken element of that left-wing tendency in the French cinema. The happy ending that is tacked on to the rest of the movie—Jean manages (with difficulty) to persuade René to go and find Yvonne—cannot disguise the fact that the young woman's object of desire is René, who of the two men is the least appreciative. This is a dark but rather modern notion of desire based on the psychoanalytic concept of *lack*: she cannot desire Jean precisely because he is at her feet. But far from being a new Gabin (Siclier 1981), Dary here comes across on the contrary as a caricature of him; once the charisma is lacking, the machismo is there for all to see, though it does not put off female desire.

Apart from this kind of settling of accounts with prewar myths, the most remarkable Occupation movies make the narrative itself hinge on female desire, in a context of tragedy or melodrama, and rarely opt for a comfortable happy ending. Madeleine Renaud's roles in Georges Lacombe's *L'Escalier sans fin* (1943) and in two movies by Jean Grémillon, *Lumière d'été* (1942) and *Le Ciel est à vous* (1943), lie at the intersection between two apparently contradictory figures: the woman of duty and the woman of desire.

Emilienne (Renaud), the social worker in Lacombe's movie, is trapped by desire in the course of carrying out her duty; she takes in and cares for Pierre (Pierre Fresnay), a hood she has fallen in love with. But the image she projects of herself (as a virtuous and deserving woman) creates an insuperable barrier that prevents him from expressing his desire for her. Once he has mended his ways, he focuses that desire on her younger sister, Anne (Suzy Carrier).

In *Lumière d'été*, we have yet another active woman who allows herself to be ensnared by passion. Cricri (Renaud), a former ballet star, has followed Patrice (Paul Bernard) to his castle in Haute-Provence, but she takes on the role of innkeeper in order to maintain the fiction of her independence. Patrice gradually falls out of love with this woman who has "sacrificed everything" for him (as she reminds him in vain). She has turned her desire into a duty, transforming herself into an ancient Greek mourner, even to the point of howling like a wounded animal when her lover is killed. From the beginning of the movie, when she is imprisoned in the cage of her veranda like a bird flapping against a window, she can embody for the audience only a negation of the desirable. Michèle (Madeleine Robinson), on the other hand, arouses male desire because, by striding across the mountains of Provence without a thought for her safety, she manifests in a physical way the independence and the thirst for freedom that fascinate the men who come near her.

Finally, *Le Ciel est à vous*, which marks the peak of Renaud's (and Grémillon's) film career, manages, in an unprecedented dialectic, to coax the woman of desire out of the chrysalis of the woman of duty. Initially a model wife, mother, and worker, Thérèse (Renaud) eventually realizes, as a result of a succession of crises that seriously undermine her relationship with her husband, Pierre (Charles Vanel), and her family, that she cannot fulfill herself just by making sure that her entourage conforms to petit bourgeois rules or by work-

Madeleine Renaud and Paul Bernard in *Lumière d'été*, 1942. Courtesy of Cinémathèque française.

ing her fingers to the bone in order to increase the household's income. Her discovery of the pleasures of flying, likened by the mise-en-scène to a veritable orgasm (after landing, as she staggers across the field, the camera shows her ecstatic face, which her husband then kisses), enables her to "lift off" from the world of women's work into the much more dangerous area—more dangerous because uncharted—of the fulfillment of her own desires, which closely combine love and "creation," that is, the transformation of the world (in this case, breaking the record for the longest distance ever flown by a woman). What is interesting about this movie is the fact that it does not try to conceal the contradictions that this causes as far as social and family relations are concerned. The film has a happy ending, but, before Thérèse's final (and unhoped-for) triumph, we observe another—tragic—outcome involving Pierre's returning home alone and being morally lynched by family and neighbors alike, who accuse him of the supposed death of his wife. This brings home to the audience, before the victory celebration that temporarily erases conflict, the thoroughly subversive nature of female desire (Sellier 1989).

This new type of theme was the perfect vehicle for actresses with exceptional dramatic talents such as Madeleine Renaud, Edwige Feuillère, Micheline Presle, Maria Déa, and Jany Holt, who became identified with some of the most powerful movies of the period. Some of these movies have already entered the cinephiles' pantheon, such as *Lumière d'été*, *Le Ciel est à vous*, *Les Visiteurs du soir*, and *Falbalas*; some remain less well-known, such as *Premier bal*, *Félicie Nanteuil*, *Secrets*, *Voyage sans espoir*, *La Fiancée des ténèbres*, and *La Duchesse de Langeais*.

Marc Allégret's *Félicie Nanteuil* (1942), which derives its power from the combined talents of Micheline Presle and Claude Dauphin, was not released until after the end of the war because of the ban on movies featuring the young Dauphin, who in the meantime had joined the Free French Forces. The film admirably reflects the Occupation's climate of guilt. Félicie Nanteuil (Presle) is a young actress far too talented for her own good, whose brilliant performances are in a completely different league from those of the pathetic ham actor Aimé Cavalier (Dauphin), who was her first teacher. She has to resign herself to paying a terrible price for her success. This story, in which Aimé's ghost prevents Félicie from ever sinking into the arms of the man she loves, Robert de Ligny (Louis Jourdan), is in fact all about the guilt felt by a woman who has tried to escape from her Pygmalion and enjoy a completely free love life. At a deeper level it portrays the desire of men to make women feel guilty should they be tempted to live their lives independently. (There were very many such women during that period.) With its brilliant mise-en-scène and direction of actors, the movie leaves the audience feeling uncomfortable because the sole aim of Félicie's display of vitality, charm, and talent would seem to be to enable the spectator to get a sadistic kick out of her being symbolically put to death. To save itself, male power is even prepared to sacrifice one of its representatives. (Aimé commits suicide.) Félicie goes on to have a successful career, but she has to pay for it by renouncing her desire. It is a way of reminding women that they cannot lay claim to everything—professional success and love.

Jacques Becker's *Falbalas* (1944) also portrays this clash between male and female desire, but at a more complex level. On the one hand, we are presented with the predatory mind-set of a leading couturier, Philippe Clarence (Raymond Rouleau), and on the other with the discovery by a bourgeois young woman from the provinces, Micheline Lafaurie (Micheline Presle), of desire and seduction in its most brutal and irresistible form. The most rewarding quality of the movie arises from its refusal to see the clash in moral terms. (In this, it is at the opposite pole from Pétainism.) The inner contradictions of the two central characters are emphasized: Micheline discovers that desire has nothing to do with the way it is described in the sentimental novels that are her staple diet; as for the womanizing Philippe, whose inspiration has been rejuvenated by the freshness of the young woman from the provinces, he cannot understand that she expects him to commit himself more firmly to her than he does to the "emancipated" women he is used to dealing with. And this acceptance by other women of a lop-sided relationship with him is in fact far from total, since one of his former mistresses commits suicide. While Philippe too ends up jumping out of a window in order to escape the intolerable reality of this female "resistance," Micheline has also changed, since she turns down the consolatory comfort she is offered by her fiancé, Daniel Rousseau (Jean Chevrier), preferring instead to face her contradictions on her own.

Edwige Feuillère, who had already before the war specialized in portraying sacrificial women in love, again endures loneliness in the title roles of Maurice Tourneur's *Mam'zelle Bonaparte* (*Miss Bonaparte*, 1941), Jacques de Baroncelli's *La Duchesse de Langeais* (1941), and Léo Joannon's *Lucrèce* (1943). Then at the peak of her stage career, Feuillère could express passion in the noblest and most moving manner and lend her film roles a subtlety that the cinema was chary of allowing actresses to express. Her noble bearing, her superb body, her sparkling or serious gaze, and her sensual mouth enabled her to escape the usual dichotomy governing female roles in the cinema: either protagonist of the drama or sexual object. And Feuillère's maturity lent her roles a charisma rivaled only, at a later date, by those played by Danielle Darrieux in Henri Decoin's *La Vérité sur Bébé Donge* (*The Truth about Bebe Donge* or *The Truth about Our Marriage*, 1952) and Max Ophuls's *Madame de . . .* (*The Earrings of Madame de . . .* , 1953).

Lucrèce is one of the very few films of the period that depicts the emergence of a woman's physical desire for a very young man whom she initially regards as a child. Lucrèce (Edwige Feuillère), a famous actress, makes the acquaintance of a young orphan, François (Jean Mercanton), who pretends to his friends at boarding school that he is her son in order to impress them. Initially furious with him, then affectionately understanding, she ends up taking him on holiday with her to "cure" him of his love for her. It is Lucrèce who gets caught out at her own game, in an atmosphere of summery abandon in the country, whereas François takes a very different course, eventually joining a gaggle of blasé young males. The refusal to allow this "incestuous" story to blossom only confirms the inequality of the sexes in a patriarchal society; the pairing of a middle-aged man with a young woman, which forms the basis of the French cinema in the 1930s, is not allowed to have its equivalent in reverse, at least not visually. And to dispel any doubts in the spectator's mind, in Joannon's movie this taboo is internalized by the woman herself: when Lucrèce realizes that she is about to succumb, after a delightful sequence in the hay, she returns to Paris without seeing François again. As in the case of Félicie Nanteuil, all that remains for her is the solitary satisfaction of her profession.

Mam'zelle Bonaparte tackles a topic that was a burning issue during the Occupation. The story it tells must have had a considerable impact on audiences, whether it brought to mind the risks involved in protecting a Resistant or, on the contrary, the reprisals that could be expected to be taken against any woman suspected of having had a relationship with a German. Under the reign of Napoléon III, Cora Pearl (Edwige Feuillère) jeopardizes her socially desirable situation (that of the "official" mistress of Prince Jérôme Bonaparte [Guillaume de Sax] — hence her nickname) by falling in love with a reprobate, the royalist Philippe de Vaudrey (Raymond Rouleau). Although their passionate relationship comes to a tragic end, it also reveals the wealth of courage and generosity of which this woman is capable once she emerges from her situation of dependence.

The movie's key scene, in which Cora takes on Lucy de Kaula (Monique Joyce) in a fencing duel, derives its effect from a "libertine" transgression of sexual roles, a typical provocation against Vichy on the part of anti-Pétainist circles in Paris. (The film was produced by Continental.) But irrespective of this whiff of scandal, the movie stresses the way a woman's desire can lead to her rejection of a patriarchal relationship and a demand for equality.

Marie Déa in *Les Visiteurs du soir* and Madeleine Sologne in *L'Eternel retour* were (almost) newcomers to the French cinema, and their success only served to highlight the public's new interest in young actresses whose register was dramatic rather than lighthearted. Déa also inspired Christian-Jaque's *Premier bal* and Pierre Blanchar's *Secrets*, two movies whose common denominator, despite their very different starting points, is the way they make the narrative hinge on the feelings of a female character and even make them the substance of the story. Nothing much happens in either film: in *Premier bal*, a young woman falls in love with a man whom her sister marries, leaves, then goes back to; in *Secrets*, a married woman allows herself to be swept off her feet in the course of one summer by her son's young tutor, but the vigilance of an old male friend helps her to "get a grip on herself." Needless to say, Déa, thanks to the naturalness of her acting and the dramatic expressiveness of her face, is primarily responsible for the power of the two movies.

While both stories attempt to give the most accurate portrayal possible of female desire, the fact that they both conclude with a renunciation reveals the limits that this theme encountered. In Christian-Jaque's film, Nicole (Déa), a tomboy with an artistic bent, fails to arouse the desire of a brilliant Parisian doctor, Jean de Lormel (Raymond Rouleau), who on two occasions prefers her flirtatious and flighty sister, Danielle (Gaby Sylvia). This echoes the clear-sighted and bitter portrayal of desire as described in *A la belle frégate*. Once Nicole has decided to write off her love for her brother-in-law, she accepts second best, the shy vet Ernest (François Périer)—whose role echoes that of René Lefèvre in the Valentin film—who has always silently loved Nicole and is docilely waiting for her.

Both the "desirable" man and the "nice" man are seen through Nicole's ironic and affectionate gaze, of the kind that a detached, disillusioned adult woman can focus on an overgrown teenager. It is she in the end who decides on the fate of both men, by sending back to his wife her brother-in-law, whom she believed loved her while her sister went missing, and rejoining her bashful lover with the promise that she will one day live up to his expectations. Once again we find here the tendency of the cinema of the time to turn women into admirable effigies who embody, against their will, all earthly wisdom, even though this particular movie amounts to more than that.

The originality of Blanchar's *Secrets* (1942) is twofold: first, his faithfulness to Turgenev's original play means we are offered a rural family chronicle that had no equivalent at the time, shot on location in an old Provençal mansion; second, the last part of the movie is taken up by a lengthy and literally Surrealist dream narrative, in the course of which Marie-Thérèse (Déa), in merrily iconoclastic fashion, acts out all the desires she has to repress in real life. As a result, the pathos-laden and discreetly moralistic ending cannot be taken seriously, and Marie-Thérèse's angelic gentleness seems to conceal very powerful drives. Even René, the demanding confidant played by Blanchar himself with rather condescending affability, loses much of his aura once we see the young woman, in her dream, brutally murdering him so she can escape with her young lover. From this point on, the movie becomes a critical meditation on all those figures of the perfect woman which the Occupation cinema, concerned as it was to regenerate itself, churned out in large numbers usually without questioning the repressive dimension of such a view.

If Roger Régent is to be believed, the "spectacular burst of light" afforded by Marcel Carné's *Les Visiteurs du soir*, on its release on December 4, 1942, also hinged on the appearance of "pure love" as embodied by Déa, an "unarmed Anne who overcomes the devil with her bare hands" (1948: 92–93). The convincing nature of the character she plays is probably due to the way Jacques

Fernand Ledoux, Marie Déa, and Marcel Herrand in *Les Visiteurs du soir*, 1942. Courtesy of G. R. Aldo, Cinémathèque française.

Prévert and Marcel Carné succeeded in merging the figure of a woman in love with a patriotic effigy, since she has generally been seen as an embodiment of spiritual resistance against the occupying power. Unlike the male characters, her father (Fernand Ledoux) and her fiancé (Marcel Herrand), who remain to the end puppets in the hands of the devilish Dominique (Arletty), Anne is depicted from the beginning of her love affair with Gilles (Alain Cuny) as defying the proprieties and patriarchal authority in the name of love, even to the point of deliberately sacrificing her own life for the salvation of her lover.

Unlike Marguerite in *Faust*, she is not a naïve and gullible young woman unaware of what she risks. Anne is, on the contrary, the most active character in the movie: her love moves mountains. Not only does she hold her own against her formidable enemy, but her lover owes her his salvation. This seminal Occupation film, which uses transparent metaphors to reflect the predicament of a defeated France (Turk 1989), offers a reversal of the balance of power between male and female figures found in prewar movies and sees female characters as a vehicle of hope for (Vichyite) regeneration — but also for national resistance. If the young Anne in *Les Visiteurs du soir* so moved audiences during the dark years, it is because she embodied the latter hope with the same enthusiasm as she expressed her love, thus temporarily demolishing the Pétainist dichotomy between desire and duty.

Jean Delannoy's *L'Eternel retour*, released ten months after *Les Visiteurs du soir*, clearly fits into the same category of "tales and legends of the dark years." Despite the fact that Jean Cocteau's fable reflects the traumatic events of the period less specifically, one cannot fail to be struck by the close similarity between Anne in *Les Visiteurs du soir* and Nathalie (Madeleine Sologne) in *L'Eternel retour*. They both embody tragic women in love who have to confront patriarchal power even unto death in order to remain true to their love. At the end of both movies, the twin images of the androgynous statue in *Les Visiteurs du soir* and the recumbent statues in *L'Eternel retour* give concrete expression to the similarity between the fates of both women.

And yet close comparison reveals subtle differences between them: not only does the blonde Sologne's statuesque beauty give the heroine conceived by Cocteau and Delannoy a clearly more effigy-like aura, but the recumbent position of the statues only serves to underline the greater passivity of their two lovers compared with those created by Carné and Prévert. Nathalie, who in the company of Patrice (Jean Marais) escapes the patriarchal authority of her husband, Marc (Jean Murat), ends up by surrendering to it and allows herself to languish in his vast castle. Traditional misogyny can also be found in the film, as embodied by Gertrude, an overpossessive and castrating mother (Yvonne de Bray), and above all by Nathalie's dark-haired rival and namesake (Junie Astor), a typical example of the woman in love seen as a praying mantis. The narrative, incidentally, highlights the young man's point of view more than the young woman's, unlike the narrative of *Les Visiteurs du soir*.

The very figure of sacrificed love, Sologne never succeeded in transcending that ossified image of herself. Although she played very different roles during this period, *L'Eternel retour* so cemented her image as a recumbent blonde that her career virtually came to an end after that initial triumph. That this should have occurred can perhaps be construed as an indication of the revenge that postwar audiences wreaked upon the female effigies they had set up during the Occupation.

At the opposite extreme from this saintly resignation to one's fate is Jany Holt. An already established actress at the beginning of the Occupation, she personified the ability of female desire to rebel. Initially in the context of dramatic comedy, as in a movie like Serge de Poligny's *Le Baron fantôme* (1942), then in a more serious register, as in André Zwoboda's *Farandole* (1944) and de Poligny's *La Fiancée des ténèbres* (1944), she has to fight to convince either the man she loves or society in general to accept her desire. With her slight yet energetic build, pointed face, high cheekbones, and dark, piercing eyes, she confronts reality with indomitable lucidity. While in de Poligny's two films her determined personality is mellowed by a kind of poetic aura, the tragic violence of the episode in *Farandole* that centers on her character (she plays a woman in love who is accused of murdering her lover's wife) comes as a surprise in an otherwise more boulevard context. The austerity of the mise-en-scène of this sequence only enhances the passion that enables her to transcend the ordinariness of her social condition.

Women's ability to face up to adversity is also emphasized in the first sequence of *Le Baron fantôme*, where the Comtesse de Saint Helie (Gabrielle Dorziat) fearlessly confronts the elements (rain, wind, a forest at nightfall) in order to take over the derelict castle that used to belong to her uncle, who has just disappeared into the depths of the ruin. The extremely funny accumulation of all the clichés of fantastic cinema only highlights the fearlessness of the character, a widow accompanied by two little girls. Ten years later, a similarly fearless Anne (Jany Holt), the foster sister who acts as a lady's companion to Elfy (Odette Joyeux), explores the ruins of the old castle. But her audacity can chiefly be gauged from the way she defends her love for Hervé (Alain Cuny), the touchy gamekeeper who turns out to be heir to the castle. Following an almost dreamlike sequence where Hervé, while sleepwalking, carries Anne off in his arms to the highest point of the castle grounds, like some Prince Charming, she persistently tries to make him aware of her love for him, whereas he remains fascinated by the pretty (and flighty) Elfy. Only rarely has the cinema offered us, without the slightest trace of misogyny, a female character so determined to fulfill her sexual desire.

The inability to choose between several objects of desire that is already characteristic of the male lead in *Le Baron fantôme* acquires a more dramatic flavor in *La Fiancée des ténèbres* (also directed by de Poligny). In it Roland Samblaca (Pierre Richard-Willm), a married man with a family and a composer whose inspiration has dried up, falls in love with Sylvie (Jany Holt), a mysterious young woman he finds wandering along the ramparts of an ancient Albigensian castle. Quite apart from the story's mystical-cum-historical window dressing, which the director seems to take with a grain of salt, the film describes various attempts by men to appropriate the young woman irrespective of her own wishes; she is torn between an old man, Monsieur Toulzac (Edouard Delmont), who believes her to be the repository of the forbidden Albigensian religion, and Samblaca, who hopes she will rekindle his musical inspiration, which burned itself out in the social whirl of Paris. Both men behave with the same thoughtless selfishness. With her tortured face framed in black, Sylvie sails through the film like some apparition whom men dispose of after use. At the end of the movie, the determined figure of the young woman strides resolutely away, turning her back on both the castle, a metaphor for an archaic and death-dealing patriarchy, and the composer, an image of male comfort surrounded by his nuclear family. It is a wrench for her to leave, but also a liberation.

Very few directors of this period attempted to depict a scene of physical lovemaking. That kind of scene, a taboo in the Pétainists' book, did not square with the much more widespread tendency of Occupation films to create women as effigies. True, the more personal directors paid little attention to the prevailing prudish atmosphere; several major films, while not necessarily renewing the codification of such scenes, allude fairly explicitly to physical desire, as in *Le Corbeau, Douce, Félicie Nanteuil, L'Eternel retour, Falbalas,* and *Les Enfants du paradis.* On the other hand, ellipsis is taken to absurd lengths in a number of Pétainist movies, such as Léon Poirier's *Jeannou* (1943), in which the young female lead can be seen to be pregnant when she returns to her father without any previous allusion to sexual relations more explicit than a kissing of hands.

The large number of unmarried mothers is matched only by the scarcity of love scenes, most often because the film begins when the "sin of the flesh" has already been committed, as in Abel Gance's *Vénus aveugle* (1940) and Maurice Tourneur's *Péchés de jeunesse* (1941). When sexual relations do take place between two characters in the course of the narrative, there is no visual allusion to them, as in Jean Delannoy's *Fièvres* (1941) and Guillaume Radot's *Le Bal des passants* (1943). In other instances, a metaphor emphasizes the sordid aspect of the act, such as the shot of a sign saying "Hotel" in André Cayatte's *Le Dernier sou* (1943) immediately after Pierre (Gilbert Gil) and Marcelle (Ginette Leclerc) kiss. In that context, the very explicit representation of the rape that the central character of Jean Delannoy's *Pontcarral, colonel d'Empire* (1942) forces his wife to endure just before he sets off to fight a duel with her lover seems to be a pleasing transgression of the prevailing prudishness, but it also points to the essential purpose of that scene: in order to be able to fight, the husband first needs to employ violence in order to reconstruct his manhood, which his wife scorned by locking him out of her bedroom on their wedding night and by cheating on him openly and publicly.

As for de Poligny, he portrays love scenes in a dreamlike register where ellipsis is replaced by metaphor; thus the still unconscious love for Sylvie (Janu Holt) experienced by Hervé (played by the young Alain Cuny) in *Le Baron fantôme* is expressed in the scene where, when sleepwalking, he goes to fetch the young woman from her bed and carries her slowly through the grounds, crossing the river on a floating tree trunk with her white figure in his arms, up to the top of the ruined castle — his domain — where he lays her down as though on an altar. In *La Fiancée des ténèbres*, the two lovers emerge from the depths of a cave into an enchanted landscape where a house awaits them; they lie down in front of the open fire like recumbent statues and whisper to each other until they fall asleep. The young woman is the first to wake up, and she leaves. These are poetic images of love with which the director tries to transcend the Judeo-Christian dichotomy between the soul and the body, at a time when it was officially promoted.

This overview of how female desire expressed itself in Occupation cinema is a far cry from the misogynistic moralism of Pétainist ideology. But there can be little doubt that the not always very conscious perception by filmmakers of the Defeat and the Occupation as a failure of the patriarchy formed the breeding ground for the new images of women as disembodied effigies one moment and desiring bodies the next, and sometimes even both at the same time — an ambivalence that may be seen as emblematic of the period.

CHAPTER 9
Gentle Male Figures and New Fathers

ALAIN CUNY'S SWEET smile in *Les Visiteurs du soir* (1942) and the sad expression of the clown-like figure immortalized by Jean-Louis Barrault in *Les Enfants du paradis* (1944–45) were strongly influenced by Marcel Carné's homosexuality, but they could also be seen to symbolize the most characteristic male figure of French Occupation cinema: the gentle male. A mere comparison of those two characters with those in Carné's prewar and postwar movies, the most celebrated of them played by Jean Gabin, reveals the extent to which, irrespective of auteurist touches, male figures underwent changes during the period under consideration.

The novelty of *Les Visiteurs du soir* for 1942 audiences is to be found, among other things, in its completely new depiction of sexual relationships: it shows a young woman, Anne (Marie Déa), compromising herself in public by the erotic way she gazes at the singing troubadour, Gilles (Alain Cuny), an element that is emphasized by Carné's cross-cutting between her face and his body seen in increasingly close shots. When the man officially betrothed to Anne threatens the troubadour, the latter resolutely refuses to pick up the gauntlet—in other words, to up the macho ante—and very meekly accepts his own weakness when faced with a "warlord."

This new male figure who is desirable because he is feminized emerges in this particular film in the person of Cuny, as a latter-day St. Sebastian tied to a cross in a mediaeval dungeon, whose singing disarms his jailor and whose body is enhanced by very tight-fitting breeches. Irrespective of this eroticization, which is no doubt also shaped by the director's homosexuality, the troubadour, who sings ballads about love and refuses to rise to macho provocation, is the only "positive" male protagonist in the movie, and his moral rehabilitation — he has already been damned when the story begins because Dominique (Arletty) and he had played at love — requires him to commit himself totally to his beloved. This is a remarkable reversal of sexual roles and of the criteria of virility and seduction.

Carné was to pick up this theme again in *Les Enfants du paradis* in a more ethereal and probably more personal mode. The sad clown Baptiste (Jean-Louis Barrault) is loved by Garance (Arletty), the ideal and inaccessible woman, because he lacks the traditional attributes of masculinity possessed by her other suitors: the gift of the gab and sexual aggressiveness of Frédéric Lemaître (Pierre Brasseur), the social and financial power of Count de Mornay (Louis Salou), or the urge to dominate shown by Lacenaire (Marcel Herrand). On the contrary, Baptiste devotes himself solely to his art, which is eminently feminine because it involves corporal flexibility and a refusal to speak. Although he falls in love with Garance the moment they first meet, he shies away from the body she offers him, thus bringing to light the link between the gentle male and a homosexual fixation on the mother. But more generally we are moved by this sexual shyness because it reflects a respect for the loved woman and a rejection of a swaggering attitude in relations between the sexes (Turk 1989; Sellier 1992).

The positive image of male weakness is a recurrent theme in Occupation cinema. Thus, when it comes to male seduction, we get something very different from the prewar period, from the gaudy uniforms of a Victor Francen or a Jean Murat, the working-class burliness of a Jean Gabin, or the patriarchal glibness of a Raimu, a Jules Berry, or a Harry Baur. The Occupation saw a proliferation of unusual male roles that gave a second chance to or made famous such "unmanly" actors as Noël-Noël (*La Cage aux rossignols*), Jean Tissier (*L'Amant de Bornéo*), and René Lefèvre (*A la belle frégate*).

There also emerged a new generation of young male leads, some of whom rose to stardom after the war, such as Bernard Blier (*Marie-Martine*), François Périer (*Premier bal*), Jean Desailly (*Le Voyageur de la Toussaint*), Jean Marais (*L'Eternel retour*), Raymond Rouleau (*Mam'zelle Bonaparte*), Paul Meurisse (*Défense d'aimer*), and Louis Jourdan (*Premier rendez-vous*). The film careers of others came to a rather abrupt end after the Liberation, namely André Reybaz, Michel Marsay, Jean Pâqui, Gilbert Gil, Gérard Landry, Jimmy Gaillard, Pierre Mingand, Georges Grey, Georges Rollin, André Legall, and Charles Trenet.

Even men who were cast as virile effigies before and after the war were notable during the Occupation for their performances in the roles of gentle males: Jacques Dumesnil (*Le Mariage de Chiffon*, *Les Ailes blanches*, *Secrets*), Jean Chevrier (*L'Assassin a peur la nuit*, *Falbalas*), and Georges Marchal (*Lumère d'été*, *Vautrin* [*Vautrin the Thief*]). Jean Marais made a very brilliant start to his career as a romantic young male lead during the Occupation, even though his relationship with Jean Cocteau and his high-pitched voice caused him to be violently attacked by collaborationist critics, who saw him as being "the most egregious example of decadent emasculation" (*La Francisque*, February 1944). In *Le Lit à colonnes* (*The Four-Poster*, 1942), a fine antipatriarchal melodrama by Roland Tual, Marais plays Rémi Bonvent, a musician serving a prison sentence for having carried out a vendetta against a gamekeeper, and who, like Fabrice del Dongo in his tower in Stendhal's *La Chartreuse de Parme*, falls in love with Marie-Dorée (Odette Joyeux), the daughter of the prison governor (Fernand Ledoux). He writes an opera for her, which her father appropriates in order to impress his daughter and his mistress. This prisoner, who composes music while fantasizing about the image of a young woman he has scarcely glimpsed and who dies tragically in a suicidal escape, having discovered that his opera has been stolen and that his beloved has got married, alludes to another sort of captivity, that of the POWs, and to the ploys those young men had to think up in order to endure waiting, separation, and humiliation.

The movie does display a certain degree of misogyny: Marie-Dorée is a scatterbrained ingénue, who remains unaware of the tragedy that is taking place under her own roof because she has a fixation on her fiancé's fine uniform. Possibly this should be interpreted as a reflection of France's obsession with women's faithfulness to their imprisoned husbands during the dark years and with what was known as their "horizontal collaboration" with the German occupying forces.

No survey of this theme would be complete without mentioning Jean Delannoy's *L'Eternel retour* (1943). In it, Marais plays Patrice, the docile and much-loved nephew of the patriarch Marc (Jean Murat). Marc asks him to find him a (young) woman capable of brightening up his old age. As the legend has it, but also as is only logical, it is Patrice who falls in love with her.

In fact they are smitten with each other before they even realize it, as a result of the first-aid that the "blonde Nathalie" (Madeleine Sologne) gives Patrice after he has been wounded by the violent Morholt (Alexandre Rignault).

Never in the film does Patrice resort to the slightest violence; he does not confront his uncle but tries by trickery to elope with the woman he loves. When he realizes that Marc has taken her back, he does not rebel. He weeps, in the belief that she has forgotten him. He ventures beneath her window but must flee after being wounded by Achille Frossin (Piéral), an evil dwarf. He allows himself to die after the "dark-haired Nathalie" (Junie Astor) convinces him, out of jealousy, that the woman he loves did not respond to his appeal. Patrice's behavior is in strong contrast to the swaggering aggressiveness traditionally expected of a man in love when dealing with his rivals. And yet there is not the shadow of a doubt in the spectator's mind about the absolute nature of his love.

Here we have the same type of lover, including his physical beauty, as in *Les Visiteurs du soir*. But unlike Carné, Jean Cocteau made no secret of his homosexuality, and his affection for Marais can be sensed in his conception of the role of Patrice. But although the creation of nonmacho male figures by certain filmmakers can be explained by their sexual leanings, the reversal of sexual roles is something that informs the Occupation cinema more broadly.

In this respect, the way Jean Tissier's career developed is particularly significant. Typecast in supporting roles in prewar movies as an asexual confidant (for example, in *Battement de coeur* and *J'étais une aventurière*) with feminine characteristics that carried overtones of homosexuality, he suddenly started being cast in leading roles during the Occupation. In Jacques de Baroncelli's *Ce n'est pas moi* (*It's Not Me*, 1941), he is both a banker and an artist; in Jean Boyer's *A vos ordres, Madame* (1942), he is cast as a character similar to that played by Michel Simon in *Circonstances atténuantes*, minus the latter's patriarchal starchiness. René Jayet's *Vingt-cinq ans de bonheur* (1943) centers on the amorous escapades of Gabriel (Tissier) with Elisabeth (Denise Grey) and Marguerite (Tania Fédor), whereas in Albert Valentin's *La Maison des sept jeunes filles* (1941), Rorive (Tissier) ends up marrying Rolande (Gaby Andreu) after long remaining unable to make up his mind which of the seven equally attractive sisters of the title he would opt for. These are all more or less boulevard comedies — Tissier was already a theatrical star — but his promotion as a desirable screen figure was unusual for French cinema, which had so long focused on the power of virile seduction.

In Jean-Pierre Feydeau and René Le Hénaff's *L'Amant de Bornéo* (1942),

Jean Tissier and Arletty in *L'Amant de Bornéo*, 1942. Courtesy of Cinémathèque française.

Lucien Mazerand (Tissier) seduces Stella Losange (Arletty), a Parisian music hall star, under the very nose of her protector, Arthur Serval (Alerme), and her young gigolo, Rastange (Jimmy Gaillard). Mazerand does this thanks to his book learning (he is a provincial bookseller passing himself off as an explorer). His sensitivity and his erotic savoir-faire (which are recognized by Stella) enable him to continue to enjoy the affections (and the body) of his mistress, even after he has been unmasked.

At a comical or melodramatic level, the singers Tino Rossi and Charles Trenet also embodied this new type of seduction despite their different styles; the Corsican singer's "schmaltz" and the young poet's "swinging" rhythms were perhaps not on a par with each other musically, but they did delineate at that time a type of man not dissimilar to that of the gentle male. At the opposite pole from the seductive aggressiveness of a Don Juan, Jean Dupray (Rossi) in Jean Delannoy's *Fièvres* (1941) ends up deciding to enter a monastery in order to escape the women he attracts despite himself. In Richard Pottier's *Mon amour est près de toi* (1943), Rossi plays Jacques Marton, who takes to the road in order to escape being harassed by his mistress and his impresario, and finds work on a barge skippered by a woman, for whom he sings and picks posies. This scandalizes Louis, the first mate (Edouard Delmont), who regards such behavior as unmanly, but it does not stop Marton winning the heart of the pretty Marie-Lou (Annie France).

Trenet, who was well known for being homosexual, never enjoyed the same sort of lady-killer image. But during the war, with the fashion for swing, which he integrated perfectly into his musical and poetic style, he became extremely popular despite venomous criticism from the collaborationist press, which accused him of being too open-minded as regards the *zazous*. His film career began in 1938 with *Je chante* and *La Route enchantée*, but dried up completely after the war, as though his image as a harmless eccentric was no longer in tune with the Zeitgeist. The four movies he made between 1941 and 1943 resemble each other not only because he sings in them but also because he introduces the character he plays — that of a gentle young man — into widely differing genres. There are, for instance, few similarities between the Prévert brothers' poetic comedy *Adieu Léonard* and Jean Boyer's two movies, the comic melodrama *Romance de Paris* and the boulevard comedy *Frédérica*, let alone Yvan Noé's Pétainist melodrama, *La Cavalcade des heures*.

The ideological meaning of such gentleness varies widely from one film to another. Whereas the Prévert brothers make a point of using the Trenet character's perpetually childlike persona to extol antibourgeois and antipatriarchal values, the singer is exploited in *Frédérica* in such a way as to reassert male solidarity in the face of the power of women, who have to content themselves with worshipping from afar the image of a creative genius they may destroy if they appropriate him.

This misogynistic hijacking of Trenet is more typical of prewar boulevard, which is not the case with the two other movies, where he embodies with disarming naïveté the image of the good son as promoted by Vichyite posters for Mother's Day. In *Romance de Paris* Georges (Trenet) succeeds in fulfilling the expectations of his mother (Sylvie) and his fiancée, Madeleine (Jacqueline Porel), while his pal Jules (Jean Tissier) — another gentle male figure — marries his sister, Jeannette (Yvette Lebon). In the more austere register of *La Cavalcade des heures*, the only person he can show affection for, well away from the social whirl imposed on him by his career, is an old beggar woman. He is the "good object" of his episode in the film, but has a price to pay. Voluntarily withdrawing from the circuit of desire (as in *Frédérica*, curiously enough), he is the counterpart of the female effigy.

From the start of his career, Fernandel played gentle characters with an awkward physique. But in *La Fille du puisatier* he is cast in the rather unattractive role of a gullible fool who is prepared to marry Patricia (Josette Day), a young woman seduced and abandoned by Jacques (Georges Grey), a good-looking officer, but who is also prepared to step aside when Jacques reappears. In *Simplet* (1942), on the other hand, a movie he codirected with Carlo Rim, Fernandel plays a character endowed with a more important status; true, he is still the village idiot, but he enjoys the protection of a wise old man, Le Papet (Edouard Delmont), a classical Pétainist figure. When the local worthies, caricatures of the much despised Third Republic, decide to expel the village idiot on the grounds that he is a disgrace to the community, they are supported by public opinion, which is keen to find a scapegoat. Simplet's latest crime has been to be discovered sleeping on the statue of a local dignitary just as the authorities unveil it ceremoniously—a touching nod in the direction of Chaplin's *City Lights* at a time when anti-U.S. feeling and anti-Semitism were rife in France. (The ludicrous village worthies ask the sculptor to shorten the nose of the statue.) But when Simplet is expelled, the village is hit by every disaster from which it had up to then been miraculously spared, and the same worthies will move heaven and earth to get their idiot back so the good times will return.

The movie is riddled with contradictory ideologies that reflect the contradictions of the period: on the one hand, we are treated to all the Pétainist clichés about the decadence of the political community, the need to put an end to internal squabbling, and a certain justification of denunciation as a weapon against "terrorism"; on the other, we find a blistering attack on the singling out of a scapegoat and on banishment, clear allusions to the policy of anti-Semitic exclusion (particularly rampant in the film industry). The gentle male figure personified by Fernandel here symbolizes all outlaws and all innocent victims of arbitrary political policies, with evangelical overtones that are in no way reactionary.

In Jacques Becker's *Goupi mains rouges* (*It Happened at the Inn*, 1942), Eugène Goupi (Georges Rollin), known as "Goupi-Monsieur" but soon relegated to the rank of "Goupi-Cravate," is a particularly provocative gentle male figure in relation to Pétainist ideology in that his total lack of aggressiveness, combined with his city education, is portrayed in a decidedly positive light compared with the alternately grotesque and dangerous paranoia of the peasants whose family he comes from. The other protagonist, "Goupi Mains Rouges" himself, is played by Fernand Ledoux, another gentle male figure, but this time in a peasant context. Doomed to the role of an outcast, he explains that he feels hostility toward the members of the Goupi family because when he fell in love with a young woman they opposed their marriage and she threw herself into a well. After playing a rather labored practical joke on his nephew from the city, he helps young people to combat the stupidity of certain members of the family and the jealousy of others. It is he too who protects the poor "simple-minded" farmhand and who eventually discovers who has murdered "Goupi Tisane." Thus the movie's positive values are embodied by the characters who refuse to accept the Goupi family's murderous tendencies, namely "Goupi Mains Rouges," "Goupi Monsieur," and the gentle "Goupi Muguet" (Blanchette Brunoy). Gentleness is shown here as a greater ability to understand the world and other people, and not as a weakness, whereas verbal or physical violence is repeatedly portrayed as a form of blindness.

We find the same connection between gentleness and intelligence in Louis Daquin's *Le Voyageur de la Toussaint* (1942), based on a Georges Simenon novel. The central character, Gilles, played by Jean Desailly in a brilliant screen début, has to face up to a gang of white-collar criminals terrorizing the small provincial town to which he has returned in order to inherit from an uncle. The success of the film resides in the contrast between the sunny vulnerability of the solitary young man and the diabolical cunning of four old lags played by Jules Berry, Louis Seigner, Roger Karl, and Guillaume de Sax. Daquin's stalwart optimism lets Gilles foil their schemes with the help of people touched by his disarming honesty. It is also thanks to his shyness and kindness that he succeeds in winning the heart of his uncle's young widow, another figure of a sacrificial lamb. (The uncle, a prewar incestuous patriarch, has died before the story starts.)

Desailly's good looks make it easy for spectators of both sexes to be won over by Gilles. On the other hand, it is harder at first to find Bernard Blier attractive, even when he was only twenty-five. Yet this is what is asked of us by Albert Valentin in his fine — and unjustly forgotten — melodrama *Marie-Martine* (1942), based on a script by Jacques Viot. As in *Le Jour se lève*, which Viot also scripted, the movie consists of a series of flashbacks, which gradually reveal the past of the eponymous central character (Renée Saint-Cyr) via the investigations of a sensationalist hack writer, Loïc Limousin (Jules Berry), who has been unscrupulously rummaging in her past. This complex narrative structure means that the spectator knows much more about her life than does the naïve musician Maurice (Blier), who remains completely unaware of the past of the young woman he takes into his home and marries. But as we spectators are allowed to delve deeper and deeper into her tragic past, we gradually realize why, with her eyes wide open, she decides to enter into a relationship with the nice Maurice, who up to then has lived only with his mother. Maurice encapsulates the whole range of "female" characteristics: kindness, devotion, trust, naïveté, innocence, purity, sensitivity, and generosity. This is why Marie-Martine, just like a man who has been through a lot, decides to take refuge in this haven of gentleness in order to lick her wounds and renounce those fantasies of passionate love, which caused her such unhappiness a few years earlier. It is tempting to draw a parallel between the modest but realistic happiness that the young woman decides to create for herself by concealing from her fiancé the dark years she has experienced, and the new state of play as regards male and female roles that was ushered in after the war, when 1.5 million French soldiers returned from their ordeal of captivity in Germany: it provided reassurance about the ability of women to suffer in silence and to accept "impaired" males.

One more remarkable example of the gentle male figure with an unprepossessing physique is Pierre Gauthier (Charles Vanel) in Jean Grémillon's *Le Ciel est à vous* (1943), a far cry from the Pétainist patriarchs of *Les Roquevillard* and *Haut-le-vent*. Pierre and his wife, Thérèse (Madeleine Renaud), are an ordinary couple of small entrepreneurs. He is initially portrayed as a good father, an endearing rather than an alluring characteristic. His naturally massive build is made to seem even heavier by the garage mechanic's overalls he wears almost all the time. And yet we see him go over the moon with admiration for an aviatrix who performs an aerial display at the local flying club. It is highly significant that in this scene, that gentle male figure should wax enthusiastic over the exploits of a woman; the episode foreshadows the moment when with a tearful smile he agrees to let his wife set off in their little monoplane in a bid to beat the women's long-distance flight record.

What is interesting about Grémillon's very subtle movie is the way it first shows us this gentle male figure in a more classically male light, where his lack of macho aggressiveness is simply a form of withdrawal: while his wife works in Limoges, he takes refuge in a recreational activity (flying) instead of repairing cars and looking after the children, with the result that his wife is forced to come back home. Only under the affectionate but iron hand of his wife is he able to turn his efforts back to the family business and ultimately to the challenge of flying records, as his wife's efficient ground mechanic.

But after it appears his wife has been lost at sea, he breaks down completely when faced with the prospect of having to deal with his children, his mother-in-law, and the neighbors' reactions all on his own, resulting in a situation where Thérèse's final triumph and Pierre's success as president of the flying club cannot disguise the dependence of this gentle male figure: outside his relationship with his wife, he is nothing. This is a neat reversal of the prevailing ideology.

In the case of Grémillon too we probably need to take into account his bisexuality, a factor that caused him to adopt an idiosyncratic attitude to sexual identity. But the fact that so many of the directors under discussion were able to express themselves in a way that they had never done before and in an area that had traditionally been—and still is today—taboo, only confirms that patriarchal power was in a state of crisis. Paradoxically, as we must not forget, despite Marshal Pétain's popularity and even though Pétainist policies drew on the most reactionary aspects of patriarchal ideology (Miller 1975), the presence of an old man as head of state only intensified that crisis, for most French people soon came to regard him as a puppet (Laborie 1990).

While the gentle male figure is defined by his refusal to enter into a relationship of domination over women, he is often associated with another, less innocent figure: that of the mothering father who, by way of contrast with the authoritarian and incestuous father of the prewar period, established himself as the final manifestation—in this case a positive one—of the castrated father. The figure of the mothering father, impregnated with female values after the trauma of defeat, was a way of regenerating male figures by exploiting to their advantage the positive nature of maternal images. This process of renovation, the various stages of which can be observed during the four years of the Occupation, foreshadowed and paved the way for the return of misogyny in the postwar period.

We find a startling number of movies in which a widowed father enjoys a relationship of trust with his grown-up children, who are often girls, in a register of extremely disinterested, unauthoritarian affection, in the very best tradition of the castrated father. The aptly named Fernand Ledoux (*doux* means "gentle") is the actor most frequently cast in this kind of role. In Christian-Jaque's *Premier bal* (1941), he plays Michel Noblet, a nutty professor type who dotes on both his daughters, while having a particularly soft spot for the one most like him, Nicole (Marie Déa); indeed she uses his Christian name when addressing him, as though to emphasize the lack of any relationship of authority between them. He awkwardly tries to influence each daughter's love life in a positive fashion, consoling the one who suffers without ever passing judgment on her, then himself suffering in silence after the shock caused by his elder daughter leaving home, and finally allowing himself to die of loneliness after his other daughter abandons him. An understanding, whimsical, and affectionate man, he is capable of recalling that he too was once in love. But while the film allows us to sympathize with him, it does not portray him in a particularly good light: the suicidal sadness that overwhelms him when his younger daughter, Nicole, leaves him forces her to break off the romance she is at last enjoying with Jean de Lormel (Raymond Rouleau), and it is his funeral that causes his elder daughter, Danielle (Gaby Sylvia), to return home in the role of repentant wife, thus forcing her sister permanently into the background.

Premier bal, which was the great success of the year 1941, portrays a contradictory father figure in that while he is movingly affectionate toward his daughters he forms an objective obstacle to the happiness of the one who is presented by the movie as the good object. In other words, *Premier bal* condemns this paternal love whose incestuous overtones prevent the "good" daughter from being happy.

In two other movies featuring Ledoux, his character's inability to exercise his fatherhood "reasonably" takes the form of truly schizophrenic behavior, which causes him to oscillate between an authoritarian fantasy and a need for affection. In Roland Tual's *Le Lit à colonnes* (1942), he plays an uncompromising prison governor who is obsessed by his reputation and melts only when he hears his daughter playing the piano. In Henri Decoin's *L'Homme de Londres* (1943), Ledoux is initially almost a caricature of a repressive father, but after discovering a treasure that was not meant for him he suddenly allows himself to become a happy father, in other words, to spoil his daughter. But he shifts so far the other way that she is embarrassed.

The mother in both these movies is reduced to the role of governess or servant and completely excluded from the circuit of feelings (let alone desire). In contrast with the virago-like female characters of prewar cinema (such as the one played by Gabrielle Dorziat in *Mollenard*), the emphasis has shifted to the patriarchal repression exercised against both wife and children.

In these three films starring Ledoux, as well as in many others, the mothering father is a clearly neurotic figure, either because his love for his daughter signals an abdication of all authority or because it coexists in contradictory fashion with a dictatorial authoritarianism. This serious imbalance always has a tragic outcome, for which the father is held to be objectively responsible because of the very excessiveness of his love.

In a comic register, Albert Valentin's *La Maison des sept jeunes filles* (1941) and Marc Allégret's *Les Petites du quai aux fleurs* (1943) follow a similar pattern, whereby a mothering father is confronted by motherless daughters of marriageable age. In both cases, the father's willingness is matched only by his ineffectualness, but the daughters are resourceful enough to manage on their own, even if they have to endure a painful moment when their father explains how he is torn between his love for them and his duty to prove his authority. In both movies, as it happens, he decides not to put the second alternative into practice.

The mothering-cum-castrated father can be found in an even more austere form, which involves devoting himself to young boys, in Maurice Tourneur's *Péchés de jeunesse* (1941), a Vichyite version of the same template. Monsieur Lacalade (Harry Baur) ends up having to agree to accommodate a whole orphanage in order to be entitled to look after his own son. In the final part of the film, we see Lacalade (who does not yet know which of the boys is his son) mothering all the lads to a degree that causes him to be called to order by a young woman teacher, Madeleine (Lise Delamare), the voice of the law. The reversal of roles here is total and ultimately eludes the Pétainist ideology that apparently inspired the initial project and that could be summed up as follows: a wealthy and dissolute bachelor redeems himself late in life by taking in a whole orphanage. This guilt-inducing version of the "inadequate" father is the counterpart of the bad father figure found in many explicitly Pétainist movies.

Toward the end of the Occupation there emerged a new development that tended to exclude the mother so that the mothering father could completely take over parental power, that is to say, recover some of his former prerogatives, however transformed. In 1944 this new configuration could be found in two film versions, one rose-tinted, the other noir.

Thanks to the light touch and optimism of Noël-Noël, who both scripted and acted in the movie, Jean Dréville's *La Cage aux rossignols* (1944) was one of the biggest hits of the immediate postwar period. Like Léo Joannon's *Le Carrefour des enfants perdus* (1943), but from a very different viewpoint, the film looks at the problem of institutions for waifs. Joannon's film flirts constantly with fascism in the way it makes the social "rescue" of the children hinge on the authority of a leader (René Dary) and makes out a group of teenagers to be a malleable horde spontaneously driven by the worst kind of destructive instincts. *La Cage aux rossignols*, on the other hand, is based on the premise that human nature needs affection in order to blossom and that it turns nasty only when love is lacking.

The sole source of love that turns the children in Dréville's movie back into human beings is Clément (Noël-Noël), their supervisor, who soon becomes their choirmaster. Music, which is at once the vehicle of and metaphor for the new educational methods advocated by the kind mentor, has connotations of the feminine, gentleness, emotion, and everything whose expression is forbidden by the codes of virility. It is thanks to music that the children escape the curse of a world without love, as personified by the terrifying patriarchal figure of the headmaster (René Blancard), and "become civilised."

Clément's girlfriend, Micheline, is not at all involved in the story; she simply reads the account he has written of his experiences, whose publication in a newspaper enables him to win through in the end. No woman is required in order to create the mothering relationship with the children, and Micheline's mother even provides an opportunity to include some misogynistic scenes in the best boulevard tradition.

The theme of the mothering father is also central to Richard Pottier's *Les Caves du Majestic*, a movie that remained little known because it was released after the war and bore the stigma of its production company, the German-owned Continental. Adapted by Charles Spaak from a Georges Simenon novel, it was Continental's last film. (Shooting began only in February 1944.) The care and resources that went into the making of the movie are evident from the very free-flowing narrative and editing, the extraordinarily wide range of actors who appeared in it, and in particular the camerawork and editing of the scenes in the Hôtel Majestic's kitchens, where elaborate dolly movements are enhanced by high-quality lighting that already looked forward to the postwar period. This sophistication is all the more remarkable because shooting took place during the darkest period of the Occupation from a material point of view, with shortages and power cuts intensifying as a result of the Allied offensive that would soon gather momentum on every front.

Comparison with Simenon's original, a Maigret novel published in 1942, reveals the considerable extent to which Spaak reworked the story; the problem of fatherhood, for example, which is central to the movie, does not exist as such in the novel. The factual elements of the story are more or less the same: Maigret (Albert Préjean) is investigating the murder of a wealthy customer of the Hôtel Majestic, Madame Petersen (Suzy Prim), whose son turns out to have been fathered not by his supposed father, an American she married when pregnant, but by a Frenchman, Arthur Donge (Jacques Baumer), a humble cook at the same hotel. The murderer is Ramuel (René Génin), an employee of the Majestic who was blackmailing Petersen by pretending to be Donge.

Spaak changed the nationality of the official father (because of the Occupation), who became Petersen, a Scandinavian and perfect French speaker (played by Jean Marchat), whereas in the Simenon original neither the American nor his secretary could understand a word of the language. But above all, Spaak completely changed the purpose of Maigret's investigation, which in the

Jacques Baumer in *Les Caves du Majestic*, 1945. Courtesy of Cinémathèque française.

detective's own words is no longer to discover the murderer but to establish which of the two men who claim to be the father should have custody of the boy, Teddy. The scenario was written at a time when the issue of fatherhood was being hotly debated in intellectual Catholic circles, not from a Vichyite point of view of how to preserve patriarchal authority but, on the contrary, in an attempt to transcend the crisis of authority by adopting a new conception of paternal responsibility, involving in particular the notion of creating life consciously (Marcel 1945/2010).

The film opens with an extraordinary scene of mothering fatherhood, in which we see Petersen (the "adoptive" father), his son, and his secretary playing at being Indians, all of them sporting Sioux headdresses. When the mother (Suzy Prim, an unmaternal figure as only a boulevard star could be) bursts in and puts an abrupt end to their games, it is as though they had been caught out by a complete stranger, as she remarks bitterly in a subsequent scene with her secretary. In other words, we have here a father who plays with his son in the most natural manner possible and with clear enjoyment, in the presence of a mother who herself realizes she is incapable of getting her son to love her. This reversal of roles, which displays more than a trace of misogyny, foreshadows the settling of scores that would take place after the war.

The most important scene in the movie comes when Maigret invites the two fathers to a dinner he has carefully prepared, which is presented as the dénouement of the affair. It turns out instead to consist of a poignant discussion of fatherhood, which includes an argument taken directly from contemporary Catholic texts (Marcel 1945/2010). "The father is the one who gives life intentionally," Petersen tells Donge, who retorts, "I conceived this child out of love." In fact Donge became a father without realizing it, following his affair with a woman who, when she discovered she was pregnant, married the wealthy businessman Petersen.

The mind boggles at the way the two men, played by two actors who worked in boulevard before the war, try to outdo each other in paternal love, which for both of them consists exclusively of trying to do what is best for the child's well-being. This gourmet dinner that Maigret, like some latter-day Solomon, has organized so as to judge the fatherly qualities of each man from his ability or otherwise to swallow his food before the fate of the child is sorted out, ends in a tie: neither of them has touched what was on his plate. (The argument was all the more convincing for contemporary spectators since food restrictions were an unfortunate fact of daily life.) Donge, the boy's actual father, who lives with his wife, Charlotte (Florelle), in a small suburban villa, nevertheless decides with a heavy heart to drop his claim to the child because he knows that Petersen can afford to give him a better upbringing, just as the true mother in the judgment of Solomon dropped her claim to her child rather than see him split in half.

After a scene in which Maigret has gone through the motions of unmasking the murderer, the movie ends with a close-up of Donge's tragic face. He has become a new effigy of frustrated paternity.

This return of the pendulum is confirmed by one of the last films that went into production before the Liberation, Robert Vernay's *Le Père Goriot*. The movie centers on two examples of fatherly devotion, literally in the case of Goriot (Pierre Larquey) toward his two daughters, and figuratively, with an implicit homosexual ingredient, in the case of Vautrin (Pierre Renoir), toward Eugène de Rastignac (Georges Rollin). While the male characters — including the escaped convict — all win the sympathy of the spectator in one way or another, the female figures can be summed up as three society ladies, all of them adulterous, who have been duped by their lovers and are solely interested in currying favor. They include Goriot's two daughters, whom Balzac, in the original novel, described as monstrous egotists, and who vie with each other in their cruelty toward the wretched old man, a veritable martyr of fatherhood.

While he is dying, the two young men living in the Vauquer boardinghouse, Rastignac and Bianchon (Jean Desailly), remain at his side in the place of his two daughters, who have gone to a dance. In the old man's delirium, the faces of the two young men are temporarily replaced by those of his daughters, but the spectator is brought back to the reality of a world where men alone stand by one another. In this scene, Rastignac utters what was to become the motto of postwar cinema: "All women are sluts!"

The other aspect of this restoration of the old order, in evidence from the Liberation onward, is to be found in *Le Bossu* (1944), directed by Jean Delannoy and starring Pierre Blanchar, both of whom had worked together two years earlier on *Pontcarral, colonel d'Empire*, a monumental example of "resistant" misogyny. On this occasion, the double smokescreen of a swashbuckling movie and an adaptation of a celebrated popular novel by Paul Féval (1858) enabled its authors to rehabilitate the incestuous father who is both mothering and heroic. Blanchar plays a two-edged role as a knight, Henri de Lagardère, who has to disguise himself as a hunchback in order to wreak vengeance on the enemies of the young Claire de Nevers (Yvonne Gaudeau), whom he took in as a baby, raised in secret in Spain, and brought back to Paris when she came of age so she could recover her rights. Ultimately she convinces her heroic guardian to marry her, for though smitten with his protégée, he is initially full of scruples because of their age difference.

The rehabilitation of the incestuous father in this film is cloaked in the new-found dignity of mothering fathers and undercover fighters. (Forced to go into hiding in order to protect the child, Lagardère alternates between guile and confrontation with his enemies, cast as usurpers.) The women (mother and daughter are played by the same, rather unappealing actress) depend totally on male power, whether it be good or evil. The only positive desire expressed by Claire is her wish to marry her benefactor. This is a particularly sly twist in the plot whereby it is the woman herself who calls for the return of the most threadbare patriarchal setup.

The narrative patterns whereby films put women in their place after the war turned out to be more complex than might be suggested by the rather naïve presumption of *Le Bossu*. But this film, which brings down the curtain on Occupation cinema with a defense of the mothering-incestuous father, demonstrates how rapidly patriarchal mentalities, which had taken a battering from the Débâcle, were coming back into their own.

ℛ

Film Analyses

ℛ LA DUCHESSE DE LANGEAIS
  (Jacques de Baroncelli, 1941)

Never in the history of French cinema were the novels of Balzac adapted for the screen as often as they were during the Occupation: seven times in four years, which is an absolute record. Critics and historians usually interpret this fashion for literary adaptation as a desire to escape into the past, at a time when many costume movies were indeed being produced. In the case of Balzac, some writers have even suggested there is an affinity between the conservatism of the legitimist novelist and the Occupation Zeitgeist, which is assumed to have been uniformly reactionary.

We are inclined to think rather that a director like Claude Autant-Lara, who specialized in period films, regarded such a detour via the past as a sharper way of getting around censorship than resorting to the "vaguely contemporary." Moreover Balzac's often cynical and even nihilist social criticism was well suited to scriptwriters, directors, and producers who wanted, for often widely differing ideological reasons, to steer clear of the sentimentality that imbued so many movies of the period, quite apart from the handful (thirty) of explicitly Pétainist films.

As the Marxist historian and philosopher Georg Lukács (1974) has demonstrated, Balzac, despite his fascination with the aristocracy, produced a fundamental critique of the social order of his time — much more than that proposed by the "socialist" writer Eugène Sue, for example. During the Occupation, a critique of that kind was entirely consistent with a very widely shared desire to call into question the social order, which Yves Chalas (1985: 38–39) sums up as follows: "Neither the right nor the left, neither Pétain in Vichy nor the collaborators in Paris nor even the Resistance had any desire to bring back what all regarded as a dangerous past. . . . On the whole the aspirations of the period were those which involved a general surpassing of the models that had resulted from the predominance of free-market capitalism." With the exception of one very loose modernized adaptation with overtones of boulevard theater, André Cayatte's *La Fausse maîtresse* (1942), all those Balzac adaptations generate the same pessimism about the prevailing social order, both public and private, as well as a gnawing aspiration for something else.

La Duchesse de Langeais, adapted for the screen by Jean Giraudoux, leaves aside the theme of political subversion that underlies *L'Histoire des treize*, the Balzac trilogy of which this novel formed part. But the author of *Juliette au pays des hommes*, who was attracted for the first time by the prospect of working for the cinema, kept his adaptation free of Balzac's misogyny and brought out instead the original's "latent feminism." This is contained notably in the theme, typical of Balzac, of the "mis-married" woman who is traumatized by her sexually brutal husband and becomes, like an ill-treated animal, dangerous to all those who approach her (compare *La Physiologie du mariage*). In Balzac's original, this trauma simply turns Antoinette, the Duchess of Langeais, into the most attractive and most cruel coquette in the Faubourg Saint-Germain, who subjects men to a sadistic game until the day when she meets a "true man," an illustrious Napoleonic general, and at last experiences love — and punishment.

In Giraudoux's version, Antoinette (Edwige Feuillère) becomes a woman "who wants to avenge all other women" and who aspires to more egalitarian relations between men and women, to an intellectual dialogue and not the immediate and total physical possession authorized by the marriage contract. She is the direct heir of Mademoiselle de Scudéry and her friends, the *Précieuses*, not as Molière depicted them but as they really were: France's first feminists (Haase-Dubosc and Viennot 1991). Balzac's Antoinette, like all the coquettes in *La Comédie Humaine*, is uneducated. In Giraudoux's version, on the contrary, she loves poetry, painting, and music — "as a woman owes it to herself," she says toward the end of the movie, regretting that her stormy love affair

Pierre Richard-Willm and Edwige Feuillère in *La Duchesse de Langeais*, 1941. Courtesy of Cinémathèque française.

with General Montriveau (Pierre Richard-Willm) has kept her away from cultural activities in Paris.

Giraudoux and Baroncelli's film in fact consists of a systematic critique of Balzac's novel. It does so in a highly original way, by dividing the movie into two relatively autonomous textual systems: on the one hand, we get the story as told by Balzac — through Montriveau's viewpoint; on the other, we are shown the affair between Antoinette and the general as Giraudoux sees it from the woman's point of view.

Balzac is present on the screen throughout the movie in the person of Ronquerolles (Aimé Clariond), who is Montriveau's friend in the novel too, but does not play at all the same role. We sense that Ronquerolles is not really "in" the film from the opening sequence, when, shot in close-up from the front in a way that does not really fit in with the general shots of the ball that is going on around him, he has fun completing the announcements made by the butler and predicting to the audience the often tragic end (usually death) of the people entering the ballroom. Now if he knows the characters' future, it is not because he has the gift of second sight, a notion that is not relevant to the textual level, but because he functions as a spokesman, not for Giraudoux but for Balzac. Throughout the film, he remains just behind the door, closely watching the story as it unfolds. Either he comments on it ironically and with Balzac's male chauvinism (for instance, by deriding in the Palais-Royal the love affair between Antoinette and the general like a barker on the Boulevard du Crime), or he openly manipulates the story by stealing a note Antoinette writes to Montriveau and replacing it with a forgery, thus drawing his friend into a humiliating trap that causes the lovers to break up—whereas in the novel this manipulation is invisible, given that the misunderstanding is of a contingent nature (a mislaid letter). When Ronquerolles gets it into his head all too late, and just as arbitrarily, to regret his manipulation, he clearly states that he acted out of male solidarity in order to save his friend from a female danger.

Having attributed Balzac's view not to the text but to a rather unattractive character who is always located on the edge of the frame (figuratively, but often also literally), the film then firmly adopts Antoinette's point of view. In so doing, it is greatly helped by the personality of Edwige Feuillère and her status as a major star of the period—though this narrative reversal cannot be reduced to the contingencies of the star system, since the characters Feuillère plays in her prewar movies are often treated in the way that Balzac treats his Antoinette.

The film career of Feuillère, who was one of the few female stars of the 1930s around whom movies were put together, centered before the war on the figure of the shrew who needed to be tamed, the dominant female who was invariably brought to heel at the end of the last reel. That stereotype applied as well to all the major roles she played during and after the war. (She is one of the very few cases, along with Fernandel, of a typecasting that was not brought to an end by the reorganization of gender relations during the Occupation.) In contrast, the movies that Feuillère shot between 1940 and 1944 are marked by a new bias in favor of the female character. In *Mam'zelle Bonaparte* (Maurice Tourneur, 1941), *L'Honorable Catherine* (Marcel L'Herbier, 1942), *Lucrèce* (Léo Joannon, 1943), and above all *La Duchesse de Langeais* she asserts herself—before succumbing to death, loneliness, or a man—much more positively than in *Lucrèce Borgia* (Abel Gance, 1935) or *L'Emigrante* (Léo Joannon, 1939).

Ronquerolles and other male commentators—overzealous spectators of this affair between the queen of the Faubourg Saint-Germain and a military hero not very familiar with high society—insist throughout the movie on the notion that the Duchess of Langeais is a callous "vamp" (though it is one of those spectators who reveals her "objective" function, which is "to avenge other women"). If the badly treated Montriveau ends up sharing that verdict, the spectator, however unwillingly, sees something quite different and comes to regard Montriveau himself as a man who can only treat a woman "the way Napoleon's armies treat towns," as Antoinette points out to him when he tries to take her by force. He is a man who soon starts behaving like a child whose toy has been taken away when Antoinette continues to withhold her body while nonetheless seeking out his company.

This critical view of male sexual mores is most strongly asserted during the extraordinary ballroom scene. Deceived by Ronquerolles's fake note, Montriveau at first believed he had achieved his ends, then discovered that the veiled woman in the cab, which an anonymous note had invited him to meet, was in fact a prostitute named Pamela. So now, in front of the assembled guests, he tells the woman who has been leading him on a few home truths. But we know full well that the general, whose pride has been hurt, is unfair in his accusations of Antoinette and that although she would like to bring him to heel she genuinely loves him and had nothing to do with the cruel practical joke that has been played on him. What is more, the crowd of guests who watch this harrowing scene but do not take part in it put the movie's spectators *en abyme* and create for them the distance of reflection. It is easy to imagine the effect that would have been produced by the same scene if it had shown only the two characters together, without witnesses and without a physical distance between them, where the private catharsis of the close-up would have had its full impact, and where the spectator would have been alone in the presence of Montriveau's excessive behavior and Antoinette's dignified reaction — a confrontation of two subjectivities where the spectacle of the emotions would have swept all before it.

This sequence, incidentally, in which a high-society audience remains detached, is like an echo of the alliance that Giraudoux's script posits between the duchess and the people, central to several scenes in the Palais-Royal: a little girl apes Ronquerolles's misogynistic jibes; the sight of a *grisette* who simply greets her lover with a kiss, temporarily releases Antoinette, who then goes to kiss the man she loves with equal simplicity; and, after Ronquerolles the manipulator has spoiled in advance a scene where Antoinette hopes to appeal to Montriveau's emotions by getting "Le Fleuve du Tage" (a fashionable ditty much mocked by Ronquerolles) played to him, a barrel-organ player and the flâneurs in the Palais-Royal gather around Montriveau to make fun of him when he tries to prevent the musician from playing the tune and some lovers from singing a duet. He has to retire in a hail of booing — like a bad actor.

This same motif of popular clear-sightedness contrasted with Balzac's male chauvinism reappears when the concierge of the building, in front of which Antoinette has been waiting in vain for Montriveau to respond to her last letter, warns the poor woman against the general's insensitivity; although he had remained devoted to Napoleon, he did not shed a tear when he learned of the emperor's death.

The leitmotif of Balzac's novel is Antoinette's punishment, since his story is told in flashback, bracketed by the episode of the convent to which she has retired and from which Montriveau, after months of trying to track her down, has come to carry her away. But whereas Balzac skates over the duchess's death, which he treats in a distant and rather ironic way, this final scene in the movie depicts at great length and with great pathos her dying moments in the arms of the man who should have been her lover. In Giraudoux's view, there can be no doubt that Antoinette is a martyr of the battle of the sexes, a victim of men with a one-track mind and of her own hopes, as vain as they were moving, for another kind of love relation.

There are similarities between this film and *Falbalas* (Jacques Becker, 1944), another critique of the male approach to affairs of the heart. In both cases, it is highly probable that at the time (and indeed for many years afterward) men — and women — who still took phallocentric values for granted may not have noticed Giraudoux's inflection of Balzac's vision. (Critics at the time, such as Roger Régent, and more recently Jacques Siclier referred to the movie as a faithful adaptation of Balzac's novel!) Even when playing opposite Feuillère, Richard-Willm, who was usually cast as an innocent man grappling with evil, might have come across to many as a sympathetic character. But in the past twenty years this film — and others of the same period, such as *Falbalas* — have become more intelligible in terms of what may legitimately be regarded as their authors' intentions.

ℛ *MARIE-MARTINE*
   (Albert Valentin, 1943)

A writer who has run out of inspiration exploits the misfortunes of a young woman, which he intends to use in a novel, but promptly hands her over to the police. He tracks her down when she is released from prison and pesters her out of cynical curiosity, in the hope of producing another best-seller. He is eventually thwarted, and the young woman is then able to live in peace with a nice musician who knows nothing of her past.

Roger Régent (1948: 150) deplores the "serious miscasting" of Renée Saint-Cyr in the title role of *Marie-Martine* but praises the theme and construction of Jacques Viot's script, while Jacques Siclier, uncharacteristically, is impressed by Saint-Cyr's performance and sees the influence of prewar poetic realism in the film. But then Saint-Cyr is not an actress greatly appreciated by French cinephiles. Françoise Ducout (1978: 118) describes her as "not quite a young woman any more, but 'ever so proper,' with just a touch of (phoney) American-style gaiety, and very cool, calm and collected, a characteristic she tries to correct by tremulous diction, sighs, simpering airs and swoonings." Roger Boussinot (1980) sees her as effective only in "tear-jerkers and bourgeois melodramas." Jean-Loup Passek (1986) describes her as "utterly well-meaning." The common denominator of all these verdicts is extreme condescension. Saint-Cyr's success throughout the 1930s and 1940s, both on the screen and on stage, suggests that in this case the public's appreciation of her was very different from that of the critics. The unsaid in the uncomplimentary remarks we have quoted is probably her "overintellectual" demeanor, at a time when the dominant figures were naïve young women (Danielle Darrieux, Michèle Morgan) or delectable sluts (Viviane Romance, Ginette Leclerc). In the patriarchal view of women, as it existed before the war (and which has not been called into question by modern critics), there is no room for thinking women; they are necessarily bluestockings, "snotty little madams," *femmes savantes*, or *précieuses ridicules*. It is no accident that it was during the Occupation that Saint-Cyr obtained her finest roles in such movies as Christian-Jaque's *La Symphonie fantastique*, Louis Daquin's *Madame et le mort*, Albert Valentin's *Marie-Martine*, and André Cayatte's *Pierre et Jean*.

In *Marie-Martine*, the scriptwriter Viot again experimented with a complex construction based on flashbacks, as in *Le Jour se lève* (but in this case they are not chronological), and once again Jules Berry is cast in a similar role as an aging and cynical ladies' man. These analogies make the principal difference between the two films, which is typical of the period, all the more striking: the hero becomes a heroine as Saint-Cyr replaces Jean Gabin.

The central conflict depicted by the movie is between a young woman and an old man; in other words, the film clearly refers back to the prewar "incestuous" couple, but in such a way as to show, from the opening sequence, the pathetic, illegitimate, and cynical nature of the patriarchal figure. Loïc Limousin (Jules Berry) spots his latest novel, *Marie-Martine*, prominently displayed in the window of a small provincial bookshop. But he learns from the bookseller (the hilarious Jeanne Fusier-Gir) that the only copy she sold was to a young woman of the same name, who turns out to be the person who unwittingly inspired the novelist.

The movie opens, then, with a denunciation of the myth of the artist and his muse, which is reduced to the sordid exploitation of a young woman's misfortunes. The construction of the filmic narrative is articulated no longer around the memories of the central character, as in *Le Jour se lève*, but around the reiterated theft of a woman's words by a writer, as a metaphor of the "symbolic violence" at the heart of male dominance (Coquillat 1982; Le Doeuff 1989/1991; Bourdieu 1996/2002).

So that the spectator should not be unaware of women's ability to master the order of the discourse, the first flashback is narrated by the young woman herself, who tells Limousin about her stint in jail and her first meeting with Maurice (Bernard Blier). Her ability to symbolize is underlined by the mise-en-scène. We see her walking across the drawing-room carpet counting the number of steps, in the presence of the mystified writer, to whom she explains the meaning of her actions: the carpet has exactly the same dimensions as the cell in which she spent three years of her life.

The symbolic violence suffered by women takes the form of real violence on several occasions: Limousin forces his way into the house where Marie-Martine has taken refuge; he wrenches secrets out of the young woman, who is haunted by her memories of prison that she has to keep from Maurice and his mother (Sylvie); the writer uses physical violence to fondle her, behavior that is brought to an abrupt end by the authority of the blind mother, who kicks the intruder out. In another flashback to the tragedy that destroys Marie-Martine's youth, the movie draws a parallel between the violence of the upper-middle-class de Lachaume (Jean Debucourt), who makes sure his young employee Marie-Martine is accused of a murder committed by his own daughter, and the violence of Limousin, who, after hearing the story of the young woman on the run, hands her over to the police. This violence perpetrated by the patriarchal order is also directed at young men, since the murder of Philippe Monthieu (Michel Marsay), a young man of means who dared prefer Marie-Martine the orphan to his official fiancée, echoes the thwarted loves of young Maurice's nonconformist uncle Parpain (Saturnin Fabre), who has chosen to become a dropout, even to the extent of preferring candles to electricity.

While denouncing the various aspects of patriarchal oppression, the movie nevertheless displays an endearing optimism, since the characters who suffer that oppression succeed in banding together to defend themselves against it (with a little help from the makers of the film). Thus the young Maurice, who is worried about the similarities he sees between the mysterious life of the young woman he loves and the heroine of the same name in Limousin's novel, decides to go and talk to the writer. But Limousin is afraid of causing a scandal and gets his young wife (Héléna Manson) to let Maurice in. She decides to ridicule her husband's personality so as to reassure Maurice. This results in a delightful sequence where shots of her furious husband, who is eavesdropping behind a closed door, alternate with an apparently innocuous conversation in which the wife describes her husband as a portly old man with a red nose who drinks too much and wears long johns and slippers while sitting by the fireside and inventing his characters' unlikely adventures.

The image of this grotesque married couple, in which the young woman calls her aging husband "Daddy," is an ironic echo of the incestuous couple found in 1930s movies — a figure that the film finally disposes of by the device of a convenient accident, to the spectator's great relief. Just as he is about to send an anonymous letter to Maurice revealing his fiancée's past, Limousin, despite the pleadings of his wife, who tries to protect the two youngsters' happiness, walks out of a café half-drunk and gets run over by a bus. The letter falls into a gutter and disappears into the sewer. This is an exemplary fate for an anonymous letter of denunciation at a time when such missives were officially encouraged.

In other words, a deus ex machina was needed to get rid of the evil patriarch for good, an unintentional way of admitting that the true defeat of the patriarchy remained problematic. However, to combat that oppression, the young couple will find another ally in the person of Maurice's elderly and blind mother (Sylvie), the one and only true love of Uncle Parpain, who was forced by his family to marry for money. Here we have a character at the opposite pole from the overbearing mother of prewar cinema and the diabolical mother-in-law of the postwar period. Her blindness is an indication that her power is not exerted in the domain of the visible. This recurrent theme of blindness in the cinema of the Occupation differs somewhat in meaning depending on whether it concerns a male, female, young, or old character. But in at least four of these films blindness expresses a positive renunciation of the most selfish forms of temporal power. Maurice's mother embodies all the most generous values of motherhood and is in no way typical of Vichyite moralism; by offering Marie-Martine hospitality without knowing where she has come from, then by kicking out the usurping writer even after overhearing Marie-Martine admitting her little secrets, and finally, on her death bed, by giving her blessing to the young couple, she organizes resistance to the moral and social oppression of women in particularly clear-sighted fashion. At the end of the film, once she has become aware of her son's typically male naïveté — the refusal of a man in love to accept the idea that the woman he loves could have had another life before meeting him — she approves of Marie-Martine's silence by urging her son never to have doubts about the woman he loves. This image of a discreet but effective solidarity between women is echoed in striking fashion by what we know about the low-profile, daily, and silent battle carried out by women for collective survival during the Occupation (Fishman 1991; Veillon 1995).

While not all the male characters in the movie collude with patriarchal oppression, they are remarkably feckless in their attempts to combat it. The anticonformist Uncle Parpain, a model of the castrated father, is an old eccentric who derides the family and authority in general. His delightful monologue is interspersed with his celebrated injunction "Hold your candle . . . upright!," whose indecent overtones in those puritan times were patent both to the actor who thought it up (Fabre) and, apparently, to audiences (Fabre 1948/1987). Although he is droll and moving, Parpain has no influence over Maurice, who, after spending the night reading Limousin's novel, rushes to see him and try to find out everything about Marie-Martine, despite his uncle's having expressly advised him not to do so in order to safeguard his happiness.

Maurice himself is an endearing male figure, but the movie constantly highlights his vulnerability and naïveté. Male kindness is accompanied by a good dose of infantilism which women need to compensate for by perceptiveness and a sometimes burdensome sense of responsibility. Such women are a far cry from the childlike creatures that the cinema of the 1930s so accommodatingly created. Marie-Martine's experiences, which the spectator is eventually able to piece together and which include a tragically terminated love affair that is at the root of all her misfortunes, symbolize what women have to renounce in order to attain something resembling happiness, but stripped of illusions. A final flashback aims to show the parallel between Marie-Martine's relationship with Maurice and the first love affair of her youth with a young man of means. The man concerned, who is fed up with the capricious behavior of his fiancée, who is from his social class, is touched by the humble and gentle femininity of the woman he encounters in the hall of his future parents-in-law's mansion.

In this initial episode in Marie-Martine's life, which is recounted by her old governess, Miss Aimée, she almost comes across as a typically Pétainist figure — an instrument of moral regeneration for a bourgeois young man. But the caricatural and sketchy tone of this episode suggests it should be taken as a tongue-in-cheek pastiche of right-thinking films of the period. This is all the more plausible because the makers of the film refuse to allow this episode to end in a happy or edifying way: the young man's sister kills her fiancé when she discovers he has been cheating on her, and her cynical father (Jean Debucourt) gets Marie-Martine to take the blame for the murder. She is sent to prison for three years. Even after his own daughter's suicide, the father refuses to reveal the truth in order to protect his good name. Bourgeois selfishness is the only law that counts, whatever Vichyite ideology would have people believe.

The relationship between Marie-Martine and Maurice, a not very good-looking provincial viola player who lives a quiet life with his blind old mother, represents in comparison a renunciation on the part of Marie-Martine of the consensual and right-thinking illusions fostered by the popular novels published by the Catholic Bonne Presse. The casting of Bernard Blier as Maurice also represents a renunciation of the romantic illusions of *l'amour fou*, a stereotype of the poetic realism of the prewar period. While tending to have a tragic ending, these films provided spectators with considerable satisfaction by enabling them to dream about Jean Gabin's love for Michèle Morgan, for example. Roger Régent never forgave Albert Valentin for casting Renée Saint-Cyr as Marie-Martine; he would have preferred Morgan.

There is nothing romantic or particularly edifying about the end of *Marie-Martine* (the title character will build her happiness on a lie), but the filmmakers condone the positive aspect of this outcome, which is above all the heroine's decision: after having a passionate love affair with Philippe, the young man of means, and experiencing its appalling consequences in a society of class and sexual oppression, she decides, fully aware of what it entails, to live a life of modest happiness with a young musician who has been ceremoniously chosen for her by his mother in a handover that admirably symbolizes the regeneration of society by the feminine, typical of the cinema of the period. The price to be paid by Marie-Martine for this realistic happiness is also her renunciation of desire: it is quite clear to the audience — particularly its female elements — that Blier is not desirable. But he has a quality which the movie valorizes: kindness. Ultimately *Marie-Martine* draws a portrait of a sick world in which men are marked by *lack* (castrated patriarchs, immature young men) and which women can hope to make more or less tolerable only so long as they themselves give up any idea of sexual desire. *Marie-Martine* is a clear-sighted movie in which, if one reads between the lines, one can detect the profound imbalances that lurk behind the call for regeneration through female figures that was characteristic of the Occupation.

✒ *DONNE-MOI TES YEUX*
(Sacha Guitry, 1943)

Sacha Guitry's films (twenty-nine features between 1935 and 1957) adopt an approach that is completely different from the one mostly found in the corpus of movies under discussion in this book, that is to say a critical view of patriarchal values. The celebrated boulevard playwright was, on the contrary, at the heart of that system of values, and remained there right up to the end of his life. But for that very reason it seemed interesting to us to analyze in detail the way the ideological collapse of 1940 affected his work and to assess the scale of that upheaval through the effect it had on an auteur so firmly entrenched in the bastion of patriarchal and libertine misogyny.

Despite the total originality of an actor who became a playwright, then a filmmaker, the roles he wrote, cast himself in, and filmed before the war conform perfectly to the dominant pattern found in the French cinema of the 1930s: the incestuous couple. Between 1935 and 1938 Guitry made ten movies with the twenty-five-year-old Jacqueline Delubac, whom he had just married at the age of fifty.

The shift in that pattern to be found in *Donne-moi tes yeux* is all the more striking because in it Guitry forms a new—and even more "incestuous"— couple with his fourth wife, the young Geneviève de Séréville. But on this occasion Guitry switches from boulevard to melodrama, portraying a patriarch whose weakness is expressed metaphorically by a fast-approaching blindness that leads him to break off with the young woman he was planning to marry. This theme and this genre, which Guitry tackled here for the very first time, were on the other hand very much of their time (compare *Vénus aveugle* and *L'Ange de la nuit*).

The opening sequence of *Donne-moi tes yeux* in the Palais de Tokyo exhibition building in Paris works as a veritable manifesto both at a political level and in the register of relations between men and women. It intermixes three motifs: the initial encounter between François (Guitry), a sculptor, and Catherine (de Séréville), the young woman who becomes his model and then fiancée; a sketch in which Floriane (Mila Parély), playing a sex object who can be bought by the highest bidder, makes a mockery of the relationships between middle-aged men and young women that were typical of prewar cinema; and a long stroll, complete with commentary, by François among the masterpieces in the Salon, which serves as a pretext for a "defense and illustration" of Guitry's ambiguous political position during that period.

Sacha Guitry and Geneviève de Séréville in *Donne-moi tes yeux*, 1943. Courtesy of Cinémathèque française.

In voice-over, Guitry compares the Salon of 1943 with that of 1871, whose masterpieces he parades before the camera (a fine example of the liberties he took with spatiotemporal continuity), and pleads for artistic creation as a form of national resistance: "What we lost on one side, we won on the other. . . . Masterpieces like that are tantamount to victory!"

This opening visit to the Salon revives the militant spirit of Guitry's very first film, *Ceux de chez nous* (1915/1939), a documentary on great living French artists made during World War I, which he showed during the Occupation after rejecting the Germans' demand that he cut the sequence featuring Sarah Bernhardt (who was of Jewish origin). This cultural nationalism, which was encouraged by intellectuals and left-wing parties after the war to counter the Marshall Plan, highlights the ambiguities of Guitry's position during the dark years, when he was prepared to make a lot of compromises to save "French culture" and proved incapable of seeing the Nazis as anything other than "France's hereditary enemy."

This melodrama on blindness also offers some original thinking on the male gaze. Before the war Guitry had already portrayed the inequality of sexual relations in such an explicit and provocative way (see *Le Nouveau Testament*,

1935) that he forced one to see it rather than merely endure it. But blindness in *Donne-moi tes yeux*, quite apart from its metaphor of castration—which also reflects, as Noël Simsolo (1988: 95) has shown, the crisis in Guitry's relationship with de Séréville—acts as a calling into question of the legitimacy of the voyeuristic gaze, which turns the other person into an object.

The first half of the movie depicts the sculptor's sexual strategy in the course of various sittings in which Catherine serves as a model for a bust. In the first sequence, the two protagonists are framed in medium close-up, which highlights François's voyeuristic gaze on the face of the young woman, who offers herself to him without looking at him. The second sitting marks a distinct change in their relationship by framing Catherine separately in a close-up filmed from the front, while a medium shot shows the sculptor at work in profile. The third sitting depicts the breakup, which is caused by François: he asks her to sit with her back to him, which she interprets as being "as if [she] was leaving." But her reaction can also be interpreted as a rejection of the voyeuristic gaze. While he laboriously explains why he has dropped the idea of sculpting a bust of her, the camera remains on Catherine's face in close-up, which has replaced the sensualist sculptor's gaze as a vector of spectator identification.

This renunciation of the voyeuristic male gaze is confirmed in the celebrated sequence where, in the total darkness of Paris streets subjected to a blackout (this exceptional direct allusion to the political and military situation is a rarity worth noting), François asks Catherine to forgive him for the suffering he has caused her and voices some doubts about their future, while at the same time confessing, "I love you." Just before that, he pretends to ogle a singer (Mona Goya) in the bright lights of a cabaret; this produces the paradox whereby illumination enables him to stage a lie, whereas total darkness alone authorizes sincerity. After his admission of love, she takes the flashlight from him so as to light the way they are going, as if she has sensed his inability to give a direction to their relationship.

Finally, after Catherine has understood the true reasons for their breakup and returns to throw herself into his arms, they are once again framed together, but most of the time with their eyes lowered or closed, as she theorizes about the new quality that François's blindness lends their love: "For you, I was just someone very nice to look at. . . . I wasn't up to it before, I was nothing. . . . I couldn't feel useful; and now here I am, needed by you. . . . It's delightful for a woman to feel she is indispensable!"

Quite apart from the typically Pétainist tone of this argument, whereby women were glad to put themselves in the service of a faltering patriarchy, the last spoken words of the film, when he takes her into his arms and says, "Turn out the light, so we'll be the same!," are a clear indication that renunciation of the voyeuristic gaze is a renunciation of the fantasy of absolute patriarchal power.

ℳ DOUCE
(Claude Autant-Lara, 1943)

Only six films made during the Occupation (out of 220) center on class antagonism (alongside some ten others that hinge on a class difference whose relevance is constantly denied). Marcel Pagnol's *La Fille du puisatier* (1940) bears the stamp of the prewar period: the antagonism between a bourgeois family and some ordinary farmers is resolved, under Marshal Pétain's gaze, by a symbolic reconciliation focused on an illegitimate baby. André Cayatte's *Au Bonheur des Dames* (1943) resolves the Zolaesque contradiction between salesgirls in a department store and their high-powered boss when he is suddenly converted to the benefits of Vichyite paternalism. Albert Valentin's *La Vie de plaisir* (1943) portrays the clash between an exclusive clan of aristocrats and an honest nightclub manager, which is resolved when the aristocratic daughter betrays her class in order to join the man she loves. Jean Grémillon's *Lumière d'été* (1942) depicts the conflict between a decadent nobleman and a young engineer, who has the support of a band of workers (an almost unprecedented situation for the period, which caused the movie to run into problems with the Vichyite censors), and the struggle results in the "people's execution" of the aristocrat. Marcel Carné's *Les Enfants du paradis* (1944) sublimates the complex network of social alliances and oppositions in a metaphysical tragedy. And in Claude Autant-Lara's *Douce* (1943), a clash between a landed aristocrat and the petite bourgeoisie, aided by the proletariat, is brought to an end, but not resolved, by an absurd tragedy.

The fact that class antagonism was seldom used as a dramatic device on which Occupation films hinged can probably be explained above all by Vichy's pressure in favor of national reconciliation. That reconciliation — against the invader — was also the main watchword of the Resistance (including its Communist wing, which declared a truce in the class war). On at least two occasions, the underground press explicitly attacked one or other of those movies, precisely in the name of national unity.

With the exception of Carné and Jacques Prévert's monumental *Les Enfants du paradis*, which was released after the war, the main critical support for most such films, apart from that of one or two "apolitical" writers (such as Roger Régent and Jacques Audiberti), came from the collaborationist press, and in particular Lucien Rebatet (whose nom de plume as a film critic was François Vinneuil) in *Paris Soir* and *Je suis partout*. And yet none of the above-mentioned movies can be likened to the very few fascistic feature films of the period (*Mermoz, Coup de tête, Le Carrefour des enfants perdus*), which were not necessarily to the liking of such committed critics, however. The only "class struggle" discourse publicly voiced (including in the underground press and the London-based radio stations) was that of the Paris fascists, who called for the death of the bourgeoisie, borrowing their class analyses from the then-banned Marxism. Hence the film critics among them were well-equipped to appreciate a cinema of conflict.

After the credit titles roll against the background of an open fire (we will return to this), the film opens with a lateral tracking shot showing the upper-class districts of Paris, with the Eiffel Tower still only half built; the date indicated is 1887, but the historical significance of this becomes clear only at the end of the movie. Deliberately or not, this very obvious model of the tower serves to underline the convention of the costume film. During the first — and most fruitful — period of his career (1942–52), Autant-Lara made no mystery about using purely conventional returns to the past as camouflage for his criticism of a contemporary social organization he rejected en bloc.

The constantly mobile camera takes us into a church and moves slowly toward a confessional, following the footsteps of a young sexton (Albert Rémy) who is prowling the nave; he stops for a moment to look at a nun meditating, then, a little farther on, picks up an umbrella that has fallen on the floor and props it up against a pew. In the darkness of the confessional, a woman whose veiled face cannot be recognized and whose whispered voice prevents us from identifying the actress, has apparently made a grave confession:

Priest: Do you see him often?
Woman: Every day!
Priest: Does he seek you out, or do you go to see him?
Woman: We live under the same roof.
Priest: Is he a relative of yours?
Woman: No . . .
Priest: A friend, a close friend?
Woman: No . . .
Priest: Is there a social difference between you? (*a pause*) A great enough difference to make marriage impossible? (*a pause*) A servant? (*a pause:*

the priest glances around him) Believe me, this marriage cannot bring you happiness!

When the unrepentant woman says she is determined to elope with the man she loves, the priest mentions hell and assures her she will not go far. "Given the state of mind [he finds her in]," he refuses to give her absolution.

The woman, of whom we get barely a glimpse, leaves the church. The sexton then discovers she has left her umbrella behind and takes it to the home of the Bonafé family, where the trusty housekeeper, Estelle (Gabrielle Fontan), recognizes it as belonging to "Miss Irène" (Madeleine Robinson). At this point, Irène appears at the top of the main staircase (a symbolic position she has to abandon at the end of the movie) and claims to remember that she did indeed leave her umbrella behind in the church. But a few minutes later, when speaking alone to her young pupil, Douce (Odette Joyeux), she scolds her for her absentmindedness. Douce, it turns out, had borrowed Irène's umbrella without her permission and left it in the church.

This transition from confessional to umbrella already encapsulates the web of sexual and class relationships that will structure the film. The two women, each in her own respective class position, are involved in a sexual relationship with a man — a relationship fraught with social transgression. The conversation reproduced above could have been attributed to either of the two women. But at the same time a strong link binds each of them to the other's future partner. This quadrille forms the basis of the whole structure of this complex film.

Douce's private tutor, Irène, went into service with the Bonafé family thanks to a discreet recommendation by her secret lover, Fabien Marani (Roger Pigaut), steward of the estate of Count Engelbert de Bonafé (Jean Debucourt) and his mother, the countess (Marguerite Moreno). Count Bonafé is decidedly an extreme case in the Occupation cinema's gallery of castrated fathers, with his pitiful demeanor and his connections with the lost war. He lost his right leg, which has been replaced by a noisy prosthesis. At the beginning of the movie, Douce complains at length about the touching contrast between that sinister noise, which accompanies her father wherever he goes and so frightened her when she was small, and the man's gentle and shy nature. Later on, the count himself, when talking privately in the library to Irène, whom he has caught putting back a volume of *Les Liaisons dangereuses*, uses Laclos's military career as a pretext to reveal that he too spent the war in the cavalry — the war of 1870, which must have reminded spectators of the film of more recent events. However, unlike Colonel Chabert (Raimu), whose arm was cut off by a saber, Bonafé "couldn't even lose his leg" in that lost war, but only in a silly show-jumping accident. What is more, this long-standing widower has been supplanted as head of the family by his authoritarian mother; when she makes her long-delayed appearance in the new elevator that raises her slowly and majestically in a medium close shot, Douce cannot resist announcing in an aside, "Gentlemen, the king!"

The presentation of each character, like that of the tutor and the countess, defines their place in the household. The way we first see Douce indicates her ambiguous and powerless position: a pan shot reveals her as though by chance—we do not even suspect her presence in the bedroom that Irène enters; we are introduced to the father by a close-up of his wooden leg, after which his rather ceremonious appearance as a door opens seems ridiculous; as for Marani the rebel, he appears for the first time outside the Bonafé mansion, resolutely facing the audience and turning his back on Irène, whom the spectator already identifies with this stifling aristocratic world.

It is in the library that the count finally declares that he is in love with Irène and that he wants to marry her and give her his name and a well-to-do life. When he gets carried away and embraces the young woman, we realize that she is overwhelmed by the opportunity that is being offered her—but also that she does not like the idea of physical contact with a man twice her age: 1943 is a far cry from the prewar period, when "incestuous" relationships went without saying (Vincendeau 1989). The tensions between Irène and her lover, who has been urging her to leave with him for Canada, have reached a breaking point ever since she forced him to return the money he stole from farm rentals, with which he had hoped to finance their trip. Despite that, later in her bedroom, when she begins to undress as soon as he touches her, we realize that she has him under her skin. The fact remains that ever since Marani enabled her to turn her back on poverty by securing her a position in such a well-to-do household she has lived in fear of becoming poor again. When the countess, who is sorting some old clothes that "will go to the poor," condescendingly offers her one piece, Irène curtly declines it as if she had just been slapped.

While the fear of lapsing back into poverty makes her young tutor feel insecure, Douce herself feels like a prisoner in her own home—and in her maidenly status. Her virginity is like the family treasure.

Returning from the discreet assignation with her lover in the course of which she refused to go to Canada with the money from the farm rentals, Irène is surprised to find Douce in her bedroom. Douce is watching for Marani, who is supposed to bring her a big fir tree for her "last Christmas as a little girl":

Douce: Do you mind my borrowing your window?

Irene: No, why?

Douce: One can see the street. . . . *I'm* a little street girl. Only a pane of glass separates us. . . .

Irene: That's quite a lot, a pane of glass.

Douce: But it can be broken.

It was through windows that wealthy nineteenth-century women peered enviously at the world outside. Douce feels imprisoned by windowpanes, whereas Irène feels protected by them. The first time we see Irène entering her bedroom, a draft blows the window wide open, and she rushes to close it. Later on, Marani, who wants to have it out with Irène despite her reluctance to do so, breaks a window to enter her bedroom, cutting his hand in the process. Finally, after Douce has eloped with Marani and the countess has ordered Irène to leave the house, the camera waits for her outside in the falling snow; we watch her through different windows as she packs her bags and briefly meets the count in a frosty and silent pantomime. He no longer wants her.

In the three movies that Autant-Lara and his usual scriptwriter, Jean Aurenche, made during the Occupation (*Le Mariage de Chiffon*, *Lettres d'amour*, and *Douce*), the extraordinary Odette Joyeux is a particularly striking emblem of female resistance and rebellion in a cinema that boasted many such figures, and Douce is her greatest role. Douce loves Marani as a man, but above all as a rebel, whereas his rebellious side is a threat for Irène, who has chosen to be submissive. The whole film hinges on this contrast between rebellion and submission — the very different rebellions of Marani and Douce, which they try in vain to bring together, and the submission of Irène, when she forces Marani to return the money from the farms. It is a submission that is always connected with money, as the Scottish servant explains, with figures to prove it, during the inauguration of the elevator, a central symbol of authority: given the short period of time she still has to live, each ride upstairs will cost the countess about twenty francs, whereas he, her servant, would be prepared "to carry her up on [his] back for forty sous — or even ten!"

Submission is everywhere, chiefly symbolized by sensorial deprivation: the muteness of the docile sexton and that which the elderly Estelle imposes on herself (and yet "she knows everything"); the deafness of the destitute old man whose home the countess forces Irène and Marani to visit with her in the course of a charitable outing. Marani, on the other hand, is "neither deaf, nor blind, nor dumb," as he angrily proclaims at the table, when he is on the point of creating a scandal and is only prevented from doing by Douce's pretending to faint.

Douce herself sees and hears everything. While supposedly in a swoon, her eyes pop open in close-up to size up the situation in a flash; trimming her Christmas tree with Marani, she watches intently for his reaction to the news of Irène's forthcoming marriage to the count; through the thin wall between her bedroom and Irène's, she can hear everything the two lovers say to each other (despite Irène's attempts to hush Marani precisely for fear of being over-heard); and when Douce plays the tune "A little love, a little hope" on her gui-tar, she "wakes up all the people in the house," who are decidedly reluctant to hear anything. In this house, the power of speech is monopolized by the count-ess. And with Marguerite Moreno's caustic performance, it is the theatrical volubility associated with the Ancien Régime that ruthlessly silences the more modern actors — quite a symbol for this age of backlash.

The submissive Irène would like to see Douce submit in turn. She gives her piano lessons (to her father's delight). But Douce is less interested in the piano, a lady's pursuit and a symbol of women's idleness or domesticity, than in a portable instrument like the guitar. When the time comes, her guitar case will serve to pack a few belongings before leaving with Marani. The handsome steward has agreed to elope with the young woman who loves him in order to get back at Irène, and at the count as well, for having taken her away from him. But according to Douce, it was actually Irène who triggered her rebellion, by unwittingly teaching her "her" song through the wall; in other words, Douce was first aroused by the sound of Irène and Marani making love through the wall between their bedrooms.

Among the actors who played leading male roles during the Occupation, Roger Pigaut is the exception that proves the rule, for there is nothing kind and gentle about him along the lines of such new young leads as Jean Marais, Gilbert Gil, François Périer, and Jean Desailly. A Communist Resistant, Pigaut had a short-lived career after the war playing idealist young rebels in movies like *Antoine et Antoinette*, *Les Frères Bouquinquant*, and *La Rose des mers*, be-fore going over to film direction when such insubordinate figures fell out of fashion. During the Occupation, he played a very similar rebel in *Sortilèges*, with dialogue by Jacques Prévert. In *Douce* the character he plays even went too far in the eyes of the censor. At the end of the hilarious scene where the countess visits a destitute elderly couple in their garret, the old woman ex-presses the hope that her benefactress will live to a ripe old age, and the latter urges her to be patient and resigned. The old woman then asks Irène, "And what about you, young lady? What should one wish you?" Marani intervenes, snapping, "Wish her impatience and rebellion!," and proudly leaves the garret, arm in arm with Irène. His remark was cut by the censors when the film came out, but Autant-Lara restored it after the Liberation.

This contrast between rebellion and submission, which structures the whole movie, gets transformed into other binary contrasts which are both concrete and symbolic:

~ Between idleness and domesticity: The countess believes that the ability to make a fire or prepare a hot meal are among the compulsory skills expected only of poor women (tasks that Irène hopes to be spared at last, when she marries the count). In Douce's mind, on the other hand, darning socks and washing her stockings herself are activities she values more than playing the piano, out of love for her man, no doubt, but above all as a way of asserting her freedom.

~ Between the elevator and the stairs: The elevator, whose installation is completed when the film opens is, like any modernization, an emblem of social power. It is via the elevator that the countess comes "on stage," and it is by inviting Irène into the elevator with him that the count begins to court her. Neither Douce nor Marani, on the other hand, ever take the elevator. They use only the stairs, just like the servants, and like all the poor who, as the countess complains on her charity errand, "always live on the very top floor." At the end of the movie Irène, who has fallen into disgrace, has to walk down the stairs carrying her own suitcase (as the countess has denied her the services of the butler).

~ Between water and fire, the film's central symbolism: Fire can be the fire of passion, but also the fire of hell with which the priest threatened the veiled young woman in the confessional. The profane version of fire is the fireplace with the Bonafés' monogram adorning the back wall — the fireplace on which the camera lingers during the credit titles and through whose flames, near the beginning of the movie, we see Douce describing the powerful yet pathetic figure of her father, the symbolic warder of her prison whom she no longer respects. It is also in front of her fireplace that the countess laments the social decline symbolized by marriages between different classes. Such wood fires are a luxury that the wealthy can afford without counting the cost, whereas wood is a precious commodity for the poor, who "hoard" it; the senile old man in his garret cries out with indignation when the countess is about to heat up the stew she has brought him, "My wood, my wood is being stolen!" "Shut up, it's a present!" says his wife, who is more willing to conform to the social order. A hotel bellboy, bringing logs to the room

where the eloping lovers have taken refuge, dispels the intimacy growing between them as he reminds Douce of the constraints of poverty
(there are no more invisible servants). And it is in telling Marani to
make a fire (using the more formal *vous* again) that Douce restores for
a time the class difference between them which he knows will never go
away. Finally, it is a fire that consumes Douce, when, after discovering
the intangible barriers that separate the sexes as well as classes, she is
preparing to go back to her family.

Water, on the other hand, symbolizes possible freedom, the high
seas, the ocean that Marani dreams of crossing to Canada. It is the sea
which is evoked by the darning egg whose inscription, "Trouville," the
seaside resort Irène has never visited, reminds her of the fleeting hopes
she had during her unhappy youth and of her impossible dream of a
little sailboat. The boat that stands on Douce's mantelpiece is beautiful but has never been in contact with water; when she wants to make
a gift of it to Irène, Irène refuses to accept it, just as she later refuses to
run off with Marani. She has already opted for the slavery of the home
and its warming fire. Finally, on the landing in front of the lovers' hotel
room, a little boy is patiently piecing together a jigsaw puzzle of a sail-
ing ship. When Irène, who has come to fetch Douce home in the hope
of sorting out the world that is collapsing around her, goes back down
the stairs having lost all hope, she accidentally scatters the puzzle with
the hem of her dress. The ensuing ellipse (a dissolve to the reassembled
puzzle) indicates that Douce and Marani have consummated their
love. But it is the same little boy whom Douce, unbeknown to Marani,
entrusts with the task of taking a note back to her family saying that
she has changed her mind and is coming back home. The note will end
up in the open fire, where the countess has thrown it.

The fire at the Opéra Comique theater, in which Douce dies so melodra-
matically, has often been problematic for spectators. In the already mentioned
British cut of the movie, the ending is purely and simply removed: Douce tells
Marani, in their box at the Opéra Comique, that she has finally decided not to
elope with him because she will always feel Irène's presence standing between
them. (In other words, she admits to him the insurmountable nature of class
differences, despite the love she feels and his desire.) We then suddenly see her
again at home, behind a window, a shot taken from the previous cut, which
ends this version.

But Autant-Lara (1974: 66) himself, in an interview with *Les Cahiers de la Cinémathèque*, says he wished he had opted for another ending, one closer to the original novel by Michel Davet — the pseudonym of a woman writer — in which Marani dies in the fire while trying to rescue Douce and "the great bourgeois façade engulfs 'the guilty woman'" (Siclier 1981: 233). On second thought, Autant-Lara probably felt uneasy about the moralizing dimension of the dénouement he had chosen, which was reminiscent of the punitive endings of so many prewar melodramas. And yet, in the context of the period and of the film itself, the ending he actually chose seems perfectly coherent and appropriate.

On the one hand, this "absurd" disaster (which was, however, historically accurate: the Opéra Comique did indeed burn down in 1887) surely stands for the debacle of 1940, which also put an end to countless individual dreams of happiness and freedom. Yet, when one takes a closer look at the sequence, the disaster is not as gratuitous as all that, since it is the symbolic consequence of Douce's incautious behavior, letting her gaze wander too much, flouting the rule of modesty that a proper young woman should observe (as Marani reminds her), and thus exposing herself to a lethal male gaze.

Indeed in the fashionable restaurant where she and Marani spend their last evening — and where we finally discover the complete lyrics and the meaning of the song heard repeatedly throughout the movie ("A little hope in you / A little love for a day / A simple farewell, goodbye and good night") — Douce keeps looking around her, thus apparently encouraging a society man (Roger Blin) to stare at her. He continues to stare at her right up to her death — a desiring and murderous gaze emphasized by the only swish pan in the film, which here replaces the usual reverse-angle cut. Later we see the same playboy seemingly spying on Douce from the wings of the Opéra Comique, while also watching the ballerinas on stage. And it is this same man who, by going through a door in a set, causes a piece of tulle to come into contact with a gas lamp, thus triggering the fatal fire.

It is, of course, hardly surprising that the same censors who decided to prevent British audiences from seeing the confessional scene also lopped off the movie's gruesome dénouement: Marani, his face blackened by smoke and his clothes in disarray, comes to tell the countess and her household that the woman they loved more than anything is dead. The countess curses the couple formed again by the tutor and the steward, and driving them from the house exhorts them to leave "together, above all together." She knows that from now on they are as inextricably bound together as they are incompatible, since their relationship has been sealed by Douce's death but divided forever in their loss of the only individual solutions open to the poor in the context of traditional European society: emigration for men, social advancement through marriage for women.

Douce is a less "feminist" movie than other great films of the period, such as *Le Ciel est à vous*, *Falbalas*, and *Marie-Martine*. But it has the great merit of articulating dialectically sexual and class oppression. It does not idealize women in the manner of the Pétainist Abel Gance (*Vénus aveugle*), any more than it does in the manner of the Communist Louis Daquin (*Madame et le mort*). It demonstrates that women's consciousness and rebellion, or else their alienation and submission, are an inextricable function of their class situation, and that social oppression and patriarchal oppression are the two sides of the same coin.

LE CORBEAU
(Henri-Georges Clouzot, 1943)

The subject of a heated controversy when it was released in 1943 as well as for a long time after the war, *Le Corbeau* is today French cinema's emblematic Occupation film, featuring on the cover of at least three books devoted to that period. Directed by Henri-Georges Clouzot for Continental, the production company in which he enjoyed important artistic responsibilities, the movie was attacked in a celebrated article in the underground *Les Lettres françaises*, which saw it as a collaborationist-inspired machine of war aimed at reinforcing the German image of France as a country rotten to the core. At the Liberation, Clouzot was criticized by the Purge Commission for having allowed his film to be distributed in Germany under the title *A Small French Town*. (The charge was dropped when it was discovered that it was erroneous.) But that damning verdict persisted in milieux close to the Resistance for a long time after the war.

It is fashionable today to pour ridicule on the *Lettres françaises* article on the grounds that it was overanxious to denounce anything that could divide France in the face of the enemy and that its political bias caused the artistic qualities of "a masterpiece" to be overlooked. Yet the article did recognize in *Le Corbeau* a "class hatred" of a particular kind, that of the anarchist right inspired by the ideas of Georges Sorel. Clouzot's movie did not go down well with Vichy either, and more particularly with the Catholic Cinema Bureau, which saw it as an "essentially pernicious" work and awarded the film its lowest rating (Siclier 1981: 453). This was not the first time that there was a convergence between two puritanisms, that of the Pétainists and that of the Resistants, two camps on opposite sides of the political spectrum but both very keen to foster an edifying image of the nation.

While admitting his sympathies with the "social side of fascism," Clouzot denied before the Purge Commission that he had entertained any of the "anti-French" intentions attributed to him, arguing—in somewhat contradictory fashion—that he had registered a first version of Louis Chavance's script in 1937 (Chavance 1937) and that he and Chavance were both determined to denounce the practice of anonymous letters during the dark years (Bertin-Maghit 1989: 224). During the Occupation, champions of *Le Corbeau*, whether the collaborationist critic Lucien Rebatet or the apolitical Roger Régent, were determined to judge the movie according to purely artistic criteria, like all those who after the war felt that Clouzot was being unfairly criticized for ideas he did not hold. In the early 1970s a left-wing critic, Marcel Oms (1973), in a closely argued analysis, saw *Le Corbeau* as a film that rigorously and systematically denounced the petit bourgeois order of the broad mass of the French people "down the centuries."

Irrespective of the controversy that erupted after the Liberation and the prejudices of every period, let us try to analyze the movie in the context of French cinema during the Occupation. For, contrary to what most film historians seem to think, *Le Corbeau* is in no way a timeless work of art, floating in the Platonic firmament of social satire. On the contrary, it is a movie firmly rooted in its time, generated by the interaction of, on the one hand, an ideology which the Resistants on *Les Lettres françaises* understood to be the right-wing anarchism of collaborationist intellectuals and, on the other, several major themes that ran right through French cinema during those four years.

The opening tracking shot of a small-town graveyard establishes in two-fold fashion the film's subtext, first, because it hints at the deadly aspect of the microsociety we are about to be shown, and second, because the problematic survival of women in childbirth (and of their babies) is one of the movie's key themes. In the first narrative sequence of the film, Dr. Rémy Germain (Pierre Fresnay) washes his hands in highly symbolic fashion after having saved the life of a woman who has given birth to a baby that did not survive and impassively advises her husband's grandmother to ask him to make her pregnant again in a few months' time. This scene introduces what will become, in the course of the movie, the theme of abortion. In this case, Germain is, objectively speaking, an abortionist; as Dr. Delorme (Antoine Balpêtré), the head doctor of the hospital where Germain works, remarks to him, "This is the third time in a month." We learn later that Germain's attitude is motivated by his own wife's death in childbirth, caused by an obstetrician who gave priority—in vain, as it happened—to the baby's life. As a result of this double loss, Germain, a brilliant brain surgeon, fled to the remote provinces and under an assumed name became a general practitioner determined to save the lives of mothers. At the same time, after finding a room with the headmaster of the local school (Noël Roquevert), he will have more than one opportunity to make it clear that he cannot stand children. True, he is not an abortionist in the derogatory sense usually applied to the word. (Indeed he is the only "clean" man in this small town precisely because he is from somewhere else, the capital.) And he gets a chance to prove it when a veiled woman, hired by his enemies, begs him to carry out the service that is frowned upon by the law. Finally, when the *corbeau* (the writer of poison-pen letters) is identified and punished, Dr. Germain allows himself to be moved when Denise Saillens (Ginette Leclerc), a supposed slut he has made pregnant, attempts to abort herself. Then, opening the window to let in those children's voices he previously had refused to hear, he abandons his misanthropic pose to envisage a positive future with a wife and children.

Both champions and detractors of the movie have interpreted, either implicitly or explicitly, the central character's last-minute change of heart as a forced touch of optimism aimed at counteracting the film's dark truth. But whether or not they like it, the whole framework of *Le Corbeau* is consonant with the most conformist, and even the most Vichyite, movies of the period: the condemnation of abortion and its corollary, the acceptance of illegitimate children, which were not themes to be found in prewar films, are a specific feature of Pétainist melodrama.

Another strong link between this movie and its period is its calling into question of the "incestuous" couple, whose unnatural character was denounced by many contemporary films. In *Le Corbeau*, the whole problem stems in the last account from a marriage between a young woman, Laura (Micheline Francey), and an old man, Michel Vorzet (Pierre Larquey), who cannot satisfy her. Moreover however much the critics may ramble on about the way Larquey is here cast against type, he was in fact an actor who had by then become a star precisely in the role of the "discredited father" that was a constant feature of Occupation movies. At the beginning of *Le Corbeau* Vorzet, when referring to his own marriage, hints that it is a mistake for an old man to take a young woman as his spouse; here as elsewhere he acts as spokesperson for the authors.

The film's voice is twofold. Dr. Germain is one of its mouthpieces. A Pari-

Pierre Larquey and Pierre Fresnay in *Le Corbeau*, 1943. Courtesy of Cinémathèque française.

sian intellectual (his apparent roots in Grenoble are just part of his camouflage), he expresses the views of the authors, "entomologists" engrossed by the hypocritical mores of a sanctimonious and reactionary *France profonde*. This reflects the deep sense of alterity felt by the urban intelligentsia, which goes back at least as far as the time when La Bruyère, in a celebrated passage in his *Caractères*, discovered the "subhuman" peasantry, and which can be traced up through Balzac and Zola to Marcel Aymé, for example (Weber 1976). The "primitive" peasantry (which Germain washes from his hands) is in fact presented, immediately after the film's opening shot of the cemetery, as a metonymy for the provincial petite bourgeoisie whose horrors are shortly to be revealed to us. The mockery aimed at traditional Catholic rites forms an integral part of the same ideology, as when a letter flutters down from a gallery in the church during a sermon or slips out of a funeral wreath on a hearse.

The philosophical voice of the film, on the other hand, is provided by Dr. Vorzet, the psychiatrist played by Larquey, almost every time he opens his mouth, in particular when he mocks his own profession, whose artificiality he denounces on his return from a psychiatrists' conference in Paris. He is fully aware, even before Germain finds out for himself, of the town's "rottenness" and everyone's little failings. (For instance, Rolande, the "little girl" at the post office, has got into the habit of "borrowing" money, allegedly to cover up an indiscretion in her handling of the cash register.) This omniscience makes him a perfect candidate (as he himself points out on several occasions) for the role of the poison pen who is sowing discord in the town.

But then comes the problem of his motive. When one has the opportunity to analyze this film with students—this is one of the methods an academic can use to test the way a text may have been understood—one invariably notices the extent to which the hermeneutic issue (Who is the poison pen?) is problematic, even when the film is over and the question seems to have been answered at a narrative level. The final explanation is indeed provided so quickly and, what is more, in two contradictory versions—the psychiatrist's wife, Laura, when accused by her husband, accuses him in turn before being bundled off to a lunatic asylum—that there remains a degree of uncertainty about the respective responsibilities of this "diabolical couple." When this concluding uncertainty is compounded by the discovery that the main culprit is the movie's philosophical spokesman and that no plausible motive is offered by the text other than his "madness" (the argument put forward by his wife as she is about to be confined), any analyst of the movie is forced to look for the key to the mystery outside the film. Once the mouthpiece of the film's misanthropy (in contrast with Germain's misanthropy, which is "cured" at the end) has been revealed to be the man who wrote the poison-pen letters, which have had the effect of exposing a general state of rottenness, ranging from Bonnevie, the hospital bursar, and its director to the subprefect himself, one ends up concluding that the "true" writers of the letters are Clouzot and Chavance. So the movie's narrative boils down to a monumental and incredibly skillful manipulation of the spectator.

Most commentators see the film's key sequence as being the scene in the classroom after the celebrated marathon dictation (which of course serves no purpose, since the poison pen is none other than the person giving the dictation). Vorzet then "proves" to Germain that there is no such thing as a single truth and that everything has two sides, a dark and a light side. (The proof offered by Vorzet is the fact that you burn your fingers if you try to stop a swinging lamp!) Now this scene, more than any other, is of the order of Freudian denial: the movie, like so many others both before and after the war (see *L'Assassinat du Père Noël*), liquidates, in no uncertain terms, that petite bourgeoisie that people like Clouzot (as well as left-wing anarchists like Jacques Prévert and Henri Jeanson before the war) saw as the perfect embodiment of stupidity and maliciousness.

A semiological analysis of this manipulation — which is extraordinary in its technical perfection, and the equivalent of which can be found in all Clouzot's greatest successes (*Quai des Orfèvres*, *Les Diaboliques*, and *Le Salaire de la peur*) — is beyond the scope of this analysis. But another dimension is worth examining closely. For the film's Manichaeism, while undoubtedly contrasting Vorzet's cynical and Germain's indignant lucidity with the "rottenness" of the small town, also contrasts, in a roundabout way, men's greed, hypocrisy, and thirst for power with what eventually turns out to be the innocence of women. This is one of the movie's surprising features in view of the unfailing misogyny to be found in many of Clouzot's subsequent films. Should this be interpreted as yet another effect of the "feminizing" context of French cinema at the time?

It would certainly seem so. Chavance's original screenplay (Chavance 1937: 3) was thoroughly misogynistic, since in it Vorzet's wife is the only guilty party: "The emotional mainspring of the whole story is that Laura is secretly in love with the young doctor. We do not know where her husband is. She becomes decidedly frustrated." It is, by the way, amusing to note that the shift which led from this absent husband to an "incestuous" and omnipresent husband went through an intermediate version — an initial shooting script written by Clouzot (possibly with Chavance) entitled "Aux frontières du mal," in which Laura is actually Vorzet's daughter! What is more, while the major themes of Occupation cinema — criticism of incestuous fathers and an idealization of women, criticism of abortion and natalism — are nowhere to be found in Chavance's first screenplay, they are emphasized to a greater extent in the finished movie than in Clouzot's first shooting script, in which there is no scene at a farm, no mention by Vorzet of the age difference between him and his wife, no attempted abortion by the pregnant Denise, and no trace, in his last scene with Denise, of Germain's key indication that he is a convert to Vichyite ideology: "We cannot sacrifice the future to the present."

The construction of all the female characters in the film, with no exception, hinges on an illusion. And that illusion is always resolved in the same way, which tends to show women in a more favorable light than men. Let's look at each of them in order of appearance. The rather unprepossessing nurse, Marie Corbin (Héléna Manson), arouses the hostility of Germain (and indeed of the spectator) in the first scene that brings them together. She would seem to be jealous of the mutual attraction that exists between the town's new doctor and her sister, the beautiful Laura Vorzet. But the nurse is soon to become a scapegoat pursued by the hateful rabble, and this scene in which the poor woman narrowly escapes being lynched enables the filmmakers to vent all their bile on that *Français moyen* whom they so loathe. Indeed champions of the movie see that scene as a "courageous denunciation" of the black-marketing shopkeeper class during the Nazi Occupation.

As for Laura Vorzet, she has sided with Dr. Germain from the start, and the first sign of a relationship between the two seems to spring up. Although it remains chaste (she is faithful to her husband, and he to the memory of his late wife), it arouses the anger of the mysterious poison pen. At the last moment, Vorzet "reveals" that his wife's shameful physical passion for Dr. Germain is the basis for the whole horrible episode (he claims she was the person who wrote the first letter): fire beneath the ice. But immediately afterward there is a second twist to the story, when Laura recovers her innocence by becoming a victim, since it turns out that her husband has had her committed without justification.

The bespectacled teenage Rolande (Liliane Maigné), the schoolmaster's younger daughter, who has a job as a post office clerk, is presented for a long time as a sly and prying liar with, above all, a perverse interest in sexual matters. But when the dénouement comes (in a scene that was added during the shooting) we realize that she is in fact supportive of her older sister, Denise, whom she helps to patch things up with Dr. Germain, and that she is basically a good sort.

It is in the case of Denise Saillens, played by Ginette Leclerc (the female star of the movie, even though she does not appear on the screen more often than Héléna Manson), that the illusion is the most egregious and manipulative: in a role tailor-made for Leclerc as an archetypal slut, she strives from the start to seduce Germain when he sounds her chest, thus causing the puritan doctor to react with disdain. Having nevertheless made love to her, he despises her (and himself) even more, and treats her like a prostitute. His harsh judgment of her seems to be confirmed by the way she disguises her physical handicap (she has a limp) by wearing an orthopedic shoe that enables her to appear "normally desirable": camouflage is no doubt the specific characteristic of women on the make who try to ensnare "honest" men (Corbin 1978). And yet all this is just an illusion, since at the end of the movie the embittered Germain is regenerated only after he has come to accept Denise, another "basically honest" woman and the mother of his unborn child.

Also worth noting is the character played by Sylvie, a silent and self-effacing cleaning woman able to mete out rough justice with her own hand, ruthlessly executing Dr. Vorzet with the razor her son used to commit suicide in the hospital after the poison pen had revealed to him how seriously ill he was. Finally,

Héléna Manson, Micheline Francey, and Ginette Leclerc in *Le Corbeau*, 1943. Courtesy of Cinémathèque française.

it is a woman (Lucienne Bogaert), sent by the local worthies to compromise Germain as an abortionist (after he has already been described as one in a poison-pen letter), who reveals to us his tragic and laudable past by recognizing him as the surgeon who once saved her life.

Ranged against these women, the true target of the movie is in fact patriarchal power, whether it be medical or political; it is these hypocritical and unscrupulous men who, in the absence of Germain, the film's conscience, are caught by the camera in the act of revealing their shameful behavior (as in the grotesque confrontation between Dr. Delorme and Bonnevie, whose hands are tied by a kind of reciprocal blackmail, or the sordid plots of local councilors, in the midst of whom Vorzet plays at being a cynical observer). The only person to emerge unscathed, probably because of his qualities as an intellectual worker with whom the filmmakers could identify, is the one-armed schoolmaster, Saillens (Noël Roquevert), another castrated father.

Paradoxically, then, *Le Corbeau* — a film reputed to be the complete antithesis of the form and substance of "Vichyite cinema" — turns out after analysis to espouse some of the leading watchwords of the period: the devaluation of patriarchy, the condemnation of the "incestuous" couple, the idealization of women, and even the promotion of natalism. The only feature in fact that sets it apart from the Vichyite cinema as a whole is its dark realism, which can indeed be attributed, as it quite reasonably was by voices from the underground, to the right-wing anarchism of the collaborationist circles in which Clouzot moved during the Occupation.

ℐ *LE CIEL EST À VOUS*
(Jean Grémillon, 1943)

A mystery surrounds Jean Grémillon's *Le Ciel est à vous*, now regarded by specialists (Sellier 1989) and a fair number of cinephiles as the director's most accomplished work: during the Occupation, it was virtually the only movie that earned praise from all critics, whatever their political coloring, from the collaborationist press to underground journals and Vichyite organs. In 1972, while U.S. feminist academics were delighted at their discovery of *The Woman Who Dared*, as the film was tendentiously titled in English, participants at a French conference devoted to a reappraisal of some forty films of the period were sharply divided over Grémillon's film: one of them, in agreement with the underground *Les Lettres françaises* and the film historian Georges Sadoul, saw it as an undoubtedly Resistant movie, while another detected in it the characteristics of a "Poujadist" cinema before the term had been coined, and yet another preferred to stress its feminist dimension (*Les Cahiers de la Cinémathèque* 1973). Even today the ideological consensus prompted by *Le Ciel est à vous* during the Occupation continues to raise questions.

It could be that this consensus has not been taken seriously enough and needs to be examined more closely in order to understand to what extent the strictly political perspective that has been generally applied to French film by most historians for over fifty years is reductive and blinkered. According to that perspective, any discernible phenomenon, thought, or act that took place in French society between June 1940 and August 1944 — and therefore any film — was a product of either the collaboration, the Resistance, Pétainism, a wait-and-see attitude, escapism or ("at best") timeless art.

Consequently a fundamental misunderstanding of the political specificities of "private life" and its representations has arisen. People tend to regard as irrelevant for an understanding of this particular past (and incidentally its cinema) the deeply felt yearning for a different relationship between the sexes — both within and outside the framework of the heterosexual couple — which, as we have learned from modern feminism, also has a political dimension, even if in France that dimension has always been, and continues to be, widely repressed. Now during the Occupation, as we demonstrate at length elsewhere, that yearning was closer to the surface of the French collective consciousness than at any other period before or since—apart perhaps from the 1960s. But paradoxically, that yearning could become the subject of a tacit consensus precisely because it was repressed. (Witness the total silence with which critics at the time greeted the sudden, spectacular feminization of movies after the 1940 defeat.) It still fell into the category of the unsaid, the "extra-ideological." Articles at the time that praised *Le Ciel est à vous* did so in essentially nationalistic or chauvinistic terms and talked about the greatness and heroism of the French woman and the French family, even though the film totally ignores such considerations. This suggests to us that we should look elsewhere for the veritable subtext of that consensus.

As Yves Chalas (1985) has observed so perspicaciously, the French longed unanimously, and whatever their ideology, to move on from the structures and values of market capitalism as embodied by the Third Republic—which was also, we should add, the period when the patriarchy ruled supreme, as can be seen from its cinema, among other things. If one accepts that hypothesis, one can better understand the consensus among (male) critics regarding *Le Ciel est à vous*, postulating that even if most of them did not allude directly to the film's plea in favor of new relations within the couple and the emancipation of women, they were sensitive to this aspiration. One can also better understand why the (male) participants at the 1972 conference failed to understand the consensus of that period, given, on the one hand, the repression even today of such aspirations in France and, on the other, the way French political thinking is focused on issues in the public sphere.

After its opening sequence, which shows a large group of children from an orphanage in black uniforms singing on an outing—which recurs at regular intervals during the movie—*Le Ciel est à vous* shows a symbolic house move: the Gauthier family (Pierre, Thérèse, their two children, and Thérèse's mother) leave the old country garage they have been running for years and settle in a nearby village. The move contains in a nutshell the movie's central issue. This antiquated garage, where father and son take one last look at the plank on which the height of the children was penciled year after year, symbolizes the old family order; it is due to be demolished to make way for an airfield symbolizing the future—the future of France and the world, but above all of the Gauthier family. The move also suggests the fragility of patriarchal rule. True, during this first narrative sequence, the family order is depicted as more or less normal: it is Pierre Gauthier (Charles Vanel), the self-important father, who

Raoul Marco, Madeleine Renaud, and Charles Vanel in *Le Ciel est à vous*, 1943. Courtesy of Cinémathèque française.

seems to run the whole show; the obedient children help out as best they can; the shrewish mother-in-law (Raymonde Vernay), a caricature of the old order and of the complaining but dependent old woman, protests having to get on to the back of the overloaded and rather rickety truck. And yet it is Thérèse Gauthier (Madeleine Renaud) who takes the wheel.

As they are in the process of moving into the large flat above the new garage, an incident occurs that hints at a chink in the patriarchal order. Jacqueline (Anne-Marie Labaye), the Gauthier's elder daughter, is a piano student (and a highly gifted one, as we soon discover). The only way to get her instrument into the second-floor flat is to hoist it up through the window. At least that is the opinion — in the absence of Pierre, who has been held up at the old garage — of the young village lads who have taken charge of the move. Confident of their strength and despite the fears of Jacqueline and her mother, they start hoisting the heavy piano. When the mother notices they seem to have misgivings, she challenges them: "Come on! Are you men or not, eh?" Almost immediately, one of the showoffs lets the rope slip, and the piano is smashed to smithereens on the pavement below. At that point Pierre arrives in the square and, discovering the disaster, tries rather pathetically to restore male authority:

"Don't anyone touch what's left of the piano! I'll see what can be salvaged!" But never again in the course of the movie will he be able to exercise that authority unchallenged.

Le Ciel est à vous deals with the oppressive weight of a patriarchal order that is beginning to lose its grip and that is embodied throughout by a woman, Thérèse's mother. This in itself is a fundamental insight: slaves internalize their master's values. But the main theme of the movie is the division of sexual roles within the couple and the contradictions that handicap a woman who tries to reconcile domestic duties — which she willingly accepts — with an independent activity.

As the Gauthiers settle into their new garage, one scene in particular illustrates the role of "superwoman" allotted to the wife and mother in any family of workers. Gauthier has agreed to spend the night repairing the car of a customer who is pressed for time. When the man arrives first thing in the morning to collect his car, he is amazed to learn that not only did the garage owner's wife spend the whole night organizing the garage while her husband was repairing the vehicle, but she is at that very moment preparing the children for school and making coffee for himself and Gauthier. This evidence of what he sees as Thérèse's exceptional energy prompts him to suggest to her that she should manage his automobile agency in Limoges. Thérèse accepts the job despite the drawbacks involved in leaving Pierre and her mother with the task of looking after the house and the children. The household needs cash, and Thérèse is dying to use her abilities elsewhere.

In Limoges she does a wonderful job as a businesswoman, and her new boss seems happy with her. Yet she cannot help worrying about what might be going on at home in her absence. When she can no longer contain herself and returns home unexpectedly, her worst fears are confirmed: the flat is dusty, her son has injured himself slightly after sliding recklessly down a banister, and Pierre is nowhere to be found. After a swift investigation, Thérèse discovers that, contrary to his promise not to let himself be tempted by the new flying club built on land where his former garage once stood, for weeks he has been taking locals up for their first flight. Before owning a garage, Pierre worked "in aviation," or, more precisely, he was the mechanic of the top fighter Georges Guynemer during World War I. Learning to fly has been child's play for him.

In Thérèse's case, on the other hand, her first contact with aviation took place toward the beginning of the movie, in an extremely "female" mode. Before the inauguration of the flying club, the star guest and crack aerobatics pilot, the beautiful Lucienne Ivry (Anne Vandène), needs a mechanic to repair her plane. The head of the club, Dr. Maulette (Léonce Corne), calls on Pierre's services. Once he has repaired the plane, he is clearly astounded by the aviatrix's feats. This arouses in his wife a curious mixture of jealousy and fear for her husband—a doubly "female" reaction. The scene she makes when she returns from Limoges to take charge of family and home again—having proved they cannot do without her—is perfectly consistent with her role as a protective mother (a role she inherited from her own mother, as we note repeatedly). And yet Thérèse, as she is constructed by the film's realistic Utopia, is not satisfied with her role as a perfect and much loved mother. She is missing "something," and when she does eventually manage to fill that gap, her discovery curiously resembles that of sexual pleasure.

Because she believes, mistakenly, that her husband has started flying again in secret, she goes looking for him at the flying club and lets Dr. Maulette persuade her to take her first flight with him. (The way he challenges her—"To get into one of those, what it mostly takes is guts"—is curiously reminiscent of her mother's challenge to the piano movers, and Thérèse's reply is amazingly "virile": "Are you trying to say I don't have guts? Hang on a minute, doctor: *I* don't have guts?!") Then Pierre turns up at the flying club and discovers, to his alarm, that his wife is "up there." When the little plane finally lands, Thérèse falls into his arms, swooning with explicitly physical pleasure: "Pierre, I'll never ever stop you from flying again."

The camera never goes up in a plane with either of the protagonists. The flying lessons Pierre now gives Thérèse, as well as the flights they make together, are completely elided from the film according to a narrative logic that has nothing to do with the difficult shooting conditions specific to the period: the action is always seen through the eyes of the "passive" member of the couple, the one who remains on the ground. First there is Thérèse's viewpoint, in the first scenes already described, when she is still a prisoner of her "woman's role"; then Pierre, following a minor accident in which he breaks his arm, gives up flying, having noticed, moreover, that his wife is a more gifted pilot than he is, and decides he will be of more use to her as a mechanic on the ground. At the point when he gives up flying and accepts the "female" role in their couple, he makes a moving declaration in which he draws a parallel between the new loving relationship he and his wife have discovered and the working relationship he had with Guynemer during the war. "I love you even more than on the day Claude was born!" he concludes with tears in his eyes.

When Thérèse decides to tackle the women's record for a straight-course flight, she sacrifices her daughter's new piano in order to finance preparations for the somewhat presumptuous undertaking. This important theme of Jacqueline's musical vocation runs like a thread throughout the film and admirably embodies the objective contradiction experienced by a woman in a patriarchal environment between Thérèse's role as mother and the pursuit of her personal projects, which clash with those of her daughter. For Thérèse's flying activity is portrayed as a passion, a "gratuitous" activity similar to an artistic one; the talent and ambition of Jacqueline, who is encouraged by her piano teacher, Larcher (played by Jean Debucourt, a "gentle male" figure par excellence), are constantly compared with her mother's love of flying. Thérèse herself is perfectly aware of the parallel but refuses to compromise: when it becomes clear that the piano needs to be sold if she is to achieve the goal she and Pierre are agreed upon, she doesn't look back.

Larcher continues to give Jacqueline lessons in secret, even after Thérèse, clinging to her role as a conservative mother while relentlessly pursuing her career as an aviatrix (this dichotomy lies at the heart of the movie), has forbidden her daughter to apply for the Conservatoire and, as though driven by class reflex, strongly urges her to follow a sensible career as a pharmacist. Larcher reveals the meaning of this contradiction toward the end of the film, since he is the only close friend of the Gauthiers to stick up for their enthusiasm for flying when all the other petits bourgeois have ganged up with the mother-in-law in heaping criticism on Pierre when it seems that Thérèse must have come down in the Mediterranean.

The movie culminates with this dramatic episode of her flight to Africa, which Barthélémy Amengual sees as the metaphor that most justifies the term *Resistant* being applied to *Le Ciel est à vous*: "In the film, . . . the achievements of big companies are contrasted with the work of tinkerers, amateurs, people who set off without a radio, poor guys who embark on tasks that are too big for them. That is precisely the kind of criticism that was leveled at a handful of political partisans and Resistants for wanting to launch into undertakings that normally required chiefs of staff, the Allies, de Gaulle in London, and an officially constituted army with the weapons it needed" (*Les Cahiers de la Cinémathèque* 1973: 37). Amengual's comments seem fully justified. The explicitly Resistant dimension of the movie is confirmed by its allusion to Louis Aragon's first Resistant poem, "Les Lilas et les roses," published in *Le Figaro* and secretly distributed throughout the country as early as 1940 (Daix 1994). In *Le Ciel est à vous*, "Le Temps des lilas et des roses" is a the title of a love song that Larcher plays on the piano at the Gauthier parents' request, and which, ignoring cultural barriers, he associates at the end of the film "with that other thing which [Thérèse and Pierre] must have discovered in order to get carried away together, to surpass [themselves], thanks to that song [they] continued to hear." During the same scene and in the same spirit, Larcher refuses to allow his mother-in-law to pass judgment on her daughter by retorting to her, "Madame, you would understand better if, in the whole of music, you liked something other than the march in *Aïda*!"—which would seem to be a subversive allusion to the use of that tune to celebrate the departure of troops to the front during World War I (see Louis Guilloux, *Le Pain des rêves*, 1942).

However, these serious considerations should not lead one, for example, to dismiss the penultimate scene of the movie as a mere comical interlude aimed at easing the tense atmosphere after many long hours of worry. At the air base in the Sahara where Thérèse has safely landed after easily beating the record, the heroine of the day is chiefly concerned about her family and says to a dumbfounded officer, "The minute I'm not there, everything's a mess!" Indeed this remark brings us back to the film's central dialectic, as it was formulated by the bisexual Grémillon in his Utopian discourse on the egalitarian couple, while at the same time marking the limits that could not be overstepped at the time (and even today to a great extent): while women can take on anything, men cannot yet manage to do the same.

Like some other movies of the period (in particular *Le Journal tombe à cinq heures* and *Madame et le mort*), *Le Ciel est à vous* comes out in favor of a "new couple" based on equality and a job outside the home for both of its members. But it remains an exceptional movie in the context of all traditional cinema, and not only in France, in that it refuses to idealize: it demonstrates that a woman who wants both to raise a family and to embark on an independent activity for her own pleasure and emancipation comes up against a host of contradictions which the film does not resolve. This can be seen, in addition to the scene in the desert, in the startling sequence in which the two children, "abandoned" by their parents who have set off to try their luck, stand looking at the marks left by the plane in the sawdust of the garage while the column of black-clad orphans comes marching by—a recurring reminder of the movie's depiction of Utopia's reverse side, as well as of the countless family tragedies caused by the war. This sequence movingly encapsulates the contradictions faced by a mother who refuses to give herself body and soul to her children, as required by a tradition that is both pernicious and deep-seated, as well as being a terrible waste of talent and happiness.

It would be absurd, of course, to argue that this Utopian dialectic is neither right wing nor left wing; the scriptwriters Albert Valentin and Charles Spaak were certainly not right wing, and Grémillon took an active part in the Resistance. But if a critic like the one writing for *L'Action française* felt in sympathy with the movie, it is not in our opinion because it displays some kind of Poujadism but because, without elaborating the slightest thesis likely to offend people's feelings directly, it proposed an ideal to which all men and women could aspire in their heart of hearts, particularly during a deeply disturbed period when values of all kinds were in a state of crisis, and irrespective of whether certain individuals felt the need to take advantage of that crisis in order to advocate the most retrograde models of society.

While *Le Ciel est à vous* is definitely left wing, it does not espouse "feminism" in the modern sense, which regards marriage, children, and even heterosexual couples as hindrances preventing women from fulfilling themselves. Such a view had at the time no social meaning for either men or women. But fifty years on, who in France can argue that *Le Ciel est à vous* no longer has any meaning for us?

ℛ *FALBALAS*
(Jacques Becker, 1944)

Falbalas, the shooting of which began on March 1, 1944, is a transitional movie on the borderline between the Occupation and the postwar period. It was in fact released after *Les Enfants du paradis*, in June 1945. Although it got excellent reviews when it came out, *Falbalas* was long underestimated by the auteurists on *Les Cahiers du cinéma*, who considered it inferior to the same director's *Casque d'Or* (*Golden Marie*), *Touchez pas au grisbi* (*Grisbi*), and *Le Trou* (*The Hole*). Jacques Becker's third feature has been gradually reassessed over the past twenty years, with increased interest in the style of its mise-en-scène and in its acute psychological description of the creative process (Naumann 1991).

On the other hand, there has been little discussion about the aspects that particularly interest us here: the way the film explains and engages with the contradictions that resulted from the Defeat and the Occupation and that were exacerbated by Pétainist ideology: a profound crisis in male identity and the patriarchal order and the emergence of autonomous female figures. What is more, *Falbalas*, like *Les Dames du Bois de Boulogne*, anticipates certain aftereffects of a war whose outcome, by the beginning of 1944, was clearly imminent. There were already the first stirrings of a reordering process which male power, after being symbolically regenerated by the Resistance, would shortly endeavor to impose on the French, and in particular on women.

While *Falbalas* is one of the few Occupation movies that bristles with allusions to the material restrictions that affected the lives of French people during the dark years (for instance, the replacement of the car by the bicycle, even in wealthy milieux), it also focuses at a very profound level on the disruption of the patriarchal order caused by the Débâcle of 1940: truncated or dispersed families, impotent or absent fathers, mothers forced to take charge of everything, orphaned children.

Micheline (Micheline Presle) is an orphan and an out-of-towner: she arrives in Paris from Reims and is put up by her aunt (Jane Marken) at her private mansion in Paris while waiting to get married to Daniel Rousseau (Jean Chevrier), the nice but rather dull son of a silk manufacturer in Lyon. She meets a friend of her fiancée, Philippe Clarence (Raymond Rouleau), who is already a well-known couturier and who gives her no peace until she yields to his advances. But while the irresistible ladies' man regards their relationship as an affair that will help his inspiration, Micheline discovers desire and love. The clash of those two contradictory forces has tragic consequences.

The phoney stability of the bourgeois family is already suggested by the "tribe" that welcomes Micheline in Paris, and whose father is nowhere to be seen; the mother (Marken) rules over a gaggle of ten children and teenagers, all of them equally loathsome, who swoop on Micheline like birds of prey. This send-up of the large and "right-thinking" family is particularly telling in the context of Pétainist ideology, which saw such families as the keystone of a "regenerated" France. This theme is brilliantly orchestrated during the game of Ping-Pong, with its mechanically rhythmical series of cuts geared to the click of the table tennis balls and the mesmerized expressions of the spectators, who are like a host of automata that bombard Micheline until she collapses. Here we see a game of skill turned into a death-dealing mechanism by the aggressiveness of a bourgeois family.

By way of contrast, the fashion house functions like a real family whose members have chosen to work together to produce great works. It cannot be said, however, that the movie was secretly influenced by the Pétainist work ethic, as expressed, for example, in the epilogue to *Au Bonheur des Dames* that André Cayatte added to Zola's original so as to advocate the kind of class collaboration peddled by Vichy. In fact the whole difference resides in Becker's point of view, which constantly keeps its distance from the fantasy of the firm as a family, in particular through the way its employees, Lucienne (Christiane Barry), Solange (Gabrielle Dorziat), and Anne-Marie (Françoise Lugagne), see their boss, Philippe Clarence. True, the great couturier introduces Solange,

Micheline Presle and Raymond Rouleau in *Falbalas*, 1944. Courtesy of Cinémathèque française.

the manager of the business, to Micheline as "his only family." But the film casts an unforgiving eye on the exploitation that lurks behind the interweaving of affectivity and work: Philippe encourages emotional dependence in order better to exploit his staff, spontaneously or cynically, depending on circumstances and on the individual. Even when he is still in the early stages of winning Micheline's heart, the Lothario's cynicism is plain for all to see in the sequence where he tells her on the telephone how lonely and desperate he is while at the same time busily organizing the trying-on of a dress in his new collection with the discreet complicity of six of his female employees. His boorishness is so stylish that audiences laugh with the character rather than at him.

The fashion house's exclusively female staff highlights the way class domination is reinforced by gender domination, and the constant shifting from the public sphere to the private sphere reinforces male supremacy. In this respect, *Falbalas* can be seen as a kind of UFO in the firmament of the French cinema, today just as much as it must have been in the past.

The spatial organization of the fashion house centers on the boss-cum-creator's office, a veritable sanctuary at the end of a succession of corridors patrolled by his employees like so many sentries protecting the artist from the outside world. A hidden staircase leads from Philippe's office to his private apartment, a holy of holies accessible only to the master's current (and usually fleeting) mistress for just as long as she inspires him. But this cocoon will ultimately smother him.

The movie's scathing criticism of the real family and of aspirations to a social organization modeled on the family is articulated through the mother figure, in both its caricatural form (Jane Marken) and its positive form (Gabrielle Dorziat). Dorziat plays Solange, who runs the fashion house like a harem and furthers the love affairs of the business's child-king in such a way as to restrict desirable women to their role as fetishes that can be renewed with each new collection. Her hostility toward Micheline is directly connected with the latter's claim to achieve the rank of subject. The loving mother is also the patriarchy's best ally and the most formidable foe of women's emancipation. But as guardian of the temple she gradually loses her footing when Philippe is confronted with the resistance of the subject-woman.

The two men that Micheline meets embody different facets of a male identity in a state of crisis. On the one hand, Micheline's fiancé, Daniel (played by the burly and reassuring Jean Chevrier), is acting on behalf of his distant and invisible father (a leading silk manufacturer in Lyon). He is a "gentle male" figure and a deeply conventional man who is head over heels in love and involves himself in domestic tasks (such as preparing the marital apartment). Indeed Micheline unintentionally points up their lack of reciprocal desire when she says to him, "Good old Daniel! Serious-minded every day of the year!" By way of contrast, we have the will-o'-the-wisp Philippe, Daniel's friend and antithesis. Highly talented and "unreliable" (above all financially), he desires women as a succession of images capable of stimulating his creativity in a never-ending process of renewal. In one case there is kindness without desire, and in the other a fetishistic desire that collects women like images.

Micheline's first encounter with Philippe is in this respect quite unambiguous. The image of the wax dummy has already been impressed on the spectator's mind, as has the important position occupied by that ersatz in the couturier's life: the movie opens with a shot of the dead Philippe sprawled on the pavement with a wax dummy in his arms, a dummy that also features in the first shot of the flashback that follows, imposingly displayed in the master's office. Now when Philippe comes out of the elevator in the building where he has just been to visit his friend Daniel, the camera shows, through Philippe's eyes, the face of a woman we initially take to be that of the dummy, motionless, wide-eyed, and framed by curly fair hair. This vision leaves the couturier speechless. He steps out of the elevator like a sleepwalker, holds the door open for the woman, then turns on his heels and follows her back into the elevator. A close medium shot shows them as the elevator rises slowly and silently toward Micheline and Daniel's future marital home. Philippe follows her through the door and, in front of a bemused Daniel, shows her around the apartment as though he were himself the fiancé. In the following sequence, we learn that during the night Philippe has designed a new collection featuring sketches of a woman who looks strikingly like Micheline.

This says everything about Philippe's love at first sight, a fetishistic fixation on an image, and the reactivation of a fantasy in which the woman herself plays no role. The elevator shaft represents Philippe's amorous abduction of Micheline, with overtones of imprisonment. This sequence highlights the ambivalence of the muse figure, a fetishistic form of the sexual relationship that is peculiar to artists and reinforces the inequality of the sexes: women are reduced to effigies that stimulate men's creativity. The image of the elevator also ties in with that of the wardrobe in which Philippe, like some latter-day Bluebeard, stashes the dresses that remind him of his successive conquests — a collection whose lethal nature is waspishly remarked upon by Lucienne, the previous mistress who experiences "shelving" for herself.

And yet Philippe, because he gives Micheline a chance to express her desire without worrying about the proprieties (another privilege of the artist), unintentionally helps her to become aware of her own desiring autonomy, which up to then has been deeply repressed by her social milieu. When Becker films both characters, he respects the impulsive and uncontrolled dimension of their reactions; thus there is nothing to suggest, before Philippe literally crashes through the door of the room where Micheline is trying on her bridal dress, that he is about to suggest that she drop everything and elope with him. Similarly Micheline's final decision not to leave with him but to return home alone is not the result of any preestablished psychological schema.

As in other Occupation movies (*Secrets*, *Les Visiteurs du soir*), female desire is shown to be autonomous, as emanating from a subject who deals with it in a gesture of freedom. At first naïvely flattered by the couturier's interest in her, Micheline allows herself a degree of coquettishness under the protection of her status as Daniel's fiancée. Very soon, however, she finds herself in a different position, following the night sequence that opens with her standing behind a gramophone as though she were on stage, singing an accompaniment to a blues tune and looking straight at Philippe, her only spectator. She has made the transition from a young woman who is gauche because she is unaware of her charm to a self-confident woman who makes no secret of her pleasure.

The choice of the Tuileries gardens as the location for the decisive scene where Micheline becomes self-aware is typical of Becker's rejection of any expressionism. There is no fatality in the way the story unfolds, just an interplay of feelings and a balance of power in an indifferent natural setting. On the other hand, Philippe's choice of such a light-filled open space marks a violent contrast with the nocturnal intimacy of his apartment, where he "conquered" Micheline the previous day, thus indicating to her that their amorous interlude was over. While Philippe and Micheline are having it out, they are observed by an old man feeding the sparrows, a Franciscan and an endearing fallen patriarch figure, in contrast with Philippe, who reveals here his belief in the patriarchy's fundamental principle: women's submission to men. The scene ends when Philippe snaps at this importunate onlooker, who is embarrassed at witnessing his boorishness. This sequence works as an ironic counterpart to the apprentices' admiring gaze in the scene where Philippe pretends over the telephone to be head over heels in love.

In this scene where they break off their relationship, a close shot of Philippe highlights his cynicism compared with Micheline's sincerity; when she announces that she "can no longer marry Daniel," Philippe replies with amazement, "But the guy loves you!," before going on to remark, "Women are all the same! Along comes the first man they meet, and they just have to make him suffer!" Like a blind woman suddenly recovering her sight, Micheline gives a start, scattering the sparrows, and runs off; she has realized that she is just an object that Philippe and Daniel can exchange and use in several mutually nonexclusive ways as long as appearances are kept up. Philippe's status as an artist enables him to poach on his friends' preserves with total impunity. But the game works only if the women agree willy-nilly to be no more than decoration.

At almost the same time, then, the female character experiences the revelation of her desire and comes to realize that the current social organization does not allow her to be in control of it. And it is one and the same man who first enables her to express that desire and subsequently informs her of her status as a mere object of male desire.

This contradiction produces the tragic ending of which the spectator is already aware and which the scenario also suggests might have been the other way around: Philippe kills himself a scant twenty-four hours after the suicide of Anne-Marie, his collaborator and twice-humiliated mistress. This suicide is portrayed as a woman's ultimate dignified reaction against the emotional manipulation she has been subjected to by Philippe.

While *Falbalas* explicitly shows the privileged position of the artist in the organization of patriarchal oppression and depicts Don Juanism as an obsessional neurosis, Becker's determination to lend credibility to the character's actual charisma—a key element if one is to understand the submissiveness of the women who surround him—does have some ambiguous effects on male and female spectators. First of all, there is the casting of Raymond Rouleau as Philippe. Rouleau was probably the most outstanding young male lead of the period (see *L'Assassinat du Père Noël*, *Premier bal*, *Mam'zelle Bonaparte*, *Dernier atout*, and *L'Honorable Catherine*), whereas one might have expected a leading couturier at the height of his fame to be played by a slightly older actor more clearly in line with the critical approach to the patriarchy that was characteristic of Occupation cinema. Instead of that, Rouleau's performance in *Falbalas* combines elegance, a lightness of touch, and a tragic gravity. He even pays tribute (perhaps unintentionally) to the prewar Jean Gabin in the closing sequences, where the dazed Philippe, who has been spurned by both Micheline and Daniel, wide-eyed and staring into space, is no more than a rag doll in the hands of his friend (compare the Gabin character facing René Lefèvre at the end of *Gueule d'amour*). This reprise, whether intentional or not, of an essential ingredient of Gabin's acting (Gauteur and Vincendeau 1993) roots Becker's character even more deeply in the spectator's desire. As in *Pépé le Moko*—but to a lesser degree—the central character's exploitation of women is partly camouflaged by a thwarted love that leads him to commit suicide.

The construction of the movie can also be interpreted as an empathic portrait of the male character: the images of Philippe's suicide, which we see in full at the end of the film, are first shown as a kind of prologue to the story (compare *Le Jour se lève*) and encourage a process of victimization that comes into its own in the postwar cinema. In the initial version of the screenplay, the narrative, also told in flashback, begins with Micheline's visit to a psychiatric hospital, where Philippe, who has gone mad, nears the end of his life. In the final version, Philippe's spectacular suicide, lamented by the women standing around him like a Greek chorus, lends an even more tragic dimension to the fate of the central male character.

The ambiguous effects of Becker's dialectical approach often manifest themselves in the film. When the creator runs out of inspiration and manhandles or insults a female model, the spectator is expected to excuse such fits of bad temper, first because the maestro is in pain, and second because the model in question is portrayed as a pretentious airhead who thinks she is entitled to give her opinion because she still—but not for much longer—enjoys the master's favors. When the couturier turns up one fine morning with drawings of the collection inspired by his encounter with Micheline, the seamstresses' complaints about being required to work overtime by this sudden change of plan are brushed aside by a remark by one of the old hands, Paulette (Jeanne Fusier-Gir): "I didn't like that collection either!" This engaging and grumpy character, played by an actress who often appeared as one of the "eccentrics of the French cinema" (Barrot and Chirat 1983), is the pet of the boss, whom she serves devotedly while at the same time telling him a few home truths. In so doing, she also helps to redeem him. Finally, after Micheline refuses to see Philippe when he comes to fetch her after deserting his fashion house the day before the presentation of his collection, the audience is tempted to side with the male character, who is staggered and crushed by her rejection, whereas she seems to be less affected.

The scales between Philippe and Micheline are not equally balanced: What influence can a young bourgeoise from the provinces possibly have when faced with the inspiration of an haute couture creator? How important are the "emotional complications" of a young woman (in Solange's words) compared with the influence of an employer with a staff of three hundred people? If Becker deliberately set out to turn Micheline into an empty shell designed to accommodate the couturier's neurosis, those spectators least likely to question the traditional patterns of sexual relations have no difficulty in belittling the central female character and in identifying with Solange when she whispers to Micheline, "This is all your fault." This is particularly true since the film (rightly) concentrates its attention on Philippe's feverish activities while Micheline busies herself—outside the narrative—with the necessarily rather futile errands of a young bride-to-be.

But despite this narrative and dramatic imbalance, Becker was perfectly aware of the importance of his female character, as can be seen in a subsequent remark he made about the movie: "The period of the Occupation marked the beginning of a certain degree of emancipation for young women from a wealthy background. Some of them took lovers before getting married. Such behaviour was previously to be found only among young women from a less well-off background: as they had less money, they were morally purer and more disinterested" (*Arts*, December 29, 1954).

Presle's performance turns this rather one-dimensional character into a moving heroine whose internal experiences can have no echo in a milieu where women have no autonomous existence. When she took on the part, she was already at the height of her career as a young female lead, in the wake of her dramatic dual role in Abel Gance's *Paradis perdu* (1939), the deceptively frivolous character she played in Marcel L'Herbier's *La Nuit fantastique* (1941), and her performance as an actress doomed to a tragic end in Marc Allégret's *Félicie Nanteuil* (1942). Becker uses both her sensuality and her dramatic abilities to construct a modern female character caught between alienating models of sexual and class identity and a desire for emancipation which was beginning confusedly to emerge. Doomed to loneliness and guilt and ejected from the narrative as a result of Philippe's suicide, she foreshadows, probably unbeknown to Becker himself, the forthcoming defeats of women in the postwar cinema.

LES DAMES DU BOIS DE BOULOGNE
   (Robert Bresson, 1944–45)

Like Robert Bresson's previous movie, *Les Anges du péché* (1943), *Les Dames du bois de Boulogne* is a "women's film" that conforms to the dominant tendency of Occupation cinema. But it is also a work that marks a transition to the postwar period and looks forward in certain ways to the new issue of the battle of the sexes.

The director chose and reworked the original story, based on an episode in Diderot's *Jacques le Fataliste*. Jean Cocteau's contribution to the writing of the dialogue was, on his own admission, completely dependent on the filmmaker's intentions. This was probably not the case with Jean Giraudoux on *Les Anges du péché*. Analysis of the way the adaptation was made is therefore highly edifying; other critics (Briot 1957; Estève 1962) have already remarked on the fact that Diderot's very short libertine story (only a few pages long) becomes a tragic narrative in Bresson's film. But a comparison of the two texts shows that Bresson has stripped the three female characters of the criminal or cynical dimension given them by Diderot. Even the mother, Madame D., who remains the least likable character, becomes weaker rather than calculating.

Hélène (Maria Casarès), who is Madame de La Pommeraye in the original story, is depicted in the first (added) scene as being duped by an unrequited passion, since it is one of her friends, Jacques (Jean Marchat), who reveals to her something she was unaware of, by way of a memorable aphorism: "There's no such thing as love, there are only tokens of love." From the start, Bresson attenuates the cool and calculating nature of Diderot's central female character, since she is shown, as soon as she appears, to be an effigy of wounded dignity in a socially unequal game of love between the sexes.

Casarès's hieratic performance (the actress remembers hating Bresson on set because he restrained her impulses as an actress) is informed by a suffering whose manifestations — silent tears and prostration — are all the more moving because they do not possess the violent side indicated by Diderot. This tragic seriousness attenuates the diabolical aspects of the machination devised by this jilted woman as a way of taking revenge on her lover, Jean (Paul Bernard). In this sense, while Hélène undoubtedly foreshadows the "evil bitches" of the postwar cinema, she still retains the authenticity and moral austerity of the female figures in Occupation cinema, opposite whom Bernard's lighthearted performance renders the male character unbearable. Bresson and Cocteau initially thought of giving Jean Marais the role of the marquis in Diderot's original story (here renamed Jean, surely no coincidence), but they had to give up that idea because Marais was shooting another film. This incident confirms in any case the fact that Diderot's libertine character was contaminated by the "gentle male" figure of the type played by Marais in *L'Eternel retour* and *Voyage sans retour*. But the rather spineless character that Bernard makes of him means that the spectator cannot take pity on a man crude enough to accept the connivance of the woman he has just left in order to conquer fresh prey.

The essential difference between Diderot's story and Bresson's film is to be found in its tone: the text portrays cynical licentiousness, while the movie suggests tragic suffering. The filmmaker takes all his characters quite seriously, whereas Diderot's prose creates the twofold distance of a *mise en abyme*. Indeed the final twist in the story (the reconciled spouses spend three years far from the capital so as to allow the scandal to be forgotten, and Madame de La Pommeraye turns out to have wasted her time) is a good indication of the light tone the writer wanted to retain, which is also helped by the comments Jacques and his master make about the literary quality of the hostess's account.

But it is the development of the character of the young woman, renamed Agnès (as a tribute to Molière?), that makes Bresson's movie seem to be more clearly involved in the problems of the Occupation. He turns her into a rebellious young woman whose artistic aspirations (classical ballet) are scotched by her fallen mother. She becomes a real character, whereas in Diderot's story she is no more than an instrument. Bresson, for instance, adds the episode in which Agnès, in order to foil the schemes of Hélène and her mother, decides to admit her past to the man she loves. She writes him a letter which he refuses to read.

In the movie, we first see the young woman in a top hat and sequined leotard doing a brilliant tap dance in a cabaret. This is a nod in the direction of both American tap dancing and the androgynous figure of Marlene Dietrich in Josef von Sternberg's films. She is an unusual and provocative character at a time of official Americanophobia. As remote from the religious or secular female effigies commonly found in Vichyite cinema (compare *Les Anges du péché*) as she is from the prewar stereotyped sluts, Agnès is a resolutely modern character. Her exuberant vitality is at the opposite pole from the hieratic reserve of Maria Casarès, who always wears long black dresses, like a priestess devoted to some cult of the dead.

But Agnès's radiant smile and the heady rhythms of her dancing contrast violently with her exhausted and disgusted attitude shortly afterward in her dressing room, where her mother urges her to get dressed so she can cater to the gentlemen who are waiting for her at home. This unvarnished observation of the way her talents as a dancer are being sexually exploited puts her straight into the category of victims of a cynical patriarchal order. And yet she is a far cry from the submissive young women of prewar melodramas. She rebels in the very first scene, smashing the pots of flowers sent by the men who take advantage of her: "I hate pots of flowers, especially when they are sent by a drunk!" Her violence, which is always ready to erupt, is depicted as the expression of a need for self-respect, which her mother implicitly denies her, solely concerned as she is with her "happiness," that is, how to sell her charms for the best price. This cynical and spineless character foreshadows the mother-cum-procuress in Yves Allégret's *Manèges* (1949), the only differences being that she retains the urbane veneer of a woman from high society "who has fallen on bad times" and that Bresson refuses to resort to caricature.

Later on, when Agnès dances — for the last time, she tells her mother — in the flat where Hélène has cloistered mother and daughter, she is curiously dressed in a kind of Central European folk dress, as though this aerial dance were the final expression of her longing for purity and straightforward happiness before being engulfed by a misfortune she feels to be inevitable. An ultimate outburst of a vital energy held in check by patriarchal oppression, this dance by a "blossoming young woman" ends symbolically with her blacking out, a presage of a more serious blacking out at the end of the movie.

Mothers, bolstered by their intimacy with their daughters, are the best guardians of that patriarchal order, whereas men are either absent or inadequate, as in most films of the period; on the evidence of the drunken roisterers and boors in the two women's flat at the beginning, and of a man (Jean) manipulated from start to finish when he thought he was experiencing a great passion, the male sex is decidedly not up to it. As for the women, they battle to survive, whether financially or emotionally, but not for the same reasons. Agnès's mother longs for a return of the old order and struggles blindly to restore it, even if it means sacrificing her own daughter. Hélène, a victim of that order which makes men incapable of fidelity in love, wreaks revenge by manipulating another woman; in the spectator's eyes, the prime victim is Agnès and not Jean, whose misfortunes we find it very hard to sympathize with, for we know that Agnès was forced by her own mother to become the hooker Hélène wanted to reduce her to in Jean's eyes.

Bresson's movie, which is party to the battle of the sexes that broke out shortly before the end of the Occupation and gathered momentum to an unprecedented degree, emphasizes the tragedy experienced by two women, one of them imprisoned by her thirst for revenge and the other caught up in the illusion of an impossible emancipation and a love affair blighted by class differences. The refined nature of the mise-en-scène, contrary to what might be deduced from a Christian exegesis, never aims to obliterate social differences. On the contrary, the austere simplicity of the costumes and the sets turns them into tokens, stripped of the picturesque, of each character's place in society. Hélène's long, dark, and low-cut dresses, her hats, and her fur muffs display her wealth and power, as do Jean's dark suits and wing collars. Similarly the silent elevator in Hélène's building and Jean's long black automobile evince the luxury of an environment in which all objects are perfectly oiled cogs in a smoothly running social machine.

By way of contrast, poor Agnès, apart from her stage costume, which she goes on sporting after the show, is allowed to wear only short skirts and dark crew-neck sweaters, always accompanied by a crumpled light-colored raincoat that she fastens with a leather belt — a reminder of the serious clothing shortage suffered by the French at the time. Bresson, incidentally, cut out a scene in which Agnès was wearing a white evening dress at the beginning of the movie. The only white dress she wears in the final version is her bridal dress, whose symbolism is thus reinforced, certainly with regard to a virginity she wins back through love, but above all in the religious register of the sacrificial lamb. This is an interpretation that is not contradicted by the highly ambiguous ending, wherein Agnès, recumbent on the bridal bed in her wedding veil, whispers (in her last breath?) to Jean, who begs forgiveness, "I'm staying." Her mother, who is always dressed in black, claims to belong to the same social class as Hélène, in an obstinate denial of her degeneration. Her hat with a veil is a reminder of her "distinguished" origins but also symbolizes her hypocrisy.

As for the sets, the telephone on Hélène's bedside table — she remains prostrate on her bed while a chambermaid comes to pick up the receiver — is the exact opposite of the one available to Agnès and her mother, which is next to the concierge's lodge: they have to come downstairs and speak standing up in the hall of the building. They live in a barely furnished little flat (pictures stand on the floor facing the wall), harshly illuminated by daylight, and with communicating rooms which enable the mother to keep a close eye on her daughter. This is a far cry from Hélène's vast reception rooms, with a grand piano, indirect lighting, an open fire, and silent servants, all in a muffled atmosphere far from the madding crowd.

Dominique Païni (1992) has shown how the scene in which Hélène arrives at the flat where the two women engage in an explicit form of high-society prostitution is organized according to an arrangement that follows the iconographic pattern of the Annunciation. From that point of view, it could be said that Bresson reverses the terms of the biblical scene. What we have here is a diabolical annunciation, and Hélène, dressed in black, is a Luciferian angel: while claiming to bring them salvation, she plunges Agnès into a much more perverse form of unhappiness, of "damnation," than the upper-class prostitution her mother has forced her to engage in. Agnès was able to rebel against the lecherous brutality of clients imposed on her by her mother, but she will prove unable to renounce her love for Jean. The devil here has taken on the guise of an angel.

If Hélène has sold her soul to the devil in order to act as a substitute for divine justice, it could also be said that Agnès, the paschal lamb, is a Christlike figure in the feminine. At first she displays a very upper-class charisma, then she becomes more and more spiritual as she goes through a series of ordeals. The significance of her change of dancing costume becomes clearer when seen from this point of view. She agrees to sacrifice herself to save a man who thereby becomes the symbol of a humanity that is both guilty and redeemed by the sufferings of the young woman. This feminine version of the Gospels breaks a major taboo for the Catholic Church (namely the Church hierarchy's fierce opposition to the ordination of women priests), but is linked to the regeneration of the moral and social order by female figures that is typical of Vichyite cinema.

The narrative is based on the (alternate) viewpoints of the two main female characters (Hélène and Agnès), and we move from Hélène's apartment to the two women's flat without ever showing Jean except in their presence. There is, however, a slightly ambivalent element in the movie, which was made (need we mention it?) by men. In 1944 anyone telling the story of a woman's revenge against a man (and that is how Hélène brings the story, if not the film, to a close) was bound to fuel the fantasy of dangerous women at the very moment when, in no way coincidentally, many women were about to suffer a terrible revenge by having their heads shaven at the Liberation (Brossat 1992).

The explicit and dominant theme of the narrative is indeed the implacable nature of that female revenge. At whatever cost to herself, Hélène carries out her designs to the end. She applies to the private sphere the terrifying founding principle of power in the public sphere: the end justifies the means. Her character is constructed in such a way as to avoid all the stereotypes (whether positive or negative) of femininity: sensitivity, generosity, and a sense of sacrifice, but also faintheartedness, fickleness, superficiality, and so on. And the male templates that Hélène adopts take on evil connotations precisely because they are embodied by a woman; determination, reserve, and self-control are here devalued because they are used for private ends (revenge for a lover's infidelity). Here we get the first glimmerings of the change that took place in female figures from the Liberation on: they were restricted to strictly "selfish" preoccupations in which their initiatives could not be interpreted as other than dangerous insofar as they took no account of the general good (that is, the patriarchal order).

In contrast to Hélène, the character of Jean, with his cowardice, his ever-changing desires, and the indecent way he exposes his emotions, seems to be constructed according to several female stereotypes that make him seem irresponsible and therefore pitiful, faced with the misfortunes he causes and endures. But the more ruthless his enemy is, the more his weakness seems excusable. And Agnès's love proves his innocence once and for all.

At the same time, Bresson's movie is about much more than this story of revenge, through the use of an aesthetic device based on the systematic generation of a meaning that goes beyond what the spectator sees and hears, in a kind of sublimation of the constraints that the censors had imposed on the French consciousness for five years by the time Bresson made his film. It is no longer a question of spectators needing to have things spelled out to them in order for them to understand, but of their understanding what is going on despite the words. In *Les Dames du bois de Boulogne*, they are always invited to identify with one or other of the characters in order to understand the hidden meaning of words or acts. This empathy, which we experience with Agnès and Hélène in turn, prevents us from interpreting the story unilaterally. Its words bathe in negativity, since the characters (in particular the mother) use language that is all the more refined when they are expressing morally shameful feelings; perhaps this can be interpreted as the expression of a schizophrenic period, when the relationship between words and thoughts was obstructed by a totalitarian power and the terror it produced.

While Hélène is particularly frightening when she puts on a show of politeness so as to trap her victims, Bresson's mise-en-scène also allows the spectator to feel empathy toward her. In the course of the story, she is more than once affected by the consequences of her own machinations, as indeed we are. This is expressed by an abrupt shift in behavior, such as when, in the scene where she plays the piano to put on a pretence of indifference toward Jean, who says he is desperate at not being able to see Agnès, she does not hear him leave. When she notices he has gone, she leaps up from her stool and runs into the hall, then down the stairs and up to the car he has just got into, and then agrees to give in to his desires. This very spectacular mise-en-scène, because of the way it contrasts with the rest of the movie (Bresson shows Hélène hurtling down the two long flights of stairs in her mansion, whereas up to then we have seen her making majestic use of the elevator), reminds us that she is a human being who conceals her humanity to protect herself from hurt.

The most moving moment in the film comes when, truthfully for once, she confesses to Jean that she would like to marry him, when he has just informed her of his decision to marry Agnès. Her confession is all the more astounding because she makes it under humiliating circumstances, those of an abandoned woman who continues to love the man who has jilted her and who tells him so just as all hope of winning him back has been dashed by his decision to marry another woman. There is in her confession a tragic humility, of which Jean shows himself quite unworthy, but which overwhelms the spectator. To lend it greater impact, Bresson reemploys the sets and the decoupage of her initial confession scene and reverses the position of the protagonists: this time it is Jean who is sitting on a sofa as he speaks, framed as Hélène was when she "admitted" to him that she no longer loved him, and it is she who is leaning against the mantelpiece, as he was in the first scene. Bresson, however, uses this similarity to highlight the contrast between the two characters: whereas Jean, relieved by Hélène's (fake) confession, walked to and fro, followed by a mobile camera, Hélène is here paralyzed by her unhappiness and has to lean against the mantelpiece. Despite the half-light, we can see she is weeping. This framing, which shows her being crucified by her solitary suffering, is reminiscent of the shot that concluded the first confession scene after the departure of her lover. It is a cry of despair directed at the audience and has all the more impact because the audience is alone in hearing it. Her fickle lover has left with a clear conscience.

In this way, Bresson's movie plunges into the heart of female suffering, which is all the more harrowing because it is silent. Compared with it, Jean's self-indulgent description of the symptoms of his despair is bound to seem derisory. Only the man and the mother (who are on the right side of patriarchal power) describe their suffering at length, whereas the two young women, who are victims of it in various ways, are not allowed to describe theirs. They have to be content to suffer in silence, or else they express themselves by scream-ing or blacking out (that is, by turning their suffering against themselves). To that extent, the spectator is prepared to grant them, despite their antagonism, the same esteem — an esteem reserved for victims who manage to retain their self-respect.

A profoundly contradictory film, *Les Dames du bois Boulogne* portrays not only the greater moral legitimacy of (young) women but also their malice in the face of a male impotence that camouflages a persistently burdensome patriarchal order, as can be seen from Agnès's fate. While denouncing that oppression, the movie also expresses fear of a world in which women alone take the initiative — a world fantasized by absent or imprisoned men during the four years of the Occupation.

Part III

THE POSTWAR PERIOD, 1945–1956

Settling of Scores

CHAPTER 10
The Destabilizing Effects of the Liberation

———————————
———————————

THE WAY HISTORIANS have looked at the Liberation has shifted considerably in the past fifty years, irrespective of the gulf that separates supporters of the Gaullist and Communist fiction that the French who resisted were alone responsible for the Liberation from their opponents, often people who had compromised themselves with the fallen Vichyite regime, who invented or believed in the dark myth of the postwar purges, or *épuration*, and who contended that the horrific crackdown carried out by the Nazis and pro-Nazi French militias during the war was no worse than the backlash of the épuration (Lottman 1986; Rousso 1987/1994). Today the disproportion between the two phenomena has been established, but certain aspects of the Liberation that slot less easily into the traditional categories of political history have yet to be properly explored; it was only thanks to the work of the philosopher Alain Brossat (1992) in the early 1990s that the widespread practice of shaving the heads of women accused of collaboration with the Germans started to be accurately assessed.

In the cinema as elsewhere, the aim of the épuration was national reconstruction rather than ideological clarification. Most directors who had made explicitly Pétainist films during the war did not get into trouble with the authorities. Only explicit collaboration with the occupying forces was punished, and often in a rather confused way, as was the case with Henri-Georges Clouzot. The charges against him were of two kinds: in his capacity as head of the scripts department at Continental, he took an active part in the Germans' policy of exerting a stranglehold on the French cinema, but it was in fact the low esteem in which his movie *Le Corbeau* (1943) was held by former Resistants that was apparently the main cause of his falling out of favor. He was accused of having deliberately made an anti-French film and of having agreed to allow it to be shown in Germany so as to blacken the reputation of the French people. (This turned out to be untrue.) The latter accusation was dropped by the Purge Commission of the Liberation Committee of the French Cinema, which handled the case. However, the Interprofessional Committee, which made the final decision, one that may be regarded as the verdict of the state rather than that of the film industry, extended the ban on his making films to twenty-four months, on the grounds that *Le Corbeau* was of a "tendentious anti-French" nature.

As for Albert Valentin, who made two movies for Continental (for which he incurred a "reprimand to be displayed at his place of work"), he was banned from making films until 1948, seemingly because the last movie he made during the Occupation, *La Vie de plaisir* (1944), was violently criticized by both the Resistance and the Vichyite press. He subsequently made a handful of films more or less in secret, before turning exclusively to scriptwriting, with some notable successes.

As regards film producers, Raoul Ploquin, who up until the war was a production manager with the German company UFA, in charge of French versions of German movies, and a member of the Vichyite Committee for the Organization of the Film Industry until November 1942, was acquitted, whereas André Paulvé, producer of some of the most courageous films of the period (*Les Visiteurs du soir, Lumière d'été*), was banned from exercising his profession until 1946, on the grounds that he had connections with a production company in Mussolini's Italy (thanks to which he was able to get around many of the restrictions imposed by the German occupying forces in France).

Quite apart from the ambiguities and inconsistency of the purges in the film industry (Bertin-Maghit 1989: 429; Ragache and Ragache 1988), the harshest treatment was meted out to actresses accused of what was known as "horizontal collaboration." Arletty and Mireille Balin were both jailed after the Liberation because each had had an affair with a German officer; as for Ginette Leclerc, she was denounced by her French lover, and after being imprisoned for almost a year had great difficulty in resurfacing after the war. This did not happen purely by chance.

In the general feeling of euphoria that accompanied the Liberation, the fact that women accused of horizontal collaboration, whether rightly or wrongly, almost always had their heads shaved struck a particularly discordant note. Brossat's (1992) book on the subject was the first to investigate and analyze this practice. He brings out the fact that this kind of misogynistic "excess" is an integral part of a "carnivalesque" ritual (in the sense understood by Mikhail Bakhtin), which enables a long oppressed and humiliated population to settle its scores before submitting to a new order of law, in this case that of the restored republic. How was it that women, mostly of working-class origin (neither Balin nor Arletty had their heads shaved), were the main target of this "cathartic" ritual? Brossat demonstrates that the fact (actual or imagined) that a woman had sexual relations with the enemy became the very symbol of the nation's humiliation in the eyes of a patriarchal society whose army had been routed and held prisoner for four years, leaving women to cope with the occupying forces on their own. Shaving the heads of women decreed to be guilty of having slept with the occupier (but who might have committed more serious crimes, punishable by prison sentences or even death) was an attempt, in a long tradition going back to the Middle Ages, to ward off the fear of female sexuality that could not be controlled (by men), to remind women that their bodies do not belong to them, and to reappropriate them symbolically on behalf of the nation after the years of interruption caused by the Occupation.

If we see the phenomenon as a collective recovery of women's bodies by a patriarchal institution that wanted to wash away the humiliation caused by the Defeat, it becomes easier to understand that this "shameful" episode of the shaven women was often initiated, in the absence of official orders or in violation of them, by the Resistants themselves (many of whom had only just jumped on the bandwagon), seen as the "natural" spokesmen for the prisoners of war (more than 1 million of them were still in captivity in 1944) and for the exiled conscripts of the Compulsory Labor Service, suffering daily humiliation and dreading they might be cheated on by their wives (Durand 1987; Eck 1994).

Women thus became the ideal scapegoat for all these fears, because their de facto independence during the Occupation fired the jealousy of those who were absent; and because they had had to take up employment, they seemed to be responsible for the difficulties men experienced in trying to get their jobs back after the Liberation. The phenomenon of the shaven women and the increase in the divorce rate in the immediate postwar period seem to have been the (barely) visible tip of an iceberg, namely a deep crisis in gender relations whose traditional equilibrium was disrupted by the military defeat and by the new responsibilities shouldered by women during the Occupation (*CLIO* 1995).

The introduction of the vote for women in 1945 (decades later than in other comparable countries) was officially linked to their role in the Resistance. Yet the Liberation ushered in an extremely conflictual period in relations between the sexes, which was fueled by fresh fears on the part of men that women would refuse to return to the marital home — in other words, to accept anew their dominated position in society. During the Occupation, they proved, often against their will, as in the case of prisoners' wives (Fishman 1991), that they were capable of ensuring the financial survival of the household as well as assuming its domestic management and the educational responsibilities traditionally allotted to them.

At the point when the political authorities "granted" (see the terms of de Gaulle's 1944 speech) women the vote, it was vital for that weakened male power to set limits on the emancipation of women. The fears and rejections expressed during that process were fueled by a French "specificity," namely the civil code introduced by Napoléon in 1804 explicitly on the basis of the subordination of women, as reflected by husbands' marital rights and the legal incapacity of their wives. Even after 1945 women continued to be regarded as minors in all areas of civil law. It was only in the 1960s that this monument of patriarchal power began to be seriously eroded (Sineau 1991/1996; Duchen 1994).

If we analyze the stances of the main women's organizations that grew up after the war and the terms of the 1946 Constitution, we can see that there was a consensus on the need to defend, as a priority if not exclusively, women's maternal role in the context of a natalist policy. Only the Communist-led Union of French Women also stood up for their right to work (Muller et al., 1985; Duchen 1994). But while politicians on both right and left were content to reestablish, more or less en bloc, the traditional division of gender relations, cultural productions contained many allusions to the crisis that this consensus was intended to conceal (Ory 1989).

The pathological sexual violence of a succès de scandale like *J'irai cracher sur vos tombes* (1946), in which Boris Vian, under the guise of a respectably antiracist American detective novel, devises a story of revenge directed entirely against women (who are personally innocent of the crime they are going to pay for), displays a disturbing parallel with the way the French avenged their national humiliation by shaving the heads of women. But quite apart from this extreme case, there are many traces of this hate-filled climate in the traditional sectors of "legitimate" and male culture (books and drama). Hervé Bazin's *Vipère au poing* (1948), the peak of misogynistic violence, was one of the most successful postwar novels. Even such more original writers, such as Sartre and Camus, who testified forcefully to the crisis in male identity that resulted from the 1940 defeat (Coquillat 1982), at no point tied it to a new conception of women's subjectivity. In his *Les Chemins de la liberté* (1945/2001), one gets the impression that Sartre gets women—handicapped, ill-treated, or pitiful—to pay for the existential malaise experienced by his male characters. This fear of women is confirmed by the terrifying female "couple" in his play *Huis-clos* (*No Exit*, 1945) and by the inexistence of female characters in Camus's novels *L'Etranger* (*The Stranger*, 1942) and *La Peste* (*The Plague*, 1947).

Even Simone de Beauvoir's first novels, which date from that period, find it hard to steer clear of misogynistic stereotypes: *L'Invitée* (1943) centers on a trio of characters later echoed by *Huis-clos*. The woman narrator, faced with the destructive effect on her relationship with her lover exerted by a young woman with whom they are both in love, kills her. Thus Beauvoir departs from the autobiographical reality on which she draws, to offer us a replay of that literary stereotype, the murderess-by-jealousy, as though to protect the male figure at all costs. In *The Blood of Others* (1945/1964), relations between men and women in the Resistance are similar to those to be found in Roger Vailland's highly misogynistic *Drôle de jeu*. But it is well known that for Beauvoir emancipation first involved identification with the male, however deep his own crisis, as the only existing model for the construction of the self. It was not until *Le Deuxième sexe* (1949) and, in the form of a novel, *The Mandarins* (1956), that she tackled head-on, and very vigorously, the question of the female subject (Moi 1994/2008).

On the other hand, film representations from the Liberation onward display a less unilateral reflection of the new setup in relations between men and women in the immediate postwar period. True, the exemplary female icons and stars of Occupation cinema suddenly vanished as films were swamped with diabolical female images, the template for which was Yves Allégret's *Manèges* (1949) and which can be found as late as 1956 in Julien Duvivier's *Voici le temps des assassins* (1956), an extreme example of the genre. But during the same period there were representations of women in the process of emancipation which, although the exception rather than the rule, possessed unprecedented vigor, as in Jacques Becker's *Antoine et Antoinette* (*Antoine and Antoinette*, 1946), Jean Renoir's *Le Carrosse d'or* (*The Golden Coach*, 1952), and Jean Grémillon's *L'Amour d'une femme* (*The Love of a Woman*, 1954).

❧ Resistance and Misogyny

Resistance films opted firmly for misogyny, which is only apparently paradoxical when one remembers a movie like *Pontcarral, colonel d'Empire*. Most such films were made by filmmakers close to Resistant circles and by virtue of that fact were claimed to be authentic. These portrayed only groups of men, never mentioning the essential role played by women, notably in such areas as material support and liaison, as attested by historians (Schwartz 1987; *CLIO* 1995; Collins Weitz 1995).

René Clément's *La Bataille du rail* (*The Battle of the Rails*, 1945), the archetype of the "authentic" Resistance movie dealing with railway workers in combat, set this unsubtle pattern for an exclusively male Resistance—even though Colette Audry coscripted the film. A woman appears only once in the movie, and in a negative light: she tries to dissuade her husband from taking risks. In a more traditional register, Raymond Bernard's *Un ami viendra ce soir* (*A Friend Will Come Tonight*, 1945) tells the story of a group of Resistants hiding in a lunatic asylum. The movie, which eschews neither Manichaeism nor wild romanticism, nor, for that matter, actors' set pieces, portrays Hélène Asselin (Madeleine Sologne), a young Jewess pretending to be a mental patient, as a fragile and unreliable woman. She falls in love with Dr. Maurice Tiller (Paul Bernard), who turns out to be a Nazi spy. When she realizes that her relationship has put the Resistants' lives at risk, she joins her lover in order to defuse the time bomb he has primed and kills him. But after succeeding in saving her comrades' lives, she does actually go mad, traumatized as she is by her unfortunate choice of lover and the murder she has just committed. She is conveniently sidelined at the very moment when the young Resistants triumphantly liberate the village.

It was Louis Daquin, a Communist, who provided the most violent example of such misogyny, which was part and parcel of the ideology of the Resistance, in *Patrie* (1945). The film takes a historical episode similar to the plot of Jacques Feyder's *La Kermesse héroïque* (1935), giving it a slant more in tune with the spirit of the times. In *Patrie*, Charles Spaak, who also scripted Feyder's movie, exalts the resistance of the Flemish people against the Spanish occupying forces. But here he is careful to reverse the sexual roles: the Flemish burghers become heroic, defending their country even when about to be burned at the stake, whereas one of the women has no qualms about denouncing her husband in order to save her lover's life. Male solidarity fortunately saves the day, and the traitor is punished by none other than her lover.

The film's caricatural version of men's heroism and women's shameful behavior is all the more surprising coming from a Communist activist (and former assistant of the "feminist" Jean Grémillon), who during the Occupation made *Madame et le mort*, a comic *policier* in praise of an emancipated woman. Perhaps such a staggering change of attitude (which fortunately affected only one of Daquin's movies) can be put down to the extreme malaise that was particularly widespread in Resistance circles at the time, as though the role of women in the underground (which as a Communist Resistant he was particularly well qualified to know) was unconsciously felt as a threat to the recovery of a positive male identity.

On the other hand, it comes as no surprise to find Yves Allégret, who was later to prove a dab hand at misogyny, making *Les Démons de l'aube* (1945), a second-rate story about an army commando in North Africa which exalts comradeship in arms against a background of female treachery. Lieutenant Claude Legrand (Georges Marchal), a recently released prisoner of war, allows himself to be led astray by his wife, who prefers dances (and her lover) to solidarity with the Resistance. Once he realizes his mistake, he leaves for Algiers, only to die with his men destroying a German gun emplacement on the coast near Toulon just before the Allied landings.

Maurice de Canonge's two-episode *Mission spéciale* (1945) is the intelligence service version of the same male heroism that does its best to ensure the continuity of the apparatus of state, which is necessarily Resistant. The only major female role is that of a sadistic German spy, Emmy de Welder (Jany Holt). In supporting roles, two women are in the Resistance, but one of them dies after being raped and tortured by the Gestapo, while the other is killed after having extracted secret documents from the German officer whose mistress she has become in order to avenge her slaughtered family. The sadistic woman is the personification of everything that is most hateful about the enemy, and the women fighting on the right side are frighteningly vulnerable. Men alone will be capable of successfully carrying out the Liberation of France. And the reassuring invulnerability of their leader, Chabrier (Jean Davy), is suggested by the fact that he is not involved with any woman.

But the great box-office success of the immediate postwar period, which thereby revealed the ideological consensus that most of the French population aspired to, was Noël-Noël's *Le Père tranquille* (*Mr. Orchid*, 1946), with technical direction by René Clément. Edouard Martin (Noël-Noël) is a quintessential average Frenchman and an ex-serviceman decorated seven times during the previous war. He is regarded by members of his family as a nice if somewhat cowardly man, who is interested only in his orchids at a time when

Left to right: José Artur, Noël-Noël, Claire Olivier (back to camera), Nadine Alari and Jean Varas in *Le Père tranquille*, 1946. Courtesy of Cinémathèque française.

France is occupied by the Germans. But it is not long before first the audience, then the children of this antihero realize they have got the apparently timid old man completely wrong: he is in fact the head of the Resistance in a whole region. The "gentle male" figure of *La Cage aux rossignols* (1944) and, by extension, of the whole Occupation cinema here becomes a decoy that masks the most traditional form of warlike virility.

The very dull mise-en-scène aims exclusively to reconstruct the image of the father, as though there was a need to convince young people and women — the other male characters are not under any illusion, since they are part of the Resistance and under Martin's orders — that not all ex-servicemen are in the mold of Marshal Pétain. The movie tries to persuade us that the wait-and-see option under the Occupation, which Pierre Laborie (1990) tells us was the attitude of a majority of the French, was simply a clever way of camouflaging the Resistant spirit. This new version of the adage "Appearances are sometimes deceptive" came at just the right time to clear the silent majority of charges of passivity during the dark years.

However, not everyone comes out of the operation unscathed: the prime target of *Le Père tranquille* is the wife of this average Frenchman, a misogynistic stereotype of a mother bogged down in everyday concerns and incapable of thinking of anything more important than the evening meal or a cough mixture. Martin's daughter, Monique (Nadine Alari), on the other hand, shifts from an attitude of indulgent affection for a father she believes to be weak to boundless admiration for the man she discovers to be a great Resistant. She marries the right-hand man of that beloved father, who has done her the great favor of letting her into the secret of his undercover activities. The father-daughter couple, which took a battering during the Occupation, is thus reconstituted as though nothing had happened.

The other relationship at stake in the film is that between father and son: the headstrong teenager believes his father to be a coward and takes to the maquis "so there's at least one person in the family who's in the Resistance!" He is later shown locked up in a pigsty by the *maquisards* to stop him getting into mischief. When he is released he joins his wounded father after he has been arrested by the Gestapo and freed by the maquisards; the son's tears show that he repents his attitude. If we read between the lines, perhaps this fantasy of a rebellious son who makes amends refers to the reality of the crisis in paternal authority that occurred at the Liberation, when a whole generation of fathers rejoined their sons, who had been left to their own devices for five years. This exemplary and discreetly Gaullist movie is built around a denial of all the contradictions of the period, and its consensual success did not augur well for the lucidity of the French at the Liberation.

These works, which are rooted in the historical moment, are often very mediocre (hence the rapid disappearance of the genre). They are chiefly interesting because they propose (or impose) an official version of the preceding period, when the triumph of the Resistance, which was exclusively embodied by men, could not be seen in isolation from the resumption by women of their status as dominated entities (Lindeperg 1997).

Noir Realism, or the Defeat of Women

It is well known that the hopes of a social revolution fired by the Resistance and the Liberation quickly petered out when confronted with the political and economic realities, both national and international, of the postwar period (Rioux 1980/1989). The *réalisme noir* school could be interpreted as the reflection of that ideological disillusionment. But such an analysis fails to take into account the main issue involved in that type of cinema, irrespective of the different individual characteristics of the scriptwriters (Jacques Prévert yet again, but above all Charles Spaak, Jacques Sigurd, Henri Jeanson, Jean Aurenche, and Pierre Bost) and directors (Yves Allégret, Henri-Georges Clouzot, André

Cayatte, Claude Autant-Lara, Julien Duvivier, Marcel Carné, René Clément, and Henri Decoin). In contrast with prewar poetic realism films, which laid the ground for the noir films and were written and directed by some of the same men, the new element that these postwar movies have in common is the correlation between the (objectively or subjectively) evil nature of women and the victimization of men. It could be said that Simone Signoret stepped into Jules Berry's shoes. Fatality was now no longer personified by the recognizable characteristics of a bourgeois dirty old man but took on the deceptive appearance of a beautiful young woman; the social context of prewar cinema was replaced by the theme of the battle of the sexes, in which women exert a destructive power over men.

Compared with Occupation cinema, the position of women also changed in the cinematic narrative. After women's emergence en masse as a subject or as a dominant point of view, the postwar cinema suddenly went into reverse: the male subject came back into his own, since many movies of that period, whether misogynistic or not, were totally or partly shaped by the narration of the central male character, for example, *Le Diable au corps*, *Le Silence de la mer*, *La Vie en rose* (*The Loves of Colette*, 1948), *Les Dernières vacances* (*The Last Vacation*, 1948), *Manon*, *Manèges*, *Le Journal d'un curé de campagne*, *Les Miracles n'ont lieu qu'une fois*, *Juliette ou la clé des songes*, *La Vérité sur Bébé Donge* (1952), and *Monsieur Ripois*.

More generally, a new figure imposed itself, that of the victimized male subject. He is very different from the tragic hero of poetic realism, in that from beginning to end the spectator is asked to pity the central character, even though he is usually young and often good-looking. Gérard Philipe (*L'Idiot*, *Une si jolie petite plage* [*Such a Pretty Little Beach*, 1949], *Les Orgueilleux* [*The Proud Ones*, 1953]), Serge Reggiani (*Les Amants de Vérone*, *Casque d'or*), Daniel Gélin (*Edouard et Caroline* [*Edward and Caroline*, 1951]), Georges Marchal (*Gibier de potence*), Jean Marais (*Orphée*, *Les Miracles n'ont lieu qu'une fois*), and Jean Desailly (*Chéri*) appear in that type of role as often as Pierre Brasseur (*Portrait d'un assassin*), Michel Simon (*La Poison*, *L'Etrange désir de Monsieur Bard*), Bernard Blier (*Quai des Orfèvres* [*Quay of the Goldsmiths*, 1948], *La Maison Bonnadieu*), and Henri Vilbert (*Le Bon Dieu sans confession*). This emphasis on male weakness, despite appearances, when faced with often overwhelmingly strong female characters, could be seen as men's paranoid interpretation of their predicament after the Liberation, when they were worried they would not be able to regain their prewar domination and experienced the emancipation of women as a bid to destroy male identity.

Michel Simon in *Panique*, 1946. Courtesy of Cinémathèque française.

Paradoxically it was the veteran Julien Duvivier, after spending the war in the United States, who inaugurated this new model with *Panique* (1946), based on Georges Simenon's novel *Les Fiançailles de Monsieur Hire*. In it, Michel Simon plays Monsieur Hire, a man who has been victimized in a redoubtably contemporary sense (he is Jewish) and has to face up to Alice (Viviane Romance), a beautiful prewar slut who has been transformed into a creature as weak as she is dangerous, mere putty in the hands of Alfred (Paul Bernard), her crooked lover. The film's achievement lies in its complex relationship with the climate of the time: its chief target seems to be the France of the BOF (*beurre, oeufs, fromages*), grocers, butchers, and so on at a time of rationing and black-marketing, who had often lent their voices to the Vichy policy of excluding Jews, Communists, foreigners, and anyone else suspected of being different from the national community. The film cleverly manipulates the spectator, first by emphasizing, through remarks made by shopkeepers who are reluctant to serve Monsieur Hire, the oddity of the man, a bearded bachelor of few words who takes photographs on a patch of wasteland before going to buy his meat and pointing out to the butcher, "Yesterday it wasn't bloody enough." (At that point he is framed between two enormous quarters of beef.) He gives sweets to children but spies quite shamelessly on the beautiful Alice as she undresses in the room opposite. On the pretext of an astrological consultation, he even seems to be intending to blackmail her. Once the spectator has been sufficiently disconcerted by this basically rather unpleasant character, the movie operates a narrative putsch by revealing the hidden side of Monsieur Hire as an inveterate romantic who for years has been preparing a wonderful cottage for some future love in the hope of exorcising an earlier "betrayal." He then becomes easy prey for the wicked bitch, who puts on a show of affection so she can get him charged with a murder committed by her lover. This unlikely narrative twist, which turns a disturbing misanthrope into a fooled lover, can be interpreted as suggesting that any man, however strong he may seem, will always be hiding his weak point: vulnerability as far as women are concerned.

The cynicism that would characterize so many postwar films is already apparent in the spectacle of a hostile crowd that causes Hire to panic and plunge to his death — a crowd that looks up from the street to the rooftops, in a kind of disturbing counterpoint to the crowd that is sympathetic toward the outlawed François (Jean Gabin) in *Le Jour se lève*. Alice's intervention has a crucial bearing on Hire's death: he mistrusts the others, but not her. And the discreet but efficient young policeman, Lieutenant Michelet (Charles Dorat), who quite early on suspects Alfred (Paul Bernard) of being the real culprit, fails to unmask the diabolical couple's framing of Hire in time to save him. A positive and familiar embodiment of the law, Michelet represents the apparatus of government after it has been regenerated by the Resistance, against the background of an unsavory society whose honor he tries to save by isolating its most rotten branches. But yet again it is the woman, because of her "excessive" emotionalism, who attracts the attention of the policeman and confirms his suspicions.

In *Panique*, Duvivier displays skillful political opportunism in the way he helps to sweep away the syndrome of the Occupation at the expense both of the cowardly and profiteering average Frenchman and above all of women; an old hand at misogyny, he had already typecast Viviane Romance in that sort of role in *La Belle équipe* (*They Were Five*, 1936), where she plays a slut who gives free rein to her desires and is therefore morally reprehensible, but who at the same time comes across as irresistible because of her sheer nerve. The new slut she plays in *Panique* has lost all her autonomy: she has gone to prison in the place of her lover, Alfred, and as soon as she is released obeys his orders by cynically seducing Hire. The film brings off the tour de force of getting the full quota of human wickedness (against a Jew in 1946!) embodied by a woman deprived of agency (she is manipulated by someone else), and the sudden moral awareness she displays in one lingering close-up is immediately cancelled out by her physical dependence on her lover. As in the episode of the shaven women, the female character serves as a scapegoat for the national community as a whole, and the ploy is all the more effective because it is largely unconscious and invisible, since in France gender relations, then as now, belong to the category of the unthought, even in the minds of most women.

The breakaway from the cinema of the previous period is all the more striking when one looks at movies by younger directors who made a name for themselves during the Occupation by helping to fashion these young and dynamic new female figures, as personified, for example, by Odette Joyeux in Claude Autant-Lara's brilliant trilogy, *Le Mariage de Chiffon* (1941), *Lettres d'amour* (*Love Letters*, 1942), and *Douce* (1943). The same Autant-Lara acquired international fame thanks to a succès de scandale, *Le Diable au corps* (1947), based on a novel by Raymond Radiguet. The scandal triggered by the book when it came out in 1923 centered mainly on the figure of the betrayed husband, a recurrent fantasy in World War I literature, which, as Mary Louise Roberts (1994: 39–40) shows, symbolized all the betrayals that soldiers in the trenches felt they had suffered. Autant-Lara's adaptation of the novel in 1947 also caused a scandal, but for different reasons. By adding an explicitly antimilitarist and pacifist dimension to the story (e.g., the scene in the hospital and the ironic coincidence of the armistice with the funeral of Marthe [Micheline Presle]) he refused to be associated with the heroic view of war and the Resistance that was predominant in the French cinema of the time (Lindeperg 1997: 288–91).

So in part the film draws upon the contradictions between Autant-Lara's antimilitarist message, carried by the male protagonist, and Radiguet's text, driven more by an exaltation of youth and sexual desire, symbols of absolute freedom. But the importance of the film's female characters shows that it also draws on what might be described as the legacy of the previous period, and the charisma of Presle, the movie's main star, who insisted that Gérard Philipe, then more or less at the beginning of his career, should play opposite her, clashes somewhat with the director's determination to show things primarily from the man's point of view. Philipe then went on to become the ideal male lead of the 1950s. Unlike the novel, the film's narrative is broken up by flashes forward to the present, showing the male hero's tragic, lonely mourning. This way the spectator is made more sensitive to the young man's desperate grief as he attends the funeral of his mistress on Armistice Day than to the objectively tragic death of the young woman in childbirth. But the final shot of the movie brings together the tragic loneliness of both central characters, when the verger, the very embodiment of clerical, militaristic, and flag-waving stupidity, appears on the steps of the church where the funeral service has just been held and says to no one in particular, "Now it's the women who're going to die. Everybody gets their turn!," as the bells celebrating the armistice ring out.

The narrative mode underlines the gulf between François's outraged conscience and Marthe's passivity, particularly in the episode where the young lover, aware of the ordeal suffered in the trenches by his mistress's husband, himself dictates to the forgetful Marthe the letters aimed at boosting the poor *poilu*'s morale. Here the theme of male solidarity makes its appearance, as a way of excluding and humiliating women. But the letter to the husband can also be read at face value, as an expression of compassion on the part of a man who managed to escape the "great butchery" because of his age, for a man who could possibly die at the front.

The same movie is notable for the emergence of a key character in the cinema of the period: Madame Grangier (Denise Grey), the evil mother-in-law — meaning always the wife's mother, since male viewpoint is the norm. From the first sequences of the film, Grey manages to whip up the spectator's hostility toward this image of a much more destructive and cynical matriarchal power than that of the traditional patriarchal authority. Yet here the "evil mother" character has a complexity which was to disappear from the later movies of the postwar period. A lingering close-up of Madame Grangier as she weeps after being caught in a lie by the young couple and left standing on the stairs lessens the film's criticism of this woman in the service of the patriarchy. The only male parental figure, François's father, Monsieur Jaubert (whom Jean Debucourt plays in a pitiful and touching manner inherited from his role in *Douce*), is exempted from any responsibility by virtue of his very weakness. But he is an ambiguous figure, ludicrous to start with, who later becomes his son's accomplice in a piece of male trickery of which the movie does not entirely approve; nothing could be more poignant than Marthe waiting alone at night on the ferry landing where she has a rendezvous with François in one final attempt to escape from her arranged marriage, with her tears falling silently into the water.

The last section of the story emphasizes the young couple's different degrees of maturity. The moment that Marthe discovers she is pregnant, François seems incapable of coping with the situation. On the train that is to take her far away from him so she can bring her pregnancy to term, she says with melancholy affection, as he puts his head on her lap, "I've two children." Then, during the final evening at a restaurant where they are supposed to celebrate their parting, he talks, with all the arrogance of a gifted and already cynical man, about the novel he will write about their affair, while she reveals to him every-thing he missed by not coming to their rendezvous at the ferry landing. Her moving clear-sightedness contrasts with her lover's offhand selfishness. The richness of the movie, and no doubt its box-office success and its reputation, spring from this complex interweaving of several layers of meaning of often heterogeneous and sometimes even contradictory origin: Radiguet's liber-tarian exaltation, Autant-Lara's antimilitaristic right-wing anarchism, and the various contradictions associated with that period of transition.

Originating in a long literary tradition that Oscar Wilde and the team of Hugo von Hoffmannsthal and Richard Strauss had previously made fashion-able in the twin figures of Herodias and Salome, an evil conspiracy between Dora (Simone Signoret) and her mother (Jane Marken) forms the central plank of Yves Allégret's *Manèges* (1949). The extremely complex organization of a series of flashbacks is designed to achieve the fusion of mother and daugh-ter in a one-sided contest between Robert (Bernard Blier), a man alone, and two women secretly conspiring to ruin him.

Another example of the same configuration, as late as 1956, consists of Catherine (Danièle Delorme) and Gabrielle (Lucienne Bogaert) in *Voici le temps des assassins* (1956) by Duvivier again. It could first be detected in Marcel Cravenne's *La Danse de mort* (1946), where Théa (Denise Vernac) and Rita (Maria Denis) gang up on their husband and father, the odious and pathetic Edgar (Erich von Stroheim), whom they betray in order to allow Rita to go off with the man she loves, a prisoner who is in Edgar's hands.

An unexpected comical variant is to be found in Jean Boyer's *Le Trou nor-mand* (*Crazy for Love*, 1952), where Javotte (Brigitte Bardot) and her aunt, Au-gustine (Jane Marken yet again), appear in a lighthearted remake of *Manèges* at the expense of poor Hippolyte (Bourvil), the village simpleton. But as this is a comedy, the amiable hero realizes that he would be better off settling for an ugly but loving wife, and the diabolical pair lose out. The young Brigitte, who starts off as a perfect slut, turns out to be — already — nothing more than a *ravissante idiote*, whom Roger Pierre has no difficulty sweeping off her feet, thus unintentionally foiling all her horrible mother's plans.

In all the films that have recourse to it, this dual figure of the wicked woman seems therefore to derive its phantasmatic effectiveness from the fact that it makes it possible to combine two logically contradictory notions, wickedness and passivity. Young women (of the kind that fascinate men) behave passively: their seductiveness operates without their being aware of it, and their physical beauty acts without their mind being involved. But their mothers, women who have lost their seductiveness along with their youth, become actively harmful, as though taking revenge for no longer being beautiful. Thus seductiveness can be seen to be a specifically female instrument of power, temporarily camouflaging a much more formidable ambition that emerges when beauty has faded. This dual figure denies the desired woman any autonomy while lending her power that she derives from her submission to the omnipotence of a mother or sister.

This matriarchal fantasy arises from a double reversal of the social reality of the period: the isolation of the housewife and her financial dependence most often put her in an unfavorable position in relation to her husband and family, but above all, the massive arrival of (young) women in the tertiary sector, at the expense of more traditional sectors such as homemaking and agriculture, gave them a new financial as well as social and psychological autonomy that made the omnipotent figure of the mother anachronistic (Ariès and Duby 1998; Prost and Vincent 1987). By resuscitating that figure so violently, the cinema tried to rope women back into being the eternal minor, traditionally confined to the private sphere.

Christian-Jaque's *Un revenant* (*A Lover's Return*, 1946), a story of revenge, takes this demeaning equation between young women and mature women to its logical conclusion, because we are introduced to the hero's old flame, Geneviève Gonin (Gaby Morlay), only when she has become a mature and submissive bourgeoise. Jean-Jacques Sauvage (Louis Jouvet), a famous choreographer, returns to Lyon, the city he left twenty years earlier after narrowly escaping an attempt on his life. He returns in order to settle a score. While the film, scripted by Henri Jeanson, runs the gamut of antibourgeois satire with some jubilation, pride of place is given to misogyny in the person of Morlay, who was still enjoying the aura of the virtuous roles she played in the Vichyite cinema. Personable enough on the face of it, Geneviève appears to be the victim of her milieu, which forced her to give up the man she loved and accept an arranged marriage. Little by little she is sadistically put on trial by her former lover, who is clearly the scriptwriter's mouthpiece and who makes her increasingly ridiculous as the film unfolds. He pretends to swear eternal love but ends up leaving her on a railway platform after urging her to leave her husband for his sake. And as he departs, he tells her he is taking her son with him as punishment for her having agreed in the past to fall back into line. The spectator, who identifies with Jean-Jacques's position as a dispenser of the law, also sees Geneviève as chiefly responsible for his past tribulations, all the more easily because she is a mature woman who is no longer as attractive or innocent as

Louis Jouvet and Gaby Morlay in *Un revenant*, 1946. Courtesy of Cinémathèque française.

she was in her youth and who compromised herself with the patriarchal and bourgeois powers that be. Geneviève thus comes across as the true face of an erstwhile deceptive passion, while the fact that she has aged serves to reveal the "true nature" of women as weak, hypocritical, and submissive.

It is tempting to interpret this story of a man who steps out of the past as a version of the soldier who, returning from captivity, sets himself up as a judge of women who are thought to have compromised themselves in order to survive during the Occupation. Thus the feeling of guilt attached to military defeat and of having left women to face the enemy on their own is turned on its head, with accusations of guilt being directed at women who remained at home while their husbands risked their lives fighting. *Un revenant* also transforms a class confrontation into sexual revenge, since Jean-Jacques, while claiming to get his own back on the bourgeois family that tried to kill him, above all punishes the woman he says he once loved, partly by making off with her son, François (a young François Périer), after deliberately getting him involved with a promiscuous actress. Thus any relationship with a woman is pure deception.

This new defensive coalition against women by men of different generations can be seen as a major change from the cinema of the preceding period.

The predominantly incestuous pattern of the 1930s pitted against each other, in a bid to possess a young woman, a middle-aged man and a young man, who usually ended up being the loser. In the postwar cinema, on the other hand, a regeneration of the patriarchy is brought about by both older and younger men teaming up to combat the harmful ascendancy of women. *Un revenant* does it in aggressive fashion, while *Le Diable au corps* relies on pathos. *Manèges* gives the theme a particularly poignant note in the person of a clear-sighted and helpless father figure, the old groom Louis (Jacques Baumer), who tries in vain to warn poor Robert (Bernard Blier) about his wife's schemes.

We find the same pattern in its raw state in Yvan Noé's *Dominique* (1950), a second-rate boulevard play directed by its author. Dominique (Michel Barbey) is a medical student who is being pressured by his family to break off his relationship with the young working-class woman he loves. He decides to leave his narrow-minded bourgeois milieu and live with her. What else is new? one might ask. However, the plot thickens when his father, who seems at first to be a particularly intolerant patriarchal figure, turns out to have engineered Dominique's decision to go and live with the young woman, to whom he has secretly been giving financial support, so that his son can shake off the castrating guardianship of the female members of the family—which, to his great regret, he himself never dared to do. Thus Noé naïvely updates the methods whereby the discredited prewar patriarchy hoped to make a comeback, namely to convince their male offspring that all their woes were caused by women's exorbitant power in the family and in society and to urge them to take control of the situation and thus liberate their oppressed fathers. As all this takes place in a boulevard context, the subject is sexual oppression. But the part holds true for the whole.

Whether or not they are combined with a paternal image, the figures of young men in the immediate postwar period all display a pathetic vulnerability that marks them out as ideal victims, no longer of their social milieu but of women who take advantage of their naïveté. Yves Allégret's *Une si jolie petite plage* (1949), scripted by Jacques Sigurd, carries out a displacement that is typical of the period, shifting from a social problem (the way children in state care are exploited by their host families) to the theme of the battle of the sexes. Pierre (Gérard Philipe) returns to the place where he spent an unhappy adolescence, only to meet an alter ego who is being exploited as he once was by another manager of the same hotel, Madame Mahieu (Jane Marken). He broods over the past and in his desperate state of mind confuses that exploitation with his abduction ten years earlier by an older woman who happened to be passing through—and whom he has just murdered because he was incapable of leaving her. Fred (Jean Servais), a sinister character who tracks him down like a detective or a jealous lover, turns out to be less of a threat to him than the painful memory of that woman. Pierre's only way out is suicide.

Like some vengeful ghost, the murdered woman manifests herself through a record that the hotel customers listen to: she was a realist nightclub singer, of the kind that tells the bitter truth about love, and when he breaks the record Pierre settles his score with that prewar myth. In such movies as *Paris-Béguin* (1932), *La Tête d'un homme* (1933), *Pépé le Moko* (1936), and *L'Entraîneuse* (1938), realist singers like Jane Marney, Damia, and Fréhel confirmed by their performances the genuineness of the emotions experienced by the spectator. It is the falsity of those emotions that Pierre in *Une si jolie petite plage* violently denounces when he destroys something that, distanced by the phonograph, is now nothing more than a hackneyed old song. Poetic realism had had its day; long live noir realism!

An unhappy childhood (which in *Le Jour se lève* created a bond between the characters played by Jean Gabin and Jacqueline Laurent) can no longer bring together young people who have been sexually exploited by older women. Pierre fails to gain the trust of the teenager who has succeeded him as a dogsbody at the hotel and who falls prey to a middle-aged female client in a relationship similar to that experienced by Pierre. As for the poor servant, Marthe (Madeleine Robinson), who sympathizes with him, she proves incapable of saving him; it is as though he had fallen under a witch's spell that made him permanently incapable of any loving relationship. The woman in question forms the structuring absence of the movie: she is already dead when the story begins, is never brought back to life in a flashback, but finally triggers Pierre's suicide. In other words, she is tantamount to an evil deity, whom he can neither leave nor even kill without causing his own death. This paranoiac mania can perhaps be interpreted as an age-old dread of a matriarchal power, modeled on the old patriarchy by divine right which men use to make emancipated women feel guilty while at the same time salving their wounded masculinity.

Even when dealing with young women, young men seem just as vulnerable. *Quai des Orfèvres* (1947) and *Manon* (1948) enabled Clouzot to resurface in style after having endured a two-year ban on exercising his profession. The evil influence of women was an eminently consensual theme that made it possible to draw a veil over ideological differences and questionable conduct.

Jenny Lamour, in *Quai des Orfèvres*, is doubtless the finest role in Suzy Delair's career. She plays a music hall singer whose ruthless ambition prompts her husband, Maurice (Bernard Blier), to commit a murder (or almost). Blier is a natural for the part of a loving, gullible husband who is both likable and weak, a petit bourgeois who has lowered himself socially out of love. A pianist in the music hall where his wife appears, he is reduced most of the time to standing by helplessly as she throws herself at various men.

The embodiment of a clear-sighted but discredited patriarchal authority, Lieutenant Antoine (Louis Jouvet) duly investigates, only to discover to his dismay that the husband is probably the culprit and that his "slut" of a wife is the sole person responsible. The audience feels uneasy throughout the movie, forced as it apparently is to choose between the victimized husband and the conscientious sleuth, because of the murder that one of them is alleged to have committed and the other is supposed to unravel. Very soon it is Jenny who emerges as the person responsible for this tragic confrontation between two honest men. But to prevent the film from implying that all women are sluts, it features Dora (Simone Renant), a lesbian photographer who is also secretly in love with the beautiful Jenny and who is prepared to compromise herself so as to make up for the mistakes Jenny has made (or her crime), and whom Antoine fondly describes as "my kind of guy."

It is worth lingering a moment on Dora, an unusual character in the French cinema. Prewar films often portrayed tragic but not very likable lesbians in supporting roles (see *Club de femmes* [1936] and *Hélène*). Clouzot here gave the role of an out-of-the-closet lesbian to an actress then at the peak of her film career and accustomed to playing attractive adult women (see *Voyage sans espoir*, *L'Ange qu'on m'a donné*, and *La Tentation de Barbizon* [*The Temptation of Barbizon*, 1946]). In other words, he lends the character a positive image, but at the same time makes it clear that it involves a psychological sex change (e.g., Antoine's remark), thus confirming the inferiority of femaleness. Men and lesbians are portrayed as victims of female seduction, bravely putting up with their unhappy condition.

What is more, Blier and Jouvet each in their own way offer a fragile and endearing image of masculinity: the young husband, who has no defense against his wife's fierce ambition, and the aging inspector, who returned from the colonies with malaria and a half-caste child whom he pampers like a mother. They are two incarnations of a very effectively camouflaged patriarchal law, which the postwar cinema set about rehabilitating: if Jenny had obeyed her husband, the nightmare would not have taken place, and only the inspector's pernickety perseverance ends up by proving Maurice innocent, after having completely demolished his alibis. Georges Brignon (Charles Dullin), the horrible old lecher who marks a concession to the notion of an abusive patriarchy, cuts a totally ludicrous figure; he has to make do with photographing his conquests in lascivious poses because he no longer has the strength to "possess" them. The last-minute discovery of the "true murderer" in the person of a completely anonymous prowler demonstrates that the film's discourse lies elsewhere.

By sparing in extremis the woman who remains the main culprit from a moral point of view, the movie allows itself the luxury of appearing to be magnanimous. Antoine speaks on behalf of the film's authors when he absolves the young couple, but it is clear in the spectator's mind that it is the husband's generosity that deserves to be rewarded. The choice of Blier to play him, with his unprepossessing looks and air of an average Frenchman, reinforces the identification of not only the male but also the female spectator, who finds it very hard to feel anything in common with the provocative and irresponsible cabaret singer or the solitary lesbian. The effectiveness of *Quai des Orfèvres*, which won the Best Director Award at the 1947 Venice Film Festival, is the result of its extremely brilliant mise-en-scène, from the construction of the narrative to the direction of actors, forming a fascinating contrast with the mediocrity of the characters and the sordid nature of the events described — a contrast that was to become Clouzot's "signature."

Manon (1949), Clouzot's update to present-day France of Abbé Prévost's eighteenth-century novel, was also a great box-office success. Yet it is difficult today to feel involved in this modern adaptation of *Manon Lescaut*. The eponymous eighteenth-century heroine, a victim of patriarchal oppression as much as she is of her own desire, is turned into a flighty young woman who at the Liberation narrowly escapes having her head shaved, thanks to Robert Dégrieux (Michel Auclair), a Resistant who betrays his comrades for the woman he loves. He becomes a petty black-market trafficker before fleeing with her to Palestine, where the two lovers die in the desert. Unlike the novel, where the hero survives to tell his "unfortunate tale," the victimization of the male protagonist in Clouzot's movie results in an interminable final sequence in which, after Manon has died, we see Robert in his death throes, stretched out on the sand with his arms forming a cross — a latter-day Christ sacrificed to make amends for the sins of the Woman.

The film consists of a series of flashbacks, like those of Jean Renoir's *Le Crime de Monsieur Lange*. A man accused of murder by the judicial authorities tries to explain the reasons for his act to those who can either hand him over or

Michel Auclair (far left) and Cécile Aubry in *Manon*, 1948. Courtesy of Lucienne Chevert and Sam Levin, Cinémathèque française.

save him. But as in *Quai des Orfèvres*, the aim is to prove to the audience that the woman alone is guilty.

The first flashback has become a classic. Amid the ruins of a town bombed during the Liberation, a group of Resistance fighters belonging to the Forces Françaises de l'Intérieur (FFI) manage to rescue a young woman, Manon (Cécile Aubry), from the clutches of a bunch of hysterical women who are intent on shaving off her hair as punishment for her "horizontal collaboration." Naked and tattooed women with shaven heads (*tondues*) are herded past the camera. Dégrieux is in charge of keeping guard over Manon until she is tried according to the rules. She tries to escape, but he catches up with her. Then she persuades him to flee with her.

The depiction of the tondues episode in a 1948 movie by a filmmaker who seriously compromised himself with the occupying forces is included with a very definite purpose, which is to recall the "horrors" of the Liberation in order to draw a veil over the much greater horrors of the Occupation. But Clouzot's way of dealing with the question has several levels of meaning. Contrary to the bulk of the evidence, he exonerates the young FFI fighters of direct responsibility for shaving the heads of suspects and blames women instead; the shaving, he shows, was the result of women settling scores with each other, and not sexist reprisals. This is not all that different from Manon's belief that the tondues were "simply" guilty of being young and beautiful and victims of the shameful jealousy of a few harpies. But in the light of what is to come later on in the movie, the scene can also be interpreted as an appeal for a united front of men on all sides (collaborators and Resistants) against women. In any case, the fact that Clouzot could already afford to take so few precautions when dealing with the still controversial themes of the purges and the black market proves that public opinion toward him had changed. (This was confirmed by the movie's box-office success.)

A typically "revisionist" film, *Manon* reflects Clouzot's determination to settle a few scores in a scandalous context of youthful passion, thus resorting to the formula Autant-Lara used in *Le Diable au corps*. The final episode in Palestine (foreshadowed by the sequence where Jewish refugees chant in Yiddish in the hold of the boat where Dégrieux and Manon have stowed away) demonstrates Clouzot's extraordinary ability to clear his reputation at little cost. Jews who have survived the genocide and are emigrating to the Promised Land replace the deported convicts who feature in the novel; later on, in the desert, the poor wretches, already exhausted from their long trek, are subjected to a surprise attack by Bedouins. This is a very good example, coming from a right-wing filmmaker, of how anti-Arab racism can replace anti-Semitism so as to draw a veil over the complicity of the French in the Jewish genocide.

These successive manipulations of recent history (and there are many other such examples in the film) make puppets of the characters, including Dégrieux, who speaks on behalf of the director and has no autonomy of his own; through the device of a voice-over, he offers up "truths" such as the following, aimed at justifying the narrator's participation in the black market: "In the gigantic free-for-all of the postwar period, I grabbed my share." But Clouzot devotes most of his attention to the character of Manon, a literal reversal of the typical female figure found in the Occupation cinema, namely the subject of the narrative and the person in charge of the community's fate. In this case, the hero-cum-narrator is the subject, while the woman is the object of his desire and cause of all his problems. The view we are given of the female character is through the gaze of the desiring male. This return to the preeminence of the male viewpoint, which can be found again and again in the postwar cinema, comes across as revenge.

As for the female figures, they are modeled on those found in Hollywood movies, with the addition of an eroticism that did not exist in prewar French cinema, but they are almost always regarded as objects. Cécile Aubry's child-like appearance, which is emphasized by her acting, makes the film's subtext perfectly explicit: women are fascinating because they are childlike, irresponsible, and thoughtless. In other words, they are attractive to men because of their ability to be nothing but bodies, interested solely in their appearance and creature comforts. The scene where Dégrieux discovers, to his horror, that Manon works in a deluxe brothel encapsulates Clouzot's theory about the relationship between men and women: women are "fit to be killed" (*bonnes à tuer*, the title of a film Henri Decoin made in 1954), but we always absolve them because they do not even realize that they make us men suffer. Quite apart from Clouzot's personal settling of scores, the film's success in 1948, whether because of or despite the ponderousness of its argumentation, is in itself a major indication of the violently conflictual nature of relations between the sexes at the time.

℀ *The Emergence of a Feminist Trend*

The wave of misogyny found in the immediately postwar cinema is not, however, the sole expression, although it is predominant, of the upheavals caused in the private sphere by the Defeat and the Occupation. In a persistent and often remarkable counterpoint to it, we find what might be called a genuine feminist trend in the French cinema, whose novelty compared with the previous period is abundantly clear: positive but often idealized female figures are replaced by representations that audaciously confront the contradictions in relations between men and women revealed by the Liberation. The most innovative of these movies tackle the issue of desire (whether liberating or alienating), relations between the couple, the articulation between the professional and private spheres of each of the sexes, the influence of education on the behavior of both, and everything that makes relations between the sexes an integral part of a given society and historical moment. It is probably this attempt — which is variously successful depending on the movie — to question relationships that were so long regarded as natural which marks the novelty and modernity of this trend. It should be seen in the light of a book published in 1948, which Pascal Ory (1989) regards — but without expanding on his judgment — as "the most influential of the whole century," Simone de Beauvoir's *Le Deuxième sexe* (see also Duchen 1994).

Although found in only a minority of films, this trend is expressed by filmmakers who differ widely from each other both artistically and ideologically, which only goes to show what a key position this issue occupied in postwar society. Some of these movies originated in Resistant or progressive circles, such as Jacques Becker's *Antoine et Antoinette* (1947), Louis Daquin's *Les Frères Bouquinquant* (1947) and *Le Point du jour* (*The Mark of the Day*, 1949), Jean Grémillon's *Pattes blanches* (1948), the young Jean-Pierre Melville's *Le Silence de la mer* (*The Silence of the Sea*, 1947), and *Les Malheurs de Sophie* (1946), *Gigi* (1948), and *Minne, l'ingénue libertine* (*Minnie*, 1950) by Jacqueline Audry, who finally got to direct after working for fifteen years in the profession.

But the feminist trend also affected less politically committed directors such as Jean Cocteau (*La Belle et la Bête* [*Beauty and the Beast*], 1946), Christian-Jaque (*Boule de suif* [*Angel and Sinner*], 1945), and Henri Decoin (*Les Amants du Pont Saint-Jean*, 1947), as well as less well known filmmakers like Paul Mesnier (*La Kermesse rouge*, 1946) and Jacques Manuel (*Julie de Carneilhan*, 1949). All these movies tackle head-on the paradoxical legacy — derived from the experience of both the Occupation and the Resistance — of female emancipation. That source of inspiration dwindled during the 1950s but continued to spawn interesting or remarkable films (*Le Château de verre, Casque d'or, Le Carrosse d'or, Les Miracles n'ont lieu qu'une fois, La Vérité sur Bébé Donge, L'Amour d'une femme*, and *Des gens sans importance*). This trend is interesting because of the complex works that made it up in various genres and styles. Some filmmakers who made an impact in that register later joined the mainstream misogynistic school (Melville, Cocteau, Christian-Jaque, Decoin, and even Becker and Renoir).

Antoine et Antoinette, whose naïve optimism is typical of the climate at the Liberation, describes the daily life of a young couple of workers (an unusual feature that can probably also be attributed to the period when the film was made). Although traces of a prewar set of themes that emerged from poetic realism can be detected, what one chiefly notices is how the movie breaks away from that tradition. The tragic atmosphere of films by Carné, Duvivier, and Grémillon and even Renoir's *Toni* has disappeared and is replaced by a less literary description of social and individual conflicts. The lecherous old grocer (Noël Roquevert) is a ludicrous "incestuous father" figure, because his age is no longer camouflaged by any trace of prestige. But above all, the balance of the movie has been tipped in favor of the female character. While Roger Pigaut (Antoine) is a likable enough young worker, he is totally lacking in the prewar Gabin's charisma, and the movie highlights the childish jealousy he displays toward his wife. Claire Mafféi (Antoinette), on the other hand, is the life and soul of the couple. Her radiant smile helps to make light of their problems, and her generosity enables Antoine to recover his pride after the embarrassment of losing a lottery ticket. He dreams of buying a motorcycle with a side-car, a vehicle that reproduces the traditional pattern of domination in a couple, whereas she would prefer more comfortable lodgings for them both. But this idealized image whereby a woman's maturity repairs the damage caused by a man's infantilism contains the seeds of its own limitations. The idealized approach was reversed, in Becker's films too, as soon as the political and ideological climate became less favorable.

Louis Daquin offers another typical example of the contradictions in the progressive male conscience of the time; after his misogynistic pamphlet, *Patrie*, he directed two movies that tackled the relations of domination between the sexes. Set in the world of river barges, perhaps a nod in the direction of Jean Vigo's *L'Atalante* (1934) — another movie with feminist overtones — *Les Frères Bouquinquant* compares a female and a male point of view, that of two lovers after the suspicious death of the woman's husband. The aim is not to oppose the two but to take into account the psychological and sociological determinations hanging over both of them. The confession of Julie (Madeleine Robinson), which takes up most of the movie, describes her sad life as a dogs-body, first seduced, then overworked by her older husband, Léon (Albert Préjean), a bargeman. The young male lead of the prewar populist cinema here becomes a slightly shop-worn Don Juan and an alcoholic and violent social sponger. Thus the film turns its back on the incestuous couple of the 1930s, replacing them with Madeleine Robinson and Roger Pigaut, a couple that had already graced the screen, but in a negative mode, in *Douce*.

In *Les Frères Bouquinquant*, Pigaut plays Pierre, a factory worker who falls in love with his elder brother's young wife and tries to rescue her from her oppressive married life so he can himself bring up the child she has had with him. The very embodiment of Communism's "new man," Pierre follows in the footsteps of both the "mothering fathers" to be found in Richard Pottier's *Les Caves du Majestic* (1944) and those "gentle male" figures who tried to put relations with women on an equal and respectful footing. He himself encounters some difficulty in doing so, because Julie is very reluctant to disregard the dominant moral code. In the very best anticlerical tradition of the French left, the movie denounces the hold that Catholic morality has over women, who are depicted as almost implausibly submissive. Perhaps this can be interpreted as an insidious leftover of left-wing misogyny.

The film nonetheless offers a remarkable analysis, put across with pathos by Robinson, of the specific oppression that weighs down deprived women, both as poor and as women (a girl from the provinces who leaves home to become a dogsbody in a bourgeois Parisian household, before doing the same work for her husband with no pay and a few beatings thrown in). The movie shows that this oppression is facilitated by the alienation women have to endure as a result of their having less access to education, which is replaced by religious control as personified by the prison chaplain to whom Julie confesses. (Jean Vilar plays this terrifying spiritual advisor.) Although it was probably unintentional, there is a revealing symmetry in the narrative between this repressive priest and Louis (Albert Jacquin), the local Communist Party representative, who preaches Communist morals to the young worker.

Daquin's second film on this social issue is *Le Point du jour* (1949), but this time the main subject is directly political in the traditional sense: the movie argues in favor of a class alliance in the coal mines of northern France between workers and executives, both committed to the postwar "production battle." Larzac (Jean Desailly) is a young Parisian engineer from a bourgeois background who gradually adapts to the world of miners. Despite some very fine near-documentary sequences, the film does not always steer clear of the pitfalls inherent in films with a social message, and the question of the relationship between men and women becomes less central. Loleh Bellon plays Marie, a superb example of an emancipated young woman, who works as a top-side grader while the men dig coal underground. She refuses to be treated as a dogsbody, a role traditionally reserved for married women in that milieu. Despite the fact that she loves her young fiancé, Georges (Michel Piccoli) — her desire is made explicit in a moving love scene in a field of weeds overlooked by a slagheap — she holds back from marriage so she can go on working. Daquin emphasizes the inflexibility of the young miners who are determined to hang on to their meager traditional male privileges, and it is the successful outcome of the political conflict that is the movie's only true happy ending.

Shot during the summer of 1948, at a time when the Communists had already left the government more than a year earlier and were having to cope with the cold war environment, the movie displays an unwavering faith in a broad policy of alliance. But Daquin also seems already to be aware of the fact that the emancipation of women, while remaining essential if life is to be changed, will take second place for the Communists compared with political issues.

Also worthy of note is a recent rediscovery, Henri Decoin's *Les Amants du Pont Saint-Jean* (1947). Scripted by René Wheeler and Jean Aurenche and shot on location in a village in the Rhône Valley, the film describes the love affair of an atypical couple, Maryse (Gaby Morlay) and Alcide (Michel Simon), two

Michel Simon, René Génin, and Gaby Morlay in *Les Amants du Pont Saint-Jean*, 1948.
Courtesy of Cinémathèque française.

down-and-outs who have been living together for fifteen years and who each
fight tooth and nail to prevent their freedom from being encroached upon by
the other. Their belated marriage is supposed to make it easier for Alcide's son
to get accepted by the bourgeois family of Augusta (the remarkable Nadine
Alari), the woman he loves, but after spending the night with him Maryse realizes how unrealistic their relationship is and turns down the offer of marriage
she gets from her lover as "reparation" for her lost virginity.

The movie clearly highlights women's courage and determination when
dealing with men who are likable enough but tend to be cowardly or violent.
Maryse ebulliently insists on her right to go to the village dance, despite Alcide's jealousy. It is only out of solidarity with Augusta, who is oppressed by
her father, that she agrees to jeopardize her independence by marrying her
long-term partner. But the rather meager wedding banquet does not turn out
well for her: all the men get drunk, and Alcide knocks her off a ladder. She dies
alone on a river bank.

Les Amants du Pont Saint-Jean is an unclassifiable film that unfortunately
did not inspire any kind of following. It would seem to have been the product
of the particular conditions of the immediate postwar period; these included
ravaged infrastructure and reduced financial resources, but they were accom-

panied by the exhilarating atmosphere of a period when all the old straitjackets seemed to be bursting at the seams and any project was feasible (thanks most notably to the notion that state aid should enable film to depend less on profitability). For despite its tragic ending, the film produces a feeling of elation, resulting probably from its creative freedom and the cheerfully iconoclastic image it puts across.

This innovative trend in the representation of sexual relations and identities found in individual films as well as the work of certain directors and which paid scant respect to the grids of interpretation since imposed by the *politique des auteurs*, seems to be associated with certain types of actors. In the immediate postwar years Jean Marais, for example, was involved in a whole series of movies of widely differing origins which nevertheless shared a propensity to offer a critical version of the initiation into masculinity. Jean Cocteau's *La Belle et la Bête* (1946), Pierre Billon's *Ruy Blas* (1947), Jean Delannoy's *Aux yeux du souvenir* (*Souvenir*, 1948), Cocteau's *Les Parents terribles* (*The Storm Within*, 1948), Delannoy's *Le Secret de Mayerling* (*The Secret of Mayerling*, 1948), Cocteau's *Orphée* (1949), Yves Allégret's *Les Miracles n'ont lieu qu'une fois* (1950), René Clément's *Le Château de verre* (1950), and Roger Richebé's *Les Amants de minuit* (1953) paint the picture of an immature young man whose encounter with a woman helps or forces him to become an adult, in some kind of reversal of the paranoiac pattern of a man victimized by an evil bitch that was the rule during that period. A number of narrative elements in many of those movies suggest more or less explicitly that he is a young man who has been prevented from moving "normally" into adulthood by war and other external events. Trapped in an infantile form of behavior by an experience that may or may not have been heroic, which forces him to adopt a caricaturally virile manner, he will succeed, with the help of a psychologically adult woman, in achieving a more responsible form of masculinity.

This pattern can be found in films with right-wing and left-wing connotations, whether the emphasis is on the restoration of a regenerated patriarchy (*Aux yeux du souvenir*) or on a crisis of masculinity (*Orphée, Le Château de verre*). This rare ability to put across the image of a vulnerable man can probably be partly put down to Marais's self-proclaimed homosexuality (insofar as that was possible in France at that time) and to Cocteau's direct influence over his career. The same is true of another remarkable character trait: the maturity of these male figures can be gauged from their ability to take feelings seriously, a traditionally female characteristic.

La Belle et la Bête marked a brilliant start to the series, but the aesthetic qualities of this fairy-tale production blinded commentators to the very con-temporary nature of the issues raised by the film. For example, surely the weak and selfish father who is prepared to sacrifice his daughter to a mon-ster in order to save his own life is the very quintessence of the castrated and unworthy fathers of the Occupation. Yet the initial misdeed committed by Belle (Josette Day), which is to have refused to leave her father to marry a young man, comes across as a throwback to the prewar figure of the incestuous couple. On the other hand, the young woman's confrontation with her mon-strous jailor, who has to win her love in order to become a man, seems to be a luminous metaphor for the task assigned to women at the Liberation, which was to sacrifice themselves so that the male identity, twisted beyond recogni-tion by the horrors of war, could reconstruct itself. Day, whose beauty, in the best fairy-tale tradition, is the expression of boundless generosity, embodies the humanity of which the Beast (Jean Marais) has been deprived, and the movie shows how this condemnation to bestiality is the cause of terrible suf-fering, which is only intensified when Belle rejects his attentions. She will have to renounce her own desire in order to love the person who needs her, and she will find happiness only at the outcome of this self-denial.

This transitional movie makes it possible to understand how the ideal female figures of the Occupation could so abruptly be turned into their oppo-site. Cocteau's film portrays the kind of ideal woman that war-battered men dreamed of at the Liberation. But the confrontation with the harsh realities of the postwar period and the inability of most men to understand the changes that had taken place would spawn that figure of male resentment: the diaboli-cal bitch. What was a pathetic admission of inadequacy in *La Belle et la Bête* (the fairy tale is also the expression of a desire to regress) would soon become, in the films of other directors and with other actors more in sympathy with patriarchal values, a wild barrage of accusations against the Other. But Marais continued to go against the general trend and pursue his register of vulnerable masculinity.

Les Miracles n'ont lieu qu'une fois provides a version of this pattern that is all the more interesting because its director, Yves Allégret, also using Jacques Sigurd as his scriptwriter, was responsible a year earlier for that veritable acme of misogyny, *Manèges*, which would tend to suggest that the essence of the period resides in contradiction. Jérôme (Jean Marais), the central character and narrator of *Les Miracles n'ont lieu qu'une fois*, starts out as a carefree and rowdy medical student who fails to see that Claudia (Alida Valli), a young Ital-ian student, is in love with him. By the time the truth dawns on him, it is time

Alida Valli and Jean Marais in *Les Miracles n'ont lieu qu'une fois*, 1950.
Courtesy of Cinémathèque française.

for her to go back home. He joins her in Italy, and they enjoy a secret "honey-moon" in San Geminiano. But it is August 1939. Jérôme is mobilized and has to go back to France alone. In 1940 he is taken prisoner and loses touch with the woman he loves. After escaping from prison, he makes a living from the black market in Paris and loses all hope of ever finding her again. At the Liberation he gets married in a fit of pique, but soon divorces. Eleven years after their "honeymoon," he finally tracks down the woman he loved in Italy, a war-ravaged country corrupted by the American occupation, and they both realize that the romantic passion of their youth has evaporated. He is furious with her and lets her go, only catching up with her at the last moment.

The film is a bittersweet account of the transition from youth to adulthood. Jérôme, who is carefree and self-confident to start with, is crushed by the steamroller of History and ends up having to abandon all his illusions. This painful transformation is personified by a female figure, at first an innocent and loving young woman whom he initiates like some Pygmalion, and who by the end of the movie has been turned into a woman of great experience, including sexually. A very explicit moment comes when we see the two lovers in physical contact again, a scene that is interrupted by Jérôme's realization that the person he has in his arms is no longer an awkward girl but an expert woman who has learned how to have an orgasm. He pushes her away with horror, unable as he is to tolerate this concrete proof that she has sought and found pleasure in other men's arms. The movie thus denounces, in a way that is sufficiently unusual for it to be emphasized, the unsaid persistence in the male mentality of a sexual permissiveness reserved for men. Jérôme's transition to adulthood is materialized by his ability to get rid of his fixation, at once infantile and paternalistic, on an image of the "innocent" woman who needs to be initiated by a man. The tragic atmosphere of the final sequence of their reunion comes as a reminder that this renunciation can only be accompanied by suffering. And the mise-en-scène ties it to the anxieties of the cold war.

CHAPTER II

Restoring the Patriarchal Order

THE YEAR 1950 marked a turning point, which was probably not unconnected with an improvement in the economic situation in general and in that
of the French cinema in particular. After the serious industrial and political
unrest that marked the end of the 1940s, the beginning of the cold war, the
exclusion of the Communists from the government, and the strikes of 1947
which were ruthlessly put down, the effects of the Marshall Plan began to
make themselves felt. As far as the cinema was concerned, the massive mobi-
lization of film industry circles resulted in 1948 in the renegotiation of the
Blum-Byrnes accords of 1946 in a way that restricted American competition:
the number of weeks reserved for the exhibition of French films in cinemas
was raised from four to five per quarter, and the government passed the first
legislation aimed at helping the film industry, on the basis of a tax on entrance
tickets. In that way, part of the operating profits of all films shown in France
was channeled into the production of French films. Although it was not until
the end of the decade and André Malraux's cultural policies that the criterion
of quality was taken into account in that redistribution, a policy of state support that had first been attempted under the Vichy regime began to be put in
place (Courtade 1978; Portes 1986; Jeancolas 1992; Sellier 1993, 1994).

However, the improved economic health of the French cinema was accompanied by an increasingly insistent determination on the part of the industry to respond to American competition on its own ground, that of big productions, most of them coproduced with Italian or Spanish companies, with the aim of reducing risks by a relative standardization of products. This entailed a more assertive classification of genres such as detective films, historical movies, and literary adaptations. But the process also resulted in greater caution in the choice and treatment of subjects for commercial reasons. In that context, misogyny was dressed up in more refined and more "international" clothes.

A striking example of this development in the French cinema was the biggest box-office success of 1950, Richard Pottier's *Caroline chérie* (*Dear Caroline*), based on a novel by Cécil Saint-Laurent, with dialogue by Jean Anouilh and a score by Georges Auric. The credit titles present these icons of middlebrow culture against a background of engravings from the period of the Revolution, preceding a cast list that puts Martine Carol right at the end of the credits and shows how little known the future star was at the time. The voice-over of Jean Debucourt of the Comédie Française embodies the "subject supposed to know" (who has lost all his illusions). Before becoming the light comedy that established Carol as a star, *Caroline chérie* was put across as a carefully made historical film, exploiting the vein, initiated by Sacha Guitry (in *Le Destin fabuleux de Désirée Clary* [*Mlle. Desiree*], 1941, and *Le Diable boîteux*, 1948), of a boulevard rereading of French history, in which the cowardice and cynicism of individuals is matched only by the chaos of events. But of course it was a more recent period that the *Caroline* series was reinterpreting in reactionary terms, via the 1789 Revolution.

In the 1950s costume films no longer served as camouflage to fool the censors as they did during the Occupation (see *Douce*). Most of them were designed to be popular entertainment that would give audiences their money's worth. The French historical movie with literary pretensions—Guitry became the uncontested master of the genre with his two box-office hits, *Si Versailles m'était conté* (*Royal Affairs in Versailles*, 1953) and *Napoléon* (1954)—did not eschew a light form of eroticism that was the hallmark of 1950s commercial cinema, all the more precious as it enabled Guitry and others to offer, in lighthearted mode, a reactionary rereading of French history.

But quite apart from such stereotypes as the vulgar greed of the populace and the dignity of the aristocracy—and of course the likening of the Chouans to the *maquisards*—*Caroline chérie* used the heroine's racy adventures as a way of pouring derision on the world of politics in general. And while freedom of morals is the only virtue advocated by the movie, it is careful to avoid lending it the meaning of a liberation in relations between men and women. The young Caroline's discovery of sexual pleasure in the film's first scene can be interpreted as agreeably licentious, but what follows deals with sex in the most conventional way. And while the beautiful Caroline can afford to be notoriously unfaithful to the man she loves, Gaston de Sallanches (Jacques Dacqmine) on no fewer than two occasions — plus performing her conjugal duties and being raped by a despicable revolutionary soldier — the end of the movie sets the record straight: Caroline allows herself to be slapped and called a "whore" by the handsome Sallanches, even though she knows that the man she loves is an inveterate womanizer. The movie never questions the unilateral right of men to seek their pleasure wherever they like. But before this restoration of patriarchal order, the (male) spectator can get a kick out of the young woman's saucy adventures with a clear conscience: that was all the Revolution's fault!

Despite that final slap in the face, the "dear Caroline" played by Carol has little in common with the sluts of the prewar cinema or the diabolical women of the postwar period. Her character, whose success spawned several sequels, introduced a new phase in the battle of the sexes as well as the class war. The choice of a woman aristocrat living at the time of the Revolution meant that any issues regarding the emancipation of women could be ruled out. And the heroine's smiling eroticism harks back to the French tradition of courtly love which has long served as an effective foil to questions about gender relations. The term *bagatelle* (literally, a "trifle") in the sense of "sexual pleasure," which was first used in the eighteenth century, says a lot about men's refusal to take seriously the pleasure that honest women are anyway not supposed to experience; in the nineteenth century, boulevard theater's obsession with the (comic) theme of adultery confirmed that typical French frame of mind which the cinema took up with gusto so it could deal with gender relations in a lighthearted mode that deliberately drew a veil over such issues as power and morals.

Serious boulevard, on the other hand (which could be likened to filmed melodrama), dealt with such issues head-on. Its most eminent representative, Henry Bernstein, had seven of his plays adapted for the screen in the 1930s, then vanished from the French cinema during the Occupation in the early 1940s (because of his Jewish origins). He reemerged only once, at the beginning of the 1950s, with Claude Heymann's *Victor* (1951). This loss of interest in Bernstein in the postwar cinema confirms that the rereading of the libertine outlook carefully drained it of the subversive dimension it could have on gender relations.

The poor reputation of filmed melodrama in France (particularly in edu-cated circles), which was accentuated by the way Pétainist cinema used it, can also be explained as a refusal to discuss gender relations in emotional and moral terms. The predominant discourse on sex in the classical French cinema gives pride of place to the male standpoint of flirtation and conquest, expressed through an eroticism that had been restricted to language in the 1930s and was broadened to include the image of the female body in the 1950s.

⚔ Jacqueline Audry, the Invisible Director

In that context, the case of Jacqueline Audry, the only outstanding woman director working in the commercial cinema of the period, is utterly fascinat-ing. It is worth noting that her work is not discussed in either the most recent histories of the French cinema (Prédal 2005; Billard 1995) or works on women filmmakers (Audé 1981; Flitterman-Lewis 1996).

Born in 1908, Colette Audry's younger sister worked as an assistant in the 1930s and made her first feature, *Les Malheurs de Sophie*, in 1946. The film was adapted, or rather hijacked, from the Comtesse de Ségur's novel by Colette Audry, who turned the edifying novel for well-behaved little girls into a de-nunciation of the education of upper-class girls—an education based solely on submission. In the second part of the movie, cousin Paul (Michel Auclair) becomes a student protester at the barricades of the 1848 Revolution, and it is with him that Sophie (Madeleine Bousset) elopes to escape the marriage of convenience her family wants to impose on her.

With her husband, Pierre Laroche, Jacqueline Audry then adapted three novels by Colette for the screen, as well as Victor Marguerite's *La Garçonne*. From the start, then, she was a feminist filmmaker in that all her movies di-rectly challenge sexual roles as defined by society. But she resorts to the smoke-screen of the costume film, and it can be argued that the success of many of her films was the result of a misunderstanding fostered by a lightheartedly erotic atmosphere that made it possible for her to criticize gender relations without clashing openly with the general climate of male chauvinism.

The first and best known of her adaptations of Colette, *Gigi* (1948), is a de-nunciation of the double sexual standard that forces women to be nothing but instruments of male pleasure. Gigi (Daniel Delorme) was born into a milieu of demimondaines and is being brought up to succeed them. But she rebels against the idea of being sold to the man she loves. Two years later, Delorme played the central character of *Minne, l'ingénue libertine* (*Minne*, 1950), which clearly demands that women be entitled to enjoy sexual pleasure. The movie

Danièle Delorme in *Minne, l'ingénue libertine*, 1950. Courtesy of André Garimond, Cinémathèque française.

shows that neither Minne's husband nor her subsequent lovers are able to give her that pleasure because society cannot imagine reciprocity in that area any more than in many others. Thanks to the sincerity and freshness that Delorme lends her character, what might have just been the story of an adulterous woman or, as seen through the prism of the period, the humiliation of a cuckolded husband at the hands of a slut, becomes a subtle but implacable description of the inequality of husband and wife in a traditional marriage. But the refined Belle Epoque atmosphere, Pierre Laroche's brilliant dialogue, and the happy ending (it is finally in her husband's arms that Minne discovers pleasure, though an incongruous shot of a cactus jubilantly subverts this conventional ending) together mean that spectators not very concerned with feminism can see the movie merely as a slightly bawdy comedy in the best French tradition.

Olivia (The Pit of Loneliness, 1951), adapted from Colette's novel of the same name, partly eludes that ambiguity because it is probably the first French film to deal directly with female homosexuality without regarding it as either an illness or a perversion. A cult movie among British and American feminists, this Jacqueline Audry film remains little known to French cinephiles. Set at the end of the nineteenth century in a kind of secular and female Abbaye de Thélème, *Olivia* features a dazzling Edwige Feuillère as Mademoiselle Julie, a paragon of a teacher who gradually reveals herself to be a tragic Don Juan figure. She is hounded by the hatred of her former lover, Mademoiselle Cara (Simone Simon), and struggles against her desire for her young pupils (not because she is homosexual but because of the inequality inherent in her status as a teacher). But she also gives of her best in her passionate relationship with the young Olivia (Marie-Claire Olivia), the nostalgic narrator of this paradise lost.

There are no men in this self-sufficient female universe, and a whole range of feelings and passions are expressed in it without any caricature or salacious innuendo. Christmas Eve, which is celebrated in true secular fashion with a dance, contains a surprisingly audacious scene, where Mademoiselle Julie in an evening dress changes partners according to the whim of the moment, then kisses one of her pupils with a sensuality that makes the young Olivia wildly jealous. But most remarkable is the fact that spectators, male and female, catch themselves identifying with her loving glances, as though Audry had succeeded in making us forget the taboo of homosexuality so she could tell us her story like any other (heterosexual) love story. It was after she made *Olivia* that some critics expressed more aggressive hostility to Audry, as though she had broken a taboo that no longer allowed her movies to be classified merely as enjoyable entertainment.

ℛ *Women in Series, Men in Gangs*

The success of comical *policier* films like André Hunebelle's *Méfiez-vous des blondes* (1950) reflected a fascination with a new form of male chauvinism. Before Eddie Constantine came on the scene, Raymond Rouleau was cast as a high-powered, charming detective playing opposite creatures whose sheer numbers gave a fair indication of their interchangeability. There is no point in lingering on the misogyny that was an essential component of such movies. But it is worth pointing out the relative novelty in France of a genre that obliged women, according to Hollywood norms, to be no more than infinitely different versions of the same model: blonde, tall, and with generous curves. That such norms were able to impose themselves on French films showed that the ideological climate had changed compared with the violence of the immediate postwar period. From then on, there was no doubt about it: a genre could reduce female figures to the state of inflatable dolls, and the public (and perhaps not just the male public) could not get enough of them.

The accumulation of images of women was the main trend of the decade, affecting the way scenarios were constructed, as, for example, in films made up of sketches that claimed to offer a representative sampling of the female sex, such as Jean Delannoy's *Destinées* (1954) and Henri Decoin's *Secrets d'alcôve* (*The Bed*, 1954). But more generally such movies as René Clair's *Belles de nuit* (1952), Max Ophuls's *La Ronde* (1950) and *Le Plaisir* (1952), Christian-Jaque's *Adorables créatures* (*Adorable Creatures*, 1952), René Clément's *Monsieur Ripois* (*Lovers, Happy Lovers!* or *Lover Boy*, 1954), and Decoin's *Bonnes à tuer* (*One Step to Eternity*, 1954), although they had very different ambitions, obeyed similar rules, which apparently went down well with audiences at the time since almost all these movies were box-office successes. On the other hand, during the same period, films built mainly around men told stories of male bonding and/or gangs of hoods, as in Georges Lampin's *Le Paradis des pilotes perdus* (1949), Henri Decoin's *Le Grand balcon* (1949), Georges Lampin's *Les Anciens de Saint-Loup* (1950), Henri-Georges Clouzot's *Le Salaire de la peur* (*The Wages of Fear*, 1953), Jacques Becker's *Touchez pas au grisbi* (1954), Yves Ciampi's *Les Héros sont fatigués* (*Heroes and Sinners*, 1955), and Claude Autant-Lara's *La Traversée de Paris* (*Four Bags Full*, 1956). It never occurred to scriptwriters to establish a similarly comparative catalogue of their male characters. Such stories of men who prefer each other's company, which exalted camaraderie and were very much in fashion during the second half of the 1930s thanks, above all, to Jean Gabin (*La Bandera*, *La Belle équipe*, and *La Grande illusion*), virtually disappeared during the Occupation (except in the tiny handful of fascistic movies). Their reappearance at the beginning of the 1950s (without any connection with the populist values of the prewar period) was just further evidence of the need that was then felt to reassert the supremacy of male values that had recently taken a battering.

The structuring absence of that malaise was Gabin's postwar career. From 1945 to 1954 the actor went through a very bad patch, which he remembered with such pain that he subsequently avoided taking the slightest risk in the handling of his image and career (Brunelin 1987: 334 ff.). That bad patch corresponded exactly to the period when there predominated a conflictual representation of gender relations which the roles Gabin played during that time (mostly in dramas and melodramas) expressed par excellence. From Georges Lacombe's *Martin Roumagnac* (*The Room Upstairs*, 1946) to Gilles Grangier's *La Vierge du Rhin* (1953), he made thirteen movies — none of them a great box-office success — which all portrayed a wound, a flaw, in short, a crisis of masculinity. This is particularly true of the best of the lot, Henri Decoin's *La Vérité sur Bébé Donge* (1952). In them, the character played by Gabin was in turn destroyed by a femme fatale (*Martin Roumagnac*); ensnared by his love for a poor waitress in René Clément's *Au-delà des grilles* (*The Walls of Malapaga*,

1948) or by the ambition of a younger woman in Marcel Carné's *La Marie du port* (1949); symbolically castrated in Lacombe's *La Nuit est mon royaume* (*The Night Is My Kingdom*, 1951), where he plays a train driver who goes blind; a man firmly turned away by a prostitute on vacation in Max Ophuls's *Le Plaisir* (1952); a husband cuckolded by the young Daniel Gélin in Jean Delannoy's *La Minute de vérité* (*The Minute of Truth*, 1952); and a prisoner of war betrayed by his wife in *La Vierge du Rhin*. All these parts made up a veritable catalogue of male fears as they crystallized after the Liberation.

But the way these films flopped at the box office to a greater or lesser degree can probably be attributed, irrespective of their variable quality, to a certain reluctance on the part of the public to see the great male star of the prewar period (and the only one with any real erotic charisma) become a prematurely aged figure and, worse, start personifying "losers." The complete flop of *La Vérité sur Bébé Donge* and, in contrast, the huge box-office success of Jacques Becker's *Touchez pas au grisbi* (1954) two years later confirmed the general public's reluctance to see an erosion of the legendary image of masculinity as embodied by Gabin (Gauteur and Vincendeau 1993).

Touchez pas au grisbi can be seen, in the context of Jacques Becker's career, as an attempt to regain popularity with the public by radically switching genres (from psychological comedy to gangster film) and by calling on the services of a popular novelist, Albert Simonin. The result was so brilliant that Becker created a veritable subgenre in the already very popular genre of gangster films; it could be called the gang film or film about men keeping themselves to themselves. It was soon followed by Jules Dassin's *Du rififi chez les hommes* (*Rififi*, 1955), Henri Decoin's *Razzia sur la chnouf* (*Razzia*, 1954), Jean-Pierre Melville's *Bob le flambeur* (1956), and Pierre Chenal's *Rafles sur la ville* (*Sinners of Paris*, 1958), to mention only the most successful of them. But as in many of Becker's previous movies, a couple is central to *Touchez pas au grisbi*, the one formed by Max and Riton (Gabin and René Dary), two world-weary gangsters whom the film portrays in a fond relationship that looks like nothing so much as a stereotype of married life. In the couple, Gabin undoubtedly plays the part of the husband, with a quiet self-confidence and benevolent authority that amounts to a veritable rehabilitation of the patriarchy, while Dary corresponds perfectly to the misogynous stereotype of the married woman, good-natured but irresponsible, not very bright but affectionate, who should not be left in the lurch for the simple reason that he is incapable of muddling through on his own.

In the rightly celebrated sequence where Max takes Riton to his secret flat, shares a rather refined snack with him, and makes their sleeping arrangements for the night, the metaphor of an elderly couple is breathtaking. But the two characters are not equally balanced. Riton has only weaknesses, whereas Max is in control of everything, including those little details that go to make the perfect hostess (the *petit vin blanc* to go with the foie gras, and the extra pajamas and toothbrush for the guest). But at the same time he is invested with the authority of a patriarch. (He reveals to Riton that his mistress is cheating on him and promises to sort things out.) That authority can also be sensed in the term he uses to indicate Riton's degrading feminization: when the latter, before going to sleep, asks his friend pathetically, "And what would you do in my place?," Max answers gruffly, "But I'd never be in your place, you poor sucker!" The ontological difference between the two characters could not be indicated more clearly.

But Becker is not content merely to portray a couple that is both pathetic and inegalitarian. He allows the female characters only one status, that of sex objects, who, when they refuse to go on being submissive, necessarily become harmful. The two comrades' plan to go into well-deserved retirement is ruined when Josy (Jeanne Moreau) betrays them. The only woman who "keeps her place" in the movie, apart from the mothering restaurant owner, is a superb and wealthy foreigner who silently offers herself to Max after having served him a delicious meal. The film seems to be saying that this is what sexual relations should boil down to for the "mature" man.

A scene that makes the spectator feel uncomfortable coming from a left-wing director who was in the Resistance is the one where the "good guy," Pierrot (Paul Frankeur), Max's unfailing friend, has no compunction about torturing a small-time crook from a rival gang in order to extract information from him. This film, which once again demonstrates Becker's skill at providing a precise description of a milieu and his subtle direction of actors, enabled Gabin to make a brilliant comeback, but, like Jean Renoir's *French Cancan* at the same date (and with the same actor), it offered a vision of gender relations at the opposite pole from that found in *Falbalas*, *Antoine et Antoinette*, and *Casque d'or*. A sign of the times, no doubt.

ℛ *Women's Melodrama: A Minor Challenge to the Patriarchal Order*

While the new differentiation of genres, borrowed from Hollywood, coincided with a generalization of the misogynistic approach, it also paradoxically allowed room for a new form of women's melodrama to emerge — a genre that flourished in Hollywood during the 1930s and 1940s (Bourget 1985). It certainly did not come like a bolt from the blue; women's melodrama did not disappear overnight after the Liberation. For example, Jean Choux's *L'Ange qu'on m'a donné* (1945, based on a 1941 scenario adapted by Françoise Giroud) cast Simone Renant in the role of Claire, a young woman who takes in and brings up a baby lost during the Débâcle. Five years later, when the father, François (Jean Chevrier), returns after the war, he claims his baby back. Claire hands over the child only very reluctantly, and then gets taken on as a house-keeper at François's château. Claire and François begin to fall in love, but the child's mother, Isabelle (Anne Laurens), who was reported missing during the Débâcle, is found in a sorry state and suffering from amnesia. The adoptive mother steps aside in favor of the actual mother so that everything can return to normal. A transitional film, *L'Ange qu'on m'a donné* is at once a late manifestation of the Pétainist melodrama and a still polite but firm appeal to women's generosity aimed at getting them to agree to return to their prewar dominated status without causing any trouble. Claire disappears at the end of the movie in favor of the "legitimate" amnesiac child-wife who spent the whole war in a psychiatric hospital; the spectator sees only a bedridden figure combing her hair, with a mirror in her hand and humming like a little girl. An effigy of narcissistic passivity, she is an ideal vehicle for the restoration of the patriarchal order.

Georges Lampin's adaptation of Dostoevski's *The Idiot* (*L'Idiot*, 1946), on the other hand, introduces a new character typical of 1950s melodramas: the sold woman. Edwige Feuillère lends the film an extraordinary radiance, especially in the scene where she describes, with a mixture of bitterness and gusto, how she was sold to a wealthy old merchant, Rogogine (Lucien Coëdel), while still a barely pubescent teenager. The movie shows how her present marriage is simply a suicidal repeat of an initial trauma that no woman can recover from. Even the evangelical gentleness of Prince Muichkine (Gérard Philipe) is incapable of reconstructing her broken identity, particularly as he prefers the virginal Aglaé (Nathalie Nattier).

A similar denunciation of the specific oppression endured by women because they are turned into sex objects is Jean Grémillon's argument in *Pattes blanches* (*White Paws* or *White Shanks*, 1949). He took a scenario by the playwright Jean Anouilh (who was prevented by illness from directing the movie himself) and turned it on its head by exploiting the sex appeal of Suzy Delair (an actress imposed on him) in the role of Odette in order to demonstrate how alienating that appeal can be both for her and for the men she ensnares. Odette, who is kept by a wealthy wholesale fish merchant, Jock (Fernand Ledoux), seduces a ruined aristocrat, Julien (Paul Bernard). By the time she discovers true love with a young rebel, Maurice (Michel Bouquet), it is too late: the femme fatale image on which she has based her power works against her, and Julien, furious at having been betrayed, kills her. Her tragic end reverberates like a virulent protest against the fate of sold women (Sellier 1989: 250 ff.).

Even René Clair, who could hardly be suspected of being a feminist, tackles a similar theme in *Les Grandes manoeuvres* (*The Grand Maneuver*, 1955), probably his best postwar movie. It is set in a small garrison town during the Belle Epoque. Michèle Morgan plays Marie-Louise, a divorced milliner; her matrimonial situation and financial independence spoke directly to French spectators of the 1950s. The bourgeois Victor (Jean Desailly) would like to marry her but cannot make up his mind for fear of what people will say. Marie-Louise falls victim to the whim of a redoubtable Don Juan, when a lieutenant of the dragoons, Armand de la Verne (Gérard Philipe), makes a wager with his comrades. During a stag party, he signs a piece of paper committing him to seduce a woman chosen at random. That woman is Marie-Louise, unbeknown to her. The wager, which is both symbolic and financial (Armand pledges to buy his friends dinner if he fails), is not unconnected with the theme of the sold woman. The fact that Armand is hoist with his own petard (he falls in love with Marie-Louise, who resists his advances despite feeling attracted to him) could be interpreted as pure convention. But the final twist—whereby she refuses to see him again after finding out about the wager, even though he has abandoned his ideas of conquest so he can establish a truly loving relationship with her—proposes a tragic vision of male-female relations wherein the masculine urge to dominate is shown to be destructive, even for the man.

The "academic" perfection of the sets and costumes, the delicate harmony of the color photography, Morgan's reserved performance, and Philipe's rather cramped charm highlight the suffocating nature of a society that ensnares the protagonists in rituals from which they no longer know how to escape. The gradual transition, as pointed up by André Bazin, from vaudeville to tragedy eloquently illustrates how the straitjacket operates: as in Max Ophuls's *Madame de ...* (1953), everything is hunky-dory just as long as everyone obeys the rules that require women to do men's bidding. Problems begin to arise when we are shown that women are victims of that situation; tragedy ensues when we realize that men too can be destroyed by a system that is supposed to guarantee their supremacy. For the only time in his career, as many critics admiringly pointed out when the movie came out (Clair 1983), René Clair dealt seriously with a love affair and, what is more, denounced the patriarchal straitjacket that prevents it from blossoming. Further proof, if proof were needed, that when an auteur is confronted with the most burning issues of the time, his or her talent is stimulated.

Criticism of the way women were being reduced to the status of sex objects, a theme that had not been on the agenda of Occupation cinema, thus returned in the 1950s as an insistent counterpoint to the predominant emphasis on the "evil slut," in a register rarely tackled before the war (see, however, Francis Carco's *Prisons de femmes* [*Marked Girls*], 1936). Jean Delannoy's *Le Garçon sauvage* (*Savage Triangle*, 1950), from a script by Delannoy and Henri Jeanson, with Madeleine Robinson; Guy Lefranc's *L'Homme de ma vie* (1951), also from a script by Jeanson, with Madeleine Robinson and Jeanne Moreau; Yves Allégret's *La Jeune folle* (*Desperate Decision* or *Revenge at Daybreak*, 1952), from a script by Jacques Sigurd, with Danièle Delorme; Pierre Chevalier's *Les Impures* (*Human Cargo*, 1954), from a script by Juliette Saint-Giniez, with Micheline Presle; Jean Gourguet's *Maternité clandestine (Illicit Motherhood*, 1953), from a script by Jean and Michelle Gourguet, with Dany Carrel—all portrayed pitiful female characters having to face up to the crushing power of men.

Françoise Arnoul was a favorite choice for these melodramas of poverty. Her sensuality says a lot about the changes that had taken place since the emergence of this genre during the Occupation. But the often ambiguous nature of movies revolving around prostitutes whose scantily clad charms are frequently on display should not be allowed to obscure the fact that women in such films are also mostly the viewpoint characters; the narrative is shown through their eyes, and the genre typically denounces the emotional, sexual, and financial exploitation of women by a group of men—the very quintessence of male chauvinist violence. But far from restricting its horizon to a description of the underworld, the genre was probably the only one to elaborate a certain social realism during the 1950s.

Arnoul was partly responsible for their box-office success in such vehicles as *Les Compagnes de la nuit* (*Companions of the Night*) and *La Rage au corps* (*Tempest in the Flesh*), directed one after the other by Ralph Habib in 1953. Less mediocre than some cinephiles would have us believe, and well constructed by their scriptwriters and adapters, Paul Andréota and Jacques Companeez, they give priority to the woman's viewpoint in their accounts of sexual and financial exploitation. *Les Compagnes de la nuit*, the more openly "feminist" of the two movies, describes the experiences of Olga, an unmarried mother who drifts from prison into prostitution because she cannot make ends meet with no job training and a child on her hands. The pimp, Jo, played with all the neces-

Georges Galley and Françoise Arnoul in *La Rage au corps*, 1953. Courtesy of Cinémathèque française.

sary cynicism by Raymond Pellegrin, uses women's maternal bonds to entrap them and has no compunction about committing a murder. It is female solidarity that saves the women from despair. Olga ends up shooting Jo in order to avenge her companions. Articulated around a long flashback, whose point of departure is the murder that the police are investigating, the movie nevertheless hints at an optimistic outcome typical of popular melodrama, since there are plenty of mitigating circumstances to suggest that Olga's sentence will be the lightest possible.

La Rage au corps, made immediately after *Les Compagnes de la nuit*, is much more ambiguous but utterly fascinating in what it tells us about the fear of female sexuality. Again using the device of the flashback, the movie purports to describe a case of nymphomania, an affliction given the seal of approval, in a prologue, by a psychiatrist. In fact what the movie portrays as a mental illness is simply a female version of Don Juanism: a woman who has a lot of sexual partners must necessarily be seriously ill!

When we first see Clara (Françoise Arnoul), she is working as a canteen waitress on a dam construction site in the mountains. She makes a play for those workers who take her fancy, including Gino (Jean-Claude Pascal), but refuses to enter into any long-term relationship. When she falls in love with the new head foreman, Tonio (Raymond Pellegrin), she has great difficulty convincing him that she is being sincere. When he finally marries her, she ends up as a housewife in a working-class area of Paris. The movie then causes her social isolation to interact with her erotic temptations; while her husband is on a business trip she makes friends with a woman neighbor, who turns out to be a prostitute. When Clara too is accosted in the street, she does not disabuse her client and takes him to a hotel. Later she tries to commit suicide, but it looks as if her husband's love and the psychiatric treatment she receives may well cure her. What is interesting about the film is its very blindness to the real problems it raises: the sexual and professional double standards that women suffer from. They are not entitled either to the sexual activity enjoyed by men or to the combination of marriage and a professional activity. If they desire men other than their husband or get bored staying at home, it means they are sick.

But Arnoul's energy is an implicit denial of the script's pathological prejudices. Quite apart from the fact that she has gone down in film history as a star of enormous sensuality, what is striking here is the maturity and intelligence of her acting and the determination she injects into the character she plays — and not just in this movie. In this she is markedly different from the characters played by Martine Carol, for example, in that she appears in film after film as a woman determined to control her own destiny. However, Arnoul's sensuality is used to distract the spectator's attention from her attempts at emancipation; the desire she experiences and arouses often camouflages the oppression she has to undergo, which is, however, rather explicitly illustrated in some of her movies. Here we have a representation of one of the major contradictions of the period: at a time when the massive arrival of middle-class women on the labor market highlighted the issue of their emancipation, the cinema preferred to focus on the theme of sexual freedom by portraying female figures of unprecedented eroticism, as though all the better to distract the spectator (and particularly the female spectator) from the other dimensions of emancipation.

℘ Women's Work: A Fictional Stumbling Block

The question of women's work in postwar French society became a burning issue because, quite apart from the upheavals of war, socioprofessional changes called into question women's traditional place in society (Duchen 1994). Although there was a relative decrease in the number of working women between 1920 and 1960, when they accounted for 34 percent of the working population, it in fact concealed major changes in the pattern of female labor.

On the one hand, the number of married working women increased steadily from the 1920s onward to reach 53 percent of the female working population by 1962. On the other hand, the professional composition of that working population changed: the number of women in a cottage industry or in agriculture fell steadily, whereas salaried women, particularly in the tertiary sector (banking, insurance, and public services), increased exponentially. In addition, the number of women employed in industry shifted from traditional sectors such as textiles to modern sectors such as chemicals and electronics. The replacement of cottage industries or family businesses by salaried employment probably marks the major change in women's employment during that period. It reflects women's greater autonomy in relation to the domestic sphere and to parental or marital power (Sullerot 1973; Lagrave 1991/1994; Duchen 1994).

All these elements point to the same trend: a change in the value of work for women, which was long restricted to the working classes and regarded by the bourgeoisie as a sign of social decline. As its nature changed, it became a means of women's emancipation. It was that development that frightened the traditional patriarchal mentality. In France in particular, where that socioeconomic change was particularly marked from 1945 on, the Napoleonic civil code, still in force, created increasingly intolerable contradictions: until 1965 a husband could still legally object to his wife's taking a job. That sociological sea change was accompanied by a new awareness, as reflected by the enduring success of Beauvoir's *Le Deuxième sexe* since its publication in 1949. (By February 1955 Gallimard had already reprinted it ninety-seven times.) Its extremely rigorous and precise analysis of the many psychological, social, cultural, and financial impediments preventing women from constructing their own identity remains totally valid today.

The French cinema of the 1950s, however dominated by the restoration of patriarchal order, displays an unprecedented and almost obsessive concern with the theme of women's work, which acts not as a background, like manual labor in most prewar movies associated with poetic realism, but as a central dramatic element around which the whole film is constructed. In most cases, the melodramatic treatment of that motif aims to convince women that they should give up the idea of working (as well as any autonomy) so they can enjoy happiness (in love and in marriage), or else abandon all hope of love if they are really keen to keep working, like the dancer played by Ludmilla Tchérina in François Campaux's *Grand gala* (1952).

The dilemma facing Jeanne (Michèle Morgan) in Jean-Paul Le Chanois's *La Belle que voilà* (*Here Is the Beauty*, 1950), adapted by Françoise Giroud from a novel by Vicky Baum, is more perverse. Also a dancer, she falls in love with

Pierre, a sculptor (Henri Vidal), who lives in the garret next to hers. But he leaves her after the first night they spend together because love, he says, prevents him from creating. In desperation after his disappearance, she ends up agreeing to go out with another man, but Pierre tracks her down and shoots her. She survives but is left with a weak heart that would normally prevent her from dancing. But she disregards the doctor's orders and instead obeys her lover and would-be murderer, who, from the prison cell where he is serving his sentence, asks her to make a success of her career so she can get him out of jail. She takes up dancing again and in order to get to the top more quickly offers herself to all the men she meets who are in positions of power. When she finally manages to get her lover released thanks to her contacts, he rejects her with disgust. All that is left open to her is to insist that she loves him and die of exhaustion.

The way the movie describes the atmosphere of classical ballet at the Opéra de Paris would seem to apply more accurately to young dancers in the mid-nineteenth century rather than in the postwar period (Robin-Challand 1983). But every new twist in the plot only goes to prove, first, that love between two artists is impossible (Pierre justifies his disappearance by pointing to the "sordid" consequences for him of getting married and having children, thus completely scotching his artistic vocation), and second, that, whatever her talent and appetite for hard work, a woman can succeed socially only by sleeping around. But the extremely contrived nature of this account of a woman's martyrdom above all reveals how difficult it is for a male conscience to take on board the sexual and professional emancipation of women.

A similar dilemma is described in Henri Calef's *Ombre et lumière* (*Shadow and Light*, 1951), which is saved from mediocrity by its brilliant actresses. Isabelle (Simone Signoret) and Caroline (Maria Casarès) are two sisters who are professionally very successful: one is a concert pianist, and the other heads a couture house. But they find themselves in love with the same man. Leaving aside its melodramatic plot, which suffers from the fact that the male lead, Jacques Berthier, is a complete nonentity, the question the film poses is once again the difficulty women have in reconciling love and professional ambitions. Whereas Caroline is left by her lover because she is clearly too engrossed in her job, Isabelle takes her place in the man's affections because she is careful to conceal from him the fact that she is a famous pianist who is taking some time off because of overwork. Isabelle suffers terrible trials and tribulations (her sister tries to get back at her by claiming she is mad) in order to deserve both love and professional success. (It is worth noting that what is involved in this case is an artistic vocation that is not incompatible with traditionally feminine qualities.)

Set in a more everyday school environment, Henri Diamant-Berger's *La Maternelle* (1949), a second adaptation of Léon Frapié's 1904 novel, is most striking. The critique of social and educational conformism contained in the original has disappeared, as has the relationship between a maternal figure and a little girl on which an earlier screen adaptation by Jean Benoît-Lévy and Marie Epstein (1933) concentrated. The central theme becomes the incompatibility between female labor and women's emotional fulfillment as illustrated by two antinomic figures. Madeleine (Marie Déa, as beautiful and moving as ever) is headmistress of a kindergarten in a working-class area who is abandoned by her fiancé, Dr. Libois (Yves Vincent), because she cannot accept the idea of giving up her job in order to get married. Enter Rose (Blanchette Brunoy), a young woman from a good social background who has been forced to work as a helper in the school after falling on hard times and who ends up winning the doctor's heart; together they adopt the little orphan girl whom Rose had taken under her wing.

Although the movie openly sets out to praise the generosity and competence of women who work, it ruthlessly fixes the boundaries within which they may legitimately exercise a profession, that is to say, either while waiting to find a husband or because they have given up the idea of marriage. By the time Madeleine realizes she has abandoned what she already had for an uncertain alternative, it is too late. The last shot of the film shows her in a state of tragic loneliness, staring jealously at her rival, who has already set up a family with the man she loves and the little orphan they have adopted.

Many scripts written at the time that were apparently based on themes not directly connected with the question of female labor ended up as movies that were totally concerned with that issue. Thus *Les Dents longues* (*The Long Teeth*, 1953), the only film directed by the actor Daniel Gélin, makes it plain from its title and synopsis that it is about (male) ambition. Apart from its very first sequences, the movie describes in a melodramatic manner the pitiful predicament of Louis and Eva Commandeur, a married couple played by Gélin and Danièle Delorme (his real-life wife). At the beginning of the film, Delorme is a photographer on the newspaper where they both work. As soon as they get married, she stops working—as is only normal, the movie seems to imply—but complains she is being neglected because her husband works too hard. The baby that arrives opportunely to keep her busy does not survive. Its death from meningitis gives rise to a very revealing scene: while the mother leans anx-

Daniel Gélin and Danièle Delorme in *Les Dents longues*, 1953. Courtesy of Walter Limot, Cinémathèque française.

iously over the baby's cradle to see if it is breathing, her young husband looks on helplessly. The close-ups of the father, emphasizing his feeling of exclusion, form an implicit justification of the system as a whole: men go out to work, while women run the household. It is all a question of competence.

The ending of the movie confirms that its main purpose is a tortured justification of the age-old sexual division of tasks, with a kind of pathetic acceptance of the fact that women get the rawer deal, but that nothing can be done about it. When Louis, ignoring the warnings of his wife, accepts the job of editor in chief after engineering the sacking of his mentor, Walter (Jean Chevrier), the camera follows Eva wandering through the streets at night, feeling desperate and suicidal, while her husband, despite being aware that she has run away from home, remains totally engrossed in preparing the next morning's edition. She eventually arrives at the newspaper's offices and finds him feverishly checking the final details of the front page on the press, surrounded by attentive editorial staff. The editing lingers insistently on the young woman's face as she looks at first with anguish, then with affection at her husband as he works. In the end she slips away without bothering him and goes to wait for him in the car. Here we have the ultimate male defense mechanism, which consists in getting the female character to legitimate the idea that the only solution open to a loving wife is to suffer in silence (Eva is in a constant state of suffering from the moment she gets married) while her husband devotes himself to his work. Strictly speaking, this is no longer a case of misogyny but a pathetic manifestation of a male mental block.

In such a context, Jean Grémillon's *L'Amour d'une femme* (1954) seemed so daring as to be dangerous. The distributors realized this and refused to release the movie, despite the Franco-Italian coproduction's prestigious cast (Micheline Presle, Massimo Girotti, Gaby Morlay, and Carette). That decision, which effectively put an end to Grémillon's career in feature films, can be explained by the movie's very unusual documentary dimension (most of it was shot on location on the island of Ouessant), but above all by the director's refusal to use the reassuring codes of melodrama; the fictional framework is reduced to a minimum, and the characters are unusually complex. Marie Prieur (Micheline Presle) is at once a doctor totally committed to her profession and a woman in love, and the film deals head-on with the legitimacy of her dual aspiration, while at the same time uncompromisingly noting the male protagonist's inability to accept that legitimacy (Sellier 1989; Lagny 1993).

Here, for the only time in his career, Grémillon wrote his own screenplay, which he based on sociological research into the loneliness of women who work. Despite pressing his point slightly awkwardly at times, he does succeed in pointing up the still glaring contradiction in French society between women's socioprofessional emancipation and men's reluctance to draw all the necessary conclusions from it.

✣ Auteurs at the Heart of the Contradictions

The lucidity shown by Grémillon is rare. Most of the time, it was fear of women's emancipation that was expressed in the cinema of the 1950s in a light-hearted or dramatic mode. All the great and less great directors of the period, from Jacques Becker, Henri Decoin, Claude Autant-Lara, and Jean Renoir to Yves Allégret, Henri-Georges Clouzot, René Clément, and Max Ophuls, conformed to that key theme.

In the comic genre, Becker's *Edouard et Caroline* (*Edward and Caroline*, 1950) was utterly typical of that attitude. The movie, brilliantly scripted by Annette Wademant (Becker's partner at the time), follows a new young couple through a single day when a quarrel has come between them. Edouard (Daniel Gélin) is a promising pianist but comes from a working-class background.

Anne Vernon and Daniel Gélin in *Edouard et Caroline*, 1951. Courtesy of Cinémathèque française.

Caroline (Anne Vernon) is a charming young woman who is quite prepared to get her bourgeois family and socialite friends to boost his career. But whether he will accept such help or not is another matter.

Starting with an intentionally trivial row about a dress and a soirée, the film encourages the spectator to identify with the husband and finishes with the couple patching things up against a background of virile and misogynistic connivance between the young pianist and an American "angel" he meets during the soirée. The fact that Becker, the director of *Antoine et Antoinette* (1947), should choose as his female protagonist an innocently idle and snobbish bourgeoise shows just how much attitudes toward such issues had regressed since the Liberation. The success of *Edouard et Caroline* also shows that he knew which way the wind was blowing.

Casque d'or (1952), on the other hand, based on a script written before the war and which Becker had been working on since 1946, was a critical and box-office failure when it came out, probably because it depicted a world nostalgically informed by left-wing values (Andrew 1990/2000), and focused on one of the finest female characters in the history of French cinema. A tale of *grisettes* and *apaches*, it is transfigured not only by the splendid love affair between the blonde Marie, "Casque d'or" (Simone Signoret), and a carpenter, Georges

(Serge Reggiani), but above all by Marie's quiet audacity: it is she who picks up the little carpenter, pursues him in his workplace, tells her pimp to get lost, and ends up defying even Félix (Claude Dauphin), the leader of the gang, to defend her freedom. The man she has chosen to love is an anti-macho par excellence. His modest and skillful craftsmanship is at the opposite pole from the aggressive idleness of the little hoodlums who hang out with Marie and her women friends. A small man of few words, Georges smiles quietly every time Marie is a bit forward, and he uses force only in self-defense. Faced with this "new man" who does not need to dominate (particularly women) in order to feel self-respect, "Casque d'or," whose demeanor is both casual and imperious, is a perfect symbol of women who decide to stand up to the world. But in this case it is female sexual desire that triggers a determination to become emancipated rather than diverting it, as in most movies of the 1950s.

Patriarchal power, whose perverse violence is perfectly embodied by Dauphin's performance as the gang leader, needs to destroy both the "gentle male" figure and the rebellious woman, who are two subversive examples of a non-sexist and nonexploitative society. The movie's power arises from the way it articulates the clashes between class and gender. But it was precisely the serene defiance of the female character that in 1952 amounted to a provocation that was too direct, despite the Belle Epoque camouflage, for (male) spectators and critics alike to stomach. If *Casque d'or* has become part of the pantheon of cinephilia, it is for aesthetic reasons that prudently keep that burning question at arm's length.

With *Rue de L'Estrapade* (*Françoise Steps Out*, 1952), Becker returned to a much more conventional treatment of male-female relations. Louis Jourdan's Hollywood good looks seemed made to measure for this romantic comedy, in which Anne Vernon again plays a woman of leisure, Françoise, whose only concern is the unfaithfulness of her husband, Henri (Jourdan), this time a racecar driver, not a pianist. Although she leaves him and moves into a student flat in the Latin Quarter, starts working as a model for a leading couturier and friend of the family, and allows a neighbor, Robert (Daniel Gélin), to whisper sweet nothings in her ear, any vague aspirations she may have had for independence vanish the moment her piqued and jealous husband comes to fetch her. At no point does Becker allow us to take seriously the young woman's suffering or desire for independence, even if her flighty husband does not come out very well. It is only in comparison with the two other men that Françoise meets, one of them Robert, who is too young and a bounder, and the other, Jacques (Jean Servais), a fetishist homosexual, that Henri turns out to be the least of three evils. But it is no doubt this disappointing movie's refusal to take the main character seriously that reduces it to the level of a boulevard comedy about bourgeois adultery.

Quite apart from this half-failure, Becker put the critics, who were unhappy about the "triviality of his themes," in a quandary. André Bazin (1983/2012: 69, 72) thought he had found the key to this mystery when he praised Becker for having, in *Rue de L'Estrapade*, "dared to see his script for what it is: nothing," and found his "true style," which is now "based totally on the direction of the actor, the internal tempo of the image, the sharpness of the details and their relationship to one another." Like most of his fellow critics, Bazin had a problem with the central issue of the six movies Becker made, from *Falbalas* to *Rue de L'Estrapade*: gender relations, or "nothing."

Each of those movies reformulates the state of those relations, as influenced by collective mentalities and the director's own sensibility. Becker wrote most of the scripts during that period in collaboration with Annette Wademant (Françoise Giroud also coscripted *Rendez-vous de juillet*). Paradoxically it was *Casque d'or*, the only one of those films set in the past, that most extensively reformulated male-female relations, as though Becker used the same nostalgia for things past to dress up the values of the Popular Front and the dream of nonsexist relations. This second point clearly has to do with a postwar issue; the referral to the Belle Epoque period operates like some sort of Utopia, given the dashed hopes of the Liberation (as expressed in a more "realistic," but also more naïve, fashion by the working-class couple in *Antoine et Antoinette*). Between those two movies, Becker (under Wademant's influence) at least gave the issue more thought, while the French cinema as a whole regressed.

To judge from movies directed by the great Jean Renoir himself, the tone of light comedy found in the French cinema during this period was particularly conducive to misogyny. *French Cancan* (1955) and *Eléna et les hommes* (*Elena and Her Men*, 1956) seem to be quite happy to turn their back on the audacity of his earlier *Le Carrosse d'or* (1953). In *French Cancan*, which is set during the Belle Epoque, the viewpoint character is Henri Danglard, the showman played by Jean Gabin, already imbued with the patriarchal self-confidence of the final period of his career. The inspired commercial idea of putting on a show of French cancan, which "enables the bourgeois to slum it without running any risks," is portrayed as a mark of Danglard's personal genius, to which the young Nini (Françoise Arnoul), whom he has saved, if not from the gutter, at least from her job as a poor laundress, has to submit if she wishes to succeed.

Although for a brief period she enjoys the delights of being his mistress (the age difference matters little when a genius is involved!), she has to take second place without making a fuss when the maestro discards her in favor of new talents, as her girlfriends and even her mother explain to her. At no point during the movie, largely because of Gabin's charisma, does Renoir distance himself in the slightest from the self-assured cynicism of the male chauvinist impresario. His celebrated affection for his characters, combined with the undeniable vitality of his direction, seem to operate here in favor of the most reactionary conception of relations between men and women. This is proof, if proof were needed, that great filmmakers too are affected by the ravages of time.

Curiously enough, the two movies Renoir made in 1959–60, *Le Testament du docteur Cordelier* (*Experiment in Evil*, 1959) and *Le Déjeuner sur l'herbe* (*Lunch on the Grass*, 1959), pick up the question again when they portray two cases of male identity in crisis. Both Dr. Cordelier (Jean-Louis Barrault) and Etienne Alexis (Paul Meurisse) suffer from being unable to enter into a true relationship with members of the opposite sex, a condition that Renoir portrays as a neurosis. In those two movies, he criticizes the male temptation to master the world intellectually, which involves a rejection of one's body and produces, with the return of the repressed, the fascist tendencies of male power. In relation to each other, the two films function as the dark and light versions of the same script and reveal a malaise that the cinema of the period both exhibits and camouflages.

Max Ophuls's career in postwar French cinema is resolutely atypical. After taking refuge in Hollywood in 1941 to escape Nazism and the anti-Semitism of the Vichy regime, he returned to France, his country of adoption, after an absence of almost ten years and made four films in succession: two episode films, *La Ronde* (1950), adapted from an Arthur Schnitzler play, and *Le Plaisir* (1952), based on three short stories by Guy de Maupassant; *Madame de . . .* (1953), adapted from a Louise de Vilmorin novel; and, after several projects that fell through, *Lola Montès* (1955), based on a historical novel by Cécil Saint-Laurent, in which the director used color and CinemaScope for the first time. *Lola Montès* flopped at the box office, and Ophuls died in 1957, after having failed to get another movie project on the road.

While he apparently had no difficulty adopting the fashion for literary adaptations (which played a key role in the "tradition of quality," but also in the work of auteurs whom the young critic François Truffaut stood up for), he seemed more directly interested than most French filmmakers in the question of relations between men and women. That characteristic can perhaps be put down partly to the fact that when in Hollywood he specialized in female melodramas. Starting with the first movies he made before the war, in Germany, then in France, Ophuls mostly gave pride of place to the woman's viewpoint, a characteristic that had already set him apart.

The first two movies Ophuls made after returning to France dealt with the relations between men and women in a cynical manner that had been absent from his previous work. Should this be interpreted as an attempt to reoccupy a niche in the disenchanted atmosphere of postwar France? *La Ronde* is a brilliant comedy about the battle of the sexes, in which Ophuls adds a new character to the play by the young Schnitzler, a master of ceremonies (Anton Walbrook), whose comments highlight the ludicrous aspect of the romantic or sexual encounters he describes and intensify the manipulative dimension of the narrative. Men and women are puppets in the game of love, where everyone is out for themselves. The image of the merry-go-round and the repetitive and circular nature of the narrative suggest "a perpetual round of desire." Only social disparities can modify the rules of the game. A cast that includes all the most brilliant actors of the time further accentuates the impression of a parade in which Ophuls was more interested in demonstrating his skill than in getting deeply involved.

Although *Le Plaisir* follows the same pattern of an episode movie, it is more darkly humorous. The voice of Jean Servais, who narrates from beyond the grave and is first heard over a black screen, lends the movie a macabre touch from the start. The proximity of pleasure with death is emphasized on several occasions. Relations between men and women, which are once again the central subject of the three stories, are treated with a certain bitterness that is alleviated only in the second and best-known tale, "La Maison Tellier," which describes an outing by the inmates of a brothel as they go to a Normandy village to attend the first communion of a niece. The impressionist enchantment of these women in their light-colored dresses against the sun-bathed countryside is shown as a kind of brief parenthesis capable of arousing tender memories. But the ambiguity of this endearing portrayal of prostitutes—in the last account good-natured young women who are satisfied with their lot—is generated by the fact that the episode operates as a refreshing breathing space between two distinctly more sordid tales. The last one in particular takes one into the thick of the battle of the sexes in all its cruelty: a highly talented young painter, Jean (Daniel Gélin), finds himself trapped by the possessiveness of Joséphine (Simone Simon), the model with whom he once fell in love. When he decides to break off their relationship, she jumps out of the window, crippling herself in the process. He is then doomed to marry her and push her everywhere in her wheelchair. This story, which is told by Jean's friend (Jean Servais), a witness to their relationship, expresses the point of view of the male and the artist, whereby any woman who abandons her role as an erotic image that stimulates the artist becomes a dangerous enemy.

Madame de . . . , which takes the viewpoint of the heroine, Louise, played in masterful fashion by Danielle Darrieux, marks a change of tone. Ophuls here allows himself to work on the spectator's emotions by telling the story of a charming and flirtatious aristocrat who is one day violently excluded from her marriage of convenience with a senior army officer, André (Charles Boyer), when she discovers love in the person of Fabrizio (Vittorio De Sica), an Italian diplomat. The movie's great strength is that it shows how this patriarchal society, which obliges women to be frivolous and irresponsible, can no longer function properly if they become autonomous subjects, no longer satisfied with the luxury and smiling faces around them. But at the same time a woman who has been brought up to play that role as a piece of window-dressing for patriarchal power is snarled by her own contradictions when she discovers the world of feelings and desire. Louise is doomed because she cannot break away overnight from her former personality. The lie she tells her lover out of habit will break up their couple and cause them both to die.

Ophuls evokes the totally superficial world of the aristocracy at the turn of the century with a stunningly light and fluent touch. But then passionate love increasingly weighs down the narrative. The dazzling smiles and the rustle of pale evening gowns as they whirl to the sound of a waltz give way to dark, austere clothes and recumbent statue-like immobility, until the moment Louise dies of heart failure. She is doubly crushed by the patriarchal system, and the contrast between the exquisite tact of her husband at the beginning of the story and his ruthless cruelty at the end, without his ever losing his impeccable manners, is chilling. But he too seems alienated by the system he defends tooth and nail, at the expense of his feelings.

Danielle Darrieux, or the Fear of Intelligent Women

Actors' roles also changed in relation to the dominant issues of the day. Danielle Darrieux's second career, for instance, reflected in singular fashion the aspirations and fears that dominated French postwar society. The youthful, daring, and movingly sincere woman who before the war expressed the still controllable dynamism of the "new women" through the reassuring medium of comedy gradually became during the 1950s a figure made formidable by her intelligence and who reflected men's fear of autonomous women. Still typecast

Henri Vilbert and Danielle Darrieux in *Le Bon Dieu sans confession*, 1953. Courtesy of Cinémathèque française.

in such light comedies as Claude Autant-Lara's *Occupe-toi d'Amélie* (*Keep an Eye on Amelia* or *Oh Amelia!*, 1949), Ophuls's *La Ronde* (1950), Carlo Rim's *La Maison Bonnadieu* (1951), and Christian-Jaque's *Adorables créatures* (1952), Darrieux soon embarked on a risky change of direction when she appeared in Henri Decoin's *La Vérité sur Bébé Donge* (1952), Autant-Lara's *Le Bon Dieu sans confession* (1953), Max Ophuls's *Madame de . . .* (1953), Decoin's *Bonnes à tuer* (1954) and *L'Affaire des poisons* (*The Case of Poisons* or *Hangman and the Witch*, 1955), Raymond Bernard's *Le Septième ciel* (*Seventh Heaven*, 1957), and Julien Duvivier's *Marie-Octobre* (*Secret Meeting*, 1958), which brilliantly rang down the curtain on this succession of dangerous women.

Darrieux's discreet physique, dignified bearing, and subtle acting seem to have predestined her to play intelligent women. But the rules of the period required that such intelligence could only be seen as an offensive weapon against men. Already in *La Ronde*, Emma gets the audience to laugh with her rather than against her when she questions her husband, Charles (Fernand Gravey), with feigned innocence, inducing him to pontificate on married men's libertine privileges, which are not allowed to be enjoyed by honest wives. As it happens, we know that she has just been unfaithful to her husband with the charming young Alfred (Daniel Gélin). In *La Maison Bonnadieu*, Gabrielle (Darrieux) hoodwinks the husband she has cuckolded (Bernard Blier) by getting the chambermaid (Françoise Arnoul) to take the blame for her own indiscretions, while in *Adorables creatures* Darrieux's character contrives to ditch her young lover (played by Gélin) when her husband offers her a tempting trip abroad.

But Elisabeth ("Bébé"), the young bourgeois woman who becomes a murderess in *La Vérité sur Bébé Donge* (based on a Georges Simenon novel), brought about a qualitative change in Darrieux's image. The ruthless embodiment of implacable justice, she allows her husband, François (Jean Gabin), whom she has poisoned, to wrestle with his conscience, leaving him no hope of reconciliation. In other words, she kills him a second time. And yet the spectator does not condemn her, as all the memories conjured up by François in the hope of understanding why she wants to kill him justify Bébé's act. This feminist dimension and the movie's tragic atmosphere probably explain why it flopped at the box office.

Darrieux's image was soon to be made increasingly complex by more explicitly evil connotations, as in Claude Autant-Lara's *Le Bon Dieu sans confession*, based on Paul Vialar's novel, which is a veritable manifesto against intelligent women. It opens with the funeral of François Dupont (Henri Vilbert), the very embodiment of the average Frenchman, who was a black marketeer during the Occupation. He was also the deluded lover of Janine Fréjoul (Darrieux), an upper-class woman who took advantage of him all his life without ever giving him anything in return, faking passion in order to get the family business back on the rails without her husband, Maurice (handsome Yvan Desny), having to work. Her duplicity in fact has the effect of absolving the male protagonist. In this sense, *Le Bon Dieu sans confession* is typical of the period: the male characters in it are weak and rather stupid nonentities, but the spectator is invited to be indulgent with them because they are victims of superior women who overwhelm and deceive them. Female intelligence is necessarily a lethal instrument aimed at men, like a kind of unconscious avowal that women probably have good reason to wish to get their own back. The highly fragmented narrative, which follows the successive viewpoints of the various characters in the story of Francis Dupont, serves to obscure the political responsibility of the man being buried (a profiteer during the Occupation) and to highlight the moral responsibility of the woman who two-timed him.

☙ The Generation Gap: An After-Effect of the War

In a highly artificial manner, but one that says a lot about the period, *Le Bon Dieu sans confession* ends with the dead man's two children examining their conscience and paying tribute to him. His son (played by Claude Laydu, the young priest in *Journal d'un curé de campagne* [*Diary of a Country Priest*]) is a medical student who blames his father for having neglected his mother, but who realizes that all his father tried to do was to be happy without failing in his family obligations. His beloved daughter (Isabelle Pia), who deliberately has a child out of wedlock because she is disgusted by the example of her parents, was sensitive to her father's generosity when he offered to take care of her child. The closing shot shows the two young people marching firmly toward a better future, in the purest tradition of Vichyite iconography, whereas the evil woman, Janine (Darrieux), is abandoned to her sad fate. (Her husband has left her because he is jealous of the dead man.) This ending, whose forced optimism is contradicted by the suffocating sadness that emanates from both the visuals and the actors, points to another conflict spawned by the war: the generation gap.

The theme of the generation gap, which first manifested itself during the Occupation in the form of a fresh interest in young people as a social group, very quickly acquired dramatic overtones, probably as a result of the unprecedented calling into question of paternal authority that emerged at the Liberation (Delumeau and Roche 1990). During the 1950s women's magazines extensively criticized the authoritarian nature of traditional educational methods, advocating instead the creation of a relationship of trust with children, and while research has shown that this change was first brought about at the initiative of mothers (Prost and Vincent 1987), it was probably, to judge from films at the time, something that was more difficult for the male sex to accept. Retreating into denial, filmmakers tended increasingly to portray overpossessive or permissive mothers, whereas male figures are systematically touching in their very helplessness.

In a sense, *Le Diable au corps* is the manifesto of that generation gap, but it also displays all its ambiguity; most movies of the period, usually made by middle-aged men, accepted that there was a crisis of authority accompanied by unrest among young people, while being careful to avoid holding anyone responsible, unless it be women.

Jacques Becker's *Rendez-vous de juillet* (1949), which chronicles the state of mind of the postwar generation, begins with a description of the difficulties parents and children have in understanding each other and ends up putting the blame on a "slut" (Nicole Courcel), who prevents her young boyfriend (Daniel Gélin) from preparing his future as a (great) man. In a more dramatic register, André Cayatte's *Avant le déluge* (1954) portrays a younger generation that is desperately unhappy about the tensions of the cold war. It accuses parents, but does not hold them all equally responsible. Françoise (Isa Miranda), a flirtatious mother who tries to hang on to her lover instead of bringing up her son, can never be forgiven, whereas Marcel (Bernard Blier), the militant but widowed father, ends up being exonerated. René Clément's *Jeux interdits* (*Forbidden Games*, 1951), on the other hand, insists right until the end on the contrast between innocent children and monstrously selfish adults, perhaps because the young heroine is only five and the adults in question are awful peasants — natural scapegoats for the modernist and anti-Vichyite France for which Clément was the spokesman.

In 1950 — decidedly a year full of contradictions — two films were released that could not have been more different ideologically and aesthetically, but which both revealed the enormous scale of the generation gap. One of them, Jean Stelli's mediocre melodrama, *Mammy*, based on a script by Albert Valentin and with dialogue by Pierre Laroche, settled the problem of the generation gap in most cynical fashion. Two well-off grandparents, "Mammy" (Gaby Morlay) and André Pierre (Pierre Larquey), have brought up their grandson, Maurice (Michel Jourdan), whose parents are dead, but their overindulgence results in the boy's being spoiled and he becomes a hood. When he returns home like a prodigal son, the grandparents allow him to be eliminated by a group of gangsters and adopt instead a young couple of delinquents, Marthe (Françoise Arnoul) and Maurice (Philippe Lemaire), whom they help to get back on the straight and narrow. In a style reminiscent of Pétainist melodramas (of which Stelli made several with Morlay and Larquey), the movie bluntly tells young people that their material (and spiritual) security depends on their submitting unwaveringly to an apparently aging patriarchy, which is nevertheless capable of remaining in control according to the age-old principle "He who loves well punishes well!"

At the other end of the artistic spectrum, but shot at the same time, is Robert Bresson's *Journal d'un curé de campagne*, based on a Georges Bernanos novel. It is seen through the eyes of a young priest who embodies a yearning for spiritual love but has to grapple with the alienating and lethal power of the rich. In an illusion to Christ's final moments, the film ends with the death of the young man in a state of total loneliness, the loneliness of a son who has been abandoned by his terrestrial fathers because their respective values are irreconcilable. No compromise is possible, and there is no room for sons in a world where power is in the hands of fathers. This tragic movie is probably the sharpest expression of the millstone around the neck of postwar France, which may be seen as lying at the root of the May 1968 explosion.

Made that same year, René Clair's *La Beauté du diable* (*Beauty and the Devil*), quite apart from its explicit and rather stilted argument about the dangers of the atomic bomb, suggests that in the eyes of the prewar generation to which the director belonged the only enviable asset is youth. The confrontation between the ideal young man, the young Faust (Gérard Philipe), and Mephistopheles (Michel Simon), the personification of old age combined with the most repulsive ugliness, does not suggest a conflict resulting from two generations' difficulty in understanding each other, but reveals, at a more basic level, the ferocious jealousy of young people felt by the old. The movie expresses the fundamental ambiguity of the way youngsters were portrayed throughout this period in the case of films made by directors who were getting on. The most explicit expression of this was Marcel Carné's *Les Tricheurs* (*The Cheaters*, 1958), in which fascination with the newfound freedom of the young is inextricably bound up with a wish to punish them, to belittle them, and to make them ludicrous or despicable.

⅋ *The New Consensus: From Le Chanois to Vadim*

In their desperate desire to deny such painful contradictions, Jean-Paul Le Chanois and other filmmakers tried to convince audiences (very successfully, it would seem) that compromises between generations and the sexes were possible, with, as it happens, some efficient help from Gaby Morlay (yet again), who headed the cast along with Fernand Ledoux, Robert Lamoureux, and Nicole Courcel in *Papa, maman, la bonne et moi* (*Papa, Mama, the Maid, and I*, 1954) and *Papa, maman, ma femme et moi* (*Papa, Mama, My Wife, and I*, 1955). Operating a kind of synthesis of her roles as a boulevard coquette in prewar movies and a Pétainist icon during the Occupation, the aging actress here portrays Gabrielle, an average Frenchwoman. She is at once the resigned and indulgent wife of Fernand (Fernand Ledoux), a teacher who cannot control his pupils in an institution for girls, and the mother of a young lawyer, Robert (Robert Lamoureux), who is more interested in finding the woman of his dreams than in a career. It is the son who tells the story in voice-over, despite his being a remarkably passive character. A nice enough young man, but intellectually dim and head over heels in love, he cannot bring himself to admit to his parents either that he has been sacked or that he wants to marry Catherine (Nicole Courcel), who works in order to be able to bring up the child of her sister, who died in childbirth. Robert is a perfect example of an unambitious and unrebellious young man, with whom the spectator is implicitly expected to identify. He has to deal with a father who is more castrated than ever, engrossed as he is by his failure as a teacher and his obsessive money worries, and who enjoys a pathetic mockery of authority since he cannot even control his class of girls.

The only people in this romantic comedy who are effective in their actions are women. Catherine, Robert's young fiancée, gets taken on as a maid in order to win over her future parents-in-law. Gabrielle (Morlay), Robert's mother, guesses what is going on and forces Catherine to admit the truth. Then it is Catherine's turn, using kid gloves, to tell Fernand, her boss and future father-in-law, who is a bit soft on her, to stop pestering her. She then urges him to go and applaud his wife's triumphant performance in an amateur production of *La Dame aux camélias* in which she appears without her husband's knowledge for fear of his ordering her not to.

Here Ledoux is once again cast in the role of a castrated father he played in *Premier rendez-vous*, but in a more pathetic and touching mode. However, it is Robert who engineers the final reconciliation with his father (who is furious at his son's marriage plans) by telling off the girls who have been causing mayhem in their elderly teacher's class. This scene, which marks the movie's real conclusion, portrays Robert, transformed by his mission to rehabilitate his father, vehemently lecturing the girls in no uncertain terms about their own mission, which is "to give their hearts" to their teacher (in other words, to their father and/or their husband) in order to preserve a crumbling patriarchal authority.

Catherine, the figure of an ideal young woman, is a perfect illustration of this itinerary: she starts by abandoning her studies so she can bring up her sister's child. In the movie's sequel, which was released the following year under the title *Papa, maman, ma femme et moi*, her little niece is written out of the story without the slightest explanation, as if her existence served only to anticipate the sole social function required of women: to be good mothers. In the second film, when the newlywed Catherine suggests she could give English lessons to compensate for her lawyer husband's slender income, her father-in-law declares, "A lawyer's wife shouldn't have to work!" Then the narrator (Robert) adds in voice-over, "The problem was swiftly solved by a pregnancy."

When one remembers that the population increase in postwar France was initially not accompanied by any policy of creating facilities to take care of children up to primary school age, at a time when the number of married women in employment was steadily increasing, it is possible to gauge the reactionary dimension of such a remark, which accurately reflects men's fears when faced with women's financial emancipation. Le Chanois, a Communist, may have been influenced by the Party's campaign, headed by Jeannette Vermeersch, against contraception, which was depicted as a device that allowed the bourgeoisie to control the working classes (Duchen 1994). But the narrative ploy used by Le Chanois is more likely an admission of a twofold male taboo: women being paid to work and the corollary of that, their ability to decide whether or not to have children.

The only paid work that Catherine "chooses" is to be a cleaning woman "in order to win over" (in her words) her future parents-in-law, something that clearly indicates that the ideal daughter-in-law is a maid. Robert is initially taken aback but is careful not to protest against his fiancée's lowly station, for it simply anticipates her condition as a married woman in the second movie; the replacement of "the maid" by "my wife" in the title in itself speaks volumes.

Oddly enough, *Papa, maman, ma femme et moi*, which is intended to chronicle the little ups and downs of an average French family by focusing on their major problem of housing at the time, shows absolutely no trace of the blatant misogyny that was so typical of the postwar cinema, whether women were portrayed as sluts or airheads. On the contrary, what we find here are figures very similar to those of the Occupation cinema: two exemplary women who band together in order to save a faltering patriarchy. Although they may not display the heroic selflessness of Louise Jarraud (Gaby Morlay) in *Le Voile bleu* or Nicole Noblet (Marie Déa) in *Premier bal* (such an attitude was no longer necessary in peacetime), they evince a similar concern to preserve or create a harmonious family atmosphere at the expense of their own self-fulfillment or their own ambitions, even though the men to whom they devote their lives are in no way exceptional. But the young women no longer enjoy the autonomy they were granted by the cinema of the dark years, almost as if any move toward emancipation now risked turning into the thin end of the wedge, since there was no longer any occupying power that could impose de facto limitations.

The huge success of these two films can in that case be interpreted as a later variant of the attempts at intimidation expressed by such movies as *Manèges*. The aim in this case, when faced with the same considerable alarm at the emancipation of women, was to try to tame them by presenting them with an image of their place in society that was both reassuring and flattering, while at the same time reminding them that there was no alternative to the traditional division of labor along sexual lines, whatever the qualities of people of either sex.

These two consensual movies were inspired by the natalist ideology and family values that were adopted after the war by organizations close to the

Communist Party. This regressive and reassuring sentimentalism, which was widely shared by French society as a whole (hence the box-office success of Le Chanois's films), is in strong contrast with the aggressive tone of the noir realism spawned by an anarchistic ideology more typically found in filmmaking circles.

But that does not explain how Brigitte Bardot, the "sex bomb" of 1956, managed to burst onto that scene. By the mid-1950s, when the battle of the sexes had been temporarily won by a patriarchy that had been regenerated, if not rejuvenated, the violently polemical figure of the "slut" was probably less necessary. The "gorgeous scatterbrain" that Bardot portrays in Edouard Molinaro's *Une ravissante idiote* (*Agent 38-24-36*, 1964), who is presented as the quintessence of the desirable woman, no doubt reflects more accurately than any amount of discourse the (temporary?) defeat of women.

"B.B.," as Bardot came to be known, dethroned all other female stars, and in particular Martine Carol, the sultry blonde of the early 1950s. Three Bardot vehicles of 1956, Marc Allégret's *En effeuillant la marguerite* (*Plucking the Daisy*), Pierre Gaspard-Huit's *La Mariée était trop belle* (*Her Bridal Night*), and Roger Vadim's notorious *Et Dieu . . . créa la femme* (*. . . And God Created Woman*), imposed a new female type, at once a "naughty girl," a "gorgeous scatterbrain," and "the warrior's rest."

What is striking today about Vadim's movie is the enormous skill with which it combines the old and the new. Its novelty at the time (an impression created by its color photography, its CinemaScope format, and its new take on the Côte d'Azur, along with Bardot's acting and the character she plays) no longer prevents us from recognizing all the features that made this box-office success (it was ranked eighth in 1956) typical of the cinema of the period. For instance, Madame Morin (Jane Marken, yet again) plays an unpleasant mother figure in the most conventional fashion, and Madame Tardieu (Marie Glory, who played young female leads in prewar movies) is recycled as an overpossessive mother and mother-in-law. We are still firmly entrenched in the fantastical matriarchy that enables patriarchs to be let off the hook. After having tried to "buy" Juliette (Bardot) in the most cynical manner possible, Eric Carradine (Curd Jürgens) manages to come through by passing himself off as a nobleminded father. The film holds women totally responsible for the evils of oldworld morality. (Madame Morin's lecherous old husband is a cripple, a condition that should be understood in both the literal and the figurative sense; only the women members of the parents' generation are actively evil.) But the movie also portrays a good old-world ethos, that of the artisans in a little fish-ing port (the not yet celebrated Saint-Tropez). It describes how modern international capitalism has been converted so that it comes to the defense of that other side of France, as embodied by the younger generation, Michel Tardieu (Jean-Louis Trintignant) and his brother, Antoine (Christian Marquand).

But the transition to modernity (both in the economy and in people's behavior) is engineered by a clever device that sweeps away the contradictions. The aim is to say goodbye for good to the national, class, and sexual confrontations that emerged from the Liberation. The fact that Jürgens plays a character called Carradine is probably a tribute to the actor John Carradine, often cast as a colorful heavy in American movies. Through this character, whose constant sense of fair play enables public and private conflicts to be resolved, the film seems to want to move on from the scores that needed to be settled with both Germany and the United States (the Blum-Byrnes agreement).

Carradine, who seems at the start to be Juliette's "tempter" when he promises to give her a sports car in return for her favors, is different from the prewar incestuous fathers in that he does not claim to be loved for himself and lays all his cards on the table. As he develops in the course of the movie, his character gains in stature; for instance, he does not take advantage of Juliette when she throws herself into his arms in a fit of pique. And he finally gives up on her, after deflecting onto himself the bullet that her jealousy-crazed husband aimed at her. At the same time, he agrees to invest in the family business instead of destroying it and convinces the bad guy, Antoine, to leave the young couple alone. Initially perceived as a corrupting influence, he thus becomes the great conciliator, and the film is given a happy ending under his close supervision. Here the movie shows the limitations of its modernity by effecting a neoliberal (in the economic and ideological sense) revamping of the previous state of affairs.

In fact the modernity in *Et Dieu . . . créa la femme*, which appealed to both the public and the critics, stemmed chiefly from Bardot herself. Most commentators at the time, including such feminists as Beauvoir (1960), hailed the arrival on the scene of a new female figure who lays claim to her sexual autonomy through a dynamic control of her body (the actress was trained as a ballet dancer), in strong contrast with the immobility of the beautiful sex object that the cinema of the time imposed on actresses with an erotic reputation.

Ginette Vincendeau (1993) has pointed out the profound ambiguity of this new image of a woman who is at once a vamp and a gamine, in Vadim's own words, "the impossible dream of married men" and a model of possible emancipation for women. Vadim's movie is built around that contradiction, which makes the Bardot character both the active subject of the narrative and an object of pure spectacle (e.g., in the sequence where she dances the mambo) aimed at men, who are shown gazing at her longingly in a very explicit cross-cutting sequence. This new and extremely "natural" eroticism, in contrast with the lascivious and affected poses adopted by Martine Carol and her like, reflected the way the male gaze approached sexual liberation, seeing it as allowing young women spontaneously to become not only desirable but capable of taking the initiative.

Et Dieu . . . créa la femme is careful not to look too closely at the question of the specificity of female pleasure: Juliette is still a virgin when she gets married (not out of principle, but because Antoine, the man she desired, is a disappointment to her) and discovers sexual pleasure in the arms of her young husband on her "very wedding night," even though the young Michel is portrayed as a shy and awkward young man (and probably himself a virgin). An "artistic" high-angle shot of the couple in bed after making love is intended to make the audience believe in what is a sudden and decisive revelation for Juliette, who mumbles, "In any case I think it's great!" Quite apart from this declaration of women's "natural" relationship with sexuality, the scene also expresses a male desire not to be burdened with the issue of female pleasure and lays down the limitations of such sexual liberation. In comparison, Jacqueline Audry's *Minne, l'ingénue libertine*, which centers on the difficulty women have in experiencing pleasure with men who are solely concerned with their own pleasure, is far more subversive.

The very beauty of the young Bardot is used in the movie as a materialization of male fantasies; they all dream of possessing her, whereas she herself dreams only of sleeping with Antoine, the absolute stereotype of the Mediterranean macho, played by Christian Marquand. What is new here is Juliette's ability to exploit male rivalries in order to get what she wants, without her being demonized by the filmic text. The movie steers clear, however, of calling into question (particularly by its portrayal of Juliette's dance and the final slap in the face she gets) the priest's admonition to the future husband: "This little thing is still like a young animal. She needs to be tamed. You're not yet a man." By the end of the film, the bashful young lover "becomes a man" by slapping his wife, and in the very best male chauvinist tradition she then meekly agrees to follow him. (Five years earlier, *Caroline chérie* had similarly ended with the heroine's being slapped without so much as a squeak of protest from her.)

Vincendeau also points to the limitations of this image of a liberated woman at a time when contraception was still illegal (it continued to be until 1967). There were limitations too at the level of the filmic narrative itself, which never allows the female character to achieve lastingly what she desires; in Vadim's movie, she has to make do with Michel, whereas the man she desires is Antoine. In her following films (*En cas de malheur* [*Love Is My Profession*], *La Vérité* [*The Truth*], *Vie privée* [*A Very Private Affair*], and *Le Mépris* [*Contempt*]), Bardot plays characters who suffer an even more radical form of punishment: death.

Finally, the ambiguity of the image of female emancipation offered by *Et Dieu . . . créa la femme* resides in the fact that, more than ever before, the woman exists only in the sphere of physical desire. True, the moral decriminalization of female desire is very much to the credit of the B.B. phenomenon, which marked a major step forward compared with the characters played by Martine Carol in *Caroline chérie* or Françoise Arnoul in *La Rage au corps*. But the novelty surely also resides in the fact that she lays claim to her right to physical pleasure instead of her social and financial emancipation.

Thus Bardot—and this is confirmed by the characters she subsequently played—rang down the curtain, through the ambiguities of sexual liberation, on the long battle to bury (temporarily) the very notion of equality between men and women that had grown out of the Occupation and the Resistance. That battle was to prove the spawning ground of the New Wave.

꙳

Film Analyses

═══════════════
─────────────────

꙳ MANÈGES
   (Yves Allégret, 1950)

Manèges was released in Paris in January 1950. It was the third film in a trilogy directed by Yves Allégret and scripted by Jacques Sigurd, the first two movies being *Dédée d'Anvers* and *Une si jolie petite plage*, which came out in 1948 and 1949, respectively. The trilogy was seen as the core product of the new French film noir by both its admirers and its detractors, who ranged from the young moralists on *Les Cahiers du cinéma* to Georges Sadoul. This was the time when French cinemas were flooded with Hollywood-made films noirs, a genre whose quality dominated postwar U.S. film production, from *The Postman Always Rings Twice* (1946) to *Angel Face* (1953).

Detractors of the French film noir most often criticized it not only for its rather stilted fatalism but for its misogyny, which was indeed so glaring in the French movies mentioned above (and in many others that cluttered screens at the time) that it could hardly fail to be noticed, even by the least "feminist" critics. But now that we can put the phenomenon in perspective, we can detect a fundamental difference between the U.S. model and the French film noir that was believed to have copied it (badly). True, at the heart of the "male melodrama" formed by the Hollywood film noir sensu stricto, we also find a hatred of women, which is both a symptom of masculinity in crisis and a strategy aimed at regaining control after the interlude of the separation of the sexes imposed by the war (Dyer 1977). In all those movies, without exception, the protagonist is in one respect or another an "average American," a category that, in the dominant ideology of the United States, could range from a small-time university professor (*The Woman in the Window*) to an ambulance driver (*Angel Face*), from a third-rate Hollywood scriptwriter (*Sunset Boulevard*) to a drifter taken on as a handyman (*The Postman Always Rings Twice*). In view of the well-known differences that exist between a "classless" society and French society, where the class struggle has a long tradition, the resemblance in this respect with the French manifestation is also striking.

But in the U.S. movies the man is always guilty: he has broken the law (if only in a dream, as in *The Woman in the Window*), under the influence, it is true, of a woman, who has to be punished. But he too has to be punished, even if he discovers that in fact he is not guilty but only thought he was (as in many films drawn from the novels of Cornell Woolrich). In most cases, the whole film unfolds — particularly through flashbacks — in the shadow of that guilt and that punishment, which is either imminent or sometimes even already in the past. (In *Sunset Boulevard*, the story is told by a dead man.) This laying the blame on men is nowadays analyzed as a more or less unconscious and specifically U.S. strategy aimed at the maintenance of authority and social order at a time when there was a proliferation of wildcat strikes that paralyzed whole cities and when it was decided to launch the cold war and carry out witch hunts against the "Commies" (Lipsitz 1981; Krutnik 1991).

In this precise respect, *Manèges*, like most French films noirs of the period, does not conform to that pattern but looks back to the great prewar movies of poetic realism. In *Manèges*, for example, the main purpose of the highly complex flashback structure is not to establish an atmosphere of U.S.-style social or metaphysical fatality but to stress the contrast between a man who is an innocent victim, and women who are "evil sluts."

Manèges opens in a hospital (long chiaroscuro corridors filmed with a wide-angle lens) where Robert (Bernard Blier) sits anxiously at the bedside of his wife, Dora (Simone Signoret). Having suffered a serious car crash, she is at death's door, unconscious, bandaged, and in a cast. In the course of several brief and impressionistic flashbacks (introduced by a veritable riot of wipes and initially shown in a not very chronological order), Robert describes his married life in voice-over. It begins with Dora's rather mysterious departure before the accident, then goes back to the period when he timidly wooed her

Simone Signoret and Jane Marken in *Manèges*, 1950. Courtesy of Cinémathèque française.

while she was still living with her mother (Jane Marken) in a seedy hotel. Then comes their wedding and their move into the flat above the thriving riding school owned by Robert. The narrative describes the mounting difficulties of Robert's business, which force him little by little to sell his horses and to let his premises to a troupe of showgirls for their rehearsals. We soon realize that his wife's expenditures—pocket money, clothes, and the refurbishment of the flat—have driven him to the brink of ruin. When his mother-in-law bursts hysterically into the hospital room, Dora, who has come back to her senses but is barely capable of speaking, orders her to tell Robert "the whole story." He then has to listen as his mother-in-law describes, with vengeful sadism, how he had the wool pulled over his eyes by the two women, who had ganged up against him from the start: his wife had never loved, let alone desired him; from day one they had regarded him as nothing more than a sucker waiting to be fleeced.

We are then shown some scenes already described by Robert from his viewpoint, but we now realize what was going on behind his back. He bashfully brings a gift (a Hermès handbag) to his future wife, but as soon as he has left their grotty hotel room, the two women collapse in a fit of diabolical giggles at his expense, shaking uncontrollably for many minutes and almost unable to pull themselves together before waving goodbye to him from their open window. On another occasion, when the two women first visit the riding school, they exchange a conniving glance that had escaped the notice of the camera when their visit was first shown, just as Dora's blissful fiancé had failed to see it.

The movie in fact has three narrators, not two: before the arrival of the mother-in-law in the hospital, after Robert has dozed off, Dora wakes up, and the decoupage tells us that for a time it will be her memories that will direct the narrative, with comments by her absent mother in voice-over. The device whereby the mother relays Dora's description of her relationship with a man more attractive than her husband reinforces one of the essential misogynistic ideas of the movie: it is the mothers (having lost their charms) who manipulate their delectable daughters so as to be able, yet again, to exploit ordinary men — unattractive men who cannot resist a beautiful young woman.

A word or two needs to be said here about the actor Bernard Blier, who shot to stardom after the Liberation (in *Le Café du Cadran* in 1946 and *Quai des Orfèvres* in 1947) and who emerged as a new male figure in French cinema, as neither a patriarch nor a young lead as understood before the war or during the Occupation, but as *le Français moyen*, or "average Frenchman." That notion, spawned by a kind of unofficial sociology, became widespread as a typical concept of national reconciliation at a time still deeply marked by the splits of wartime (resistance vs. collaboration) and of the postwar period (the violent strikes of 1947 and the sacking of the Communist ministers). But the concept also comprises, in a subtle but decisive fashion, the exclusion of women from the social scene; no mention was ever made of any *Française moyenne*. Whether in the cinema, in newspaper cartoons, or in cabaret shows, representations of that consensual average person were invariably male and embodied a certain political and intellectual mediocrity as well as common sense and quiet stability.

It is precisely the "innocent masculinity" of an unprepossessing average man on which the women in *Manèges* prey. All of the women, without exception, are stupid and nasty. Nowhere is there, as in many U.S. films noirs, a gentle and pure-hearted woman who represents the other course which the hero could and should have chosen in order to avoid the fatal outcome that beckoned him.

Several sequences take place in the local bistro. The most important of these, the first part of which is recounted by the mother-in-law and procuress, starts with a remark she spits out with malicious relish: "And you didn't notice a thing, you idiot!" Robert is sitting at a table with the two women, describing

Bernard Blier and Simone Signoret in *Manèges*, 1950. Courtesy of Cinémathèque française.

among other things his harrowing experiences as a prisoner of war and his attempted escape, which came to nothing. The women are clearly bored stiff; the mother-in-law comes out with platitudes like "You should stop thinking about all that," while Dora makes eyes at a man sitting at the bar (Frank Villard). Suddenly Louis (Jacques Baumer), the riding school's old groom, an honest and reliable man with whom Robert has a filial relationship, bursts into the bistro to tell him about the first in a long series of disasters: a horse has fallen sick. Robert rushes out. In the dénouement of the scene, which has already been recounted from Dora's point of view, her mother slips away, leaving her daughter free to be accosted by the man, François, who later becomes her lover.

This scene, which shows an average Frenchman trying to describe his unpleasant memories of the stalag to a wife who is not listening to him and is planning to cheat on him, throws a particularly harsh light on the film's misogyny—and that of the many French movies that resembled it during that period. What we have here is a prisoner's fantasy: "So that is what our wives were up to while we were rotting in the stalag (or while on Compulsory Labor Service, in a concentration camp, or even in the maquis). But we know all about that. We have confounded them, and now they had better step back into line—or beware of the consequences" (which are harsh in *Manèges*).

Confirmation of this interpretation can be seen in the fact that Dora's relationship with François has already been recounted in Dora's hospital room while Robert dozed off, so that the episode might almost be Robert's dream. For male spectators this could be read as an illusion to the paranoia of the absent (sleeping) man who was nevertheless capable of imagining the reality of adultery, for which he would take his revenge when he returned, notably by means of the ceremonies involving public humiliation (shaven-headed women) mentioned elsewhere.

It matters little in fact whether or not the filmmakers themselves experienced this cuckolding: it was still very much in the air. But at the time such matters were still too recent to be spelled out in a movie, always supposing that any commentator was capable of undertaking that kind of critique of male reasoning as such. Such a hypothetical interpretation would have been all the more difficult at the time because the film conceals its revenge against women behind a different discourse—a discourse of class *ressentiment*, which was more respectable at the time and more in line with the spontaneous tendency in France to highlight sociopolitical antagonisms and to regard as negligible, and as old hat, antagonisms in the category of gender relations.

This Français moyen and his little business are subject to attacks which, socially speaking, come from both below and above. From below they are carried out by the two women, whose social background is disreputable; we gather this from the hotel room where they start out, but also from Dora's ignorance of good manners: when eating at a posh restaurant with her future lover (who is himself from a working-class background but has lost more of his rough edges), she looks puzzled when she is served an orange with a knife and fork. François, incidentally, serves as a vehicle for several barbs directed at women. In his relationship with Dora, he deplores her "emptiness" and the fact that all she can think of is jumping into bed (a reversal of the usual stereotype). After he goes to work for Robert, he turns out to be Robert's ally against Dora: he thinks Robert is a nice man and tries to get Dora to feel ashamed of her selfishness. But the Other also persecutes Robert from above—the bourgeois snobs who are customers at his riding school, above all the women, including one particularly curt and loathsome individual who complicates life for Robert unbeknown to him by swiping François from under Dora's nose.

Then there is the troupe of showgirls, impossibly ridiculous and hysterical when they first come into contact with the horses but to whom Robert is forced to rent out his riding school when business is bad. They rehearse a ludicrous equestrian act for a nightclub, the sort of club patronized by upper-class night owls at any period in history, but which in the popular imaginary of the time smacked of the scandalous *vie parisienne* under the Occupation: collaborators and black marketeers living it up while ordinary people suffered in a stalag or elsewhere.

As can be seen, this broadside against an average Frenchman, caught in a pincer movement between the wealthy who crush him and the survivors from the underworld who resent his modest success, is consubstantial with a broadside against masculinity. Masculinity is embodied by the riding school and its horses (about which "women don't understand a thing," as Dora is proud to proclaim) and by the character of Louis, the trusty mothering groom who keeps his eyes open and who, mistrusting the fair sex, sees through the mother and daughter's little game, but who can only keep his mouth shut, given the extent to which his employer and friend has been blinded by love.

When the bailiffs are knocking on the door and the riding school is about to be sold, Dora prepares to run off with a rich man she has spotted (at the riding school) as a replacement for her husband, who has been sucked dry. And when this new sucker gives her the heave-ho at the last minute, she falls back on a third candidate (discovered by her mother) just before being seriously injured in a car crash.

When Dora's mother comes to the end of her account, the scales have finally fallen from Robert's eyes. After Dora has been operated on, the surgeon comes to tell Robert (while ignoring his mother-in-law) that his wife is out of danger but will be paralyzed for the rest of her life. The cuckold can now wreak his revenge; with a callousness we had never suspected of him, he announces this news to his mother-in-law, whose face is made grotesque by tears and smudged mascara (an echo of the image of Dora disfigured by her injuries and bandages). He tells her that for him it is all over, but that she can look forward to a new and caring life: "You'll be able to push the wheelchair!" As he walks down the stairs toward the camera, we see the harridan going into a fit of rage as she recedes into the background. In other words, "All sluts, but they'll pay for it." Then, as if to drive the point home, a nurse appears at the top of the steps and seems to side with the mother-in-law by hurling insults at Robert as he walks away. "All in it together."

Manèges is undoubtedly one of the most powerful films of the period, thanks to the acting, its marvelous decoupage and mise-en-scène, the complexity and coherence of its narrative, and the pertinence of its dialogue. It is also surprisingly revealing in its portrayal of the less acceptable aspects of male attitudes during the postwar period and is a movie that leaves a decidedly nasty taste in the mouth—a kind of masterpiece of ugliness.

ℛ *LE JOURNAL D'UN CURÉ DE CAMPAGNE*
(Robert Bresson, 1951)

This film cannot be analyzed today without reference to the controversy it caused, following François Truffaut's celebrated 1954 article in which he launched a scorching attack on "a certain tendency in French cinema." In that article, Truffaut discussed the problem of literary adaptation and compared the way Robert Bresson adapted Georges Bernanos's novel *Le Journal d'un curé de campagne* with the version by Jean Aurenche and Pierre Bost (which had been turned down by Bernanos a few years earlier). While Truffaut's criticism of Aurenche and Bost, those champions of "French quality," remains pertinent, one is struck by the dishonesty of his remarks about Bresson's exemplary faithfulness to Bernanos's original, combined with his somewhat fetishistic view of literature (Truffaut 1987). It was also on the issue of the transition from book to film that André Bazin (1983/2012) had based his 1951 analysis, but he did so to demonstrate more subtly how Bresson was able to express the priest of Ambricourt's spiritual quest by using his own language, which was often very different from Bernanos's literary style, in a Christian perspective espoused by the writer, the filmmaker, and the critic.

But this focusing on the question of literary adaptation, which continues to be hotly debated by French film critics, has rather pushed into the background an aspect we would like to emphasize here: the considerable degree to which the movie is in tune with its time. Its radical stylistic novelty (even compared with *Les Dames du bois de Boulogne*, made six years earlier) is in the service of a point of view never previously found in the French cinema: the assertion that a young man's perception of the world and of society is entitled to exclusive legitimacy.

This aspect is highlighted by Bresson's adaptation of the novel (which involved considerable changes, Truffaut notwithstanding). For example, in the version finally released (a third shorter), the director cut out all the scenes that showed — from a perspective of social criticism — shopkeepers as "bad objects" defended by the young priest's superiors in the Church hierarchy (Briot 1957). Also cut at the editing stage or in the course of the adaptation were the numerous conversations and theological considerations involving Bernanos's central character, either alone or with the other protagonists. Bresson offers the spectator a less intellectual character closer to the world of childhood, particularly through the repeated inserts showing a school exercise book in which the priest writes down his thoughts in the regular handwriting of a good pupil.

Claude Laydu and Nicole Ladmiral in *Le Journal d'un curé de campagne*, 1951. Courtesy of Roger Corbeau, Cinémathèque française.

The film also constantly returns to a close-up of the priest's face, whose extreme youth is doubly signified by the features of the actor, Claude Laydu, and by the very fact that he was an unknown actor at the time, who is being born cinematically before our eyes. Bresson's character has been largely stripped of the social and intellectual context stressed by Bernanos and becomes a pure embodiment of youth, in that he has no power and simply asks to love and be loved.

The radicalism of Bresson's movie is remarkable when you compare it with contemporary films based on a narrative by a young protagonist, such as *Le Diable au corps* (1947), adapted from Raymond Radiguet's novel by Aurenche and Bost for the director Claude Autant-Lara. In it, François (Gérard Philipe) recalls past events when the narrative begins, which puts him in a position of omniscience compared with the spectator. In addition, the first-person narrative occasionally gives way to a narrative present to enable the spectator to benefit from a broader point of view (or knowledge) than that of the narrator. As in most traditional movies that use this device, Autant-Lara takes liberties with the single point of view in order to put the spectator in a position of omniscience. There is nothing like that in *Le Journal d'un curé de campagne*;

while it is one of many movies in the postwar period wherein the narrative is conducted by a central male character, it is radically different from them not only because it refuses to use flashbacks but also because it sticks totally to the narrator's point of view. The priest writes in his exercise book as the story unfolds; in his knowledge of events, he has no advantage over the spectator, just as, conversely, Bresson scrupulously respects the limitations of the narrator's point of view and thus refrains from putting the spectator in a more comfortable position than his central character. The upshot of this narrative rigor is nothing less than a materialization of human finiteness and a rejection of the ordinary filmgoer's deceptive feeling of omniscience — a rejection of the cinema as "distraction" in the sense used by Pascal.

The constant alternation between the priest's extradiegetic voice over images of what he recounts or words he writes in his exercise book and images with a diegetic sound track prevents spectators from immersing themselves in the fiction, forces them to keep a Brechtian distance, particularly as the inexpressive voice of the extradiegetic narrator takes the heat out of the most dramatic scenes, except — and we shall return to this — in the central scene with the countess. In most of the other scenes narrated in a direct style, and often containing gaps, the priest replies to his interlocutors with a silence that could be described as a rejection of the thick and fast dialogue that was part of the brand image of the cinema of the period. Bresson demonstrates instead the issues of power and of destruction, the alienation involved in that other kind of verbal communication (including the manipulation of characters by scriptwriters). Those who use speech as a weapon against the priest of Ambricourt designate themselves as instruments of a social power, whereas the priest's silence expresses his obstinate stand on another plane, that of evangelical love.

The world we see through the eyes of the priest is one that is divided and "not reconciled" (to quote the title of a 1965 film by Jean-Marie Straub and Danièle Huillet). Bresson's lighting gives one the impression of a world plunged into the limbo of purgatory or the shadows of darkness, even during the daytime. He systematically opts for *contre-jour* shots when filming outside: low-angle shots show the stark and twisted silhouettes of trees against a faintly lit sky. And most of the time human faces loom in close-up out of the enveloping darkness, like faint glimmers in a murky universe. The camera movements, by lingering on the characters' faces, further emphasize their isolation in an environment shorn of all picturesque elements. Interiors are reduced to the geometrical lines of a wall, window, door, or ceiling. The cross motif is repeated in a prison-like pattern of window crossbars, gate railings, and banister or bed uprights to such an obsessive extent that it is difficult to interpret the dark cross that fills the final shot solely, as a voice-over suggests, as a sign of grace.

The split that divides this world is also expressed by the confrontation of the priest with various father figures, such as the curate of Torcy (André Guibert), the count (Jean Riveyre), the canon (Gaston Séverin), and the parishioner Fabregars (Léon Arvel). Apart from this last (and more episodic) case, none of these characters is openly hostile to the young man. This makes their inability to come to his aid all the more heart-rending; whenever they meet, however well-meaning they may be, one can only observe that they do not belong to the same world. All these mature men are firmly rooted in a society where they have had to compromise; they exist in a context of power, order, and property.

The priest's first conversation with the curate of Torcy had already indicated, in the shape of a generation gap, two completely opposing conceptions of the priesthood. As the curate remarked, "In my time, they trained parish bosses, in other words masters! Nowadays, they send us choirboys who want to be loved for themselves: a true priest is never loved — he has to keep order."

Both the canon, however, and the curate of Torcy are capable, unlike the count, of recognizing the existence of that other world which they cannot enter. It is the curate who finally reveals to the young priest his "place" on the evangelical itinerary: the Garden of Gethsemane — in other words, total solitude. The scene is filmed in a low-angle shot in a ruined shack whose dark and massive covering of branches weighs down on the two despondent men. Quite apart from its Christian dimension, the position of the young man is that of a child abandoned by his father.

The movie harps more than once on the fate of this child who was already marked, before coming into the world, by a legacy of alcoholism. In a manner very different from a Darwinian viewpoint or a piece of social denunciation by Zola, this reference to his fraught past is used only as a way of better symbolizing his abandonment. The young man belongs to a lost generation, in the strongest sense of the term, as is confirmed by the only euphoric episode in the film, when he meets a handsome "angel" on a motorbike, the count's nephew Olivier. From the moment it starts, this sequence marks a change from the general tone of the movie with its long shots of an open landscape beneath a vast and clear sky, illuminated for the first time by the light of the sun. The young motorcyclist pulls up just behind the priest and, with a smile, offers him a lift. There follows a series of close-ups of their two happy wind-swept faces, seemingly cleansed of the grim cares of the real world. For the first and last time, the spectator sees the priest as a young man full of life. This scene can also be seen as a hymn to male camaraderie, which takes on curious overtones when Olivier refers to "the lost soldiers of the Foreign Legion" as the only people, along with poor priests, who deserve to be saved by God. But everything about this episode — the trusting exchange between the two young men as they sit on the railway platform, the quietly attractive demeanor of the sporty young man in a polo-neck sweater, and the framing of the two men in an exceptionally bright light — has a symbolic significance wherein the notion of happiness is associated with a flight from society and a community of young men who risk their lives together. This is proof *a contrario* that there can be no happiness in this world for these young rebels against their fathers.

This insistent metaphor of abandoned childhood can be interpreted as a forceful expression of the conflict between generations in a postwar period marked by a crisis of paternal authority. Fathers have organized the world according to temporal values that are rejected out of hand by sons in search of the absolute. The latter die literally as a result of the legacy they reject: the young priest's stomach cancer and his fellow seminarist's tuberculosis are interpreted as the price to be paid for the alcoholism and malnutrition bequeathed by their parents. Bresson, incidentally, decided to introduce the character Louis Dufrety (Bernard Hubrenne), a young defrocked priest with tuberculosis, only at the end of the movie, whereas he appears throughout the novel via his exchange of letters with the priest of Ambricourt. He thus redoubles the representation of a younger generation that has been dealt a death blow, the issue at the center of the movie.

In the course of the final episode, the elliptical image of the doctor saying goodbye to the young priest and closing the door of his office after telling him he has cancer represents the final manifestation of a death-dealing paternal authority. It takes us back to Bresson's pet issue of a philosophical, and not psychological, struggle between fathers and sons. In Bernanos's novel, on the other hand, this episode gives rise to a very lengthy discussion between the priest and the doctor, who is himself terminally ill. Bresson preferred to leave out this character almost completely in order better to highlight his own view of a world divided between those possessing knowledge and lost children. The priest manages, however, to make a number of inroads into the unlivable world that fathers have constructed, and which they defend tooth and nail, by tackling the "weakest link": women.

Three female characters of different generations and different classes do indeed brighten the tone of the movie, not in the edifying spirit of Occupation cinema but in a more ambiguous and darkly humorous register that was characteristic of the postwar period. Séraphita, the farmers' little girl, Chantal, the count's daughter, and the countess herself in turn engage with the priest in a dynamic and open relationship that is very different from his interaction with father figures.

Séraphita (Martine Lemaire), who is as apparently angelic as her name would suggest and can recite the mystery of the Eucharist without stumbling, is seemingly no more than a perverse child who teases the priest, but turns out to be a little devil like her counterpart in *Le Corbeau*. But the priest's silent suffering soon puts an end to what can eventually be seen as an awkward attempt by the little girl to imitate the nastiness of adults. In a nocturnal sequence full of pictorial allusions (between Ruysdael and Rembrandt), she becomes the child Virgin to whom the poor priest in distress appeals for help. She washes his face as he lies in a mixture of mud, blood, and vomit, then raises him up and takes him by the hand to lead him home.

Chantal (Nicole Ladmiral), the count's daughter, is portrayed throughout the film as a figure who rebels against the loveless and dishonorable world of adults. Her father wants to send her away because she has discovered he is having an affair with the primary school teacher, and her mother turns a blind eye so as to be left in peace. But Chantal's rebelliousness expresses itself in a need to make others suffer in return, in other words, from the priest's point of view, through a perverse urge to turn two wrongs into a right. Like the teacher, a barely glimpsed figure who writes anonymous letters in an attempt to protect herself, the young Chantal can conceive of her own acts solely as a form of revenge against those she cannot control, be it her father or the priest. She thus qualifies as yet another in the long string of "evil bitches" portrayed by the French postwar cinema. But Bresson reworks that vengeful stereotype and turns her into a desperate figure whom the priest tries to protect against herself.

Opposite her, and in counterpoint, the countess (Marie-Monique Arkell), a mother brokenhearted by the death of a little boy she loved too much, displays, behind her apparent resignation to her fate as an abandoned wife, a total indifference to the suffering of others, and in particular her daughter's. It is thanks to the priest that she achieves humaneness before dying. She too is a character built on a stereotype of the period: the woman who is remarkable for her dignified submissiveness. But Bresson draws a clear distinction between lethal submission to a familial and social order and true renunciation of the world. As seen through the eyes of the narrator, who imposes his own scale of values, the female characters escape becoming misogynistic stereotypes, and their behavior comes across as a pathetic, desperate, or heroic reaction to patriarchal domination.

The second meeting between the priest and the countess marks the dramatic climax of the movie. In a confrontation between two forms of suffering, the scene derives its intensity from the enclosed space in which it is played out: the countess's little boudoir, between a fireplace into which she ends up throwing the portrait of her son, and a French window, which is standing ajar and leaves them exposed to indiscreet eyes and ears (Chantal lurks outside it without their noticing), as if the two protagonists were walking a tightrope between two possibilities for destruction.

If the countess is able finally to attain the kingdom of love offered her by the priest, it is because she has already shut herself away from the world (a voluntary reclusion represented by the position of her boudoir in the internal layout of the château). The only barriers to be broken down are internal barriers, whereas the father figures, including the priests, seem incapable of imagining themselves outside the temporal world. Women are therefore more open to evangelical love because most of the time, as a result of their social status, they are bereft of a relationship of power with the world. Their dominated situation makes them sensitive to different values from those cherished by men.

One last female figure who confirms this hypothesis is the partner of Dufrety, the priest's former fellow seminarist who gave up the cloth for health reasons. This woman (Yvette Etiévant), who is one of the last people the priest talks to before dying, embodies in her poverty and humility the evangelical love that expects nothing in exchange. (She admits to the priest that she refused to get married to her partner so as not to prevent him from being reordained should his health permit it.) Kneeling at the foot of the bed on which the priest is lying, she is reminiscent of the holy women at the foot of the Cross as she engages in a rather conventional defense of the "female" values of humility and sacrifice.

The inner workings of the movie show very well how Bresson did not construct his film independently of the issues of the cinema of his time but integrated them into his own truth, that is to say, the observation of the ontological loneliness of a younger generation that thirsts for love in a world completely alienated from temporal values. Eschewing both social satire and psychological investigation, Bresson describes in almost materialistic fashion the relationship between the exclusion of young people deprived of love and the thoroughly patriarchal nature of the social order. In that context, sexual relations come across as undermined by the predicament of domination and alienation experienced by women. That explains the paradisiacal evocation of a community of young men, a regressive fantasy that takes shape as a reaction against their fathers' refusal to leave them the tiniest corner of the habitable world. The leitmotif of the château's imposing gates that parsimoniously open to admit the young priest introduces this major theme of exclusion into the filmic text and indicates, without offering any hope of reconciliation, the extreme violence of the conflict of values that separated generations at the time.

Bresson's movie speaks for the younger generation, which sets it apart from the dominant cinema of the 1950s that was mostly the work of middle-aged men. That kind of cinema, referred to as being of "French quality," privileged the theme of the young man who falls prey to women, thereby confusing the issue at stake in the conflict which Bresson tackles head-on with an energy driven by despair, the generational conflict resulting from the war, which pitted all forms of patriarchal power, whether spiritual or temporal, against young people who had come to realize during the Occupation that the emperor had no clothes. In other words, Bresson's movie is a fine demonstration of the critical dimension possessed by "masterpieces," insofar as the inventiveness of their creation forms part of a questioning of dominant representations, bringing to light what those representations strive to conceal or falsify: the contradictions and conflicts that rock society.

ℛ LE CARROSSE D'OR
(Jean Renoir, 1952)

This movie, shot in Italy, marks Jean Renoir's return to Europe after the success of *The River* in the United States. (It was also in Italy that he had hoped to shoot *La Tosca* but was forced by the outbreak of war to halt production and leave for Hollywood in 1940.) *Le Carrosse d'or* was the final stage of Renoir's return to France after his years of exile in Hollywood. The film, a Franco-Italian coproduction, was shot in Rome with a mainly European crew, and yet it is regarded by historians as a French movie, probably because of its director's strong personality and the presence of French technicians in key jobs (such as cinematographer Claude Renoir and sound engineer Joseph de Bretagne).

The script was freely adapted from a short play by Prosper Mérimée, *Le Carrosse du Saint-Sacrement*, published in 1825 as part of *Théâtre de Clara Gazul*, a pastiche of Spanish theater initially intended to be read. *Le Carrosse du Saint-Sacrement* is the only play in the collection to have been performed during Mérimée's lifetime as well as after his death. Henri Meilhac and Ludovic Halévy used it as a basis for their libretto of Jacques Offenbach's 1868 opera, *La Périchole*, which served as a pretext for a satire of the Second Empire that no longer had much to do with Mérimée's play.

Five scriptwriters are credited as having worked on the adaptation of *Le Carrosse d'or*, including Renoir himself, two Italians, one Englishman, and a Frenchwoman, Ginette Doynel, who is also credited as being responsible for continuity. Renoir clearly claimed to be responsible for the adaptation and presented Anna Magnani and Vivaldi as his main collaborators on the movie, which was "shot in Italy and in English by a French director" (Renoir 1974: 272). Compared with Mérimée's play, the biggest change is no doubt the viewpoint chosen by Renoir, which from the start is that of the female lead, Camilla. She is based on la Périchole, a famous actress who was kept by the viceroy of Spain's Latin American colonies in the eighteenth century and inspired Mérimée. The movie concentrates on the actress herself, whereas the play centers on her clash with the viceroy (with an advantage in favor of the male character, who is on stage throughout).

In the play, the other two men (Captain Aguirre and the toreador Ramon) are no more than mentioned by the jealous viceroy, the actress's official lover. The commedia dell'arte troupe is an invention by Renoir, who works into his film a confrontation between the world of the court and the world of popular theater (the characters are listed separately on the credits), which does not exist in Mérimée's play.

The screenplay is more diversified, involving a mixture of nationalities, social milieux, and professional worlds. The Italian troupe has just arrived in the New World, where the Spanish occupiers have subjugated the indigenous population (represented by Indian peasant spectators in the pit of the open-air theater), while at the same time aping the Old World in its most ridiculous aspects (powdered wigs, minuets, and ladies' vapors). The world of bullfighting is the counterpart of commedia dell'arte in the register of popular entertainment, whereas Felipe, the Spanish captain who has returned from captivity with the Indians, invokes the simplicity of their lifestyle, which he has decided to share far from the greed of the conquistadors, fascinated by the gold of the New World.

The movie, which was shot at Cinecittà with an Italian, French, and English cast and which exists in "original" versions in those three languages, makes no bones about being a cosmopolitan effort, in which Anna Magnani's colorful presence contrasts wonderfully with the sophistication of the English actor Duncan Lamont. Magnani, the only true star in the cast, was then at the peak of her career. Her fame was built more on her performances as an actress than on her erotic dimension as a woman. By making her the very embodiment of theater, Renoir remained totally in keeping with the legend of that modern diva.

The movie's ambitions, which also involved its use of color and music, did not prevent it from being a box-office and indeed critical flop when it came out. It was only later that it came to be regarded as the masterpiece of Renoir's postwar output. Critics subsequently analyzing the film, influenced by Renoir's own comments, tended to emphasize the issue of the relationship between theater and life, or more generally between art and life, and to see it as the director's "artistic legacy" (François Truffaut, quoted in Bazin 1992: 277) and an "open Sesame" to the whole of Renoir's work (Eric Rohmer, quoted in Bazin 1992: 279).

But comparison with one of Renoir's prewar box-office failures, *La Règle du jeu*, is illuminating in more than one sense. While the structure of the screenplay is also based on a confrontation between a female character and three men from three different worlds, the fact that Renoir relies on a female character in his plea for art seems to us to be highly typical of the postwar period. Camilla achieves a true status as a subject, which is not entirely true of Christine in *La Règle du jeu*, partly because she is flanked by other female characters of comparable importance (Geneviève, Lisette). One could argue that the narrative principle of Renoir's 1939 movie is a refusal to allow the point of view of one character to take precedence over that of others (theorized by Octave's celebrated remark, "Everyone has their reasons"). The principle of *Le Carrosse d'or*, on the other hand, is the deliberate decision to favor Camilla's point of view at the expense of the male characters. That is the movie's chief novelty.

The theatrical setting stressed at the beginning and end of the film (by a curtain rising and falling, as in *Les Enfants du paradis*) gives precedence to Camilla's world, all the more so as she takes her final bow alone in front of the curtain. The chief dramatic mainspring of the film is the process whereby Camilla becomes aware of the pitfalls of philandering. The narrative describes her three love affairs in a deliberately repetitive way, where seduction is immediately accompanied by a male desire for possession, which triggers a reaction of rejection in Camilla. The mechanisms of sexual conquest are unraveled from a woman's point of view, and their repetition, despite the three men's differences of status and temperament, leads Camilla and the spectator to draw a radical conclusion: love and creative work are incompatible, at least for a woman.

And yet the first picture we have of Camilla is of an actress discouraged by the difficulties of her profession and ready to marry Felipe, a young Spanish nobleman who has come to seek his fortune in the New World and with whom she struck up a friendship on the ship. Marriage is thus presented as a kind of refuge that is made to seem very attractive in view of the exiled troupe's misadventures. The young Spaniard embodies love in its tender and protective version. It is thanks to him that the troupe manages to improve the rather Draconian conditions the innkeeper tries to impose on them.

The first performance marks a climax in the confrontation between Camilla and "men." The mise-en-scène spatializes the battle that takes place between the actress and the toreador, two professional show people, for control of the audience. Just as "Colombine" comes on stage, Ramon and his male entourage make such a remarkable entrance into the "auditorium" (the courtyard of the inn) that a rival scene is created for the public, who forget the theater and manifest their enthusiasm for the king of the arena. Male-female difference is emphasized by the dark clothes worn by Ramon and his comrades and the contrasting multicolored costumes of Colombine and the actors. The toreador responds to the ovations by adopting the motionless pose of an idol, whereas Camilla busies herself on stage, furious at having the audience's attention snatched from her. The balance of power between them shifts when she delivers her lines with her back to the audience, reversing in her turn the spatial relationship between stage and auditorium in order to highlight the public's rudeness. When the toreador realizes what is going on, he deigns to sit down so as to set an example. Camilla turns around and, not without a few acid remarks, starts to sing, facing the audience, which is now once again attentive. But she soon transgresses the symbolic barrier of the footlights and accosts the toreador: "Hey, you! Stop staring at me like that—I'm not the bull!" Thus she makes explicit Ramon's ploy: he has come not to admire but to seduce. She singles him out as the symbol of an utterly crude and swaggering virility that cannot see the difference between seduction and the domination of women. The toreador's roar of laughter—he is a good loser—brings this first clash to an end with a woman's victory of which the audience is at once the arbiter and the prize. Renoir emphasizes the superiority of Camilla's acting over the sheer physical presence of the toreador. It is by denouncing the language used in the seductive maneuvers of which she is the target that she neutralizes them, ranging the force of her intelligence against the unspoken intentions behind the toreador's swaggering behavior.

But this denunciation of the seductive gaze is also a *mise en abyme* of a central device used by the dominant cinema, which makes it possible to carry spectators off into fiction through identification with the gaze of a character, granting them voyeuristic control of the Other and of the world. Through Camilla, Renoir denounces the alienating nature of this hypnotic gaze so typical of the cinema, in contrast with the more distanced nature of the playgoer's relationship with what takes place on stage. In a way, Camilla places herself in a Brechtian position: she calls on the spectator's intelligence to counter the fascination exerted by the toreador, that great manipulator of crowds. The sound of applause reaches the ears of the viceroy, who decides to invite the troupe to perform at the palace, despite the courtiers' opposition to this intrusion of popular culture into the holy of holies of aristocratic power.

In Act 2, after the performance before the court, the meeting between Camilla and the viceroy takes place in a spirit of subversion. Young, attractive, and unmarried, with a mistress in tow whose infantile behavior is meant to be emblematic of women of her class, the viceroy uses Camilla's presence as a pretext to rail against the constraints of life at court. He leads her to a secluded balcony, not to flirt, as she suspects, but to take off his wig; a loud burst of reciprocal laughter seals their connivance at breaking the rules. Still dressed as Columbine (a servant), she enables him to escape into a world he sees as offering greater freedom. But when the whole troupe bursts into the shed where Camilla and the viceroy have taken refuge, purportedly to admire the coach, the actress realizes she is being called to order. The pomp and circumstance of power are not for her, and the theatrical world has its rules and constraints too.

It is also a theatrical performance that brings together Camilla's three suitors: the viceroy concealed behind a blind; the toreador, a one-man claque in the audience; and Felipe eyeing her greedily from the wings before departing for the army. The three men, whatever their respective ranks, are equally subjugated by the actress, who, protected by the footlights, is untouchable. But as soon as she goes into the wings, trouble starts: her row with Felipe over a necklace given her by the viceroy degenerates into a fistfight and symbolically interrupts the performance, as though already suggesting an incompatibility between the profession of actress and love in the exclusive form it is understood by the three men.

And yet, in Act 3, that contradiction seems to have been resolved, since we find the whole troupe staying in a spacious villa lent by the viceroy, who has come to visit Camilla, his mistress. The private dinner shared by the actress and her aristocratic protector makes clear their reciprocal fascination. Camilla admires the viceroy's mastery of social codes, like an actor who knows his part backward and is capable of improvising at will without ever being affected, or so he claims, by such vulgar feelings as jealousy. He offers the fascinated actress the possibility that she may acquire his urbane manner if only she places herself in the hands of a man as skillful as he. Camilla sees this urbanity as the symbol of a seductive force that could transfer into real life the powers of the actor on stage. Each in turn, whether consciously or not, puts on an actor's performance that fascinates the other. Amorous seduction becomes a metaphor for the theater, with the playful and ephemeral dimension which that implies.

But already they are no longer on completely equal terms, as Camilla asks the viceroy to teach her high-society manners, whereas the reverse does not take place. Camilla is not Columbine, and in any case commedia dell'arte is not a desirable model for a viceroy; it is just a way of slumming. He admires the actress's vitality, her spontaneity, and her love of all the pleasures that life can afford—everything, to be precise, that the social milieu of the court prevents women from enjoying.

The viceroy's gift to Camilla of the coach that is coveted by everyone at court has the effect of materializing in the following sequence the contradictions inherent in their relationship. The increasingly exasperated comings and goings of the viceroy between the council chamber, where his peers are trying to create trouble for him, and the antechambers in which, on the one hand, Camilla is waiting impatiently to get her coach and, on the other, the viceroy's official mistress is determined to insist on her prerogatives, are the spatial symbol of the inability of this representative of power to control the situation. Caught between two stools, he ends up abdicating before the council, after which he is publicly humiliated by Camilla, who, in defiance of etiquette, bursts into the chamber to tell him she is breaking off their relationship. This is the supreme humiliation whereby the private sphere (women) intrudes into the public sphere (men), and it is compounded by the fact that an actress, that most despised of social categories, here comes to tell an aristocrat a few home truths.

For Camilla, however, this is a Pyrrhic victory: although she has won a battle in the war of the sexes, taking her insolence so far as to drive to the bullfight in the viceroy's golden carriage and to throw to the toreador the necklace the viceroy had given her, she cannot win in the class war. She will soon have to submit to a power which the viceroy represents—insofar as he respects its rules—but does not possess.

Everyone plays a role, and the way the narrative unfolds interests Renoir only insofar as it enables him to orchestrate Camilla's confrontation with these three men, who symbolize three types of seduction that can appeal to a woman: political and financial power, bravery, and protective affection. And yet each of them demands exclusivity, and this "objective" male solidarity is portrayed in spectacular fashion. When Ramon and Felipe proceed from the room to duel and end up in the chamber where Camilla and the viceroy are confiding in each other, the latter stand and face the intruders, who freeze when they recognize them. Camilla demands that they explain themselves, but before they are able to do so the viceroy changes sides, steps between the two duelists and demands an explanation from Camilla on their behalf. Camilla, now alone and facing three men, draws the only possible conclusion from this spatialization of the confrontation: she sends them all packing.

This scene implies that women are not allowed to conduct several love affairs at the same time, and it also portrays the instinctive solidarity that springs up between men, whatever their milieu or rivalry, in order to enforce that ban. There is a parallel between this sequence and an earlier scene where Camilla, who has been parked in an antechamber in the palace, urges the viceroy — in vain — to dismiss her rival, who is facing her symbolically in the symmetrical antechamber of the council chamber. In the end it is the actress who has to back down.

Left on her own, Camilla first rebels against the patriarchal order that is eroding her freedom; her challenge is symbolized by the golden carriage she wants to keep after falling out of favor with the viceroy. But the carriage also embodies the corruption that lies in wait for her if she prefers material wealth to the spiritual wealth of the theater.

The epilogue is an act of faith by Renoir at the height of his powers, but it is also an admission — perhaps an involuntary one — that a frontal rebellion against the patriarchal order is impossible because that order also inextricably involves class domination. Casting the bishop, played by Jean Debucourt, in the role of the deus ex machina of classical theater (in the final scene of *Tartuffe*, for example), the epilogue enables Camilla to return to the protective world of the stage and ceremoniously play out, before the highest representative of the social order, her renunciation of the world. (She gives her coach to the church.) There are many similarities between the mise-en-scène of the epilogue and that of taking the veil: Camilla, dressed in black for the first time, stands on the bishop's right and publicly kisses his ring as a token of her obedience, before his announcement that she will sing in the church during a service of reconciliation to which all the classes of colonial society have been invited. (Only the Indians do not attend this final salvation.) Then the camera tracks back to reveal the footlights and the curtain that comes down on the preceding scene, while Don Antonio, the good patriarch who manages the troupe, asks Camilla to come on stage.

However, this epilogue, which sanctifies art through an alliance with the religious institution (an alliance that must have seemed rather surprising to any French spectator familiar with Renoir's prewar ideological sympathies), can also be interpreted in a different way which puts into perspective the "progressive" message of the movie as it emerges from the above analysis. The role of the bishop (played by Debucourt with all the required unctuousness), as he takes Camilla under his lofty protection in exchange for the golden coach, invites the spectator to draw a parallel between the way the clergy devote their lives to the church by making a vow of poverty, chastity, and obedience and the sacrifice Camilla makes in order to remain worthy of her art. The golden coach is clearly a metaphor for all "worldly goods," including carnal love (*eros* as opposed to *agapè*, spiritual love).

This concept of sanctification, which has been so typical of the Western approach to art and artists since the end of the nineteenth century (since Impressionism in fact), throws light on the whole film a posteriori: Camilla is a good object because she is an artiste, and the three male characters who are contrasted with her are bad objects, less because they embody various aspects of patriarchal power than because of their position in civilian society as compared with the charisma of the artiste. The toreador, the officer, and the viceroy are each in his own way incarnations of bad power. The toreador fascinates the crowds by appealing to their basest instincts (the torture and killing of the bull) as opposed to the sublimation proposed by a theatrical performance. The officer is the military arm of the law and of the colonial order, and his last-minute conversion to the delights of the indigenous civilization remains completely abstract, or else acts as a foil to Camilla. As for the viceroy, his talent is restricted to various and not always successful attempts to misappropriate public funds for his personal profit.

These three characters suffer, however, from being no more than effigies in the service of a thesis (the toreador and the officer in particular). And their cardboard nature is reinforced by the linguistic handicap in this European co-production, in which two of the leading actors are British and a third Spanish, playing opposite an Italian actress under the direction of a French director.

The film argues in favor of the sacred dimension of art, which leads Renoir here to reduce the historical context of the story to a purely decorative backdrop. The Spanish colonial society in a South American territory is portrayed in an extremely formal fashion, where colorful harmonies play a more important role than social relationships. The first theatrical performance by the troupe in the courtyard of the inn, for example, draws an audience of Indians who are as colorless as they are picturesque, instead of the working-class whites of colonial society one might have expected. (That intermediate class does not feature at all in Renoir's movie, as though colonization were simply an abstract process involving the appropriation of an indigenous society by a European power.) In the confrontation between Camilla and the toreador, the indigenous spectators are tantamount to hostages. The issue at stake in that scene, which is the ability of this or that performer to attract the favors of the audience, does not for Renoir involve presenting an image of the public with which spectators can identify. On the contrary, these passive and easily manipulated natives reflect a rather contemptuous view of colonized peoples, but also of cinema audiences. As Renoir later said, "People think painting is secret, but the cinema is much more secret: a film is not made for the 6,000 people in the Gaumont Palace, it is made for three people out of those 6,000" (*Cinéastes de notre temps* 1970). Thus the limitations of this film are perhaps to be found in Renoir's desire to favor, through formal contrasts (the bright colors of commedia dell'arte, the gilt décor of the court), a harmonious vision of art at the expense of a critical investigation of the world. *Le Carrosse d'or* indisputably generates a jubilatory effect that Renoir himself attributed partly to the "collaboration of Anna Magnani and Vivaldi" (1974: 272). But it cannot be said that this movie, like *La Règle du jeu*, strives to take into account the reasons of each of the characters. The dialectical complexity of that earlier film (which was so difficult for spectators to stomach in 1939) has here given way to a viewpoint that is certainly more appealing but also more narcissistic, in the sense that art has become the only yardstick Renoir uses to organize his world.

ࣷ *LA VÉRITÉ SUR BÉBÉ DONGE*
(Henri Decoin, 1952)

Henri Decoin has a poor reputation in the eyes of "specialists" — cinephiles, critics, and historians. A worthy representative of the much-derided "French quality," he is acknowledged to be a skillful director but thought not to possess any "personality," let alone any Weltanschauung.

That verdict is partly deserved. But to anyone interested in something broader than the cult of the auteur as understood by *Les Cahiers du cinéma*, Decoin's output is fascinating: more than any other French director (except perhaps Maurice Tourneur after his return to France), he had an instinctive sense of which way the wind was blowing. In 1937 *Abus de confiance* expressed both the misgivings of the patriarchy about the advancement of women and the monarchist nostalgia of the conservative intelligentsia in the light of the threat from the Popular Front. In 1941 *Premier rendez-vous* was one of the first movies to point to the discredit of the father figure and express faith in a regeneration of masculinity by women. In 1945 *La Fille du diable*, a film about "normalization," clearly told young people — and in particular rebellious young women — that it was time to step back into line and that the heroism of the Resistance, as symbolized by an anarchist-gangster (Pierre Fresnay), was no longer a suitable model. (He ends up converting to the consensual values of a pacified society.) In 1947 *Les Amants du Pont Saint-Jean*, one of Decoin's most appealing movies, is a portrayal of the rather "wild dream" of new relations in the couple spawned by the Liberation.

But it was in 1952 that Decoin made his finest film, *La Vérité sur Bébé Donge*, from a novel by Georges Simenon. In the whole history of French cinema, this is probably the film that displays the keenest psychological acuity and social insight in laying bare the battle of the sexes in the well-guarded milieu of the grand bourgeois patriarchy, which it does with a stylistic starkness worthy of Robert Bresson. Here again, Decoin acts as a kind of barometer of his time: the battle of the sexes was at no time as intense on French screens — and probably in Frenchmen's minds — as it was between 1945 and 1955.

The exceptional qualities of the movie can also no doubt be put down to the fact that the experienced Decoin managed to bring together a particularly brilliant team of collaborators: scriptwriter Maurice Aubergé (who worked on Jacques Becker's *Falbalas*), composer Jean-Jacques Grunenwald (*Antoinette et Antoinette*, *Les Dames du bois de Boulogne*, *Le Journal d'un curé de campagne*), cinematographer Léonce-Henri Burel (Abel Gance's *Napoléon*, *Boudu sauvé des eaux*, *Le Journal d'un curé de campagne*), production designer Jean Douarinou (*Un carnet de bal*), and a cast dominated by Jean Gabin and Danielle Darrieux in roles where one can sense a degree of commitment on the part of those two *monstres sacrés* that had become rare since the end of the war.

Although this film, like many of those we have chosen to analyze here, tries to reflect everyone's reasons in a spirit similar to that of Renoir or Grémillon, it nevertheless adopts a class and above all gender viewpoint that was highly unusual and radical for the French cinema of the time and indeed of today. The movie is one of the last of its genre, the French film noir, which was noted even at the time by some critics, like Georges Sadoul and François Truffaut, for its misogyny. But in that register Decoin's movie is completely at odds with *Manèges*, the masterpiece of the genre, which it does, however, resemble in plot and narrative form. Indeed *La Vérité sur Bébé Donge* contradicts point by point the myths accredited in *Manèges*. And it does so above all through a reversal of gender roles. In Decoin's film, it is the husband who is at death's door in a hospital room evocative of a death row cell, and it is his wife, a ghost-like figure, already in mourning with a dark tailored suit and hair in a strict bun, who pays him a brief visit every day under pressure from in-laws intent on keeping up appearances. Whereas in *Manèges*, Allégret and Sigurd change Robert, a simple fellow hoodwinked by women into a hardened man disgusted by female treachery, in Decoin's movie, the dyed-in-the-wool male chauvinist François Donge (Gabin) ultimately glimpses the truth of male alienation. And whereas Robert's Dora suffers a punitive fate, here it is Elisabeth Donge, called "Bébé" (Darrieux), who pours arsenic into her husband's coffee. The male central character is here the only narrator (contrary to Allégret's film, where women take over the narration in order to taunt Robert), and the story he has to tell is, objectively, a "self-indictment"; whatever the blind-spots of the voice-over, the flashbacks themselves demonstrate quite unambiguously that murder was the only way out for Bébé.

Donge is a captain of industry: he runs a tannery in Annonay as well as various subsidiaries with his brother, Georges (Daniel Lecourtois). He is also a confirmed bachelor who is adored by women. Emblematically his relations with them exclude any genuine emotional ties but often comprise a distinct financial or professional interest (a society woman who acts as a go-between for a deal, a private secretary who is as competent as she is sexy).

Yet François realizes that a concentration of capital can take place only through a marriage of convenience and a dowry. The Marquise d'Ortemont (Gabrielle Dorziat), a matchmaking friend of the family and the personification of the patriarchal and bourgeois economy, offers to arrange an advantageous marriage for him, as she has already done for his brother. But François turns down the unprepossessing candidates with dowries whom she proposes, thus placing the interests of his libido above those of capitalist rationality. One of the more interesting aspects of the movie is this suggestion that the interests of the financial father and the libidinal father do not always coincide.

In the very first flashback, which describes how François and Bébé first meet, the latter discovers the authoritarian and libertine nature of this man of action when he admonishes her, a perfect stranger, for having bought up the entire stock of Turkish delights in a Paris sweetshop, where he had come to shop with one of his current mistresses. Both were in fact intending to give the Turkish delights to the same person, the two brothers' future mother-in-law.

Already fascinated from afar by the willful and thick-skinned François, Bébé sees him join one mistress in a taxi, then kiss another one on a railway platform before boarding the train that will take them both, separately, to the Ardèche. From the first, then, she knows what sort of person she will be dealing with, and what appeals to her is precisely the challenge he represents for a sensibility such as hers, at the opposite pole from that of this go-getter.

Since all the flashbacks are narrated by François's inner voice as he lies in hospital, these initial liberties taken with narrative viewpoint (François does not know that Bébé is observing him from afar) are the first sign of the clear-sightedness François has acquired on his hospital bed since his wife "put something nasty in [his] coffee." In the event, his clear-sightedness has tragic overtones, since it is now too late in every respect, but it constitutes the disruption that empowers the narrative: François sees himself from his wife's point of view, which is in fact that of the movie itself.

Thus the man speaking identifies himself with a woman, and in fact his body has been reduced to a position of "female" dependence by the poison. Never before had Gabin the actor succeeded in emasculating his character to such an extent, and never had his virility — as shown in the flashbacks — been as odious as in this, his first role as a self-confident capitalist (which looked forward to many others, notably under the direction of Denys de La Patellière). The movie picks up the features of the prewar Gabin myth but shows them from a critical perspective, as Jean Grémillon had already done in *Remorques*.

Shortly after Bébé bumps into François in Paris, we are shown the first in a series of receptions in Annonay which will structure the film; the last of them takes place in the present, outside of François's narrative, on the very evening of his death and his wife's arrest. During the first reception, the innocent and romantic Bébé ("No one has ever succeeded in calling me Elisabeth," she says, almost as a challenge) engages in a duel-like flirtation with this man who fascinates her, an exchange interrupted at various points — whenever one of Bébé's "naïve" questions embarrasses this "male machine" (Feigen Fasteau 1975) — by the constraints of a game of bridge in which François takes part inattentively (and always in the role of the dummy, *le mort* in French, an emotionally perfect definition of the man).

From the start, the two characters are seen to be different in every way: Bébé is a sensitive dreamer, never afraid to speak her mind and always ready to probe her own feelings and those of others; François, who has blocked off his own feelings and keeps those of others at arm's length, believes in two things only, immediate sensual pleasure ("life") and work. (Later on in the movie, we see this mogul getting his hands dirty at his own factory.) In other words, the difference between the two protagonists is the difference, typically, between men and women under patriarchy.

Their paradoxical alliance stems from the fact that each sees the other as a challenge, though not one of the same order. Bébé is prepared to risk all in an attempt to penetrate François's armor and to reveal to him the passionate and romantic love she feels so naturally as a woman. In François's case, the challenge is more of a gamble: Bébé is a stubborn little animal who makes a change from the blasé women he usually consorts with. But in marrying this young virgin, he does not seriously flout the conventions of his milieu. For while his wife is poor, it is Jeanne, Bébé's elder sister and his brother's bride, who will inherit; the fortune will stay in the family. In addition, this marriage between an already middle-aged man and a young maiden — a "baby" — repeats at the level of social appearances the "incestuous" couple which was typical of prewar cinema but which here has disastrous consequences.

Their first meeting concludes with a kiss, which sums up Bébé's impetuosity, and leads straight to the altar via an editing ellipse that sums up François Donge's willfulness. The brilliant sequence of their church wedding is simply a whispered continuation of their game of questions and answers, with Bébé persistently setting the same embarrassing riddles, as she will continue to do in the hope of breaking through François's defenses: "What is a couple?" "What is love?" "What is desire?" To which the ever uncommunicative François replies, "Do you think this is the right time for that?"

Thus begins a marriage placed under the sign of the father: a hideous portrait of François and Georges's father, whose bulging eyes seem to follow Bébé wherever she goes, is given pride of place on the wall of their bridal chamber. Bébé finds this silent presence difficult to bear, whereas her husband does not "even see him any more." The painting is moved down to François's study. One of the most moving scenes in the movie comes when François is woken in the middle of the night to find Bébé, in a kind of suicidal impulse prompted by her despair at the destruction of her dreams of love, lugging upstairs the enormous portrait of the father to put it back in their bedroom.

Bébé's sex life begins during her brief honeymoon in a luxury hotel on the Côte d'Azur, where, in reply to a remark by François about their future as a couple, she says, "I think I don't want any [children] at all." It comes to an end when, having discovered to her horror that François has resumed his affair with his secretary, she asks him to make her pregnant there and then; he slaps her in the face and takes her by force. This scene is not only the climax of the drama but also contains the movie's most subversive argument, which is repeated more than once and which holds that the maternal instinct is sometimes no more than a last resort for women who cannot communicate with their husband. The ground covered between these two scenes, between a libertarian rejection of motherhood and a resigned acceptance of that condition, must surely be the most typical experience of millions of women under patriarchy.

As for the honeymoon episode (which includes off-screen business appointments at regular intervals, and which François has arranged to have interrupted by a phoney urgent telegram), it pinpoints another running sore: the sexual connivance, irrespective of class difference, which bonds men together against women. The only sequence in the movie where we see a worker is the one that depicts, in comic fashion, a voyeuristic elevator attendant who is titillated by François and Bébé necking in his lift. Indeed this is the only time in the whole film François shows any affection, for immediately after the ellipse that suggests the couple's first intimacy we see that he has gone back into his shell, causing Bébé to worry that she has been a disappointment to him. When she expresses alarm at the fact that he has exposed her in a state of undress to the leering elevator attendant by opening the bedroom door to receive the scotch he ordered, François lectures his newlywed wife: it is only normal for a man to want to see her in bed. The elevator attendant would simply like to be in his place. In other words, "We men are all skirt-chasers, and it's normal for a servant to be jealous of his master who has a beautiful wife in his bed as a sign of wealth."

The battle has begun. To start with, Bébé gives as good as she gets. Her response to the phoney telegram and the curtailed honeymoon is to pretend she has sprained her ankle so François will be forced to carry her over the marital threshold. It is only when Jeanne says she is surprised to see him "so romantic" that he realizes he has just done something that expresses a feeling he does not want to feel—and plonks Bébé on the floor.

Following the birth of the baby that was conceived in a moment of anger and despair, Bébé's life becomes "more normal." While bringing up her child, who remains off-screen throughout, Bébé is seen only when she makes an appearance at one of the lavish annual receptions organized by the Donges. Her relationship with her husband, which is "serene" on the surface, boils down to muttered provocations, such as "Now *there's* a beautiful woman for you," to which François replies with a glance that says in substance, "You're on!"

In fact, and despite his "disinterested" marriage to the impecunious Bébé, there is only a surface discrepancy between the capitalist and the libertine in him. While the practice of sexual double standards is for this grand bourgeois just a kind of game (it is precisely because he has lots of mistresses that what he does with them "is of no importance," as he bluntly explains to Bébé), his hanky-panky is almost always connected with money, since all women (except Bébé, as it happens) have their exchange value. At the point when matters are coming to a head, François is having an affair with the wife of Dr. Jalabert (Jacques Castelot), who has secured major funding from him for his new clinic in return for looking the other way. It is in that same clinic that François spends the last week of his life. And the corruption that underlies the doctor's nervousness in the face of his medical task is a perfect embodiment of that patriarchal-cum-bourgeois reality principle against which Bébé's dreams of an ideal love have come to grief.

The scenes that take place in the present, in and around the clinic where François lies dying, are articulated around a gradual rapprochement between Bébé and the gentle investigating magistrate (Marcel André), who in a way represents her destiny. But the magistrate does not at all conform to the cliché image of his profession. In a sense, the whole of the movie is constructed around this convergence between Bébé and the magistrate, since the first time we see him he is sitting next to François during a game of bridge, in the countershot to the duel-like flirtation already mentioned.

The magistrate hangs around François's hospital room in the hope of getting a chance to talk to the man he believes, despite denials from the family, to have been the subject of an attempt on his life. Seeing and greeting Bébé Donge when she comes to pay her daily visit to her husband, he gradually becomes closer to her and toward the end of the film has a surprising conversation with the woman whom he alone addresses by her real Christian name, Elisabeth. Of all the characters in the movie, he is the only one who understands why Bébé murdered her husband. After questioning her very considerately, he asks if he may kiss her on the cheek. This figure of a good father who understands women's motivations seems to have stepped out of some older and more humane order (possibly because it is more rural); the horse-drawn carriage that is the emblem of this magistrate and which he ends up persuading Bébé to ride in for a talk, sticks out like a sore thumb amid the gleaming motor vehicles of 1952. As for the kiss on the cheek he gives her when bidding her farewell, it comes like the blessing of a superior law (but one that is totally secular and republican) through which the movie tries to absolve the poisoner, possibly for fear that spectators would confuse her with the "evil bitches" that appeared so often in French movies of the period.

When compared with Simenon's novel, it becomes clear that the film is an original creation by its makers, but above all that it belongs very much to the period when it was made. Although the narrative framework of the novel, written in 1940, is broadly the same as that of the movie, no scene or even snatch of dialogue is borrowed from Simenon. Moreover, while Simenon's story is mainly told from the point of view of the hospitalized François Donge, who is prepared to understand his wife, the problem of their relationship as a couple boils down in the final analysis to the twofold sexual inadequacy of Bébé, "who never knew how to make love" and whom François never desired anyway (but without any suggestion of cause and effect). In Simenon's novel, their marriage takes place without there having been any question of love at first sight and without any challenge being taken up by either party; it is more a case of rivalry between brother and sister. Finally, the character of François has absolutely no charisma and could not be further from the Gabin image. (One imagines him rather being played by Bernard Blier!)

In Simenon's story, Bébé's implied frigidity is not her fault: as a child, she was traumatized by a kind of "primal scene," when she unintentionally witnessed two servants making love. What results from this sexual perspective (François married "by mistake" a woman who cannot satisfy him) is the implicit "normality" of the character and behavior of the husband, who married a clinical "case." Although there is the occasional dig at male insensitivity, it is nevertheless the unfathomable female soul that stands accused. And Simenon opts for a happy ending that was of no interest to Decoin and Aubergé: François survives Bébé's attempt to poison him and attends her trial. Although she benefits from extenuating circumstances (implicitly her childhood trauma), she is sent to prison for some time while François picks up the pieces of his life again in the hope (which Simenon describes as ludicrous) that she may one day come back to him. As for the investigating magistrate, he is described as a smug and self-important man "whose political opinions are extremely rightwing," and who understands nothing at all about the unseen side of the case, even as it is imagined by Simenon. In short, Decoin, Aubergé, and their colleagues turned a kind of poor man's *Madame Bovary* into a film worthy of a novel by Virginia Woolf.

La Vérité sur Bébé Donge was a box-office flop — by 1952 the short-lived fashion for French films noirs had faded, and the movie undoubtedly qualified as one — but it enjoyed a real succès d'estime. Nonetheless critics at the time offered an egregious example of how the phallocentric discourse evaded gender issues. In the view of Raymond Barkan, author of a very enthusiastic review in the *Progrès de Lyon* newspaper, François Donge is undoubtedly one of those men who treat their wives badly, but the true subject of the movie is "the daily confrontation of two human beings in marriage" and "a study of marital strife." Marc Sonnet, writing in the same newspaper four days later, talked about "the marital failure of the couple" and "the tragedy of an abortive marriage." The message, in other words, is that both parties are at fault.

That is no doubt true, the optimistic reader must be thinking, but mores have moved on since then. Today anyone can see what is at issue in this movie: the oppression of women within the marriage institution and the tragic alienation of men.

And yet . . .

In a weekly aimed at an educated middle-class readership (*Télérama*), it was still possible in 1989 for a columnist to write as follows when the film was revived on television: "We shall never know 'the truth about Bébé Donge.' The truth is a complex and ambiguous thing. As in real life, we do not understand why people behave as they do. Bébé loves François. François lives with Bébé without caring about her. Bébé is wounded and no longer loves François. François begins to love Bébé. This itinerary of a couple is based on incommunicability."

More than in the case of any other true or false masterpiece of French cinema before the New Wave, spectators and critics of *La Vérité sur Bébé Donge* still have their work cut out for them.

ℛ *LOLA MONTÈS*
(Max Ophuls, 1955)

With *Lola Montès*, Max Ophuls moved one step further in his denunciation of the suffering inflicted on women by the patriarchal system, in particular when it claims to worship them. But while the young Turks on *Les Cahiers du cinéma* and a handful of the most innovative filmmakers of the time immediately recognized the superlative qualities of the maestro's final work, what has attracted the attention of traditional cinephiles, as always, is the extraordinary virtuosity of Ophuls's mise-en-scène.

The violence of the movie's denunciation, however, caused it to be rejected by audiences, who expected to see something quite different, since it had been advertised as the story of a "scandal queen" played by Martine Carol, the most popular female star of the time in France. The police had to step in more than once at the Marignan cinema, and the exhibitor was forced to make a public announcement before each showing warning the audience that they were about to see a movie that was "out of the ordinary" and that they still had time to get their money back.

Lola Montès (the adaptation of which Ophuls wrote with Annette Wademant, who worked on several of Jacques Becker's screenplays) is indeed a vitriolic satire of the type of film that Carol usually appeared in under the direction of her husband, Christian-Jaque, of which *Nana*, shot the previous year, was a perfect example. This U-turn in the image of the star (very symbolically, this is the only movie in which she is not a platinum blonde) was bound to disconcert the public. Carol's career never recovered from it.

Ophuls's denunciatory intentions are made clear from the start in a complex manner: the metaphor of the circus symbolizes — as the ringmaster (Peter Ustinov) later specifies — the kind of wild animal or monster to which the femme fatale is reduced in order to be offered up to the delectation of the public. The tinsel of the circus is a down-market version of the luxury which the variety artiste (or its modern version, the film star) is meant to attain. The ringmaster, played in fascinatingly ambiguous fashion by Ustinov, is the first to enter the arena, on a red carpet, cracking his whip to summon a richly colored cortège dominated by the diva herself, as motionless as a gilded statue, literally mummified and already reduced to a mere image of herself. In this very first sequence, the star's double alienation is on show: Lola is activated like a marionette by a man whose costume is evocative of the ringmaster, the lion-tamer, and the officer; in other words, it combines various images of authoritarian male power. Now that any distinction between her private and public life has been abolished, she is expected to serve up slices of her own life to the public. But this alienation fades into the background from time to time and reveals a struggling and suffering human being. Ophuls allows us to hear in asides (and to see) her expressions throughout this performance-cum-ordeal.

He also allows the fallen woman and the spectator to escape from the dereliction of the present through flashbacks, which on each occasion belie the misrepresented version of Lola's life imposed by and for the show. Here the garish decorations of the circus are replaced by the warm colors of memory. First we have the autumnal hues that accompany the end of her affair with the virtuoso pianist and composer Franz Liszt in the marvelous mobile cocoon of his celebrated caravan, an image of reassuring freedom that is the opposite in every way of the circus's gilded cage. When, in this first flashback, she

Martine Carol and Peter Ustinov in *Lola Montès*, 1955. Courtesy of Cinémathèque française.

conjures up the image of another free woman, the novelist George Sand, and Sand's affair with Liszt, Lola contradicts the image of a "man-eater" that the show makes her out to be; her breakup with the composer contradicts all the clichés about the excesses of romantic passion and women's possessiveness. It is she who suggests they part when their relationship seems to have run out of steam, and she retains him for one final and very affectionate embrace, just as he is preparing to slink away.

The movie is then constructed according to a counterpoint between the ringmaster's patter and the "real" memories of Lola Montès, a woman who has tried to find freedom in a patriarchal society. The authoritarian order she rebels against is embodied (yet again) by an overbearing mother figure. The presence of this misogynistic stereotype in an openly feminist film shows that you can only go so far and no farther. Lise Delamare plays this quietly frightening mother, who packs her daughter off to an overcrowded dormitory so she can spend the night undisturbed with Thomas James (Yvan Desny), the young officer who is accompanying them back from India on a boat. Her mother then plans to marry Lola off to an elderly and gouty baron, a sordid deal in which the dowry comes in the form of firm young flesh. But she is hoist with her own petard when her lover, Thomas, takes pity on her daughter in distress and marries her. But the daughter herself is disenchanted soon enough: her husband takes to drink, cheats on her, and beats her! She survives only by running away, at which point her scandalous career begins.

While the memories conjured up for the spectator illustrate above all the audacity of a woman who simply demands to be able to live a free life, the image of the bad mother is not the only limitation that can be detected in

Ophuls's viewpoint. The final flashback, which is also the longest, describes Lola Montès's sojourn in Bavaria and her affair with the elderly King Ludwig I (Anton Walbrook). This episode is described as the only time Lola enjoys some form of happiness, thanks to the love of this rheumatic and half-deaf old man, a caricature of a monarch who is booed by his subjects, but is the only man with whom Lola actually establishes a relationship of trust.

The first rumblings of a rebellion put an end to their affair. Lola, in the best tradition, makes her exit in order to save the monarchy. This episode, which is worthy of *Sissi l'impératrice* or of a magazine catering to the fascination with royalty, is of interest to us chiefly because of the parallel it suggests between the old king and a young student (Oskar Werner), who already appeared at the beginning of the episode and who helps the dancer to leave the country and suggests she start a new life with him. Lola turns down his generous offer, and the spectator is led to understand that after she and the old king have broken up against their wishes, everything has become meaningless for her.

This curious reappearance of the "incestuous" couple does not signal a re-habilitation of the dominant pattern of prewar cinema; it is no longer a case of Pygmalion's relationship with the young virgin he is sculpting (Lola Montès has already "experienced everything" when she meets the old king), but rather of an association between two human beings buffeted by life (hence the in-sistence on the king's physical and political decline) and caught up in a cut-throat power struggle, who are relieved to lay down their arms for a moment. Moreover, although Lola's first meeting with the king gives rise to an erotic gag (she rips open her bodice to reveal her cleavage to the king, who seems to have doubts about her beauty), the rest of the movie puts less emphasis on her seductiveness and his prestige than on their mutual affection. (The king com-missions a portrait of Lola from the slowest painter in the Academy of Fine Arts so as to tie her down to him; then he reads *Hamlet* to her while sipping his tea; finally, she accompanies him to the doctor to have his deafness treated.)

This idyllic relationship, which is abruptly interrupted by riots, is the only positive portrayal of relations between men and women in the film. We are given the unusual spectacle of lovemaking between a woman who is tired of causing scandals and an old man tired of wielding power. But the palace the king has built for her, a vast gilded cage that the rioters attack with stones, says a lot about the suffocating limitations and the fragility of that happiness.

The ambiguity of Ophuls's attitude to the fate of the fallen woman can be sensed in Lola's final meeting with the young student. She turns her back on the haven he is offering her and prefers to plunge into "the hell of the circus," which the ringmaster has predicted, as though total degeneracy were the only appropriate fate for her. The melodramatic nature of the epilogue reminds us that nothing is more moving to the general public than the misfortunes of a woman who had been promised every kind of happiness. At that point, spectators of the movie experience a pleasure that is not so far removed from that of circus-goers: they revel in Lola's misfortunes.

There is also something ambiguous about the fate that the movie reserves for the ringmaster played by Ustinov, who is a veritable theoretician of the star system of his day. He pays Lola a visit when she is at the height of her fame (the meeting is shown in a flashback) and explains to her his plan to make money out of the exceptional product she has become as a "scandal queen." His intelligent cynicism is as disturbing to Lola as it is to the spectator, particularly as he also makes it clear how much he admires her and is physically attracted to her. A doomed couple, united only "for worse," Lola and her ringmaster are bound together by an affectivity that can be detected during the show in their little asides, which both flaunt and camouflage the financial exploitation to which Lola is subjected.

The climax of the film expresses this intricacy in a startling way: the ringmaster is told by the doctor who has just examined Lola not to remove the safety net for her acrobatic leap that is the star turn of the show, but he gets around that order by publicly asking Lola to make the decision — in other words, by forcing her, if she does not want to lose face, to have the safety net removed even if it means risking her neck, so that the spectators get their money's worth. But after he has manipulated her in criminal fashion, after her fall, filmed from Lola's point of view as a kind of suicide, we find him standing next to the cage where the degraded dancer holds out her hands through the bars so that men can pay a dollar to kiss them. He says to her in an aside, before launching into his sales pitch for this new attraction, "I was very scared, you know, I couldn't live without you." It is only later that the double meaning, both emotional and financial, of that remark sinks into the mind of the spectator, who is still reeling from the shock of the preceding sequence.

In an interview with *Les Cahiers du cinéma*, Ophuls admitted, "Lola Montès made me want to tell stories by taming them." At a conscious level, this is an allusion to the difficulties he had to overcome as regards the screenplay (adapted from a romantic novel by Cécil Saint Laurent) and the film's technical aspects (CinemaScope and color), but the remark can also be interpreted as an admission by Ophuls that he identified with the constantly whipcracking character played by Ustinov. And the fascination that the ringmaster exerts over both Lola Montès and the spectator prompts one to speculate that the filmmaker saw himself as an inextricable combination of demiurge subjecting actors and filmgoers to his omnipotent desires, and an artist exploited by merchants. This was an eminently contradictory position in that it led him both to denounce the exploitation of beauty at the heart of the star system and to lend his aura as an auteur to the cynical master of ceremonies, and to denounce too all the forms of oppression suffered by women in a patriarchal and mercantile society at the same time as he encouraged us to enjoy the sight of a woman who allows her own decline to be put on display. The final movie by a filmmaker who placed the viewpoint of women at the heart of his endeavors, *Lola Montès* encapsulates all the ambiguities of the male gaze, which creates beauty while portraying in masterly fashion the misfortune of being a woman.

℘

Conclusion

═══════════════════════
═══════════════════════

WE BEGAN WRITING this book with the idea that the general public's interest in the stories told by films must surely be meaningful in a way that deserves a less contemptuous attitude than that of the formalist tradition. And
we posited that there is a connection between the stories people went to watch
"at the flicks" and History with a capital H—in other words, that fictional
films had a lot to say about the period in which they were made.

But we, along with many other film historians, believed that filmic representations are governed by a different time frame from that of political and
social history, one that historians of mentalities used to describe as *la longue
durée*. We discovered, however, that on at least two occasions in recent French
history, the Defeat and the Liberation, filmic representations, in the symbolic
domain that characterizes them, had reacted immediately and massively to
those two major political upheavals.

It remains to be seen whether this was due to the intensity of the traumas
suffered by French society at the time or to the cinema's extreme sensitivity to
sociopolitical events. Possibly the only way to find out more about this would
be to study a different and less turbulent historical period, for example, the
early days of the Fifth Republic. But other factors might then distort any such
analysis, in particular the French cinema's changed status following the intro-

duction in 1956 of state aid aimed at improving the quality of movies and the resulting emergence of auteur films.

In any case, what we detected in the movies of the time cannot be described as a reflection of some social reality; the cinema seems rather to play a role in the construction of a collective imaginary, but in a manner that confirms the close interconnection between the private and public spheres. Otherwise, how would it be possible to understand the new complexion of filmic representations following the Defeat? French movies from 1940 on tell us that the emperor — the all-powerful patriarch of the prewar period — has no clothes, that he is impotent, unworthy, or incapable, just as, when the time came to regain control five years later, they tell us just as massively and bluntly that active women are a lethal threat to (patriarchal) society.

Perhaps the most surprising aspect of this immediate interaction between family stories as recounted by the cinema and political History with a capital H is the way it confirms that patriarchal power is intuitively perceived as a principle of one-sided domination that expresses itself simultaneously in the state and in interpersonal relations. In other words, neither those who produced movies nor those who watched them (to mention only that aspect of cultural production) really believed in the basic principle of the patriarchal discourse, which is the distinction between the public and private spheres, even when they defended it tooth and nail.

Another surprising conclusion we came to is that even though the people who made films during the period we studied, at least in the directing and scriptwriting departments, were almost exclusively male, their work, particularly after the great upheaval of the Defeat, displayed in an often complex way something that could be defined, culturally speaking, as a "woman's point of view"; in other words, they resorted to ways of thinking and feeling that the male world traditionally treats with condescension, if not scorn. The new importance of melodramas during the Occupation — whose characteristics need to be distinguished from the social inscription of "women's cinema" that Hollywood made for a female public — arises from the way they use "feminine" values in a process of regeneration of the masculine directed at society as a whole.

The nondifferentiation of audiences in gender terms remained a constant of film consumption in France and was characterized in the postwar period by the way women spectators internalized the most misogynistic representations, as can be judged from the success of such movies as *Manèges* and *Touchez pas au grisbi*. It can be interpreted as an indication of one of the broadly shared cultural features of gender relations, resulting in a blind spot that can still be observed today, especially in France.

NOW THAT WE have come to the end of our exploration of French cinema, which has proved to be full of surprises, we feel almost as if we discovered a universe full of unexpected treasures. As cinephiles, we had assumed that the movies concerned would be chiefly interesting from a historical point of view, that they would not really be worth studying except as vestiges of a bygone age. What surprised us was that we acquired a genuine taste for such films, not only because of the greatly varied range of actors and actresses they featured (compared with the greater uniformity of physical and psychological types to be found in traditional Hollywood cinema) but also because of the stories they told, which were spawned by an "adult" culture, whereas the U.S. cinema, aimed at the general public, was often hamstrung at the time by the Hays Code, a form of censorship that treated spectators as though they were children.

One criticism often leveled at French movies is that they are too talky and are frequently little more than filmed theater. True, classical French cinema does tend to resemble a large repertory company because of the way it features the same group of actors. But it is perhaps this proximity with the theater — the result of Parisian centralization, whereas New York is a long way from Hollywood, not only geographically but culturally — that explains why so many French films of the period still speak to us today much more than many cult Hollywood movies.

While the very young men who wrote in *Les Cahiers du cinéma* and later made New Wave films had their reasons for preferring Gary Cooper and Rita Hayworth to Jean Gabin and Danielle Darrieux, we feel, having concluded our exploration, that it is regrettable that every generation of French cinephiles since then has followed in their footsteps "as one man" — indeed! It seems clear to us today that this ostracism can no longer be justified, unless it be the result of force of habit and received ideas that, when it comes to taste, have an impact that is all the more forceful because it acts by unconscious osmosis.

It only remains for us to hope that our readers, irrespective of the interest they may have had in following this journey into France's recent history, will acquire or reacquire a penchant for watching French films of the period for their entertainment value. We shall no doubt be criticized, particularly with respect to the third part of the book, which focuses on the years 1945–56, for resorting too systematically to an analysis of screenplays at the expense of a discussion of formal cinematic characteristics, which also contribute to the production of meaning. As regards that specific period, we were faced with a historiographical problem whose scale became clear to us only as we progressed in our task of viewing the films: the extraordinary dearth — given the diversity of cinematic output — of research work into the years 1945–56, a veritable lost continent in the history of French cinema. We were therefore forced to do the initial spadework without always being able to carry out a sufficient degree of in-depth analysis. It is to be hoped that other scholars will take up the torch after us.

But our chief aspiration is that we will have succeeded in making a breach in the wall of formalism, which has for so long kept French film studies in a dangerous straitjacket. There is, of course, no question of denying the internationally recognized historical contribution made by those various schools from which we ourselves emerged. But we hope to have convinced our readers that form can be of interest or generate emotion, both for those who create it and those who are its recipients, only when it produces meaning in a sociocultural context that it helps to create. And because we are above all individuals with memories, our love of films made in the recent or distant past is governed not by the degree to which they stand out from their period but, on the contrary, by their ability to make us understand where we have come from. Similarly our appreciation of other cultures also arises from our desire to comprehend the Other as a way of throwing a particular light on ourselves.

While allowing for the specific characteristics of the French cultural heritage, we have attempted to introduce two research approaches that are employed in Britain and the United States and that seem to us to be very fruitful. One of these is cultural studies and its concern with the cultural field that lies outside the norms of the dominant culture. As regards the cinema, this involves transcending auteurism (which once played an indispensable role of cultural legitimation) in order to study filmic representations without any aesthetic bias and see them as a series of cultural productions whose significance for the society of the time we have attempted to understand. We do so not out of any spirit of leveling that considers third-rate movies to be as important as masterpieces but with the aim of understanding films in a vast intertext that gives them meaning, and not in the haughty isolation of a gem extracted from the dross of run-of-the-mill cultural productions.

The other Anglo-U.S. critical approach we have found to be relevant to our area of research, gender studies, was perhaps even more foreign to the French intellectual tradition. The veritable taboo that surrounded the issue in France was all the more effective because it cloaked itself in an illusion of transparency: relationships between the sexes were thought to be a question of nature, an "always already there," like something that existed before culture and society came into being. On closer examination, it becomes clear that this "natural" element protects the eminently social system of patriarchal domination. But this increasingly prickly refusal to allow gender issues to be examined (the excesses of the U.S. conception of what is or is not politically correct provide a convenient excuse) has also had an unfortunate effect on research, in particular on the study of cultural productions like the cinema and literature, which use interpersonal relations as their basic symbolic material.

Since the first edition of this book in 1996, a number of scholars of both sexes and across both the Channel and the Atlantic have taken up the study of this or that period of pre–New Wave cinema in the perspectives of gender and cultural studies. Foremost among these, Ginette Vincendeau has continued to break new ground, her most important work for our purposes being her book on the French star system (2000), especially the chapters on Jean Gabin, Brigitte Bardot, and Jeanne Moreau, to which has been added in the French edition (2008) a chapter on Annie Girardot (the three actresses having begun their careers in the early 1950s). Vincendeau has also recently published works on Marcel Pagnol (2009) and Fernandel (2012). We must also mention two inspiring books by Susan Hayward, one on Simone Signoret (2004), the other on 1950s costume dramas (2010); Kelley Conway's (2004) well-documented book on the *chanteuses réalistes* of the 1930s; Vanessa R. Schwartz's (2007) very innovative work on cultural and economic exchanges between French and Hollywood cinema in the 1950s. Among young scholars, Gwénaëlle Le Gras (2010) published a book on Michel Simon and "the art of disgrace"; Jonathan Driskell (2008) submitted a PhD on female French stars of the 1930s; and Delphine Chedaleux (2011) has written on young male and female stars of Occupation cinema. Finally, several collective works attest to the interest of an increasing number of scholars of both sexes for this period and these approaches, one under the editorship of Raphaëlle Moine (2002/2008) on French film genres, and another, very recent volume, edited by Le Gras and Chedaleux (2012) with contributions dealing with "classical" French cinema and the articulation between genres and actors and actresses. We ourselves produced in 2009 a slim volume proposing a comparative study between two stars of the 1930s, Katharine Hepburn and Edwige Feuillère (Burch 2009), and a study of letters from the mass readership of *Cinémonde* as a way into ordinary female spectatorship (Sellier 2009). While the periodic contacts between French and

British scholars of both sexes, combined with long-standing interest in mainstream French cinema on the part of British scholars, have favored the development of this type of research, in the United States the academic study of French film is still characterized by a tendency to regard French cinema—and European film in general—essentially as art cinema, privileging an aesthetic and auteurist approach. Let us hope the publication of our book in English will encourage scholars across the Atlantic to take a fresh look at French cinema. Finally, we hope this book will also demonstrate the pertinence of a gender approach to cinema as a tool for rendering obsolete the questionable division between mainstream and auteur films.

References

Added, Serge. 1992. *Le Théâtre dans les années Vichy*. Paris: Ramsay.

Agel, Henri. 1967. *Les Grands cinéastes que je propose*. Paris: Editions du Cerf.

Andersen, Thom, and Noël Burch. 1994. *Les Communistes de Hollywood*. Paris: Presses Universitaires de la Sorbonne Nouvelle.

Andrew, Dudley. 1984. *Film in the Aura of Art*. Princeton: Princeton University Press.

———. (1990) 2000. "*Casque d'or*, Casquettes, a Cask of Aging Wine." In Susan Hayward and Ginette Vincendeau, eds., *French Film: Texts and Contexts*. London: Routledge.

———. 1995. *Mists of Regret: Culture and Sensibility in Classic French Film*. Princeton: Princeton University Press.

L'Anneau d'or. 1945. "Revue internationale de spiritualité familiale," ed. Canon Henri Caffanel. Paris (only one issue appeared).

Aragon, Louis. 1944. *Aurélien*. Paris: Gallimard.

Ariès, Philippe, and Georges Duby. 1998. *History of Private Life*, vol. 5: *Riddles of Identity in Modern Times*. Translated by Arthur Goldhammer. Cambridge, Mass.: Belknap Press.

Arletty. 1971. *La Défense*. Paris: La Table Ronde.

Arnoul, Françoise, and Jean-Louis Mingalong. 1995. *Un Animal doué de bonheur*. Paris: Belfond.

Arsand, Daniel. 1989. *Mireille Balin ou la beauté foudroyée*. Lyon: La Manufacture.

Association Peuple et Culture. 1963. *Regards neufs sur le cinéma*. Paris: Editions du Seuil.

Audé, Françoise. 1981. *Ciné-modèles, cinéma d'elles*. Lausanne: L'Âge d'homme.

Audibert, Louis. 1995. "Cinéma et Guerre." In Jean-Pierre Azéma and François Bédarida, eds., *1938–1948: Les Années de tourmente. De Munich à Prague, Dictionnaire critique*. Paris: Flammarion.

Audiberti, Jacques. 1996. "Le Mur du fond." In *Ecrits sur le cinéma*. Paris: Editions Cahiers du cinéma.

Autant-Lara, Claude. 1974. Interview in *Les Cahiers de la Cinémathèque*, no. 9. Perpignan.

Azéma, Jean-Pierre, and François Bédarida, eds. 1992. *Vichy et les Français*. Paris: Fayard.

———, eds. 1993. *La France des années noires*. 2 vols. Paris: Seuil.

Badinter, Elisabeth. 1997. *XY: On Masculine Identity*. Translated by Lydia Davis. New York: Columbia University Press.

Bakhtin, Mikhail. 2009. *Rabelais and His World*. Translated by Hélène Iswolsky. Bloomington: Indiana University Press.

Balzac, Honoré de. (1829) 1987. *La Physiologie du mariage*. Paris: Gallimard.

Bard, Christine. 1995. *Les Filles de Marianne*. Paris: Fayard.

Barrot, Olivier. 1979. *L'Ecran français 1943–1953: Histoire d'un journal et d'une époque*. Paris: Editeurs Français Réunis.

Barrot, Olivier, and Raymond Chirat. 1983. *Les Excentriques du cinéma français*. Paris: Henri Veyrier.

Bataille, Georges. 1967. *La Part maudite*. Paris: Editions de Minuit.

Bazin, André. (1958) 2009. *What Is Cinema?* Translated by Timothy Barnard. Montreal: Caboose.

———. (1983) 2012. *French Cinema from the Liberation to the New Wave, 1945–1958*. Translated by Bert Cardullo. New Orleans: UNO Press.

———. 1992. *Jean Renoir*. Translated by William H. Simon. New York: Da Capo Press.

Beauvoir, Simone de. (1949) 2011. *The Second Sex*. Translated by Constance Borde and Sheila Malovany-Chevallier. New York: Vintage.

———. (1958) 2005. *Memoirs of a Dutiful Daughter*. Translated by James Kirkup. London: Harper Perennial Modern Classics.

———. 1960. *Brigitte Bardot and the Lolita Syndrome*. Translated by Bernard Frechtman. London: André Deutsch and Weidenfeld and Nicolson.

Bertin-Maghit, Jean-Pierre. 1989. *Le Cinéma sous l'Occupation*. Paris: Olivier Orban.

Billard, Pierre. 1995. *L'Âge classique du cinéma français*. Paris: Flammarion.

Bloch, Marc. 1957. *L'Étrange défaite*. Paris: Armand Colin.

Boggio, Philippe. 1993. *Boris Vian*. Paris: Flammarion.

Bordeaux, Michèle. 1987. "Femmes hors d'État français, 1940–1944." In Rita Thalmann, ed., *Femmes et fascismes*. Paris: Tierce.

Bourdieu, Pierre. (1979) 1984. *Distinction: A Social Critique of the Judgment of Taste*. Translated by Richard Nice. Cambridge, Mass.: Harvard University Press.

———. (1996) 2002. *Masculine Domination*. Translated by Richard Nice. Palo Alto: Stanford University Press.

Bourget, Jean-Louis. 1985. *Le Mélodrame hollywoodien*. Paris: Stock.

Boussinot, Roger. 1980. *L'Encyclopédie du Cinéma*. Vol. 2. Paris: Bordas.

Bove, Emmanuel. (1945) 1986. *Le Piège*. Paris: La Table Ronde.

Breton, Emile. 1984. *Femmes d'images*. Paris: Messidor.

Briot, René. 1957. *Robert Bresson*. Paris: Editions du Cerf.

Brossat, Alain. 1992. *Les Tondues, un carnaval moche*. Paris: Manya.

Browne, Nick. 1982. "Deflections of Desire in *The Rules of the Game*: Reflections on the Theater of History." *Quarterly Review of Film Studies* 7, no. 3.

Brunelin, André. 1987. *Gabin*. Paris: Robert Laffont.

Burch, Noël. 1993. *Revoir Hollywood*. Paris: Nathan.

———. 2009. "La Garce et le bas-bleu." In Noël Burch and Geneviève Sellier, *Le Cinéma au prisme des rapports de sexe*. Paris: Vrin.

Burch, Noël, and Geneviève Sellier. 2009. *Le Cinéma au prisme des rapports de sexe*. Paris: Vrin.

Les Cahiers de la Cinémathèque. 1973. "Le Cinéma de Vichy." No. 8 (Winter).

———. 1977. "Le Cinéma du sam'di soir." No. 23–24 (Winter).

Camus, Albert. (1942) 1989. *The Stranger*. Translated by Matthew Ward. New York: Vintage.

———. (1947) 1991. *The Plague*. Translated by Stuart Gilbert. New York: Vintage.

Carné, Marcel. 1989. *La Vie à belles dents*. Paris: Belfond.

Chalas, Yves. 1985. *Vichy et l'imaginaire totalitaire*. Arles: Actes Sud.

Chavance, Louis. 1937. "Le Corbeau: L'Oeil du serpent. La Frontière du mal." Original scenario in *Fonds Louis Chavance (1923–1945)*. Paris: La Cinémathèque française.

Chedaleux, Delphine. 2011. "Jeunes premiers et jeunes premières dans le cinéma français sous l'Occupation." PhD diss., Université de Bordeaux-III.

Chirat, Raymond. 1981a. *Catalogue des films français de long-métrage 1929–1939*. Brussels: Cinémathèque royale de Belgique.

———. 1981b. *Catalogue des films français de long-métrage 1940–1950*. Luxembourg: Editions de l'Imprimerie Saint-Paul.

Cinéastes de notre temps. 1970. TV documentary. Episode: "François Truffaut: Dix ans, dix films."

Clair, René. 1983. Catalogue of René Clair exhibition at the Cinémathèque française, January–March 1983. Paris: Cinémathèque française.

CLIO (Histoire, Femmes et Sociétés). 1995. "Résistances et Libérations en France 1940–1945." No. 1. Toulouse: Presses Universitaires du Mirail.

Cocteau, Jean. 1987. *Lettres à Jean Marais*. Paris: Albin Michel.

Cointet-Labrousse, Michèle. 1987. *Vichy et le fascisme: Les Hommes, les structures et les pouvoirs*. Brussels: Complexe.

Collins Weitz, Margaret. 1995. *Sisters in the Resistance: How Women Fought to Free France 1940–1945*. New York: John Wiley and Sons.

Comte, Bernard. 1991. *Une utopie combattante: L'École de cadres d'Uriage 1940–1942*. Paris: Fayard.

Conway, Kelley. 1992. "La Femme-spectacle du cinéma français des années 30: *Prix de beauté, Zouzou, Le Bonheur*." Mémoire de DEA, Université de Paris-III, Sorbonne Nouvelle.

———. 2004. *The Chanteuse in the City: The Realist Singer in French Film*. Berkeley: University of California Press.

Coquillat, Michèle. 1982. *La Poétique du mâle*. Paris: Gallimard.

Corbin, Alain. 1978. *Les Filles de Noce*. Paris: Aubier-Montaigne.

Corvin, Michel. 1992. "Le Boulevard en question." In Jacqueline de Jomaron, ed., *Le Théâtre en France*. Paris: Armand Colin.

Courtade, Francis. 1978. *Les Malédictions du cinéma français*. Paris: Alain Moreau.

Daix, Pierre. 1994. *Aragon*. Paris: Flammarion.

Daquin, Louis. 1980. *On ne tait pas ses silences*. Paris: Les Éditeurs français réunis.

de La Bretèque, François Amy. 1977. "Les Belles histoires du sam'di soir: Les Stéréotypes narratifs." *Cahiers de la Cinémathèque*, no. 23–24 (Winter).

Delumeau, Jean, and Daniel Roche. 1990. *Histoire des pères et de la paternité*. Paris: Larousse.

Dinnerstein, Dorothy. 1978. *The Rocking of the Cradle and the Ruling of the World*. New York: Harper and Row.

Driskell, Jonathan. 2008. "Female Cinematic Stardom in 1930s French Film." PhD diss., King's College, University of London.

Dubief, Henri. 1976. *Le Déclin de la Troisième République 1929–1938*. Paris: Seuil.

Duby, Georges, and Michelle Perrot, eds. 1991. *Histoire des femmes en occident*. 5 vols. Paris: Plon.

Duby, Georges, and Michelle Perrot, eds. 1994. *A History of Women in the West*, vol. 5: *Toward a Cultural Identity in the Twentieth Century*. Translated by Arthur Goldhammer. Cambridge, Mass.: Belknap Press.

Duchen, Claire. 1994. *Women's Rights and Women's Lives in France 1944–1968*. London: Routledge.

Ducout, Françoise. 1978. *Les Séductrices du cinéma français 1936–1956*. Paris: Henri Veyrier.

Dufrancatel, Christine. 1979. "La Femme imaginaire des hommes." In Arlette Farge, Christine Dufrancatel, and Christine Faure, eds., *L'Histoire sans qualités*. Paris: Galilée.

Duquesne, Jacques. 1966. *Les Catholiques français sous l'Occupation*. Paris: Grasset.

Durand, Yves. 1987. *La Vie quotidienne des prisonniers de guerre dans les Stalags, les Oflags et les Kommandos, 1939–1945*. Paris: Hachette.

Dyer, Richard. 1977. "Homosexuality and Film Noir." *Jump Cut*, no. 16.

Eck, Hélène. 1994. "French Women under Vichy." In Georges Duby and Michelle Perrot, eds., *A History of Women in the West*, vol. 5: *Toward a Cultural Identity in the Twentieth Century*. Translated by Arthur Goldhammer. Cambridge, Mass.: Belknap Press.

Ehrlich, Evelyn. 1985. *Cinema of Paradox: French Film Making under the German Occupation*. New York: Columbia University Press.

Ellenstein, Jean, ed. 1980. *Histoire de la France contemporaine*, vol. 6: *1940–1947*. Paris: Editions sociales.

Elsaesser, Thomas. 1984. "Pathos and Leave-Taking." *Sight and Sound* 53, no. 4.

Estève, Michel. 1962. *Robert Bresson*. Paris: Seghers.

Fabre, Saturnin. (1948) 1987. *Douche écossaise*. Paris: Ramsay.

Faure, Christian. 1989. *Le Projet culturel de Vichy*. Lyon: Presses Universitaires de Lyon.

Feigen Fasteau, Marc. 1975. *The Male Machine*. New York: Dell.

Les Femmes dans la Résistance. 1977. Proceedings of UFF Conference. Paris: Éditions du Rocher.

Ferro, Marc. (1977) 1988. *Cinema and History*. Translated by Nancy Greene. Detroit: Wayne State University Press.

Fishman, Sarah. 1991. *We Will Wait: Wives of French Prisoners of War 1940–45*. New Haven: Yale University Press.

Flitterman-Lewis, Sandy. 1996. *To Desire Differently: Feminism and the French Cinema*. New York: Columbia University Press.

Flock, Jennifer. 1995. "Jacqueline Audry et l'inscription de la féminité dans le cinéma français de l'après-guerre." Master's thesis. Paris: Université de Paris-III, Sorbonne Nouvelle.

Ford, Charles. 1972. *Femmes cinéastes*. Paris, Denoël.

Fraisse, Geneviève. (1989) 1994. *Reason's Muse: Sexual Difference and the Birth of Democracy*. Translated by Jane Marie Todd. Chicago: University of Chicago Press.

———. 1992. *La Raison des femmes*. Paris: Plon.

Francos, Ania. 1978. *Il était des femmes dans la Résistance*. Paris: Stock.

Freud, Sigmund. (1907) 2003. *Gradiva: A Pompeiian Fancy / Delusion and Dream in Wilhelm Jensen's Gradiva*. Translated by Helen M. Downey. Los Angeles: Green Integer.

Garçon, François. 1984. *De Blum à Pétain*. Paris: Editions du Cerf.

Gauteur, Claude, and Ginette Vincendeau. 1993. *Jean Gabin: Anatomie d'un mythe*. Paris: Nathan.

Goldmann, Lucien. (1970) 1976. *Cultural Creation in Modern Society*. Translated by Bart Grahl. New York: Telos Press.

Gorz, André. 1988. *Métamorphoses du travail: Quête du sens, critique de la raison économique*. Paris: Galilée.

Guéhenno, Jean. 1947. *Journal des années noires*. Paris: Gallimard.

Guillaumin, Colette. 1995. *Racism, Sexism, Power and Ideology*. London: Routledge.

Haase-Dubosc, Danielle, and Éliane Viennot, eds. 1991. *Femmes et pouvoirs sous l'Ancien Régime*. Paris: Rivages.

Harvey, Sylvia. (1978) 1998. *Woman's Place: The Absent Family of Film Noir*. In E. Ann Kaplan, ed., *Women in Film Noir*. London: British Film Institute.

Haskell, Molly. 1987. *From Reverence to Rape: The Treatment of Women in the Movies*. Chicago: University of Chicago Press.

Hayward, Susan. 2004. *Simone Signoret: The Star as Cultural Sign*. London: Continuum.

———. 2010. *French Costume Drama of the 1950s: Fashioning Politics in Film*. London: Intellect.

Hayward, Susan, and Ginette Vincendeau, eds. 1990/2000. *French Film: Texts and Contexts*. London: Routledge.

Huston, Nancy. 1979. *Jouer au papa et à l'amant: De l'amour des petites filles*. Paris: Ramsay.

———. 1992. "La Belle et le bellum." *La Lettre internationale* (Spring).

Jakobson, Roman. (1928) 1977. "Problèmes des études littéraires et linguistiques." In *Huit questions de poétique*. Paris: Seuil.

Jeancolas, Jean-Pierre. 1983. *15 ans d'années trente*. Paris: Stock.

———. 1992. "L'Arrangement Blum-Byrnes à l'épreuve des faits." *1895*, no. 13.

Kaplan, Alice Y. 1986. *Reproduction of Banality: Fascism, Literature and French Intellectual Life*. Minneapolis: University of Minnesota Press.

Kaplan, E. Ann. 1983. "Ideology and Cinematic Practice in Lang's *Scarlet Street* and Renoir's *La Chienne.*" *Wide Angle* 5, no. 3.

Kaussen, Valérie. 1992. "La Figure de la cocotte dans le cinéma français des années trente." Master's thesis. Paris: Université de Paris-III, Sorbonne Nouvelle.

Kirby, Lynn. N.d. "French Film and the Foreign Horizon." Unpublished manuscript.

Krutnik, Frank. 1991. *In a Lonely Street: Film Noir, Genre, Masculinity.* London: Routledge.

Laborie, Pierre. 1990. *L'Opinion française sous Vichy.* Paris: Seuil.

———. 1992. "Vichy et ses représentations dans l'imaginaire social." In Jean-Pierre Azéma and François Bédarida, eds., *Vichy et les Français.* Paris: Fayard.

———. 1993. "Les Symboles sexués dans le système de représentation des Français 1940–1944." Paper presented at the IHTP, Paris, January.

Lagny, Michèle. 1993. "Le Réalisme imaginaire du cinéma de la Quatrième République." *Conférences du Collège d'histoire de l'art cinématographique,* no. 4 (Spring).

Lagny, Michèle, Marie-Claire Ropars, and Pierre Sorlin. 1986. *Générique des années 30.* Paris: Presses universitaires de Vincennes.

Lagrave, Rose-Marie. (1991) 1994. "A Supervised Emancipation." In Georges Duby and Michelle Perrot, eds. *A History of Women in the West,* vol. 5: *Toward a Cultural Identity in the Twentieth Century.* Translated by Arthur Goldhammer. Cambridge, Mass.: Belknap Press.

Lang, Robert. 1989. *American Film Melodrama: Griffith, Vidor, Minnelli.* Princeton: Princeton University Press.

Le Boterf, Hervé. 1995. *Harry Baur.* Paris: Pygmalion Editions.

Leclerc, Ginette. 1963. *Ma vie privée.* Paris: La Table Ronde.

Lederer, Wolfgang. 1970. *Gynophobia ou la peur des femmes.* Paris: Payot.

Le Doeuff, Michèle. (1989) 1991. *Hipparchia's Choice: An Essay Concerning Women, Philosophy, etc.* Translated by Trista Selous. Oxford: Basil Blackwell.

Le Gras, Gwénaëlle. 2010. *Michel Simon, l'art de la disgrâce.* Paris: Scope.

Le Gras, Gwénaëlle, and Delphine Chedaleux, eds. 2012. *Genres et acteurs du cinema français 1930–1960.* Rennes: PUR.

Lemerige, Françoise. 1994. "Introduction à l'analyse des œuvres de Balzac adaptées au cinéma sous l'Occupation." Master's thesis. Université de Paris-III, Sorbonne Nouvelle.

Leon, Abram. 1971. *The Jewish Question: A Marxist Interpretation.* Atlanta: Pathfinder Press.

Lévy, Claude. 1974. *La Libération, remise en ordre ou révolution?* Paris: PUF.

Lewin, Christophe. 1986. *Le Retour des prisonniers de guerre français.* Paris: Publications de la Sorbonne.

Lindeperg, Sylvie. 1997. *Les Ecrans de l'ombre: La Seconde Guerre mondiale dans le cinéma français.* Paris: CNRS Éditions.

Lipsitz, George. 1981. *Class and Culture in Cold War America: "A Rainbow at Midnight."* New York: Praeger.

Loiseau, Jean-Claude. 1977. *Les Zazous.* Paris: Le Sagittaire.

Lottman, Herbert. 1986. *The Purge: The Purification of the French Collaborators after World War II.* New York: William Morrow.

Louis, Marie-Victoire. 1994. *Le Droit de cuissage, 1860–1930*. Paris: L'Atelier.

Lukács, Georg. 1974. *The Theory of the Novel*. Cambridge, Mass.: MIT Press.

Marcel, Gabriel. (1945) 2010. *Homo Viator: Introduction to the Metaphysic of Hope*. Translated by Emma Craufurd and Paul Seaton. South Bend, Ind.: Saint Augustine's Press.

Maugue, Annelise, 1987. *L'Identité masculine en crise au tournant du siècle, 1870–1914*. Paris: Rivages.

McMillan, James. 1981. *Housewife or Harlot: The Place of Women in French Society, 1870–1940*. Brighton, U.K.: Harvester Press.

Metz, Christian. (1973) 1974. *Film Language: A Semiotics of the Cinema*. Translated by Michael Taylor. Chicago: University of Chicago Press.

Miller, Gérard. 1975. *Les Pousse-au-jouir du maréchal Pétain*. Paris: Seuil.

Modleski, Tania. 1988. *The Women Who Knew Too Much: Hitchcock and Feminist Theory*. London: Routledge.

Moi, Toril. (1994) 2008. *Simone de Beauvoir: The Making of an Intellectual Woman*. Oxford: Oxford University Press.

Moine, Raphaëlle. (2002) 2008. *Cinema Genre*. Translated by Alistair Fox and Hilary Radner. Oxford: Blackwell.

Muel-Dreyfus, Francine. (1996) 2001. *Vichy and the Eternal Feminine: A Contribution to a Political Sociology of Gender*. Translated by Kathleen A. Johnson. Durham, N.C.: Duke University Press.

Muller, Martine, et al. 1985. *Etre féministe en France: Contribution à l' étude des mouvements de femmes 1944–1967*. Paris: IHTP.

Mulvey, Laura. (1975) 1981. "Visual Pleasure and Narrative Cinema." In *Visual and Other Pleasures*. Bloomington: Indiana University Press.

Naumann, Claude. 1991. "Une métaphore de la création cinématographique: *Falbalas*." In Claude Beylie and Freddy Buache, eds., *Jacques Becker*. Locarno: Editions du Festival international du Film.

Nizhny, Vladimir. 1963. *Lessons with Eisenstein*. Translated and edited by Ivor Montagu and Jay Leyda. New York: Hill and Wang.

Oms, Marcel. 1973. "*Le Corbeau* et ses quatre vérités." *Cahiers de la Cinémathèque*, no. 8, Winter.

Ory, Pascal. 1985. *L'Anarchisme de droite*. Paris: Grasset.

——. 1989. *L'Aventure culturelle française, 1945–1989*. Paris: Flammarion.

Païni, Dominique. October 6, 1992. Lecture on "Ciné-peinture" (cinema and painting). Paris: Musée d'Orsay, Paris.

Passek, Jean-Loup. 1986. *Dictionnaire du cinéma*. Paris: Larousse.

Petro, Patrice. 1989. *Joyless Streets: Women and Melodramatic Representation in Weimar Germany*. Princeton: Princeton University Press.

Polan, Dana. 1986. *Power and Paranoia: History, Narrative, and the American Cinema, 1940–1950*. New York: Columbia University Press.

Portes, Jacques. 1986. "Les Origines de la légende noire des accords Blum-Byrnes." In "Cinéma et société," special issue of *Revue d'histoire moderne et contemporaine*, April–June.

Prédal, René. 2005. *Le Cinéma français depuis 1945*. Paris: Nathan.

Presle, Micheline. 1994. *L'Arrière-mémoire, conversation avec Serge Toubiana*. Paris: Flammarion.

Prost, Antoine, and Gérard Vincent, eds. 1987. *Histoire générale de l'enseignement et de l'éducation en France*. Vol. 4. Paris: Seghers.

Quéval, Jean. 1962. *Jacques Becker*. Paris: Seghers.

Ragache, Gilles, and Jean-Robert Ragache. 1988. *La Vie quotidienne des écrivains et des artistes sous l'Occupation, 1940–1944*. Paris: Hachette.

Rebatet, Lucien. 1941. *Les Juifs en France*, vol. 4: *Les Tribus du cinéma et du théâtre*. Paris: Nouvelles Éditions Françaises.

Régent, Roger. 1948. *Cinéma de France sous l'Occupation*. Paris: Éditions d'Aujourd'hui.

Renoir, Jean. 1974. *Ecrits, 1926–1971*. Paris: Belfond.

———. 1989. *Renoir on Renoir: Interviews, Essays, and Remarks*. Translated by Carol Volk. Cambridge: Cambridge University Press.

Rioux, Emmanuelle. 1987. "Les Zazous, un phénomène socio-culturel sous l'Occupation." Master's thesis. Université de Paris-X Nanterre.

Rioux, Jean-Pierre. (1980) 1989. *The Fourth Republic, 1944–1958*. Translated by Godfrey Rogers. Cambridge: Cambridge University Press.

Ripa, Yannick. 1995. "A propos des tondues durant la guerre civile espagnole." *Clio*, no. 1.

Roberts, Mary Louise. 1994. *Civilization without Sexes: Reconstructing Gender in Postwar France 1917–1927*. Chicago: University of Chicago Press.

Robin-Challand, Louise. 1983. "Les Danseuses de l'Opéra." PhD diss., Université de Paris-VIII, Saint-Denis.

Romance, Viviane. 1986. *Romantique à mourir*. Paris: Vertiges du Nord/Carrère.

Rosanvallon, Pierre. 1993. "L'Histoire du vote des femmes: Réflexions sur la specificité française." In Georges Duby and Michelle Perrot, eds., *Femmes et histoire*. Paris: Plon.

Rouquet, François. 1993. *Une épuration ordinaire (1944–1949): Petits et grands collaborateurs de l'administration française*. Paris: CNRS Éditions.

Rousso, Henry. (1987) 1994. *The Vichy Syndrome: History and Memory in France since 1944*. Translated by Arthur Goldhammer. Cambridge, Mass.: Harvard University Press.

Rubin, Gabrielle. 1977. *Les Sources inconscientes de la misogynie*. Paris: Robert Laffont.

Sabria, Jean-Charles. 1995. *Le Cinéma français. Tome 1: Les Années 50*. Paris: Centre Georges Pompidou/Ircam.

Said, Edward W. (1978) 2003. *Orientalism*. New York: Pantheon.

Sartre, Jean-Paul. (1945) 2001. *The Age of Reason*. Translated by Eric Sutton. London: Penguin.

Schor, Ralph. 1985. *L'Opinion française et les étrangers en France: 1919–1939*. Paris: Publications de la Sorbonne.

Schwartz, Paula. 1987. "Redefining Resistance: Women's Activism in Wartime France." In *Behind the Lines: Gender and the Two World Wars*. New Haven: Yale University Press.

Schwartz, Vanessa R. 2007. *It's So French: Hollywood, Paris, and the Making of Cosmopolitan Film Culture*. Chicago: University of Chicago Press.

Sellier, Geneviève. 1981. "Ces singuliers héritiers du cinéma français des années trente." *Cinéma 81*, no. 268.

———. 1989. *Jean Grémillon: Le Cinéma est à vous*. Paris: Librairie Klincksieck.

———. 1992. *Les Enfants du paradis: Étude critique*. Paris: Nathan.

———. 1993. "Le Précédent des accords Blum-Byrnes." *Le Monde diplomatique*, November.

———. 1994. "L'Après-guerre: Contradictions d'un auteur." *La Pensée*, no. 300 (Autumn).

———. 2009. "Le Courrier des lecteurs de Cinémonde dans les années 1950: La Naissance d'une cinéphilie au féminin." In Geneviève Sellier and Noël Burch, eds., *Le Cinéma au prisme des rapports de sexe*. Paris: Vrin.

Siclier, Jacques. 1957. *La Femme dans le cinéma français*. Paris: Editions du Cerf.

———. 1981. *La France de Pétain et son cinéma*. Paris: Henri Veyrier.

Simsolo, Noël. 1988. *Sacha Guitry*. Paris: Cahiers du Cinéma.

Sineau, Mariette. (1991) 1996. "Law and Democracy." In Georges Duby and Michelle Perrot, eds., *A History of Women in the West*, vol. 5: *Toward a Cultural Identity in the Twentieth Century*. Cambridge, Mass.: Belknap Press.

Sohn, Anne-Marie. (1991) 1994. "Between the Wars in France and England." In Georges Duby and Michelle Perrot, eds., *A History of Women in the West*, vol. 5: *Toward a Cultural Identity in the Twentieth Century*. Cambridge, Mass.: Belknap Press.

Studlar, Gaylyn. 1993. *In the Realm of Pleasure: Von Sternberg, Dietrich and the Masochistic Aesthetic*. Urbana: University of Illinois Press.

Sullerot, Évelyne. 1973. *Les Françaises au travail*. Paris: Hachette.

Theweleit, Klaus. 1987–89. *Male Fantasies*. 2 vols. Minneapolis: Polity Press.

Truffaut, François. 1987. *Le Plaisir des yeux*. Paris: Cahiers du Cinéma.

Turim, Maureen. (1990) 2000. "Poetic Realism as Psychoanalytical and Ideological Operation: Marcel Carné's *Le Jour se lève* (1939)." In Susan Hayward and Ginette Vincendeau, eds., *French Film: Texts and Contexts*. London: Routledge.

Turk, Edward Baron. 1989. *Child of Paradise: Marcel Carné and the Golden Age of French Cinema*. Cambridge, Mass.: Harvard University Press.

Vailland, Roger. 1945. *Drôle de jeu*. Paris: Buchet-Chastel.

Vanoye, Francis. 1989. *La Règle du jeu*. Paris: Nathan Université.

Veillon, Dominique. 1995. *Vivre et survivre en France 1939–1947*. Paris: Payot.

Viennot, Éliane, ed. 1995. *La Démocratie "à la française," ou les femmes indésirables*. Paris: Publications de l'Université de Paris-VII.

Vincendeau, Ginette. 1985. "Community, Nostalgia and the Spectacle of Masculinity." *Screen*, no. 26.

———. 1989. "Daddy's Girls: Oedipal Narratives in 1930s French Films." *Iris*, no. 8.

———. 1993. "L'Ancien et le nouveau: Brigitte Bardot dans les années 50." In "20 ans de théories féministes sur le cinéma," special issue of *CinémAction*, no. 67.

———. 2000. *Stars and Stardom in French Cinema*. London: Continuum.

———. 2008. *Les Stars et le star-système en France*. Paris: L'Harmattan.

———. 2009. "'Le Petit monde' de Marcel Pagnol." In Pierre Beylot and Raphaëlle Moine, eds., *Fictions patrimoniales sur grand et petit écran*. Bordeaux: Presses Universitaires de Bordeaux.

———. 2012. "Fernandel: De l'innocent du village à 'Monsieur tout le monde.'" In Gwenaëlle Le Gras and Delphine Chedaleux, eds., *Genres et acteurs du cinéma français, 1930–1960*. Rennes: PUR.

Walker, Janet. 1999. "Textual Trauma in *Kings Row* and *Freud*." In Janet Bergstrom, ed., *Endless Night: Cinema and Psychoanalysis, Parallel Histories*. Berkeley: University of California Press.

Warner, Marina. 1976. *Alone of All Her Sex: The Myth and the Cult of the Virgin Mary*. London: Weidenfeld and Nicolson.

———. 1985. *Monuments and Maidens: The Allegory of the Female Form*. London: Weidenfeld and Nicolson.

Weber, Eugen. 1976. *Peasants into Frenchmen: The Modernization of Rural France, 1870–1914*. Palo Alto: Stanford University Press.

Williams, Linda. 1988. "Feminist Film Theory: *Mildred Pierce* and the Second World War." In Deidre Pribram, ed., *Female Spectators: Looking at Film and Television*. London: Verso.

A

Index

Page numbers in *italics* indicate illustrations.

Haskell, Molly, 54
Hatred. See Mollenard
Haut-le-Vent, 101, 109, 125, 129, 146, 172
Hays Code, 343
Hayward, Susan, 345
Hayworth, Rita, 343
Heart of Paris. See Gribouille
Hélène, 26, 35, 84, 256
Hepburn, Katharine, 345
Hérain, Pierre de, 101, 109
Her Bridal Night. See Mariée était trop belle, La
Here Is the Beauty. See Belle que voilà, La
Her First Affair. See Premier rendez-vous
Heroes and Sinners. See Héros sont fatigués, Les
Héros sont fatigués, Les, 275
Herrand, Marcel, 96, *159*, 159, 165
Hess, Johnny, 140, 144
Hessling, Catherine, 30, 48
Heymann, Claude, 271
Histoire des treize, L', 181
History of Private Life, 16
Hoffmannsthal, Hugo von, 251
Hole, The. See Trou, Le
Hollywood, 342, 343
Holt, Jany, 61, 111, 119, 155, 160, 161, 163, 243
Homme de Londres, L', 98, 99, 130, 174
Homme de ma vie, L', 280
Homme de nulle part, L', 30, 128
Homme qui vendit son âme, L', 115
homosexuality. *See* Carné, Marcel; Cocteau, Jean; Marais, Jean; Trenet; Charles
Honegger, Arthur, 87
Honorable Catherine, L', 50, 117, 183, 224
Honorable Catherine, The. See Honorable Catherine, L'
Hôtel du Nord, 69
Hubrenne, Bernard, 316
Hugon, André, 35, 37, 129
Huillet, Danièle, 314
Huis-clos, 241
Human Cargo. See Impures, Les
Hunebelle, André, 274

Idiot, L', 246, 278
Illicit Motherhood. See Maternité clandestine
Illustration, L', 141
Impures, Les, 280
incest and incestuous desire, 17, 18, 20, 23,
26, 27, 29–34, 37, 40, 63, 72, 92, 93, 96, 97, 98, 156, 191, 197, 205, 210, 330, 338. *See also* father figures and fathers
Inconnus dans la maison, Les, 98, 108, 110, *111*, 111, 114
Inévitable Monsieur Dubois, L', 115, 117
Invitée, L', 241
Isn't Life a Bitch? See Chienne, La
It Happened at the Inn. See Goupi mains rouges
It's Not Me. See Ce n'est pas moi
I Was an Adventuress. See J'étais une aventurière

Jacques le Fataliste, 226
Jacquin, Albert, 263
Jayet, René, 119, 147, 167
Jeancolas, Jean-Pierre, 125, 269
Jeannou, 101, 110, 162
Jeanson, Henri, 119, 144, 148, 207, 245, 252, 280
Je chante, 169
Jensen, Wilhelm, 63
Je suis partout, 116, 195
J'étais une aventurière, 50, 167
Jeune folle, La, 280
Jeux interdits, 297
J'irai cracher sur vos tombes, 240
Joannon, Léo, 17, 19, 24, 50, 117, 123, 156, 175, 183
Jourdan, Louis, 93, 118, 155, 165, 289
Jourdan, Michel, 297
Journal d'un curé de campagne, Le, 246, 296, 297, 312–19, *313*, 328
Journal tombe à cinq heures, Le, 217
Jour se lève, Le, 19, 40, 44, 45, 66–73, *70*, 81, 99, 131, 171, 186, 187, 224, 248, 255
Jouvet, Louis, 60, 252, *253*, 256
Joyce, Monique, 121, 157
Joyeux, Odette, 138, 161, 166, 196, 198, 249
Julie de Carneilhan, 261
Juliette au pays des hommes, 181
Juliette ou la clé des songes, 246
Jürgens, Curd, 301
Justin de Marseille, 19, 20

Kaplan, E. Ann, 122
Karl, Roger, 171
Kaussen, Valérie, 18, 141
Keep an Eye on Amélie. See Occupe-toi d'Amélie